LAW AS A LEAP OF FAITH

LAW AS A LEAP OF FAITH

Essays on Law in General

JOHN GARDNER

OXFORD
UNIVERSITY PRESS

Great Clarendon Street, Oxford, OX2 6DP,
United Kingdom

Oxford University Press is a department of the University of Oxford.
It furthers the University's objective of excellence in research, scholarship,
and education by publishing worldwide. Oxford is a registered trade mark of
Oxford University Press in the UK and in certain other countries

© J. Gardner, 2012

The moral rights of the author have been asserted

First Edition published in 2012
First published in paperback 2014

Impression: 1

All rights reserved. No part of this publication may be reproduced, stored in
a retrieval system, or transmitted, in any form or by any means, without the
prior permission in writing of Oxford University Press, or as expressly permitted
by law, by licence or under terms agreed with the appropriate reprographics
rights organization. Enquiries concerning reproduction outside the scope of the
above should be sent to the Rights Department, Oxford University Press, at the
address above

You must not circulate this work in any other form
and you must impose this same condition on any acquirer

Crown copyright material is reproduced under Class Licence
Number C01P0000148 with the permission of OPSI
and the Queen's Printer for Scotland

Published in the United States of America by Oxford University Press
198 Madison Avenue, New York, NY 10016, United States of America

British Library Cataloguing in Publication Data
Data available

Library of Congress Control Number: 20129354

ISBN 978–0–19–969555–3 (hbk.)
ISBN 978–0–19–871388–3 (pbk.)

Printed and bound by Lightning Source UK Ltd.

Links to third party websites are provided by Oxford in good faith and
for information only. Oxford disclaims any responsibility for the materials
contained in any third party website referenced in this work.

PREFACE

In this book I have collected nine essays published over the past fifteen years, adding two previously unpublished ones (Chapters 8 and 11). It is hard to know where the subject 'law in general' ends,[1] but I have taken quite a strict view of it in compiling this material. I have left out a few essays on the borderline of the subject, as well as a couple that I just don't like so much. Most of the previously published essays have been slightly corrected for inclusion in the book. Those forming Chapters 7 and 10 have been subjected to some more material changes.

My attempts to write an introduction that would paint the bigger picture were unsuccessful, because there is no bigger picture. I don't have a theory of law, let alone what Ernest Weinrib calls a 'comprehensive theoretical position...[with] broad philosophical vistas'.[2] I have quite a lot of thoughts about law in general and I can only hope that they turn out to be consistent with one other. That they form any more perfect union than that is neither likely nor desirable. Philosophy is not the art of compiling as many little thoughts as possible into as few big thoughts as possible, but the art of wearing every thought down to its rightful little size and then keeping it in its rightful little place. So the main mission of this book, as I see it, is *unbundling*: separating out disparate thoughts that have often been regarded, mistakenly, as part of some package deal.

The marketing of ideas in package deals appeals to many law students, at any rate in the English-speaking world. Quite apart from making it a lot easier to come up with boilerplate text that can be learnt for the exam, the package deal approach allows one to think of philosophy on the familiar model of an adversarial trial, whether individual litigation such as *Hart* v *Dworkin*, *Posner* v *Weinrib*, and *Raz* v *Finnis*, or class actions such as *Positivism* v *Natural*

---

[1] Go straight to Ch 11 to find out what I mean by it.
[2] Ernest Weinrib, 'Why Legal Formalism?' in Robert P. George (ed), *Natural Law Theory* (Oxford 1992), at 352.

Law and *Formalism v Realism*. This whole way of thinking about what is going on is a blight on our subject, and the source of many miserable exam answers. I try here to break free from it. Although I do not hesitate, in what follows, to engage in a cross-examiner's ruthless exposure of falsehoods, especially pernicious ones, you will also find me scouring assiduously for truths across many supposedly rival positions and traditions, including some that the lawyers among you may imagine to be those of my 'opponents'.[3] I am such an intellectual squirrel (way beyond a mere fox) that I don't care at all where or how I get the little truths that I hoard away in the following pages. I may even occasionally snatch them from under the hedgehog's very nose.[4]

As these remarks suggest, many of the essays included here were originally written with pedagogical objectives in mind, responding to perennial misconceptions on the part of my students. You will struggle to find any conspicuously novel ideas about law in the book. Most of the novelty that there is lies in the way in which the ideas are explained and combined. A lot of my thinking is owed, directly or indirectly, to H.L.A. Hart. In what follows, I often attempt to elaborate Hartian ideas, to remove Hartian hesitations, and to reformulate Hartian misstatements. Sometimes (eg in Chapter 9) I even give Hart a long-overdue makeover. But the book is not a defence of Hart's thinking as such, and indeed begins as far away from Hart as it is possible to go, with some Socratic and Kierkegaardian theological meditations on norms and normativity. Why so *outré*? Hart erred, in *The Concept of Law*, in thinking of all norms on the model of social norms. In Chapter 1 I am bending over backwards not to make, or encourage, the same mistake. I am shifting the paradigm of normativity as far away from Hart's 'hats in church' norm as it is possible to go. 'Sacrifice your first-born son' is the one that gets

---

[3] See, notably, my attempts to settle the totally cross-purposes class action known as '*Positivism* v *Natural Law*' in Chs 2 and 6.

[4] An allusion to Ronald Dworkin, *Justice for Hedgehogs* (Cambridge, Mass 2011), itself alluding to the verse by Archilochus: 'Fox knows many,/Hedgehog one/Solid trick' or (more freely) 'Fox knows/Eleventythree/Tricks and still/Gets caught:/Hedgehog knows/One but it/Always works'. Guy Davenport (ed & trans), *Carmina Archilochi: The Fragments of Archilochus* (Berkeley 1964).

most of the attention here. This opens the way, I hope, to a cleaner understanding, later, of the (limited but crucial) ways in which specifically social norms figure in law, and also of the various kinds of non-social norms that also have their part to play in a full understanding of the law's modality.

The quest for that cleaner understanding becomes a major preoccupation in Chapters 3 and 4, reprised for new purposes in Chapter 11. Chapter 11 reflects broadly on the social aspects of law, those which allow sociologists to claim ownership of it as subject of study. The chapter mounts a defence of Hart's (in)famous claim to have been doing both sociological and philosophical work. Chapter 3 explains, more specifically, how customary law (and case law) can be accommodated in (and cannot be accommodated without) an understanding of law as 'positive' (ie made by people). Chapter 4, under cover of studying the nature of constitutions, investigates the essential place of a customary 'ultimate rule of recognition' in every legal system. Here we confirm (and even toughen up) Hart's claim that there is no legal system without at least one social norm.

In Chapters 5–10, by contrast, social norms as such are not so much in the foreground. The concern in these chapters is mainly with other ways of classifying norms, and in particular, over and over again, with the contrasts between (a) norms that exist because they are good and norms that exist because they are made (of which social norms are only one sub-type); and (b) general norms (aka rules) and particular norms (especially the ones that I call 'rulings'). These distinctions are introduced in Chapter 2, along with several others that recur throughout the book. Chapter 2 is indeed a big unbundling exercise, to which the reader who only wants a whistle-stop tour of the main themes of the book should now turn. Then, for another bout of aggressive unbundling, she should move straight to Chapter 6. These twin essays, in a way the signature essays of the volume, ironically invoke and preserve the infernal textbook classifications 'legal positivism' and 'natural law' that they also attempt to deflate. This is also a pedagogical move. Labels like this are pretty arbitrary. But how can anyone be cajoled to stop thinking of a 'legal positivist' or a 'natural lawyer' as an all-purpose bogeyman if we puritanically refuse to use the bogeyman's name to designate anything at all?

Here are some other ways of combining chapters, for those with more specific fish to fry. Chapter 3 and Chapter 5 both explore aspects of the role of collective agency in the law. Chapter 3 considers the collective agency of legislatures and courts. Chapter 5 considers the agency of the law itself, through its officials. I am not sceptical about either the agency of legislatures or the agency of law itself. But they call for very different analyses, which I try to provide. Chapter 1 could also be read with Chapters 5 and 6 for those attempting to delve deeper into the vexed question of how it is possible to treat law as 'normative' (ie made up of norms) while regarding it as risible, immoral, despicable, etc. This requires some definitive *contrasting* of law with morality (Chapter 6) but also some reflection on the definitive way in which law *invokes* morality (Chapter 5). This invocation ('law's moral claim') represents, I argue, an important necessary connection between law and morality.

So do the connections explored in Chapters 7 to 10. In Chapter 7 the attention shifts to one particular moral ideal, that of legality (or 'the rule of law') and its necessary connection with law. Chapters 8 and 9 explore some misunderstandings of this same ideal, which are associated with misunderstandings of the very nature of law. From the end of Chapter 9 and into Chapter 10, we move to a different moral ideal, that of justice, and we do some more deflating and some more unbundling. Yes, there is a necessary connection between law and justice, but (a) not the big one that some people hope for; and (b) not to be confused with the more intimate connection between law and legality. Perhaps whistle-stop tourers finished with Chapters 2 and 6 would find Chapter 9 the quickest way to sample this part of the book.

For those who don't have time even for the whistle-stop tour, here is the slideshow. In other words, here is a list of some of the principal theses that are defended or supported in the book, with brief location information.

¶ All law is made by people (Chapters 2 and 7), but not all is made intentionally, or even knowingly, and in particular not all is made by legislating (Chapters 2, 3, 4).
¶ Some sound legal reasoning (usually by the higher courts) is capable of making new law, often accidentally (Chapters 2, 3, 7).
¶ The content of all law is the content it was given by its makers and changers (including those who make and change law by applying it), never mind what content they ought to have given it (Chapters 1 and 2).
¶ This includes the law that determines who counts as an ultimate maker or changer of law (what Hart calls 'rules of recognition') (Chapter 4).
¶ There are therefore no moral criteria (necessary or otherwise) for establishing what the law on any given matter says (Chapters 2 and 8).
¶ Nevertheless, there are necessary (conceptually necessary) connections between law and morality (Chapters 2 and 5–10).
¶ A necessary connection: law by its nature holds itself out as morally binding, even though that may be a mistake or a pretence (Chapter 5).
¶ Another necessary connection: legal reasoning is moral reasoning with one or more legal premises (Chapters 2, 7).
¶ Also, there is a moral ideal for law, the ideal of legality or the rule of law, law's answerability to which is conceptually determined (ie is part of the very concept of law) (Chapters 7–9).
¶ And there is also, although more indirectly, a conceptual connection between law and justice (Chapter 10).
¶ Both the connection between law and legality, and that between law and justice, confirm that law is a modal as opposed to a functional kind; ie it is distinguished by how it does what it does, not by why (Chapters 8–11).
¶ All of this, and more, is true of law in general (Chapter 11).

For valuable conversations about and comments on the various topics, mostly at the time of original writing but some more recently, my thanks go to Larry Alexander, John Attanasio, Nick Barber, Jes Bjarup, Bruno Celano, Jules Coleman, Sylvie Delacroix, Michelle Dempsey, Julie Dickson, Sionaidh Douglas Scott, Luís Duarte d'Almeida, Doug Edlin, Richard Ekins,

Timothy Endicott, John Finnis, Robbie George, Les Green, Ken Himma, Elisa Holmes, Tony Honoré, Matthias Klatt, Maris Köpcke Tinturé, Matt Kramer, Niki Lacey, Grant Lamond, Brian Leiter, the late Neil MacCormick, Tim Macklem, Margaret Martin, José Juan Moreso, Mark Murphy, Hans Oberdiek, Peter Oliver, Joseph Raz, Charles Silver, Nigel Simmonds, Tomasz Stawecki, Shiv Swaminathan, Victor Tadros, John Tasioulas, Massimo la Torre, Isabel Trujillo, and Wil Waluchow.

Les Green, Tony Honoré, Niki Lacey, Tim Macklem, and Joseph Raz each deserve a further mention for their contributions to my wider jurisprudential education over the years. Tim in particular has been a source of endless intellectual support, for which I am very grateful. Alex Flach has helped patiently and beyond the call of duty with the process of turning all that jurisprudential education into a book, and I benefited from the hard work of Bethan Cousins, Briony Ryles, Emma Brady, Binesh Hass, and Janet Walker during the book's production. The biggest thanks of all go to my family, Jenny, Henrik, Annika, and Audra, who have tolerated the whole business with good humour and, in the case of the younger members, with exactly the kind of wild indifference to all rules and rulings that a philosopher of law needs to keep him on the level.

In its original version, Chapter 4 was dedicated to the memory of Neil MacCormick, and I renew that dedication here.

ACKNOWLEDGEMENTS

'Law as a Leap of Faith' first appeared in Peter Oliver, Sionaidh Douglas Scott and Victor Tadros (eds), *Faith in Law* (Oxford 2000) and is reprinted here by kind permission of Hart Publishing.

'Legal Positivism: 5½ Myths' is based on a lecture given at Notre Dame Law School in April 2001, and was first published in *American Journal of Jurisprudence* 46 (2001), 199. It appears here, with minor corrections, by courtesy of the journal's editors.

'Some Types of Law' began life as a lecture to the European Academy of Legal Theory in Brussels in September 2005. It was first published in Douglas E Edlin (ed), *Common Law Theory* (Cambridge 2008). © Cambridge University Press, reproduced with permission.

'Can There be a Written Constitution?' grew from a lecture in July 2008 to mark 25 years of Southern Methodist University's Law Program in Oxford. It later appeared in *Oxford Studies in Philosophy of Law* 1 (2011), 162.

'How Law Claims, What Law Claims' is reprinted from Matthias Klatt (ed), *Institutionalized Reason: The Jurisprudence of Robert Alexy* (Oxford 2012).

'Nearly Natural Law' is an amalgamation of parts of my Natural Law Lecture delivered at the University of Notre Dame in March 2007 and parts of my Petrazycki Lecture delivered at Warsaw University in May 2007. It was first published in *American Journal of Jurisprudence* 52 (2007), 1 and reappears here, lightly re-edited, by courtesy of the journal's editors.

'The Legality of Law' was a plenary lecture at the IVR Congress in Lund in August 2003. It was published in *Ratio Juris* 17 (2004), 168. It appears here (partly rewritten) with permission of Wiley-Blackwell. © Blackwell Publishing Ltd 2004.

'The Supposed Formality of the Rule of Law' is previously unpublished, but draws in places on the text of a lecture by the same name delivered at the University of Auckland in March

2010 under the auspices of the Legal Research Foundation and the New Zealand Society for Legal and Social Philosophy.

'Hart on Legality, Justice, and Morality' is adapted from an article of the same name in *Jurisprudence* 1 (2010), 253. Material is re-used here by kind permission of Hart Publishing.

'The Virtue of Justice and the Character of Law' is based on a public lecture given at University College London in November 1999 and written up in *Current Legal Problems* 53 (2000), 1. It is reprinted here with various changes.

'Law in General' is previously unpublished material.

CONTENTS

1. Law as a Leap of Faith	1
2. Legal Positivism: 5½ Myths	19
3. Some Types of Law	54
4. Can There be a Written Constitution?	89
5. How Law Claims, What Law Claims	125
6. Nearly Natural Law	149
7. The Legality of Law	177
8. The Supposed Formality of the Rule of Law	195
9. Hart on Legality, Justice, and Morality	221
10. The Virtue of Justice and the Character of Law	238
11. Law in General	270
Index of Subjects	303
Index of Names	313

I
Law as a Leap of Faith

1. The Socratic challenge

Euthyphro: I would say that what all the gods love is holy...
Socrates: The point which I want to resolve first is whether the holy is beloved of the gods because it is holy, or holy because it is beloved of the gods.[1]

Socrates' challenge is not merely diverting sophistry. It seriously threatens the fabric of theism. The threat becomes particularly clear if we translate the underlying puzzle into the Judaeo-Christian idiom of a single all-powerful and all-knowing God.[2] On the one hand, we are told that whatever this God commands is the right thing to do by virtue of God's commanding it. This is an aspect of God's omnipotence. On the other hand, we are reassured that whatever this God commands is commanded because it is the right thing to do. That is an aspect of God's omniscience. But these propositions about God and His commands cannot both be true at once. Either this God makes a constitutive[3] difference to what we should do or He does not. So which is it to be?

---

[1] Plato, 'Euthyphro' in Benjamin Jowett's edition of the *Dialogues* (Oxford 1871), vol 2 at 84.

[2] For simplicity I am adopting all the trappings of this tradition here, notably the capitalization of God and the use of male pronouns to identify Him.

[3] I will ignore the possibility that God makes a merely *epistemic* difference to our reasoning, ie merely assists our *knowledge* of what we should do without affecting what we should do. I ignore this possibility because (a) it eliminates God's practical authority (in favour of purely theoretical authority) and therefore makes a mockery of God's supposed omnipotence; (b) it takes all the force out of the Biblical example of Abraham and Isaac (discussed below), which illustrates nothing worth dwelling on unless it illustrates that God can command what would be, apart from his commands, truly abhorrent actions; and (c) there is no obvious reason to believe that a believer's knowledge of God's commands is generally more reliable or less vague than his or her knowledge of what he or she ought to do apart from God's commands, and so the general case for treating God as a theoretical authority in such matters is hard to grasp. On the distinction

For obvious reasons, neither alternative is wholly appetizing for theists. Either God's commands are supposed to make it right to do what would, apart from God's commands, be wrong, in which case we may ask why we are supposed to give God's commands any rational credence, or else God's commands only make it right to do what is right anyway, in which case God seems to be condemned to rational redundancy. Faced with these apparent alternatives, Christian theologians have gone to extreme lengths to shake off the Socratic puzzle. Kierkegaard, for example, began boldly enough by grasping the first horn of the dilemma, holding that God's commands can make it right to do what would, apart from those commands, be wrong. The crux of the matter, he explained in *Fear and Trembling*, lies in understanding the difference between two points of view. For Abraham to kill Isaac was wrong from the *moral* point of view, but nevertheless right from the *religious* point of view, in virtue of the fact that God commanded it.[4] When the question arises of whether someone should take the religious or the moral point of view, however, that question is not open to rational deliberation. Within each point of view there are reasons, but there are no further independent reasons to take one or the other point of view. It is a non-rational although (and thus?) courageous leap which brings a person to one or the other, and from the one to the other.[5] Neither position is absolute except in its own relative eyes, and neither therefore answers absolutely to the other. Nevertheless those who make the courageous leap to occupy the religious point of view, albeit without independent reason to do so, now find themselves paradoxically within grasping distance of an absolute or non-relative position. This absolute position, occupied only by those whom Kierkegaard dubs 'Knights of Faith', is a position in which 'my contrast to [finite, moral] existence constantly expresses itself as the most beautiful and secure harmony with it'.[6] For the Knight of Faith, in other words, the rational struggle

---

between practical and theoretical authority, see Joseph Raz, *The Morality of Freedom* (Oxford 1986), 28–31 and 52–3.

[4] *Fear and Trembling* (trans Hong & Hong, Princeton 1983), eg 55 and 68–9.
[5] Ibid 48–9.   [6] Ibid 50.

between the moral and the religious is extinguished, nay *transcended*, in the condition of divine grace.

The Knight has felt the pain of renouncing everything [for the sake of religion], even the most precious thing in the world, and yet the finite [mere morality] tastes just as good to him as to one who never came to know anything higher... he has this security that makes him delight in it as if finitude were the surest thing of all. And yet, yet, the whole earthly figure he presents is a new creation... He resigned everything infinitely and then he grasped everything again by virtue of the absurd.[7]

The promise here seems to be that the dilemma to which Socrates draws attention is dissolved if and only if one can reach that true oneness with God, which, as the ultimate absurdity of life, no investigation that would satisfy Socrates or any mere philosopher can reveal or explain or accept. Reasoned argument is useless in the sight of God; only faith will do. And where reason ends and faith begins even the truly contradictory can be the case: as a Knight of Faith, Abraham can fully reconcile the rightness of his act with its wrongness, without sinking back into relativity. There is no more struggle between competing points of view. The very categories of right and wrong are transcended in the absoluteness of God. It is probably already clear from the difficulty I am having in expressing this idea that I find it painfully obscure. But then again, approaching the issue by reasoned argument, presumably I am *bound* to find it painfully obscure. That is Kierkegaard's whole point. The obscurity of it all to me only goes to show that I am no Knight of Faith, for Knights of Faith glory in the absurd, rather than shrinking from it in Socratic bafflement and disdain.

On his way to this extraordinary dissolution of the Socratic dilemma, Kierkegaard quickly dismisses a simpler dissolution. One might argue that God is none other than a personification of goodness, and His commands therefore none other than imperatively expressed encapsulations of rightness. It is true, therefore, that God's commands are right. But they are neither His commands because right, nor right because His commands.

[7] Ibid 40.

There is no explanatory order to be found, no possible logical priority as between these apparent alternatives identified by Socrates, because a command's being God's is exactly the same property as its being right. God's command is therefore right *in being* God's and God's *in being* right. Kierkegaard rejects this dissolution on the ground that, in his view, it fails to save God from redundancy. In this solution 'God comes to be an invisible vanishing point, an impotent thought; His power is only in the ethical, which fills all of existence'.[8] But Kierkegaard is too quick with this dismissal. In fact he is too quick, in general, to anticipate imminent news of God's moral redundancy.

How so? *Pace* Kierkegaard, it does not follow from the fact that God has the power to command us to do what would otherwise be wrong that God has the power to command us to do wrong. The mere fact that, but for God's commands, Abraham is wrong to kill Isaac does not show, as Kierkegaard assumes it does, that God commands Isaac to do wrong. One need not change from one point of view to another, nor embrace the absurd, to believe that killing Isaac is wrong if God did not command it and right if God did. Both of these propositions may be ordinary moral propositions and both may be sound without paradox or absurdity. The temptation to doubt it comes of an underestimation of the sheer totality of God's omniscience. God, being omniscient, knows not only what is the right thing for His people to do independently of His commands, but also what is the right thing for them to do *given* His commands. He also knows that these two need not be identical actions. He knows, for example, that there may be value, on occasions, in people showing that they have faith in Him through obedience to His commands, even commands to do what would otherwise be wrong. This expressive value may tip the balance, making an action that would otherwise be wrong into a right action. It would be wrong for Abraham to kill Isaac if God did not command it, but remember that God's command to kill Isaac is a test of Abraham's faith. If it is valuable for Abraham to show his faith, then it may be right for him, now that God has commanded it, to kill Isaac. All of these may be

[8] Ibid 68.

regarded as ordinary moral propositions. There is no logical discontinuity requiring a shift from one point of view to another. If Abraham does shift into a religious point of view for the purposes of identifying and acting on God's commands, this does not mean he has abandoned the moral point of view. For the moral point of view may itself require him to take the religious point of view, given the moral value of faith.

If this is so, then the Socratic dilemma may be dissolved in the simple way that I indicated, and without Kierkegaard's extraordinary manoeuvres. God is none other than a personification of goodness, His commands are rightness itself. Being omnipotent, God may command any action and thereby make it right for those commanded to do it. But, being omniscient, He commands only what is right. It does not follow that His commands are redundant, merely highlighting what would be right anyway, quite apart from His commands. Because God does not only command what would be right apart from His commands. He commands what is right *given* His commands, and that, as just explained, need not be the same thing at all.

You may object that the key move here lies in the assumption that faith in God can have moral value, and that this assumption is self-undermining in view of the other elements of the picture presented above. God tells Abraham to kill Isaac as a test of faith. The command, as explained above, is right taking account of the value of that faith, although wrong without it. But why, given that He commands something that would apart from His command be wrong, does God *deserve* this faith? What can be the moral value in having faith in a God who commands, effectively, that one have faith in God? Indeed what can be the *rationality* of this? Aren't we forced back to Kierkegaard's manoeuvre of making Abraham's rectitude depend on a *non-rational* leap of faith? Doesn't the Socratic dilemma therefore simply reassert itself in a new guise?

Not quite. Many moral reasons share the following structure: being a friend is a reason for acts of friendship, being a judge is a reason for judicial acts, being a citizen is a reason to do one's citizenly duty, etc. These reasons may appear to lift themselves by their own bootstraps. But of course they do not quite do so. They presuppose that one may have a reason for being someone's friend, or for being a judge, or for being a citizen. But that reason may be something quite modest. One has a reason to make friends with someone just in case, for example, one enjoys their company. One has reason to be a judge just in case it would be a good career move. One has reason to become a citizen just in case this will allow one to escape persecution elsewhere. This need not be a moral reason. Nor need it be a reason to perform, separately, any of the particular acts which, as a friend or as a judge or a citizen, one must then go on to perform. These further acts are made rational, and indeed in some cases morally required, by the fact that one is a friend or a judge, not by the reason one had to become a friend or a judge in the first place.

Things are no different with faith in God. It is true that apart from his faith in God Abraham is morally wrong to kill Isaac, and with it he is morally right to kill Isaac. But his reason for having faith in God need not be, as it stands, a reason to kill Isaac. His reason for having faith in God may be something quite unrelated to Isaac's living or dying. He may have escaped from some terrible disaster or plague by apparently miraculous means. More prosaically, he may have witnessed the long and successful life which faith in God brought to someone else. This is a reason for having faith in God. And given that one has faith in God for this reason, God's commands are reasons for doing what is commanded even though, apart from God's commands, the fact that faith in God could bring a long and successful life would not have been any kind of reason for doing the thing that God commanded (eg killing one's son). Thus God's commands are not morally redundant for those who have faith in Him, and yet the leap of faith which gives God's commands their constitutive importance in determining what is the right thing to do need not be unsupported by reasons.

Faith in a God who sometimes engineers a test of one's faith by commanding one to do something awful, which apart from that command one has absolutely no reason to do and every reason not to do, can therefore be fully and normally rational. This does not mean that Abraham himself faces no dilemma, that rationality all points one way for him. It does not mean, for example, that there are some extra moral reasons to prefer his faith in God over his love for his son. There are reasons for his faith in God, no doubt, and reasons, we may be equally sure, for him to love his son. Given that he has faith in God and love for Isaac, his is an ordinary moral dilemma, in which two incommensurable moral duties are pitted against one another, one a requirement of faith in God and the other a requirement of love for Isaac.[9] That is the whole point of God's test: it is to place Abraham in this moral dilemma and see whether he chooses faith in God over the love of his son. If Abraham chooses faith in God, he is not transcending moral reasons. He is acting on moral reasons, reasons which his faith gives him, a faith he holds, no doubt, for reasons. If the reasons for his faith are undefeated by his reasons for loving his son—and since the two are *ex hypothesi* incommensurable the answer is that they cannot but be undefeated—then he is morally right to kill Isaac in view of the fact that God commanded it, and God commanded it in view of the fact that, for Abraham as a faithful subject of God, it is morally right. Of course, if the test leads Abraham, on the contrary, to abandon his faith, then he is wrong to kill Isaac: whatever else it can do, on the argument just sketched out, faith cannot lend its justifications to the faithless.

2. From God to the *Grundnorm*

The Socratic challenge to theism should strike a chord with legal theorists. Its logic is replicated every year in a thousand undergraduate examination essays pitting the tradition of legal positivism against the natural law tradition. In the tradition of legal positivism, law is binding because it is posited. In the natural law tradition, on the other hand, law is posited because it is binding. Since it surely cannot be both, one must choose between positivism and natural law (thus far the second-class candidate). Or else

---

[9] Some think of Abraham's dilemma as pitting 'Faith' against 'Reason'. But the dilemma as presented here is even-handedly rational; ie both alternatives in the dilemma are supported by reasons. To repeat, Abraham has reasons to love Isaac, as well as reasons to have faith in God. For those reasons he has faith in God and loves Isaac. The resulting dilemma is *within* rationality, between the duties of faith and the duties of love. As for 'Reason' with the God-like capitalization, it is hard to know what this is unless it is just rationality, ie the capacity and propensity to be guided by reasons, including those mundane ones discussed in the text above (reasons for faith and reasons for love, reasons of faith and reasons of love, etc).

one must revel in law's ultimate absurdity, its fundamental contradiction, as Kierkegaard gloried in religion's (a first- or a third-class script, depending on whether the contradiction is made apparent on purpose or by accident). But are these truly the alternatives? Or can we have law on the same terms as, according to my explanation, we can have God, namely without contradiction as both the (positive) source of right and the (natural) repository of it?

We can indeed. Kelsen already gives us the key to understanding the law in this way. At first sight this may seem surprising, because of all modern theorists of law, Kelsen came the closest, in his official account of the relationship between law and morality, to Kierkegaard's view of the relationship between religion and morality. Kelsen describes law and morality as constituting distinct and independent rational points of view. When the question arises of whether someone should take the legal point of view or the moral point of view, however, Kelsen can see no overarching rational point of view from which the question should be asked or answered. One might expect it to be a moral question whether one should take the legal point of view. But for Kelsen it might as well be a legal question whether one should take the moral point of view.[10] Officially, Kelsen makes no point of view answer to any other, rationally speaking. I say 'officially' because, as Raz has shown, Kelsen was not able to honour this doctrine consistently with his analysis of the legal point of view.[11] In an attempt to honour it he was apparently drawn more and more towards a Kierkegaardian glorification of the absurd in his later work, at the expense of his earlier, and more Kantian, exegesis of the Pure Theory.[12] This later work, in which law was said to be based upon a *fiction* of its own rightness,[13] clouded Kelsen's earlier insights. For those insights depended on the fact that, in the

---

[10] *General Theory of Law and State* (trans Wedberg, Cambridge, Mass. 1945), 374.

[11] 'Kelsen's Theory of the Basic Norm' in Raz, *The Authority of Law* (Oxford 1979), at 134–7.

[12] For the full story see Iain Stewart, 'Kelsen and the Exegetical Tradition' in Richard Tur and William Twining (eds), *Essays on Kelsen* (Oxford 1986).

[13] Kelsen, 'The Function of a Constitution', written in 1964 and translated by Iain Stewart for *Essays on Kelsen*, above note 12. See especially the discussion at 117: 'A fiction in this sense is characterized by its not only contradicting reality

earlier exegesis of the Pure Theory, what is commanded by law is ultimately identical with what is right. Therefore, just as a theist may dissolve the Socratic dilemma of theism by holding that God just is goodness personified, so a Kelsenian resolves the structurally identical dilemma of positivism and natural law by holding that law is rightness institutionalized. The question of whether legal rules are posited because right, or right because posited, thus ultimately evaporates without absurdity in the logic of the earlier Kelsenian legal system.

It is important to stress the word 'ultimately' here. That is because it is well known and cannot be denied that all individual laws, for Kelsen, have whatever normative force they have merely because posited. Regarding individual laws, Kelsen subscribes to a particularly hard-line version of legal positivism's definitive 'sources thesis',[14] according to which the 'bindingness' of a law is entirely a matter of its being made by an official authorized to make it by a higher law. Thus Kelsen is rightly associated by many with the view that we lawyers should grasp the first horn of the Socratic dilemma, and hold that law is binding because posited, not posited because binding. But Kelsen is also famous for the thesis that the ultimate source of validity for any legal system is what he called the system's *Grundnorm*, its basic norm. It is ultimately by the grace of the *Grundnorm* alone that all positive law is valid. And the *Grundnorm* is neither right because posited nor posited because right, for it is not posited at all. Its validity is, rather, a presupposition of those who treat posited law as valid *qua* law.

So what exactly is this presupposition? As Kelsen often stated it, it is the presupposition that the historically first constitution is valid.[15] But 'valid' here is a notoriously problematic term. This validity cannot *ex hypothesi* be validity endowed by some further authorizing norm. For *ex hypothesi* we are talking of the historically first constitution and this cannot, by its very definition, take its validity from any other positing act. It cannot take its validity

---

but also containing contradiction within itself'. Similarly: Kelsen, 'On the Pure Theory of Law', *Israel Law Review* 1 (1966), 1 at 6.

[14] On which see Raz, 'Legal Positivism and the Sources of Law' in *The Authority of Law*, above note 11. Also Ch 2, following.

[15] eg *General Theory of Law and State*, above note 10, 115.

from its sources. It must, instead, be valid *on its merits*. For 'sources' and 'merits' exhaust the possible ways of validating anything. The *Grundnorm* must therefore be interpreted as the presupposition that the historically first constitution is meritorious, and that this merit is inherited by whatever positive law the first constitution authorizes. The presupposition of the *Grundnorm* therefore brings might and right into a necessary, definitional alignment. Like the *Grundnorm* itself, what is authorized by the *Grundnorm* is neither right because authorized nor authorized because right. Again, there is no explanatory order to be found. For in the presupposition of the *Grundnorm* is the identification or fusion, in the juristic consciousness, of authorization and rightness. The *Grundnorm* is, in this sense, the juristic God.[16] Under the authority vested by the *Grundnorm* we must, of course, often do what apart from that authority we should or need not do. In law, the sources therefore often seem to require us to depart from the merits. But with the *Grundnorm* presupposed the merits are brought back into line. For the *Grundnorm* by its nature lends its merit to whatever sources it authorizes. Like God, the *Grundnorm* can make it right, by its demands, to do what would otherwise be wrong.

Kelsen himself had notorious difficulty conveying this point. On the one hand he was anxious to distance himself from the natural law tradition by denying that the *Grundnorm* is a moral norm. On the other hand his normative rationalism prevented him from denying that the *Grundnorm*'s validity turns on its merit or value by shifting instead to a practice-based or empirically grounded foundation for the legal system of the kind that Hart later endorsed.[17] Although this led to some wavering on Kelsen's

---

[16] Kelsen himself makes the comparison very briefly in ibid at 110–11. I think he errs (theologically) in regarding God as more akin to the first Constitution, and therefore as having a basic norm presupposed behind Him, which says something like 'the commands of God are valid'. See Sections 3.3 and 3.4 below for closer consideration of this difficult point. And see Raz, *The Concept of a Legal System* (Oxford, 1970), for the argument that there need be no *Grundnorm* behind the first Constitution either; ie that the most basic legal norm can itself be a positive norm of the system.

[17] See Hart's famous note comparing his 'Rule of Recognition' with Kelsen's *Grundnorm* on pages 245–6 of *The Concept of Law* (Oxford 1961).

part throughout his career, there is an important passage in the *General Theory of Law and State* in which he steers a course between empiricist positivism and natural law in the following terms:

> The essential characteristic of positivism, as contrasted with natural law theory, may be found precisely in the difficult renunciation of an absolute, material justification, in this self-denying and self-imposed restriction to a merely hypothetical, formal foundation in the basic norm.... Any attempt to push beyond the relative-hypothetical foundations of positive law, that is, to move from a hypothetical to an absolutely valid fundamental norm justifying the validity of positive law... means the abandonment of the distinction between positive and natural law.[18]

This passage is easily misconstrued. One may think it cuts against my claim that the *Grundnorm* is a juristic God—for after all, God is surely absolute if He exists? But this passage in fact captures Kelsen's affirmation of what I said. In legal science or legal theory, which is Kelsen's subject-matter in this passage, the *Grundnorm* is a mere hypothesis. But in the juristic consciousness it is not a hypothesis but a presupposition. Studying the nature of law theoretically, we must understand how it looks from the inside, but that is different from actually standing inside it. What is relative in legal science is absolute in law itself. What legal science interprets as a norm which is valid hypothetically—ie only if one presupposes the *Grundnorm*—is, from the perspective of one who *does* presuppose the *Grundnorm*, simply right. What is hypothetical in the view of legal theory is absolute in the view of law. It is exactly the same as with theism. What is relative for me as a student of theism, namely the presupposition of the existence of God as a personification of goodness, is necessarily absolute in the view of the faithful whose faith I am studying. So rather than driving a wedge between positivism and natural law, the *Grundnorm* ultimately reconciles them. With the presupposition of the *Grundnorm* merely hypothesized, law is valid on its sources alone. With the *Grundnorm* presupposed those sources necessarily have absolute merit. By virtue of the *Grundnorm*, their

---

[18] *General Theory of Law and State*, above note 10, 396.

authorization entails their rightness and their rightness entails their authorization. For the two properties are one and the same.

And just as the question arises of whether God deserves one's faith, so the question arises of whether the *Grundnorm* deserves one's allegiance. Just as one may have reasons for faith in God, so one may have reasons for allying oneself with the *Grundnorm*. Just as one's reasons for having faith in God may be non-moral reasons, so one's reasons for respecting the law may be non-moral reasons. Just as those who have faith in God thereby automatically acquire new moral reasons irrespective of whether their original reason for having faith in God was a moral reason, so those who ally themselves with the *Grundnorm* automatically acquire new moral reasons irrespective of whether their original reason for allying themselves with the *Grundnorm* was a moral reason. Therefore, just as the faithful may have moral reasons to do on the basis of God's commands what, apart from God's commands, they would have no moral reason to do, so those who ally themselves with the *Grundnorm* may have moral reasons to do on the basis of legal rules what, apart from these legal rules, they would have no moral reason to do. And just as the moral reasons mentioned here to do what God commands have no application to the faithless, so the moral reasons mentioned here to follow legal rules have no application to those who do not ally themselves with the *Grundnorm*, or who, to put it another way, do not have faith in law. My own belief is that such faith need not be irrational or arational any more than faith in God need be irrational or arational. It may be ordinarily rational. People may have faith in the law for the simple reason that the law has served them well, providing the facilities and services that they needed at the time when they needed them. When their faith in the law is rationally defensible, their law-abidingness is *ceteris paribus* rationally defensible too. But by the same token lack of faith in the law may be rational for those who had unfortunate dealings with it, and a general practice of abiding by the law need have no rational attraction for those who lack faith in law.

3. Loosening the analogy

Lest too much is made of these similarities between theistic and legalistic belief, let me mention five important and closely interrelated dissimilarities between God (seen as goodness personified) and the *Grundnorm*, dissimilarities which the above remarks inevitably tended to suppress.

3.1. Where God is concerned, it can be morally right to do on His command what would be morally wrong without it, *only* if one is faithful. Only faith can fill the apparent logical gap. One may, of course, have instrumental reasons for becoming faithful (eg fear of eternal damnation) but once one is faithful the logical gap can only be filled non-instrumentally by the expressive value of faith itself. Regarding the law, things are more complicated. Faith in the law, held for whatever reason, is one of the things which can fill the apparent logical gap between what one should do apart from the law and what one should do in the light of it. But instrumental considerations can also fill that logical gap in part. The classic (although not the only) case is that of the co-ordination problem in which any one of several alternative actions would be justified apart from the law but only one of these is justified given the law. Here it is the law's ability to eliminate transaction costs by getting us to act in harmony which fills the apparent logical gap.[19] This does not depend on faith in the sense discussed above, or anything analogous to it. Of course these co-ordination-based reasons arise only if people in general have faith in the law as a way of solving problems—otherwise the law will fail to establish a co-ordinating practice. But given that people in general do have this faith in the law, its instrumental co-ordinating reasons apply even to those who are faithless, who do not ally themselves in the slightest with the *Grundnorm*. They too should join in the law's solution, where applicable, to reduce transaction costs. Of course, these considerations do not apply across the whole body of the law. Not everything which the law does is an example of successful co-ordination, or of some other instrumental achievement. But my view is that these considerations

---

[19] See eg John Finnis, 'Law as Co-ordination', *Ratio Juris* 2 (1989), 97.

do not apply *at all* in the case of God. Only those who have faith are, to my mind, ever affected by God's commands. God's authority, to put it another way, is exclusively inspirational rather than instrumental. If one is not inspired by God then God has no authority over one at all. Not so the law, where some authority is instrumentally justified and other authority expressively justified; ie justified as an expression of the faithful's faith. In this respect an atheist is in a different moral position from an anarchist. An anarchist is morally permitted to deny authority to the law where, were she to have faith in law, that fact in itself would lend the law its authority over her actions. But the anarchist is morally wrong to deny authority to the law where its authority over her is instrumentally justified; eg through the benefits of co-ordination. Whereas it seems to me that an atheist, even if she is wrong to deny God's existence, is morally permitted to deny Him any authority over her actions at all.

3.2. In the case of God, to know Him is to love Him. Cognition of God entails moral commitment. Not so the *Grundnorm*. Kelsen struggled with this point throughout his career.[20] He struggled to find a way in which lawyers, for example, could enjoy cognition of the law without any personal commitment to it. He clearly believed that this was possible. He believed that one could be an anarchist who is a perfectly competent lawyer, or at any rate a perfectly competent scholar or teacher of law.[21] So, fundamentally, he needed to find two different ways in which the *Grundnorm* could be presupposed—fully, if you like, and on the other hand merely *arguendo*. He never quite succeeded in this, although successors like Raz and MacCormick have fared much better.[22] The point I am making is merely that this divide cannot even intelligibly be sought in the case of God. The reason is not simply that God is goodness personified in the eyes of the faithful. After all, as I argued, something very similar is true of the *Grundnorm* in the

---

[20] See his testimony to his own problem with this in the notes of *The Pure Theory of Law* (trans Knight, 2nd ed, Berkeley 1967), at 204.

[21] Ibid 218n.

[22] Raz, 'Kelsen's Theory of the Basic Norm', above note 11, 137ff, MacCormick, *Legal Reasoning and Legal Theory* (revised ed, Oxford 1994), 275ff (discussing Hart rather than Kelsen, but to much the same effect).

eyes of its faithful. The reason, rather, is that of God's comprehensively overarching role in the universe, if He exists. This role is such that merely recognizing His existence amounts, necessarily, to laying oneself down before Him. Nobody need feel the same about a legal system. One may see that a legal system exists, and what it involves, without in the slightest laying oneself down before it. For example, one may look up French law to discover how things are done in France. When one does so, to borrow Raz's terms, one presupposes the *Grundnorm* in a detached rather than a committed way, or, to borrow MacCormick's terms, one has the cognitive internal attitude to law without the volitional internal attitude. To know the law is not to love it even though the *Grundnorm*, if for any reason we *do* come to love the law, necessarily fuses for us the merits and the sources of law.

3.3. The *Grundnorm* does not command directly, for it is not an agent but a norm. It merely authorizes agents to command. All legal authority, even constitutional authority, is thus for Kelsen legally subordinate authority. God, on the other hand, commands directly. There is disagreement among faiths and among interpreters of faiths about whether He also commands *in*directly; eg through His officers on earth. Some hold that these officers are merely conduits through whom God issues His own commands. Others hold that these officers issue their own commands, by delegated authority from God. Still others hold that God's officers are fallible interpreters of God's commands. The question is interesting and important because it bears on the relationship between the merits and the sources of religious doctrine. If God delegates authority, does it follow that His officers on earth also share, by God's authority, the definitional goodness which He personifies? Are they, within the scope of their offices, likewise personifications of goodness? The matter bears on the Kelsenian view of law because, given that the *Grundnorm* does not command directly, we need to know whether those whom it authorizes to command are always necessarily commanding meritoriously just because of their authorization. Kelsen's very appealing answer is that they are. Within the law, by virtue of the *Grundnorm*, source-based authority is the only merit that counts. The *Grundnorm* makes legal officials infallible when they act within the scope of their authorization, even though what they command was, for example, in their own discretion rather than dictated by the first constitution, and whether or not what they commanded is a matter of interpretation of some existing law. It does not, of course, make legal officials infallible regarding what should be done apart from what they command. They often make mistakes in determining where the merits of the case lay before they gave judgment, or issued their instructions, etc. The *Grundnorm* makes them infallible regarding only what should be done given what, with the *Grundnorm*'s authorization, they command. Their lawful rulings are, to put it simply, dispositive in the eyes of the law.

3.4. The fact that legal authority is all more or less subordinate opens the way, you might say, for selective faith in law. Couldn't one have, for example, faith in the courts but none in the legislature, or faith in old law but not in newer law? Yes, one could. The question is whether this makes the *Grundnorm* drop out of the picture. For the importance of the *Grundnorm* surely resides in the fact that it entails the coincidence of all sources and all merits, so that on the doctrine of the *Grundnorm* one would expect faith in the law, like faith in God, to be an all-or-nothing affair, in which picking and choosing is unintelligible? Doesn't the possibility of picking and choosing in one's faith make the *Grundnorm* redundant? This is a premature conclusion. The fact that one may through the detached presupposition of the *Grundnorm* know law without loving it is what explains the possibility of picking and choosing where one will put one's faith. Cognition of the *Grundnorm* with detachment allows one to identify laws and understand them complete with their claim to meritoriousness *in advance of commitment to them*. Not so God and His commands. Since to know God is to love him, one has no logical space to pick and choose with His commands. His role in the life of the faithful is, for that reason and that reason alone, all or nothing. It is not that He would be redundant if we could pick and choose. It is that He would be something much less extraordinary than what, if He exists, by His nature He must be.

3.5. You may say that now we have come, at last, to the crunch. Law plainly exists. But God's existence is everywhere and always in doubt. In admitting that there are cases in which faith in God is rational we surely assumed God's existence. For there can be no reason for anyone to have faith in a non-existent God. In case of a non-existent God, faith is reduced to superstition. Of course, such superstition may be excusable. People who act on justified but false beliefs can often be excused their consequently erroneous actions.[23] But the issue here is whether faith in God can lend *justification*, not mere excuse, to the faithful. There is a short answer. The short answer is that we *obviously* assumed God's existence. After all, the Socratic puzzle with which we started assumes God's existence. For if God does not exist, then God does not command, and if God does not command, then there can be no puzzle about the constitutive difference that his commands make. So there was never any hesitation in this discussion so far as the assumption of God's existence is concerned. But personally, as I am sure I have made tolerably clear, I think the assumption is false. I do not believe that goodness is personified anywhere in the universe. I have, in that sense, no knowledge of God. But of course I can grasp the *idea* of goodness personified, and hence hypothesize the presuppositions of a believer in such a thing. It is no different from what I do as a philosopher of law when I daily hypothesize the presuppositions of lawyers. One must be careful not to confuse detachment and hypothesis. We noted above (3.2) that one cannot presuppose God's existence in a detached way as one can presuppose the *Grundnorm* in a detached way. But it does not follow that, as a philosopher, one cannot hypothesize the believer's committed presupposition of God in the same way that one hypothesizes the lawyer's detached presupposition of the *Grundnorm*. The capacity of the human intellect for hypothesis and its capacity for detached presupposition are quite different. Ronald Dworkin's *Law's Empire* tells us that, as lawyers, we cannot presuppose the validity of the first constitution non-committally—we must be committed to the whole history of the constitution. The same book tells us that, as legal theorists, we cannot hypothesize the presuppositions of lawyers without endorsing them.[24] So not only lawyers but also

---

[23] See my 'Justification and Reasons' in A.T.H. Smith and Andrew Simester (eds), *Harm and Culpability* (Oxford 1996).
[24] The moves are sketched in *Law's Empire* (Cambridge, Mass. 1986), 11–15.

legal theorists can only talk about law while being committed to it. Dworkin is wrong even on the first point. Law is not God and happily lawyers need not, in their professional capacity, be true believers. But Dworkin's error is deepened by his failure adequately to distinguish the two points. Even if law were God, so that lawyers would have to be true believers, it would not follow that only true believers could be *philosophers* of law.

2
Legal Positivism: 5½ Myths

1. Isolating legal positivism

The label 'legal positivism' is sometimes attached to a broad intellectual tradition, distinguished by an emphasis on certain aspects of legal thought and experience (namely the empirical aspects). This way of using the label is well-suited to work in the history of ideas, in which the object of the exercise is to trace the ways in which philosophical themes were reprised and reworked as they were handed down from one generation to the next. In such work there is no need to identify any distinctive proposition that was advanced or accepted by all those designated as 'legal positivists', for the label attaches by virtue of common themes rather than common theses. But things are different when the label 'legal positivism' is used in philosophical debate. In philosophical debate our interest is in the truth of propositions, and we always need to know which proposition we are supposed to be debating. So there is nothing philosophical to say about 'legal positivists' as a group unless there is some distinctive proposition or set of propositions that was advanced or assumed by all of them. In philosophical argument, to put it another way, 'legal positivists' stand or fall together only if they are united by thesis, rather than merely by theme. There is neither guilt by association nor redemption by association in philosophy.

In this chapter, I intend to treat one and only one proposition as the distinctive proposition of 'legal positivism', and to designate as 'legal positivists' all and only those who advance or endorse this proposition. The proposition is:

> (LP) In any legal system, whether a given norm is legally valid, and hence whether it forms part of the law of that system, depends on its sources, not its merits.

In philosophical argument it matters not which proposition is given which name; it matters only which is true. On the other hand, I obviously did not choose this proposition (LP) at random to carry the famous 'legal positivism' branding. In the first place, I wanted to bring my use of the label into a tolerable extensional alignment with the use of the label familiar from the history of ideas. Those commonly said to constitute the dominant historical figures of the 'legal positivist tradition'—Thomas Hobbes, Jeremy Bentham, John Austin, Hans Kelsen, and Herbert Hart—do not converge on many propositions about law. But subject to some differences of interpretation, they do converge unanimously on proposition (LP). Secondly, proposition (LP) is the one that contemporary self-styled 'legal positivists'—such as Joseph Raz and Jules Coleman—bill themselves as subscribing to *qua* legal positivists, and the correct interpretation of which they debate when they debate among themselves *qua* legal positivists. Finally, my use of the label makes literal sense of the label itself. What should a 'legal positivist' believe if not that laws are *posited*? And this, roughly, is what (LP) says of laws. It says, to be more exact, that in any legal system, a norm is valid as a norm of that system solely in virtue of the fact that at some relevant time and place some relevant agent or agents announced it, practiced it, invoked it, enforced it, endorsed it, or otherwise engaged with it. It is no objection to its counting as a law that it was an appalling norm that those agents should never have engaged with. Conversely, if it was never engaged with by any relevant agents, then it does not count as a law, even though it may be an excellent norm that all the relevant agents should have engaged with unreservedly. As Austin famously (if perhaps too brashly) expressed the point, 'the existence of law is one thing; its merit or demerit is another'.[1]

We see here how the contrast between 'sources' and 'merits' in (LP) is meant to be read. 'Source' is to be read broadly such that any intelligible argument for the validity of a norm counts as source-based if it is not merits-based. The two categories, in other words, are jointly exhaustive of the possible conditions of validity for any norm. But are they also mutually exclusive? You may say that there is a problem of overlap which prevents us from

---

[1] John Austin, *The Province of Jurisprudence Determined* (ed Rumble, Cambridge 1995), 157.

classifying some arguments for the validity of a norm as either source-based or merits-based, for they mention conditions of both types. On the one hand, (i) we have arguments that attempt to validate certain norms by relying on *merit-based tests of their sources;* eg by relying on the fact that they were announced or practised by Rex, together with the fact that Rex is a noble king. On the other hand, (ii) we have arguments that attempt to validate certain norms by relying on *source-based tests of their merits*; eg by relying on the fact that they are reasonable norms, together with the fact that some other norm (validated only by its source) instructs us to apply all and only reasonable norms.

The legal positivist tradition has been united in regarding arguments of type (i) as invoking merit conditions of a type which cannot possibly be among the conditions of its legal validity. The question of whether Rex is a noble king (or whether the regime in Lilliput is a just one, etc) obviously bears on the moral significance of his (its) pronouncements and practices, but the answer to such questions cannot, according to legal positivists, affect the legal status of those pronouncements and practices. This is not to deny, of course, that they can make a merely *causal* difference to legal status: maybe the fact that Rex is a noble King explains why his subjects, or his officials, have come to regard his word as law. But it is *his word* that they regard as law. For his word to be regarded as law it must be possible to regard his word as law without reopening the question, when his word is heard, of whether he is a noble king. Thus Rex's nobility, according to legal positivists, cannot make a *constitutive* difference to Rex's ability to affect legal validity. So our approximation (LP) should be reformulated more exactly to read:

> (LP*) In any legal system, whether a given norm is legally valid, and hence whether it forms part of the law of that system, depends on its sources, not its merits (where its merits, in the relevant sense, include the merits of its sources).

As far as arguments of type (ii) are concerned, the tradition has been more divided. Those who have come to be known as 'soft' or 'inclusive' legal positivists allow that in some legal systems norms may be legally valid in virtue of their merits (eg their reasonableness), but only if other legally valid norms happen to pick out those merits as relevant to legal validity.[2] Others, known correspondingly as 'hard' or 'exclusive' legal positivists, deny this. They hold that a law which declares that (say) all and only reasonable laws shall be valid does not legally validate any further norms, in spite of appearances. Rather, it delegates to some official (say, a judge) the task of validating further norms himself or herself by *classifying* them as reasonable. On this 'hard legal positivist' view, the validity of the further laws in question comes not of their reasonableness (their merit), but rather of the fact that some relevant agent classified (declared, treated, invoked) them as reasonable (their source).[3]

In what follows, I will for the most part bracket the internecine debate between 'hard' and 'soft' legal positivists and leave (LP★) ambiguous in respect of it. Where necessary, I will default to the 'hard' version, since that is the version I support myself. I will leave it to the reader to make the modifications needed to accommodate the soft version, where relevant. These modifications should not alter much what I have to say. That is because the problems I will be surveying—and it will largely be a second-hand survey—are apt to afflict hard and soft legal positivists alike. In general, they are not problems of legal positivism's own making. They are problems of systematic misrepresentation by others. Have the members of any tradition of thought ever had their actual philosophical commitments so comprehensively mauled, twisted, second-guessed, crudely psychoanalysed, and absurdly reinvented by ill-informed gossip and hearsay, as the legal positivists? Has any other thesis in the history of philosophy

---

[2] This possibility was clearly envisaged by Herbert Hart in *The Concept of Law* (Oxford 1961), 204, and was relied upon in the postscript to the book's second edition (Oxford 1994) at 250. (Subsequent references are to the first edition unless otherwise specified.) In the meantime 'soft' legal positivism had been proposed by Philip Soper in 'Legal Theory and the Obligation of a Judge: The Hart/Dworkin Dispute', *Michigan Law Review* 75 (1977) 473; David Lyons, 'Principles, Positivism, and Legal Theory', *Yale Law Journal* 87 (1977) 415; and perhaps most influentially by Jules Coleman in 'Negative and Positive Positivism', *Journal of Legal Studies* 11 (1982) 139.

[3] This was clearly Kelsen's view: see *The General Theory of Law and State* (New York 1961), eg at 134–6. The most influential contemporary exponent of the 'hard' legal positivist view is Joseph Raz: see his 'Authority, Law and Morality' in Raz, *Ethics in the Public Domain* (rev ed, Oxford 1995), further defended in Scott Shapiro, 'On Hart's Way Out', *Legal Theory* 4 (1998), 469.

been so widely and so contemptuously misstated, misinterpreted, misapplied, and misappropriated as (LP★)? Well, actually, I can think of a few. Something like this is apt to happen whenever a label is used in both philosophy and, relatedly, in the history of ideas. 'Natural lawyers' will feel some sympathy, as they often suffer similar indignities. Nevertheless, there are special and interesting lessons to be learnt from the catalog of myths about legal positivism that have gradually built up to give it a whipping-boy status in so much legally related literature.[4] Some of these lessons, not surprisingly, are lessons about law itself.

2. Why so misunderstood?

But before we come to the myths, let's just stop to ask ourselves what it is about legal positivism that made it so ripe for misrepresentation. I think there are two principal factors.

First: Proposition (LP★), although a proposition about the conditions of validity of certain norms that may be used in practical reasoning, is itself normatively inert. It does not provide any guidance at all on what anyone should do about anything on any occasion. Sometimes, like any proposition, it does of course serve as the minor (or informational) premise in a practical syllogism. If someone happens to acquire a duty to determine what the law of Indiana says on some subject on some occasion, then the truth of (LP★) affects how she should proceed. According to (LP★), she should look for sources of Indiana law, not ask herself what it would be most meritorious for people in Indiana to do. On the other hand, (LP★) is never a major (or operative) premise of any practical syllogism. That means that *by itself* it does not point in favour of or against doing anything at all. I don't just mean that it provides no moral guidance. It provides no legal guidance either. It merely states one feature that all legal guidance necessarily has, viz. that if valid *qua* legal it is valid in virtue of its sources, not its merits.[5] Lawyers and law teachers find

---

[4] See Fred Schauer, 'Positivism as Pariah' in Robert P. George (ed), *The Autonomy of Law* (Oxford 1996).

[5] Ronald Dworkin's talk of 'the grounds of law' in *Law's Empire* (Cambridge, Mass. 1986), at 4ff, intentionally elides the distinction I am drawing here. Both the claim

this comprehensive normative inertness in (LP*) hard to swallow. They think (rightly) that legal practice is a practical business, and they expect the philosophy of law to be the back-room activity of telling front-line practitioners how to do it well, with their heads held high. When a philosopher of law asserts a proposition that neither endorses nor criticizes what they do, but only identifies some necessary feature of what they do, lawyers and law teachers are often frustrated. They automatically start to search for hidden notes of endorsement or criticism, secret norms that they are being asked to follow. They refuse to believe that there are none.[6] They cannot accept that legal philosophy is not wholly (or even mainly) the back-room activity of identifying what is good or bad about legal practice, and hence of laying on practical proposals for its improvement (or failing that, abandonment). In this fundamentally anti-philosophical climate, a thesis like (LP*), which is inertly informative, is bound to become egregiously distorted.

Second: To make (LP*) a revealing proposition about law one has to believe that there is some *alternative* to validating norms according to their sources. One has to believe that some norms are valid depending on their merits, or else one won't see the contrastive purchase of (LP*). Instead, (LP*) will just strike one as rehearsing a general truth about norms—that all norms are made valid by somebody's engagement with them—and hence as revealing nothing special about law. All the torchbearers for the legal positivist tradition that were mentioned above agreed that, by default, the validity of a norm depends on its merits: the fact that a norm would be a good one to follow is, by default, what

---

that legal norms are valid on their sources and the claim that legislation constitutes a source of valid legal norms are treated by Dworkin as *legal* claims. But only the second is a legal claim. The first is a claim about what *makes* the second a legal claim. To be exact, 'legislation is a source of valid legal norms' is a legal claim only if the norm it mentions (viz. the norm of legislation-following) is itself being held out as valid on the strength of its sources rather than its merits (eg on the strength of the fact that legislation is identified as a source of law in a constitutional document or judicial practice).

[6] For a particularly clear expression of this refusal, see Gerald Postema, 'Jurisprudence as Practical Philosophy', *Legal Theory* 4 (1998), 329.

makes it valid. All agreed, for instance, that this is true of moral norms.[7] Legal norms, they agreed, are special (although not unique) in defying this default logic of norm-validation. How on earth do they defy it? It is a matter of deep wonderment to many philosophers.[8] Alas, many lawyers and law teachers and students do not share the wonderment. For many in these lines of work think—being especially affected by a feature they see every day and take for granted in legal norms—that whether *any* norm is valid can depend only on its sources. They assume that moral and aesthetic norms are the same: just like legal norms, they can only be validated by the beliefs or endorsements of their users, or by social conventions or practices, etc. When one proposes a moral or aesthetic norm, such people often react in classic positivist fashion by asking 'Who says?' or 'On whose authority?' (as if the validity of a moral or aesthetic norm would depend on somebody *saying* it or *authorizing* it), rather than by asking what is the merit of the norm. Such general normative positivists—and they have always dominated the Critical Legal Studies movement and similar pseudo-radical camps—naturally cannot see what (LP★) has to offer in illuminating the distinctive nature of law.[9] So if legal positivism is to illuminate the distinctive nature of law, the thinking goes, (LP★) cannot be all there is to it. There must be more. And there begins the myth-spinning.

---

[7] Kelsen is an apparent exception. He normally reserved the label 'morality' for a specialized order of posited (conventionally or ecclesiastically validated) norms rivaling law. Nevertheless, his work always presupposed the possibility of genuine moral norms valid on their merits. I defended this reading of Kelsen in Ch 1.

[8] As Hart expressed the wonderment: 'How are the creation, imposition, modification and extinction of obligations and other operations on other legal entities such as rights possible? How can such things be done?' See Hart 'Legal and Moral Obligation' in A.I. Melden (ed), *Essays in Moral Philosophy* (Seattle 1958), 82 at 86.

[9] When legal positivists are labelled simply as 'positivists', or it is otherwise insinuated that they tend to share the broader philosophical positions of eg Comte or Ayer—beware! It is usually the pot calling the kettle black. And nowhere more spectacularly than in the work of Stanley Fish: eg 'Wrong Again', *Texas Law Review* 62 (1983), 299 at 309ff, especially note 31.

3. The myths

3.1. The value of positivity

My chapter title says I will cover 5½ myths about legal positivism, and I will begin with the half-myth. At the inception of the legal positivist tradition—in the work of Hobbes and arguably that of Bentham—we find an (LP★)-inspired optimism about the value of law. Insofar as legal norms are valid on their sources rather than their merits, this fact alone is held to endow legal norms with some redeeming merit even when they are (in every other respect) unmeritorious norms.[10] Their redeeming merit is their special ability to settle matters that cannot be settled one way or the other on their merits. Believers in this claim are sometimes known as 'normative legal positivists' but here I will call them 'positivity-welcomers'.[11] That is because they need not endorse (LP★) and hence need not be legal positivists in the sense I am exploring. As positivity-welcomers they merely endorse.

> (PW) To the extent that (LP★) is sound, it identifies something not only true about legal norms, but meritorious about legal norms as well.

Those who are both legal positivists and positivity-welcomers are less frustrating to lawyers and law-school dwellers than other legal positivists. For such people give (LP★) some immediate and invariant practical significance of a kind that warms our legal hearts. They tell us that the positivity of law is not only something we have to live with, but also something we can be proud of. Thanks to the truth of (LP★) combined with the truth of (PW), they say, it is always in one respect meritorious—and hence *ceteris paribus* justifiable—to advance a legal solution (however otherwise

---

[10] See eg Thomas Hobbes, 'Questions Concerning Liberty, Necessity, and Chance' in W. Molesworth (ed), *The English Works of Thomas Hobbes* (London 1839–1845), vol. v, at 194. For thorough documentation of Bentham's complex views on the built-in merit of law, see Gerald Postema, *Bentham and the Common Law Tradition* (Oxford 1986).

[11] Prominent examples of positivity-welcomers today: Neil MacCormick, 'A Moralistic Case for A-moralistic Law', *Valparaiso Law Review* 20 (1985), 1; Tom Campbell, *The Legal Theory of Ethical Positivism* (Aldershot 1996); Jeremy Waldron, 'Normative (or Ethical) Positivism' in Jules Coleman (ed), *Hart's Postscript* (Oxford 2001), 410. I erred on the side of excess in the list of legal positivists I classified as positivity-welcomers in my review of Campbell's book in *King's College Law Journal* 9 (1998), 180.

unmeritorious) to a moral or economic problem that would be intractable on its merits alone.

This rather self-congratulatory conclusion has not been common ground among the leading figures of the legal positivist tradition, and in particular the philosophical maturing of the tradition in the twentieth century led to its abandonment by the tradition's most important modern torchbearers, among them Kelsen, Hart, and Raz. Hart is an especially interesting case. Hart agreed with those who say that all laws have a redeeming merit which comes of their very nature as laws. However, he did not trace this redeeming merit of all laws to their positivity. He traced it instead to the fact that, in his view, laws are not merely norms but *rules*; ie norms capable of repeated application from case to case. This fact of their normative generality, he thought, means that wherever laws go a kind of justice (and hence a kind of merit) automatically follows, for the correct re-application of any law entails that like cases are treated alike.[12] My own view, contrary to Hart's, is that there is no justice (and more generally no merit) to be found in the mere fact that like cases are treated alike.[13] But be that as it may, Hart's belief that all laws have some redeeming merit has everything to do with the fact that in his view laws are general norms and nothing to do with the fact that in his view they are posited norms. These two qualities are unconnected.[14] Notice that as it stands, (LP★) is not a proposition specifically about *laws*. It is a proposition about what makes norms valid as *legal norms*, and hence as part of the law. It includes within its scope non-general legal norms such as the ruling that Tice must pay $50 to Summers in damages. This too is valid as a legal norm on its sources, according to (LP★), even though it is not a norm capable of repeated application and hence would not

---

[12] See Hart's 1958 essay 'Positivism and the Separation of Law and Morals' in his *Essays in Jurisprudence and Philosophy* (Oxford 1983), 49 at 81; also *The Concept of Law*, above note 2, Ch 8.
[13] See Ch 10 below.
[14] Some of Bentham's remarks cited by Postema, above note 10, suggest that for him the only built-in merit of laws lies in their *combination* of generality and positivity, which is why I said that he was only *arguably* a supporter of (PW).

be a law, according to Hart—and hence would not share in the value that Hart ascribes to all laws.

Some legal positivists go further, as Raz does, and deny that there is any built-in merit in all laws, let alone in all legal norms.[15] Observers of such debates often ask: 'If legal positivists disagree among themselves about whether the positivity of legal norms lends them any value, why is it that they all mysteriously agree in making such a *fuss* about the positivity of law? Doesn't it reveal that they all think it *important* that legal norms are posited norms?' True enough. Philosophers who defend (LP★), like all other philosophers, are offering an interpretation of their subject matter that plays up the true and important and plays down the true but unimportant.[16] But what is important about legal norms, even what is important for their evaluation, need not be something that lends value or merit to them. Notice that the positivity of law could also be evaluatively important as a ground of *abhorrence* for law, as something that automatically drains merit out of each legal norm rather than adding merit to it. Anarchists, for example, can turn their arguments against submission to authority into arguments against respect for law only by endorsing (LP★) as a stepping stone. Only if legal norms are posited by someone do they count as exercises of authority. Anarchists who do not endorse (LP★) therefore should not have a blanket opposition to respecting legal norms *qua* legal. That anarchists do typically have a blanket opposition to respecting legal norms *qua* legal shows that they are typically legal positivists. Would one suppose that this in turn showed a secret belief, on the part of all such anarchists, that all legal norms, or all laws, have a built-in redeeming merit?

If not, then one should not jump to that conclusion regarding non-anarchistic legal positivists either. It is open to them to hold, for

---

[15] See Raz's assembled arguments in 'The Obligation to Obey the Law' and 'Respect for Law' which appear as Chs 12 and 13 of Raz, *The Authority of Law* (Oxford 1979). These add up to a rebuttal not only of law's built-in rational appeal, but also (by the same token) of its built-in merit.

[16] Which shows that it is a mistake to follow Ronald Dworkin in contrasting 'interpretive' accounts of law's nature with 'descriptive' ones, unless one happens to share Dworkin's idiosyncratic 'constructive' view of interpretation. Cf Dworkin, 'Legal Theory and the Problem of Sense' in Ruth Gavison (ed), *Issues in Contemporary Legal Philosophy* (Oxford 1987), 9 at 13–14.

example, that the truth of (LP*) is evaluatively important precisely because (LP*) brings out a single feature of legal norms that leads anarchists to find laws invariably (in one respect) repugnant and some of their opponents to find laws invariably (in one respect) attractive. Nor are these—invariable repugnance and invariable attraction—the only possible evaluative reactions to law's positivity. Perhaps the positivity of law sometimes makes law more repugnant and sometimes makes it more attractive and sometimes makes no difference at all to law's value, depending on what other conditions hold. Only if a law is meritorious in some other ways, say, does its positivity lend it additional merit. I am not advocating this position. I am only saying that the truth of (LP*) must be granted, at least *arguendo*, before the argument over this position can even begin. This shows why philosophers of law might regard the positivity of legal norms as evaluatively important without thereby being predisposed to the (LP*)-inspired but not (LP*)-entailed thesis (PW).

3.2. The rule of law

Legal positivists are sometimes identified as placing a particular emphasis on the ideal of the rule of law (or *Rechtstaat*) as opposed to other ideals of government. No doubt on some occasions this is just another way of saying that legal positivists are relative enthusiasts for law, in that they see some built-in redeeming merit in legal norms *qua* posited. This is the half-myth that we already considered under heading 3.1, involving the extra thesis (PW). But on at least some occasions the association of legal positivism with the rule of law is clearly supposed to suggest a different point not implicating (PW). It is supposed to suggest that legal positivists insist on the evaluation of laws according to their 'form' (eg their clarity, certainty, prospectivity, generality, and openness) as opposed to their content (eg what income tax rate they set, or what limits on freedom of speech they authorize). The label 'rule of law' is used to designate the former clutch of 'content-independent' evaluative criteria.[17]

---

[17] See eg Hugh Collins, 'Democracy and Adjudication' in Neil MacCormick and Peter Birks (eds), *The Legal Mind* (Oxford 1986), 67 at 68; Kenneth Winston, 'Constructing Law's Mandate' in David Dyzenhaus (ed), *Recrafting the Rule of Law* (Oxford 1999), 290ff.

It is hard to disentangle the various confusions that underlie this myth. First, it is not clear in what sense clarity, certainty, and so on, are aspects of a law's 'form', although I will persist here in so classifying them to avoid a long side-track.[18] Second, it is not clear how the relevant distinction between the form of a law and its content is supposed to relate to the distinction drawn in (LP★) between source-based criteria of normative validity and merits-based criteria. Should those who think that norms are legally valid according to their sources and not their merits be herded together with those who think that norms are legally valid according to their form rather than their content?[19] This herding together seems muddled. While the former position is the legal positivist one captured in (LP★), the latter is a classic *anti*-legal positivist position often associated (fairly or unfairly) with Lon Fuller.[20] To hold a norm legally valid according to its formal merits (clarity, certainty, etc) rather than according to the merits of its content is still to hold it valid according to its merits, and this puts one on a collision course with (LP★).

This point is spelled out by Hart in a passage towards the end of *The Concept of Law*.[21] Alas, Hart later went on to court confusion on the same point by suggesting that legal reasons (including legal norms) are distinctive in being reasons of a content-independent type.[22] Unlike moral and economic norms, their validity cannot be affected by their content. In saying this, Hart cooked up a red herring the scent of which still lingers.[23] The validity of

---

[18] The classification is challenged in detail in Ch 8 below.

[19] See eg Dworkin, *Taking Rights Seriously* (London 1977), 17: legal positivists' criteria of legal validity have to do 'not with [the] content [of norms] but with... the manner in which they were adopted or developed'.

[20] 'Positivism and Fidelity to Law: A Reply to Professor Hart' *Harvard Law Review* 71 (1958), 630. I say 'fairly or unfairly' because arguably Fuller is not talking about the conditions of legal validity at all, and so is not engaging with (LP★). Arguably he is talking about the conditions under which (admittedly valid) law deserves no respect among legal officials.

[21] In *The Concept of Law*, above note 2, 202–7.

[22] 'Commands and Authoritative Legal Reasons' in his *Essays on Bentham* (Oxford 1982), 243 at 254–5.

[23] I am not doubting the value of the idea of content-independence in framing or solving other philosophical problems. For example, the notion does help to illuminate (as Hart observes) the difference between norms and other reasons. For

legal norms *can* depend on their content so long as it does not depend on the *merits* of their content. That a certain authority has legal jurisdiction only to change the criminal law means that, by virtue of their content, its measures purporting to create new causes of action in tort do not create valid legal reasons. Conversely, and by the same token, the validity of legal norms cannot depend on their merits even if their merit does not lie in their content but lies rather in their form, eg in the extent of their compliance with rule-of-law standards. Hart should have said, to get to the real point, that legal reasons (including legal norms) are reasons of a distinctively *merit*-independent type. They take their legal validity from their sources, not from their merits, and their merits for these purposes include not only the merits of their content but also the merits of their form (as well as the merits of the person or people who purported to make them or the merits of the system within which they were purportedly made, etc). Thus, as Hart had correctly explained in his earlier engagements with Fuller, a legal norm that is retroactive, radically uncertain, and devoid of all generality, and hence dramatically deficient relative to the ideal of the rule of law, is no less valid *qua* legal, than one that is prospective, admirably certain, and perfectly general.[24]

The conflation of the form-content distinction with the source-merit distinction is compounded, in many discussions of the relationship between legal positivism and the rule of law, by numerous other confusions. In the background of such

---

more sweeping (although I think unsuccessful) objections to the philosophical value of the idea of content-independence, see P. Markwick, 'Law and Content-Independent Reasons', *Oxford Journal of Legal Studies* 20 (2000), 579.

[24] But isn't this insistence on the possibility of legal validity without conformity to the rule of law at odds with Hart's view, already mentioned at above note 12, that all laws (being not only norms but *rules*) have a built-in element of generality? No, it isn't. For the absence of this element of generality, as we saw, does not affect the legal validity of any norm, in Hart's view. It only affects whether it is a valid *law* as opposed to a legally valid norm of a non-general type (eg Tice must pay $50 to Summers). Either way, its legal validity turns on its source, not its generality. Apart from which, the minimal generality required to achieve 'rulishness' clearly falls well short of the measure of generality expected by any credible version of the rule-of-law ideal. One cannot congratulate oneself on having conformed to the generality clause of the rule of law merely by virtue of the fact that the norm one made was a rule.

discussions seems often to lurk the further assumption that the apt ways of evaluating any norm are dictated by the conditions of its validity. Thus, if we suppose that all conditions of legal validity are source-based, we are limited to source-based criticisms of the law; if we endorse 'formal' conditions of legal validity, we are limited to 'formal' criticisms of the law, and so forth. Why should this be so? It implies that the only criticism one can properly make of a supposed legal norm is that it is legally invalid. But far from being the only proper criticism of a supposed legal norm, *this need not be any criticism at all*. Agreeing that a norm is legally valid is not incompatible with holding that it is entirely worthless and should be universally attacked, shunned, ignored, or derided. There are substantive moral debates to be had—independently of the normative inert (LP★)—about the attitude one should have to legally valid norms. In these debates the whole gamut of possible attitudes is on the table. Remember the anarchists we encountered above, who went as far as to regard the fact that a norm is posited is actually part of the case for attacking it, shunning it, ignoring it, or deriding it? Even for positivity-welcoming legal positivists, who combine (LP★) and (PW) and conclude that legally valid norms necessarily have some redeeming merit, this is still only a *redeeming* merit. It does not affect the possibility of attacking, shunning, ignoring, or deriding the same legal norm on the ground of its many more striking and important *demerits*. Those demerits may obviously include the demerits of its content (eg what income tax rate it sets or what limits on freedom of speech it authorizes), as well as the demerits of what we are calling its form (its lack of clarity, uncertainty, retroactivity, lack of generality, and obscurity).

And why, to bring out one final confusion under this heading, should these last two dimensions of criticism be regarded as rivals? That one believes that lack of clarity, uncertainty, retroactivity, lack of generality, obscurity, and so forth are demerits of a legal norm does not entail that one denies that there are further demerits in the same norm's content (eg that it sets a too-low rate of income tax or a too-high protection for freedom of speech). Nor does it suggest that one regards the former demerits as more important than the latter. One may well think, to be sure, that the former demerits are in a sense *more peculiarly legal* demerits than the others. As a believer in (LP*), one is committed to agreeing with Hart that the law's living up to the rule-of-law values that Fuller called the 'inner morality of law' cannot be among the conditions for the legal validity of any norm. But so long as they are not held to be among the conditions for the legal validity of any norm, one is not debarred from agreeing with Fuller that these values constitute law's special inner morality, endowing law with its own distinctive objectives and imperatives.[25] Legal positivism is not a whole theory of law's nature, after all. It is a thesis about legal validity, which is compatible with any number of further theses about law's nature, including the thesis that all valid law is by its nature subject to special moral objectives and imperatives of its own. It is a long way from this thesis, however, to the conclusion that valid law answers *only* to its own special objectives and imperatives, and not to the rest of morality. A more credible assumption is that law's inner morality, if it has one, adds *extra* moral objectives and imperatives for legal norms to live up to, *on top of* the regular moral objectives and imperatives (eg avoiding the infliction of pain, not deceiving its addressees) that every practice or activity should live up to as a matter of course. Naturally, this addition of extra moral objectives and imperatives can give rise to extra conflicts. Sometimes laws that have meritorious content can accordingly be made morally questionable by the fact that there is no way to make them sufficiently clear, certain, prospective, general, or open. Thus—true enough—the pursuit of some other sound governmental ideals may sometimes be slowed down by adherence to the ideal of the rule of law.

But this is no reason to imagine that those who subscribe to the ideal of the rule of law have no commitment to any potentially conflicting ideals of government, or that they automatically regard potentially conflicting ideals as subordinate, or that they do not regard the law as answering to any ideals apart from the specialized ideal of the rule of law.[26] In particular, none of the leading figures of the legal positivist tradition subscribed (to the best of my

---

[25] Hart, *The Concept of Law*, above note 2, 202.
[26] Friedrich Hayek did much to encourage the view that allegiance to the rule of law requires a suppression of all other ideals for government and law: cf. *The*

knowledge) to any views resembling any of these. And even if they had, for the reasons I have given, this could have had no philosophical connection with their being legal positivists.

3.3. Positivistic adjudication

In some quarters legal positivists are thought to be committed to a distinctive view about the proper way of adjudicating cases, according to which judges should not have regard to the merits of cases when deciding them. This conclusion generally comes of combining an endorsement of (LP*) with the widespread assumption that judges are under a professional (ie a role-based moral) obligation to decide cases only by applying valid legal norms to them.[27] But the latter assumption is not shared by legal positivists in general and is directly challenged by several of the tradition's leading figures. The simplest way to challenge it is to rely on its systematic and unavoidable collision with another pressing professional obligation of judges, namely their obligation not to refuse to decide any case that is brought before them and that lies within their jurisdiction. If judges are professionally bound to decide cases only by applying valid legal norms to them, the argument goes, then there are necessarily some cases that they should refuse to decide, for there are necessarily some cases not decidable only by applying valid legal norms. This in turn is so precisely because of the positivity of legal norms. There are inherent limitations on the ability of agents to anticipate future cases in which the norms they create may be relied upon, and to shape the norms they create in such a way as to settle across the board which cases they apply to.[28] Insofar as legal norms are the creations of agents—ie insofar as they are the posited norms that (LP*) tells us they are—these inherent limitations inevitably give rise to some gaps in the law.

When I speak of 'gaps' here, I do not mean that the law is silent regarding some cases. Closure rules (such as 'everything not forbidden by law is permitted by law') are perfectly capable of

---

Road to Serfdom (London 1944), 54ff. However, Hayek's arguments to this effect were uniformly fallacious.

[27] Cf Dworkin, *Law's Empire*, above note 5, 6–8.
[28] As explained at length by Hart in *The Concept of Law*, above note 2, 121–32.

preventing legal silence.[29] Rather, the gaps I have in mind arise (i) in cases in which a given legal norm is neither applicable nor inapplicable, but rather indeterminate in its application; and (ii) in cases in which valid legal norms conflict so that two rivals (eg one forbidding a certain action and the other requiring the same action) are both applicable at once and there exists no third legal norm that resolves the conflict. No closure rule, however ingenious, can guarantee to eliminate these latter types of gaps.[30] They are endemic to law, in all legal systems, thanks to the positivity of law. This makes it inevitable that if judges are to decide all cases validly brought before them, they will sometimes have to go beyond the mere application of posited (including legal) norms. And once they have exhausted all the normative resources of posited norms, what else is there for them to rely on but the merits of the case and hence of the various norms that might *now* be posited in order to resolve it?

The picture presented here—which is mainly attributable to the work of Hart and Raz, but also owes something to Kelsen— makes legal positivists the natural enemies of the mythological 'legal positivist' view that judges should not have regard to the merits of cases when deciding them. Except by withdrawing from judges the requirement to decide every case validly brought before them, legal positivists cannot but ascribe to judges the role of determining at least some cases at least partly on their merits, and hence cannot but expect of them that they will go beyond the task of merely applying valid law. This brings out the important fact that, in dealing with the full gamut of human decision, source-based and merit-based norms are apt to call upon each other's services at frequent intervals. At least sometimes,

---

[29] Cf Kelsen's denial of the possibility of legal gaps *in the sense of silences* in 'On the Theory of Interpretation', *Legal Studies* 10 (1990), 127 at 132. As Kelsen rightly observes, deontic logic supplies automatic closure rules for cases in which the law fails to do so. Since these defaults are not valid on their sources but are necessary truths, they are not valid as legal norms according to (LP★). This reminds us that the view according to which judges should *only* apply legal norms is in one respect absurd. At the very least, they also need to apply the norms of logic, which are valid on their (intellectual) merits.

[30] Joseph Raz, 'Legal Reasons, Sources, and Gaps' in Raz *The Authority of Law*, above note 15, 70ff.

relying on source-based norms is warranted because it provides one way of resolving cases that cannot be completely resolved on their merits. On any view, this provides at least part of the justification (such as it is) for having legal systems. It is this fact, you will recall, that positivity-welcomers inflate to yield their conclusion that all laws have some redeeming merit just in virtue of their positivity. What they less often notice, however, is that the reverse point also holds with similar force and on similar grounds. At least sometimes relying on some or all of the merits of a case is warranted because it provides a way of resolving cases that cannot be completely resolved according to the applicable source-based norms. This does not necessarily turn into a constant buck-passing exercise. The source-based norms may obviously narrow the issue such that it can now be resolved on the merits even though, without the intervention of source-based norms, it would not have been resolvable on the merits.

This proposal invites a modification of the myth under consideration. Are legal positivists at the very least committed to the view that judges should, *if possible*, decide cases by applying source-based norms? Should judges resort to deciding on the merits only as a fallback, when legal norms cannot settle the matter? This idea has some moral appeal. But it is still not one that has any natural affinity with legal positivism. As I explained, (LP★) is normatively inert. It only tells us that, insofar as judges should apply legal norms when they decide cases, the norms they should apply are source-based norms. But that leaves completely open the vexed questions of whether and when judges should only apply legal norms. Some legal positivists—one thinks particularly of Bentham—happen to be enthusiasts for limiting the role of judges in developing the law.[31] It would be better, on this Benthamite view, if judges stuck to merely applying the law, so far as possible, and left law-making activities by and large to the legislature. Is (LP★) implicated in this view in any way? No. Bentham's preference for the legislature to make the law and judges to apply it is in fact totally independent of his legal

---

[31] See Postema, *Bentham and the Common Law Tradition*, above note 10, at 197, citing Bentham's manuscript remark that '[no] degree of wisdom...can render it expedient for a judge...to depart from pre-established rules'.

positivism. One could equally be a legal positivist enthusiast for judges to be the main law-makers. Moreover, endorsing (PW) changes nothing on this front. Unlike (LP★), (PW) is obviously not normatively inert. It does have some implications, even taken on its own, for what some people should sometimes do. But it still does not bring us any closer to the conclusion that legislatures should make the law and judges should so far as possible only apply it. For (PW), like (LP★), is completely indifferent as between legislative and judicial sources.[32] It holds that the positivity of legal norms endows them with some redeeming merit, whatever their demerits. If it is truly the *positivity* of legal norms that supposedly endows them with this redeeming merit (and not some other feature), then the merit in question necessarily remains constant as between enacted and judge-made legal norms. For judge-made legal norms are no less posited than their enacted counterparts. This is acknowledged in the very idea that judge-made law is judge-*made*; ie is legally valid because some judge or judges at some relevant time and place announced it, practiced it, invoked it, enforced it, endorsed it, accepted it, or otherwise engaged with it.

3.4. Judicial legislation

Legal positivism militates against the assumption that judges should only and always apply valid legal norms. This is sometimes held to be a reason to abandon legal positivism. This suggestion lay at the heart of Ronald Dworkin's first critique of Hart's work. Dworkin agreed with Hart that judges cannot but decide some cases at least partly on their merits. However, he refused to concede that this could possibly involve judges in doing anything other than applying valid legal norms. If they did anything other than applying valid legal norms they would be part-time legislators, Dworkin said, and that would lay to waste the important doctrine of the separation of powers between the

---

[32] This remains true when it is formulated as the thesis that 'the law ought to be such that legal decisions can be made without the exercise of moral judgment': Jeremy Waldron, 'The Irrelevance of Moral Objectivity' in Robert George (ed), *Natural Law Theory* (Oxford 1992). Judges can help to make the law like this no less than legislatures.

legislature and the judiciary. It would also condemn the law to violations of the rule-of-law ban on retroactive legislation, for the law made by judges would necessarily be applied by them retroactively to the cases before them. On these twin grounds, Dworkin felt impelled to reject (LP*). He famously concluded that the validity of *some* legal norms depends on their merits, rather than their sources. It depends, in his view, on their merits as moral justifications for other (source-based) legal norms.[33]

Even if we grant the premises, we may marvel at the conclusion. Why should the fact that the law would inevitably fail to live up to certain ideals if (LP*) were true be a reason to deny (LP*), rather than a reason to admit that the law inevitably fails to live up to certain ideals, or perhaps a reason to wonder whether one has exaggerated the ideals themselves?[34] But never mind that familiar challenge to Dworkin's conclusion. Instead, I want to focus on Dworkin's premise according to which (LP*), at least in Hart's hands, turns judges into part-time legislators. Here we see a fresh myth that is sometimes wheeled out, in combination with the myth just considered under heading 3.3, to effect a kind of pincer movement against legal positivists as a group. Either legal positivists agree that judges should not decide cases on their merits (absurd!), or they become committed to the view that judges are part-time legislators (intolerable!).

---

[33] *Taking Rights Seriously*, note 19 above, Ch 2. I omit the further and independent claim that source-based legal norms are 'rules' and merit-based ones are 'principles'. Hart used the word 'rule' in its ordinary sense simply to mean 'general norm'. Principles are general norms and hence count as rules in Hart's sense. Dworkin, on the other hand, gave 'rules' a special technical meaning: they are general norms that cannot be either more or less weighty. His claim that all source-based norms must be rules in this special technical sense is mistaken. Source-based norms are more or less weighty in proportion to the importance of their source: one owed to the Supreme Court has greater weight than one owed to the Court of Appeals, etc.

[34] For (LP*)-independent reasons to think that law inevitably fails to live up to the ideal of the rule of law, properly understood, see my 'Rationality and the Rule of Law in Offences Against the Person', *Cambridge Law Journal* 53 (1994), 502. For (LP*)-independent reasons to think that some people exaggerate the ideal of the rule of law, and so read conformity as violation, see Timothy Endicott, 'The Impossibility of the Rule of Law', *Oxford Journal of Legal Studies* 19 (1999), 1.

The latter myth—Dworkin's myth—has at its source the mistaken assumption that all law-making is necessarily *legislative* law-making. It is fair to point out that Hart accidentally encouraged this mistaken assumption. He said that, in cases in which a case cannot be decided by applying only valid legal norms, the judge has 'discretion' to decide the case either way.[35] Technically this is correct. The case is *ex hypothesi* unregulated by law in respect of its result and that makes the result legally discretionary. But talk of 'discretion' is also misleading here. It suggests a judge who is entitled, consistently with his or her professional obligations, to give up legal reasoning and instead simply to reason morally or economically or aesthetically, or maybe even not to reason at all any more but simply go with his or her gut instinct, the toss of a coin, etc. But giving up legal reasoning in this way, at least at this early stage in the process, would admittedly be a violation of a judge's professional obligations. For judges admittedly have a professional obligation to reach their decisions by legal reasoning. And even in a case which cannot be decided by applying only existing legal norms, it is possible to use legal reasoning to arrive at a new norm that enables (or constitutes) a decision in the case, and this norm is validated as a new legal norm in the process.

Obviously, legal reasoning, in this sense, is not simply reasoning about what legal norms already apply to the case. It is reasoning that has already-valid legal norms among its major or operative premises, but combines them non-redundantly in the same argument with moral or other merit-based premises. To forge a (legally simplified) example: (1) the Civil Rights Act of 1964 gives everyone the legal right not to be discriminated against in respect of employment on the ground of his or her sex (source-based legal norm); (2) denying a woman a job on the ground of her pregnancy is morally on a par with discriminating against her on the ground of her sex, even though there is no exact male comparator to a pregnant woman that would allow the denial to count as sex-discriminatory in the technical sense (merits-based moral claim); thus (3) women have a legal right not

---

[35] *The Concept of Law*, note 2 above, 128.

to be denied a job on the ground of their pregnancies (new legal norm); now (4) this woman P has been denied a job by D on the ground of her pregnancy (proven fact); thus (5) D owes P a job (a further new legal norm, but a non-general one).

This is a classic example of legal reasoning. Naturally, I have sidelined some possible complications. In particular I have ignored conflicting legal norms that may inhibit judicial delivery of new legal norms by this kind of reasoning. If a previous judicial decision establishes norms inconsistent with (3), then the rules of *stare decisis* applicable in the legal system in question may affect what a judge faced with the facts in (4) has the legal power to do. Perhaps she may overrule the earlier decision. Or perhaps she has scope to distinguish the earlier decision; ie to rely on and hence validate a norm narrower than (3) which is consistent with the earlier decision, but which still reflects the moral force of (2), and which still yields (5). Or perhaps not. These questions depend on the local legal norms establishing her powers as a judge. These norms set source-based constraints on the judge's use of merits-based legal reasoning. If the judge violates these constraints, different legal systems cope differently with the violation. Some may have a *per incuriam* doctrine similar to the common law one that eliminates the legal validity of norm (3) but leaves norm (5) legally valid until the case is appealed. Others may have different solutions. The possibilities are endless.

But none of this detracts from the main point. The main point is that the reasoning from (1) to (5) is an example of specifically legal reasoning—reasoning *according to law*—because the existing legal norm in premise (1) plays a non-redundant but also non-decisive role in the argument. Because the existing law is not decisive the judge necessarily ends up announcing, practising, invoking, enforcing, or otherwise engaging with some new norm or norms (which may, of course, be modifications of existing legal norms), in this case the norms in (3) and (5). In virtue of (and subject to) the judge's legal powers to decide cases on this subject, these new norms become legally valid in the process, at least for the purposes of the present case. If the judge sits in a sufficiently elevated court, then, depending on the workings of the local *stare decisis* doctrine, the new norms may also become legally valid for the purposes of future cases, subject always to future judicial powers of overruling and distinguishing. But that future validity does not turn these new norms into legislated norms even if they have exactly the same legal effects as legislated norms. In creating new legal norms by legal reasoning, or according to law, the judge plays a different role from that of a legislature. For a legislature is entitled to make new legal norms on entirely non-legal grounds; ie without having any existing legal norms operative in its reasoning. A legislature is entitled to think about a problem purely on its merits. Thus, it can enact laws against pregnancy-related denials of employment without having to rely on the existing norms of the Civil Rights Act (or other specifically legal materials) to do so. But not so a judge. Barring special circumstances, a judge may only create this new legal norm on legal grounds; ie by relying on already valid legal norms in creating new ones.

This is not the only difference between legislative and judicial law-making, but for our purposes it is the most important.[36] Dworkin may object that it is a merely verbal quibble. His arguments were directed against judicial law-making, he may say, whether we bless it with the name of 'legislation' or not. But that is not true. Dworkin's arguments were based respectively on the moral importance of the separation of powers, and the rule of law's ban on retroactivity. What is really morally important under the heading of the separation of powers is not the separation of law-making powers from law-applying powers, but rather the separation of *legislative* powers of law-making (ie powers to make legally unprecedented laws) *from judicial* powers of law-making (ie powers to develop the law gradually using existing legal resources). Similarly, the only morally credible rule-of-law ban on retroactive legislation is just that; namely a ban on retroactive *legislation*, not a ban on the retroactive change of legal norms, even when that change is made in accordance with law. In short, the distinction I drew between legislation and judicial law-making, far from being a merely verbal one, is a distinction of great significance in many moral (and some legal) arguments—

---

[36] It is explored most fully in Raz 'On the Autonomy of Legal Reasoning' and 'Legal Rights', both in Raz, *Ethics in the Public Domain*, above note 3.

notably the classic moral arguments based on the separation of powers and the rule of law that Dworkin himself invokes.

It is also entirely consistent with (LP★). According to (LP★), norms are made legally valid by someone's having engaged with them. A judge's engagement with norms by mounting a defense of them partly in terms of other legal norms is one such type of engagement. It differs in deeply important ways from the legislative engagement that consists in the norm's straightforward (legally undefended) pronouncement. So it is a myth that legal positivists must become believers in judicial legislation as soon as they agree that legal norms do not settle every case.

3.5. Interpretation

It is sometimes hinted by critics, and widely believed by students, that legal positivists must favour particular methods of legal interpretation. They must be supporters of interpretation using only the resources of the legal text itself.[37] Or maybe believers in interpretation according to the original intention of the lawmaker.[38] Why these particular methods of interpretation? Because presumably the act of positing that legally validates a norm under (LP★) must also identify the norm that it validates. And it may seem that there are only two aspects of the positing act that are suitable candidates for this identificatory role: the text in which the norm is posited and the intention of the agent who posits it. So presumably legal positivists have to choose between the rock of 'textualism' and the hard place of 'originalism'. Or so the popular mythology goes.

A preliminary but telling objection to confronting legal positivists with this Hobson's choice is that it already assumes that the legally valid norms mentioned in (LP★) must be posited *articulately* (ie in words) and *intentionally* (ie with a view to positing a norm).

---

[37] See eg Fish, 'Wrong Again', above note 9, 309–10. Cf Dworkin, *A Matter of Principle* (Cambridge, Mass. 1985), who kindly observes at 37 that 'not even' legal positivists sign up to this 'textualist' view—even though they 'seem the most likely' to do so!

[38] See eg Michael Freeman, 'Positivism and Statutory Construction: An Essay in the Retrieval of Democracy' in Stephen Guest (ed), *Positivism Today* (Aldershot 1996), 11 at 21.

But that is by no means the shared assumption of believers in (LP*). The 'command' versions of (LP*) espoused by Bentham and Austin admittedly did embrace this assumption. But Hart went to great pains to distance himself from it. He argued (I think successfully) that in all legal systems at least some valid legal norms are posited and hence validated by being practised or used rather than by being articulated, and that the relevant uses of these norms need not be regarded or intended as norm-positing acts by the relevant users.[39] Yet presumably these norms often need to be interpreted too. When that is so, what would it mean to interpret them 'using only the resources of the text itself' or 'according to original intention'? Neither proposal makes sense. So presumably there are other proposals for the interpretation of practice-validated norms that *do* make sense. Why not apply these other proposals, whatever they may be, to articulate and intentional acts of law-making, such as legislation, too? Why not, for example, interpret all these acts, in their norm-creating aspect, just as they were interpreted by others at the time when they were performed (which need neither be a textualist nor an originalist interpretation)? That meets the condition that the act of positing that legally validates a norm under (LP*) must also identify the norm that it validates. The norm is identified as the norm that certain others, observing the acts of positing in question, took those acts to be creating.

The reason why this won't do regarding legislation and other acts of intentional law-making, it may be said, is this. To have the power to make law intentionally—as it is sometimes put, to be an *authority*—one must surely have the power intentionally to determine what law one makes, at least up to a point.[40] And that surely requires interpreters to give credence to what one meant (originalism) or, alternatively, to limit attention to the words one chose to convey what one meant (textualism). It will not do to give the power to determine what norm one created entirely to others who observed one's norm-positing act, by making their interpretation authoritative, rather than one's own. But *why* will this

---

[39] *The Concept of Law*, above note 2, eg 113, 149–50.
[40] Raz, 'Intention in Interpretation' in *The Autonomy of Law*, above note 4, 249 at 256–60.

not do? So long as one can work out more or less how the relevant others will read what one says or does, one can also adapt what one says or does to anticipate their readings. If one can work out that the relevant others are perverse types who will always read 'cat' to mean 'dog', one can make the dog-regulating laws one means to make by passing a Cat Regulation Act. By this feedback route, one has the power intentionally to determine what law one makes even though the norm for interpreting that law does not refer to one's intentions (ie is not originalist), and gives one's text a quirky meaning (ie is not textualist). All of this depends, to be sure, on the assumption that one can work out more or less how the relevant others will read what one said or did. But in a legal system this condition can normally be met by having (source-based) legal rules of interpretation. These rules will be used by interpreters (eg by judges) and can therefore be relied upon in advance by legislators and other law-makers to work out, backwards, how they should speak or behave in order to be held to have made the law that they are trying to make.

So the widely different norms of interpretation adopted and practiced in different legal systems need not differ in the measure of ability they give to law-makers intentionally to shape the laws that they make. As long as the local norms of interpretation can be grasped by the law-makers (or by those drafting statutes or judgments on their behalf), the laws can be intentionally shaped by anticipating how they will be interpreted by others and drafting them accordingly. It does not follow, of course, that we should be indifferent as between different possible norms of interpretation—that we should not care, for example, whether traditional British strict construction in reading statutes prevails over the more relaxed American approach. Possibly one of these approaches makes for all-round better judicial decisions that the other, or possibly neither is as good as some third approach, or possibly a mixture of approaches would be best of all, etc. My point is only that *this* desideratum—the achievement of all-round better judicial decision—is the proper basis for selecting (and legally validating) norms of interpretation. In selecting such norms one need not be inhibited by the need to build in a special respect for the law-maker's words or the law-maker's intentions because, thanks to the feedback loop I mentioned, that can largely look after itself whatever norm one adopts or practises.

I say 'largely' because, of course, there is a proviso. Since legislators and other law-makers are no more clairvoyant than the rest of us, they can only adapt their law-making to norms of interpretation already in use or proposed. So the considerations just mentioned do have a certain conservative leaning. Insofar as law-making agents are to be treated as *authorities* regarding the norms they made, there is a reason to apply to those norms the interpretative norms that were knowably applicable to them *at the time when they were made*.[41] But how significant a constraint is this? One must remember that most legal norms, even when intentionally made, were not made by just one agent in one fell swoop. They were made by a succession of legal engagements. When people ask their lawyer or their law teacher 'What does the First Amendment have to say about this problem?' they don't normally mean to restrict attention to the norm created by the original agreement on the text back in 1789. They mean to ask about the *law* of the First Amendment, which includes the original 1789 sources *plus* the often conflicting pronouncements, arguments, and practices of countless judges in First Amendment cases over the intervening centuries. Since a great deal of this intervening law-making was itself intentional, the question is not only one of treating the Congress of 1789 as an authority, but also one of treating the Supreme Court of 1926 as an authority, and indeed as an authority regarding how to treat the Congress of 1789 as an authority, and then of treating the Supreme Court of 1968 as an authority regarding both the Congress of 1789 and the Supreme Court of 1926, and regarding the legally proper way to relate them, and so forth. It follows that the limited conservative implications of the principle of deference to authority are so limited as to be rarely worthy of any real moral anxiety. They point to nothing like 'originalism' or 'textualism' conceived as interpretative doctrines that would freeze the First Amendment or the Civil Rights Act at the time of enactment, or limit the range of background context that could bear upon its meaning.

---

[41] Ibid 271.

In all of this I have been granting another very common assumption that supporters of (LP*) need not, and often do not, share. I have been granting that the interpretation of legal norms belongs exclusively to the law-applying stage of legal reasoning, as opposed to the law-making stage. Recall that we started with the question of how (LP*) would have us *identify* the norms that are validated according to source-based criteria, and we took this to be where the question of interpretation fits in. But that is already a mistake. Interpretative activity straddles the distinction between the identification of existing legal norms and the further use of them to make new legal norms. To the extent that a judge can determine what the First Amendment means by relying exclusively on the relevant source-based norms (ie by relying on the text of the First Amendment together with judicial interpretations of it and judicial interpretations of those interpretations and applicable laws of precedent and interpretation), that judge is merely identifying the First Amendment in interpreting it. But to the extent that the judge is left with conflicts among or indeterminacies in the applicable source-based norms—including those of precedent and interpretation—the process of legal interpretation necessarily takes him beyond the law. The assembled ranks of source-based norms took the judge so far, but at a certain point they left the meaning of the First Amendment unclear, to be settled on the merits. At that point, settling the meaning of the First Amendment means *giving* it a meaning. It necessarily goes beyond norm-application to norm-alteration.

Remember our example of legal reasoning about sex discrimination under the Civil Rights Act? There our imaginary judge started with (1) an interpretation of the Act according to which it gives people a legal right not to be discriminated against on grounds of sex in employment. From that starting point, in combination with a moral premise, our imaginary judge ruled (and thereby made it the law) that (3) a woman has a legal right not to be denied a job because she is pregnant. Was this in turn an interpretation of (1)? Maybe. Maybe we forgot to mention that, according to our imaginary judge, (3A) a woman has a legal right *under the Civil Rights Act* not to be denied a job because she is pregnant. That judges talk like this has been understood by Dworkin and many others to suggest that all they are doing is applying the norms already in the Civil Rights Act when they arrive at conclusion (3A).[42] But it does not suggest that at all. It suggests that they are *interpreting* the norms already in the Civil Rights Act when they arrive at (3A), and that could mean *either* applying them *or* developing them. Some acts of interpretation are concerned with settling the law in the sense of identifying what it already says, but other acts of interpretation, like that captured in (3A), are concerned with settling the law in the sense of getting it to say something new.[43] According to (LP*), the difference between the two cases is the difference between wholly *source-based* modes of interpretation (looking to existing conventions of interpretation, or to some person's or constituency's actual understanding, etc) and partly or wholly *merits-based* modes of interpretation (looking to what would make the norm morally defensible, or more fit for its intended purpose, etc). Predictably—and much to the frustration of lawyers and law teachers all over the world—(LP*) has nothing at all to say on the subject of what the balance ought to be between these two families of interpretative considerations, for, here as elsewhere, (LP*) has nothing to say on the subject of where law-making should end and law-applying should begin. It merely says that whatever law is applied also has to be made, for unless it is made (either beforehand or in the process of application) there is nothing valid to apply. Interpreting it, however, can be making it and/or applying it.[44]

---

[42] See eg Dworkin, *Law's Empire*, above note 5, at 6.

[43] As Bentham explains robustly in *Of Laws in General* (ed Hart, London 1970), 162ff.

[44] Some student resistance to this picture seems to come of the following line of thought: (i) one must identify what norm one is interested in before one can ask about its validity according to (LP*); but (ii) one cannot identify what norm one is interested in without first eradicating the indeterminacies and other gaps in its application that (LP*) makes inevitable, and hence without completing its interpretation. But this argument works only if there can be no such thing as an identifiable norm with built-in indeterminacies. If one says, as all legal positivists who have thought about the matter must say, that one is interested in the validity of norms *complete with* their indeterminacies, then one assumes the opposite. There is of course a genuine dispute to be had about just how indeterminate a norm can be before it stops being a norm at all. But clearly it does not stop being a norm merely because there are *some* actions, the normative status of which it leaves

3.6. The 'no necessary connection' thesis

Finally, I come to the jurisprudence student's favourite myth about legal positivism. Apparently legal positivists believe:

> (NNC) there is no necessary connection between law and morality.

This thesis is absurd and no legal philosopher of note has ever endorsed it as it stands.[45] After all, there is a necessary connection between law and morality if law and morality are necessarily *alike* in any way. And of course they are. If nothing else, they are necessarily alike in both necessarily comprising some valid norms. But there are many other necessary connections between law and morality on top of this rather insubstantial one, and legal positivists have often taken great pains to assert them. Hobbes, Bentham, Austin, Kelsen, Hart, Raz, and Coleman all rely on at least some more substantial necessary connections between law and morality in explaining various aspects of the nature of law (although they do not all rely on the same ones).

So how arises the myth that, as the leading legal positivists, they must all deny all such connections? It seems to arise from Hart's early work. In a much-cited footnote, Hart mistook Bentham's and Austin's ringing endorsements of (LP★)—notably Austin's remark that 'the existence of law is one thing; its merit or demerit is another'—for endorsements of (NNC). Then by hint and emphasis he seemed to endorse (NNC) himself.[46] But a few pages later he admitted that he did not really endorse it. For even in this early work he advanced the proposal (mentioned under heading 3.1 above) that every law necessarily exhibits a redeeming moral merit, a dash of justice that comes of the mere fact that a law is a general norm that would have like cases treated alike.[47] For Hart this built-in dash of moral merit in every law

---

unclear. This is the respect in which it is misleading (although not false) to frame (LP★) as a thesis about the *identification* of legal norms, rather than their validity.

[45] Although it is billed as 'the quintessence of legal positivism' in the student textbook, Howard Davies and David Holdcroft, *Jurisprudence: Texts and Commentary* (London 1991), 3.

[46] 'Positivism and the Separation of Law and Morals', above note 12, 57–8.

[47] Ibid 81. See text at note 12 above.

clearly forges a necessary connection between law and morality. So his apparent endorsements of (NNC) must be read as bungled preliminary attempts to formulate and defend (LP*), which, like Bentham and Austin, he really did endorse.

How does (NNC) differ from (LP*)? In two respects (LP*) is the broader of the two propositions and in two respects the narrower. Let me begin by explaining how it is narrower. First, (LP*) is narrower than (NNC) in that it is concerned only with the conditions of legal *validity*. Studying the nature of law involves—as my remarks over the last few pages have amply demonstrated—studying much more than the conditions of legal validity. That some people mistake an account of the conditions of legal validity for an account of the whole nature of law (and hence mistake legal positivism's distinctive *thesis about* law for a comprehensive *theory of* law) may come of the fact that one can question the validity of a certain putatively valid law by asking 'Is this really a law?' and that question in turn is easily confused with the much more abstract (and pretentious) question 'What is law?'[48] But, in fact, once one has tackled the question of whether a certain law is valid there remain many relatively independent questions to address concerning its meaning, its fidelity to law's purposes, its role in sound legal reasoning, its legal effects, and its social functions, to name but a few. To study the nature of law one needs to turn one's mind to the philosophical aspects of these further questions too. To these further questions there is no distinctively 'legal positivist' answer, because legal positivism is a thesis only about the conditions of legal validity.

Proposition (LP*) narrows (NNC) further in that it restricts its attention to one specific connection that is sometimes thought to hold between a law's validity and its moral merits, namely a relationship in which the former *depends* upon the latter. This is a one-way relationship. Legal positivists deny that laws are valid because of their moral merits. But they do not deny the converse proposition that laws might be morally meritorious because of their validity. As we saw, some legal positivists—Hobbes, Bentham, and Hart the most prominent among them—have regarded

---

[48] This confusion is another one that is courted in Dworkin's opaque question 'What are the grounds of law?': *Law's Empire*, above note 5, at 4.

valid laws as necessarily endowed with some moral value just in virtue of being valid laws, never mind how morally odious in other respects. (NNC) rules this view out. On the other hand, (LP*) is compatible with it but does not require it.

At the same time, (LP*) is broader than (NNC) in that it is concerned not only with the connection between a law's validity and its *moral* merits, but with the connection between a law's validity and *any* of its merits. Legal positivists line up equally against views according to which the validity of a law depends upon, for example, its economic or aesthetic merits. Moreover—as we saw under heading 3.2 above—legal positivists must also reject views according to which the validity of a law depends upon its merits purely as a means; ie its fitness for its purpose (be that purpose meritorious or unmeritorious). Thus, as we saw, the thesis that insufficiently clear or insufficiently certain norms lack validity is a classic *anti*-positivist thesis.

Finally, unlike (NNC), (LP*) does not limit its embargo to supposedly *necessary* connections between a law's validity and its merits; ie to those that are supposed to exist by law's very nature. At any rate, it does not do so as I have expressed it. But here we have, you will recall, the most important point at which legal positivists differ in their interpretation of (LP*), so I had best say that in this respect (LP*) is only *arguably* broader than (NNC). According to the so-called 'soft' legal positivists, there may be laws, the validity of which depends on their merits, but only if the 'merits' test in question is set by some other law, the validity of which does *not* depend on its merits. Thus, according to soft legal positivists, there is no law that depends for its validity on its merits just in virtue of the nature of law, ie necessarily. However, there can be laws that depend for their validity on their merits in particular legal systems because other laws of those legal systems so dictate; ie contingently. Hart endorsed this view. But personally, as I mentioned near the beginning, I side with those 'hard' legal positivists who reject it. In my view, no law depends for its validity on its merits *full stop*, whether owing to the very nature of law (necessarily) or merely owing to what other laws say (contingently). To capture the hard as well as the soft legal positivist position—quite apart from its other dimensions of over- and under-inclusiveness—(NNC) should not discriminate between necessary and contingent connections.

4. Legal positivism for natural lawyers

The myths I have been concerned with here are myths often peddled about legal positivism as an intellectual tradition. My first aim has been to counteract the common but philosophically disreputable tendency to find leading writers in that tradition guilty by association. Since they are legal positivists, the thinking goes, they *must* espouse such-and-such a silly 'legal positivist' thesis. But by and large, as we have seen, the leading figures found guilty by this method do not espouse the silly theses with which they are thus associated. What they do espouse in common is thesis (LP*), which is often misrepresented by critics as some quite different and much sillier thesis, or at least held out as having some much sillier theses among its implications. That is why my second aim here, and perhaps the philosophically more important of the two, has been to identify what is and what is not an implication of (LP*). The main tendency we encountered—running through several of our myths—was a tendency to assume that (LP*) must have implications of its own for what at least some people (eg judges, governments) should do. In fact, it has no such implications. It tells us how the legal validity of any norm in any legal system falls to be determined—namely, by its sources—but leaves open whether and when and why any of us should ever bother to have or to follow any valid legal norms. To show that valid legal norms are ever worth having or following, and in what way, always requires a separate argument, regarding which (LP*) is in itself entirely agnostic.

Our friends in the natural law tradition tend to balk at the idea that we can study the validity of legal norms in the agnostic way envisaged by (LP*); ie without deciding in advance whether (at least some) valid legal norms are going to be worth having or following. It is not that natural lawyers cannot see the possibility of, or interest in, studying the validity-conditions of certain norms in the practically noncommittal sense of 'validity'. Sure, the rules of a game can be valid *qua* rules of the game without having any significance for what anyone should do except to the extent that they fancy playing the game. But law is not a game. It purports to bind us morally; ie in a way that binds even those of us who do not fancy playing. So why not go straight to the question of whether it succeeds in doing so? Why begin by asking about its legal validity in the thin, practically noncommittal sense found in (LP*), and only then go on to ask whether it is valid law in the thicker sense of being morally binding on at least some people? According to this critique, the problem with legal positivism is not that it has silly answers of the kind peddled in its name by the myth-spinners. The problem, rather, is that it has a distracting and prevaricating *question*, which is the question of what determines legal validity in the thin, practically noncommittal sense of 'legal validity'.

There are indeed two inflexions of 'legally valid', and they correspond to two senses of 'legal'. In most European languages other than English there are two words for law corresponding conveniently to these two senses of 'legal': *lex* and *ius*, *Gesetz* and *Recht*, *loi* and *droit*, and so on. Legal positivists need not deny that there is a moralized sense of 'law' captured in the second term in each of these pairs.[49] They need not deny that in some contexts 'legality' accordingly names a moral value, such that in the second moralized sense of 'valid law', laws may be more or less valid depending on the extent to which they exhibit legality, and hence depending on their merits. Nor need they deny that one must capture this moral value of legality, whatever it is, in order to tell the whole story of law's nature. As in any other field of human endeavour, understanding the nature of the endeavour in full admittedly means having an ability to tell success in the endeavour from failure. Perhaps law does have a special way of succeeding, as these European languages seem to suggest. Maybe the ideal of the rule of law, for example, does represent a moral ideal distinctively for law, such that one does not fully understand the nature of law until one understands that at least part of its success, if it were ever successful, would lie in conformity to this ideal. Or maybe the relevant ideal of legality is something quite different. But picking out the relevant ideal(s) is irrelevant to the truth or the

---

[49] Hart explicitly pointed it out in *The Concept of Law*, above note 2, at 203–7, although he went too far in speaking of there being two *concepts* of law here.

importance of (LP★). For (LP★) tries to answer another question. What is included in this field of human endeavour, to which the natural lawyer's proposed criteria of success and failure apply? What makes something a candidate for being accounted a success or failure in these terms? What is this *lex*, such that it ought to be *ius*? Legal positivism naturally supplies only part of the answer. To be exact, legal positivism explains what it takes for a law to be legally valid in the thin *lex* sense, such that the question arises of whether it is also legally valid in the thicker *ius* sense; ie morally binding *qua* law. In doing so, legal positivism admittedly does not distinguish law from a game, which is also made up of posited norms. To distinguish law from a game one must add, among other things, that law, unlike a game, purports to bind us morally.[50] That has implications, no doubt, for what counts as successful law, and hence for what one might think of as law's central case.[51] But this does not detract from the truth or the importance of (LP★), which is not a thesis about law's central case but about the validity conditions for all legal norms, be they central (morally successful) or peripheral (morally failed) examples.

---

[50] See Ch 5 for detailed discussion of what this means.
[51] The most important study of which—taking (LP★) for granted, although remaining studiously unexcited by it—is John Finnis's *Natural Law and Natural Rights* (Oxford 1981).

3
Some Types of Law

Laws can be classified in various ways. They can be classified according to the legal systems to which they belong (English, Roman, International, etc) or according to the subject matter that they regulate (contracts, property, torts, etc) or according to their normative type (duty-imposing, permission-granting, etc). In this chapter I will be concerned with the classification of laws—and hence of law as a genre—in only one dimension. It is the classification of laws according to how they are made. This is already a philosophically partisan and some may say question-begging enterprise. For some laws, say some people, are not made at all. They are not artefacts. They have no agent(s) who serve as their originator or creator or author. By demystifying some of the intriguing ways in which laws are made, I hope to remove some of the appeal of this view.

In my first three sections I consider, respectively, legislated law, customary law, and case law. In the fourth section I discuss common law. How does it fit in? In the final section I conclude that all the types of law discussed here are types of positive law. For there is, I suggest, no other type of law but positive law.

1. Legislated law

In a way (to be explained at the end of this chapter) legislated law is paradigmatic law. So it is not surprising that some writers simply equate law-making with legislating. For example, Ronald Dworkin reads the claim that judges sometimes make law as the claim that judges are part-time legislators. He therefore treats criticisms of the latter claim as biting no less against the former.[1]

---

[1] He treats criticisms of retroactive legislation as criticisms of retroactive law-making more generally; and he treats criticisms of unelected legislatures as criticisms of unelected law-makers more generally. See 'Hard Cases' in Dworkin, *Taking Rights Seriously* (London 1977), 81 at 84–6.

Here Dworkin takes his cue from John Austin, whose 'command theory' of law attempted to explain all law-making on the legislative model.[2] As H.L.A. Hart demonstrated, however, Austin's account is seriously impoverished as a general account of law-making.[3] Some non-legislative modes of law-making that we will be discussing below (in Sections 2 and 3) cannot be squeezed into Austin's account without considerable artifice.

Indeed, even as an account of *legislative* law-making, Austin's account is distorted. A command always purports to impose a requirement to act, but legislation, as Hart pointed out, often purports to confer a power or grant a permission instead.[4] Austin's attempt to squeeze such non-mandatory legislative acts into the logic of commands is an embarrassment to his thinking.[5] Yet his 'command theory' is in some other ways a decent first stab at a general account of the nature of legislation. For commands do share three important features with legislative acts. First, a command, like a legislative act, is the act of a single agent. Second, a commander, like a legislator, acts with the intention of effecting one or more normative change(s) by that very act of commanding or legislating. Third, a command, like a legislative act, is a way of making normative changes expressly; ie by expressing or attempting to express the normative changes that one intends thereby to make.

Some people remember Hart as having argued that commands should be *contrasted* with legislative acts in respect of the second (and hence the third) of these features. Did Hart not criticize Austin's 'command theory' precisely for losing sight of law's normativity? Did he not object to Austin's representing the legislator as 'the gunman situation writ large'? Yes, he did.[6] But he never denied that all commands are express attempts to impose a requirement, and in that respect to effect a normative change. He merely showed by his discussion of the gunman situation that commands need not be attempts to impose *obligations;* ie *categorical*

---

[2] *The Province of Jurisprudence Determined* (ed Rumble, Cambridge 1995), 35–6.
[3] *The Concept of Law* (Oxford 1961), 43–8.
[4] Ibid 27–33.   [5] Ibid 33–5.
[6] Ibid 7.

requirements.[7] In this respect, commands differ even from those legislative acts to which they are most similar, namely legislative acts creating mandatory legal norms, which are all by their nature categorical.[8] Yet this thesis allows (and indeed presupposes) that commands and legislative acts are similar in other salient respects. They are alike enough to be worth contrasting. I just mentioned the three most important features in respect of which they are alike. Commands and legislative acts are norm-changing acts that are alike in respect of their agency, their intentionality, and their expressness.

In what follows I shall say no more about these features as features of commands. I will explore them only as features of legislative acts. They turn out to be the three features that give most help in distinguishing legislative law-making from other kinds of law-making. Let me consider them in reverse order.

Legislated law is expressly made. Legislated law includes law contained in written constitutional documents, as well as that contained in everyday statutes, regulations, and by-laws. It also includes law contained in proclamations, edicts, directives, orders-in-council, etc. In some legal systems it may also include treaty law. Its first hallmark is that it is expressly made. Under some conditions, I suppose, legislation might conceivably be expressed in gestures or pictures. But typically legislative law is articulated law. It is expressed in words. Here, for the sake of simplicity, I will talk as if all legislation is articulate legislation, but what I am about to say could readily be adapted to cover instances of inarticulate legislation as well.

---

[7] Ibid 82. A categorical requirement is one that applies irrespective of the prevailing personal goals of the person to whom it applies. As Hart puts it, 'the conduct required by [rules of obligation] may...conflict with what the person who owes the [obligation] may wish to do' (ibid 87). The commands of the gunman, in Hart's example, make an implicit appeal to a prevailing personal goal of the person commanded, viz. the goal of staying alive.

[8] Another way to put the point, which Hart avoids but which chimes with his remarks at ibid 112–13: the law claims to bind its subjects morally, whereas many commands speak only to the prudence of the commanded. For more discussion of law's moral claim, see my 'Law's Aims in *Law's Empire*' in Scott Hershovitz (ed), *Exploring Law's Empire* (Oxford 2006), as well as Chapter 5 following.

Articulate legislation (hereafter simply 'legislation') is articulated by the legislator in the form of a legislative text. The text may be written or oral and may be made up of declarative or imperative sentences or both. One understands legislated law by understanding the legislative text that creates it. Of course, there is a great deal of variation between different legal systems when we come to the question of *how* one is to understand the legislative text. Different legal systems may have dramatically different canons of legislative interpretation. Some may require or permit a more literal approach, others a more 'purposive' approach, to construing the legislative text. Some may require or permit more atomic interpretation of words or sentences or paragraphs in the legislative text; others may require or permit greater attention to the wider textual context in which the words or sentences or paragraphs appear. Some may require or permit the interpreter to seek interpretative help in some or all of the debates that led up to the legislation's enactment, whereas others may regard this as cheating. All of this concerns the proper *mode* of interpretation for legislated law. None of it should distract us from the fact that, where legislated law is concerned, the legislative text is always the primary *object* of interpretation.[9] Whatever changes to the law one ultimately finds contained in the legislation, and however one sets about finding them, one presents them as contained in the legislation only by presenting them as entailed by an interpretation of the legislative text (or some part of it, such as a phrase or sentence or paragraph).

What one is looking for in interpreting a legislative text are the changes that it makes to the law, which are normative changes. The changes may include the introduction of new legal norms or the modification or elimination of old ones. To simplify, I will restrict my attention to the legislative creation of new norms. But

---

[9] I am simplifying. Legislation is a speech-act. As J.L. Austin says of speech-acts more generally, '[t]he total speech-act in the total speech-situation is the *only actual* phenomenon which, in the last resort, we are engaged in elucidating'. Austin, *How to Do Things with Words* (Oxford 1962), 148. So the ultimate object of interpretation is strictly speaking the act of legislating. My point is that the act of legislating is the act of enacting a text, meaning that the interpretation of the text has primacy in the interpretation of the legislation.

what I will say also applies, *mutatis mutandis*, to the modification and elimination of existing legal norms.

So (to simplify): what one is looking for in interpreting a legislative text are the legal norms that it creates. A common mistake is to confuse a legislated norm with its formulation. Thus a lawyer may refer to 'the words of the rule'.[10] This cannot be taken literally. Rules do not have words. What the lawyer really means is the wording of the legislative provision that creates the rule. It is tempting to think of this as the wording of the rule because legislated norms, unlike other legal norms, are canonically formulated. In the event that other purported formulations of the norm would give it inconsistent content (ie would point to its being a different norm) the formulation in the legislation prevails in settling what norm it is. Yet still the legislative formulation should not be identified with the norm that it formulates. For two rival norms can be identically formulated. This is why the legislative formulation often needs to be interpreted to find out which of two rival norms it formulates. Conversely, two rival formulations can be formulations of one and the same norm. Otherwise one could not interpret part of a legislative text by reformulating it consistently with itself, as lawyers often do.

Another way to put this is to say that the legislative text is not the *only* possible object of legislative interpretation. The law created by the statute—the statute's legal effect—is itself a second possible object of interpretation. The two come apart most obviously when intervening interpreters (eg judges in the highest court) use their legal power to interpret the legislative text in a way that binds successor interpreters.[11] Then the legal norms created by the statute are rendered more determinate (and in that respect are changed) by an exercise of interpretative authority,

---

[10] See eg *Three Rivers District Council v Governor and Company of The Bank of England* [2001] UKHL 16 at para 154 per Lord Hobhouse.

[11] Compare *In re Spectrum Plus Ltd* [2005] 2 AC 680, where Lord Nicholls suggests that when courts are interpreting legislation they cannot be bound by the intervening interpretations of other courts. Why not? According to Lord Nicholls: (a) earlier court decisions bind only inasmuch as they effect a change in the law; but (b) interpretation leaves its object unchanged. The error in (b) is exposed in Joseph Raz's 'Interpretation without Retrieval' in A. Marmor (ed) *Law and Interpretation* (Oxford 1995).

even though the formulation in the legislation remains the same. When this is true, a successor interpreter interprets the legal effect of the statute by interpreting the legislative text in the light of the cases that interpret the legislative text, cases which may themselves sometimes call for interpretation. We will discuss the creation and interpretation of case law in Section 3 below. For present purposes, the only point that matters is this: even where interpretation of the law in the statute requires interpretation of intervening case law, the legislative text remains the primary object of interpretation in the sense indicated earlier. Whatever legal norm one ultimately finds in the legislation, one still presents it as a norm found in the legislation only by presenting it as entailed by an interpretation of the legislative text, albeit now an interpretation of the text shaped by other interpreters' intervening interpretations of the same text. If the text drops out, so that the cases start to be treated as *independent* authorities for the legal norms they left behind, then those legal norms are no longer legislated legal norms. Then we are dealing with pure case law.[12]

Legislated law is intentionally made. Just as a promise is made with the intention of creating obligations by the very act of promise-making, so legislation is enacted with the intention of changing the law by the very act of enacting it. Witness the 'prayer' at the start of every (United Kingdom) Act of Parliament:

Be it enacted by the Queen's most Excellent Majesty, by and with the advice and consent of the Lords Spiritual and Temporal, and Commons, in this present Parliament assembled, and by the authority of the same, as follows...

This prayer removes one possible ambiguity that would otherwise afflict many of the ensuing legislative texts read literally. Declarative sentences in legislative texts (eg 'Any person who

---

[12] Gerald Postema puts the same point thus: 'Some laws [are] valid in virtue of having been explicitly made by an authorised lawmaker; others [are] valid in virtue of incorporation into the common law. The class to which a given law [is] assigned [is] not determined solely by the way it came into being, but by its present mode of validity.' Postema, 'Philosophy of the Common Law' in Jules Coleman and Scott Shapiro (eds), *The Oxford Handbook of Jurisprudence and Philosophy of Law* (Oxford 2002). Postema attributes the point to Matthew Hale.

libels the Prime Minister commits an offence') are often capable of being read literally as reports of legal norms that (according to the text's author) already exist. On that reading any legal change effected by the Act would have to be regarded as an accidental legal change, a side-effect of the legislature's attempt to state the law as it is.[13] Thanks to the prayer, this reading of the Act is ruled out. 'Any person who libels the Prime Minister commits an offence' means 'It is *hereby made* an offence for any person to libel the Prime Minister.' The Act—as the prayer makes clear—is intended as an act of norm-creation on the part of the legislator, in this case Parliament (or the Queen in Parliament, as the institution is more accurately known).

In the literature on legislation, there is much discussion of whether an institution (for example, Parliament) is capable of having intentions.[14] Doubts about whether Parliament is capable of having intentions often stem from the well-known difficulty of using Parliamentary intentions as a guide to the interpretation of statutory texts. When courts say that they are interpreting statutes according to 'the intention of Parliament', this is widely accepted to be an empty courtesy. Parliament usually had no intentions concerning the meaning, application, use, or effect of the statute in question, because the members of Parliament who debated the statute and voted on it—even those who supported it and voted in favour of it—invariably had diverse and conflicting intentions concerning its meaning, application, use and effect. Indeed, some members of Parliament possibly had no intentions at all concerning any of these matters (they were just lobby fodder who voted when they were told to by their political masters). All of this is true and important. One could design a constitution for Parliament which would determine whose intentions on matters

---

[13] Occasionally, legislatures do include a provision in which 'for the avoidance of doubt' they attempt to state or otherwise to preserve the law as it is apart from that provision. Consider eg the UK's Mental Capacity Act 2005 s62: 'For the avoidance of doubt, it is hereby declared that nothing in this Act is to be taken to affect the law relating to murder or manslaughter or the operation of section 2 of the Suicide Act 1961 (*c*. 60) (assisting suicide).'

[14] Notable doubters: Dworkin, *Law's Empire* (Cambridge, Mass. 1986), 336; Jeremy Waldron, 'Legislatures in Legal Philosophy' in his *Law and Disagreement* (Oxford 1999), 21 at 43.

such as the meaning, application, use and effect of a statute were to be regarded as constituting Parliament's intentions on these matters, in the event of conflicting intentions among ordinary members of Parliament. There has been a halting move in that direction in recent English law.[15] But for the most part there are no such rules, and hence Parliament has no such intentions.

So Parliament often has no intention to make the particular changes in the law that it ends up making when it legislates. What does not follow is that, when it legislates, Parliament has no intention to change the law. Worries about the diverse and conflicting intentions of individual Parliamentarians do not apply to this more humble intention. Barring the occasional misfire (eg an accidental stumble through the voting lobby by a drunken Parliamentarian) all of those who participate in Parliament's changing of the law intend to participate in it. Even those who vote against a certain piece of legislation have the intention to participate in changing the law, should they end up on the losing side in the vote. More precisely, they intend that the law be changed if that be Parliament's intention, where what counts as Parliament's intention depends in turn on the actions and intentions of at least some members of Parliament.[16] So (in a way that will be further explained below) the law-changing intentions of individual members of Parliament both constitute and refer to the law-changing intention of Parliament itself, Parliament being the institution that does the legislating.

Some people deny that institutions (such as Parliament) can be agents. They insist on reading apparent references to institutional agency (eg to Acts of Parliament) reductively, as elliptical references to the agency of the individual human beings who go to make up the institution. On this view it is not the legislative institution, but rather its membership, that does the legislating.

---

[15] *Pepper (Inspector of Taxes)* v *Hart* [1993] AC 593 was the move; the halting started in *R* v *Secretary of State for the Environment, Transport and the Regions ex parte Spath Holme Ltd* [2001] 2 AC 349.

[16] This is sometimes called a 'conditional' intention, suggesting that somehow it is not quite a complete intention. But there is nothing incomplete about it. See John Gardner and Heike Jung, 'Making Sense of Mens Rea: Antony Duff's Account', *Oxford Journal of Legal Studies* 11 (1991), 559 at 567–8.

We will engage with this thought in a moment. At this point we are tackling a cross-cutting question: whoever does the legislating, does he or she or it intend to change the law in the process? The answer is clearly yes. An agent acts intentionally inasmuch as it does what it does for (what it takes to be) reasons. Those who legislate, whether they be human beings or institutions, must do so for (what they take to be) reasons for and against changing the law. If they did not, there would be no sense in having legislative debates, in which supposed reasons for and against changing the law are presented, weighed, and challenged. Indeed, there would be no sense in having wider public debates about legislative policy, nor the general elections in which these debates are brought to a head. Such debates make sense only on the footing that whoever it is that legislates will, in legislating, respond to at least some supposed reasons for and against changing the law. These debates make sense, in other words, only on the footing that legislation intentionally effects legal change, exactly as the prayer in UK Acts of Parliament would have us believe it does.

Legislation is the act of one agent. The preceding remarks already foreshadow what comes next. Legislation is always the act of one agent. The agent may be a human being (eg Big Brother) or an institution (eg Parliament). The actions of an institution like Parliament depend on, but are not reducible to, the actions of those human beings who go to make it up. Thus an institution with no human beings in it (with no human members and no institutional members that in turn meet this condition) cannot act. Yet when an institution does act through its members, its acts are distinct from those of its members. Members of Parliament argue their points, table amendments, and cast votes. These are things that Parliament as an institution cannot do. On the other hand, it is Parliament, not its membership, that legislates. Analogously, the members of an orchestra play their instruments, watch the conductor, and follow the score. But only the orchestra—concertedly—plays the symphony.

What turns a mere collection of human beings (musicians, politicians) into a concerted agent (an orchestra, a legislature), the actions of which depend on, but are not reducible to, the actions of those human beings who go to make it up (its members, officials)? We can distinguish natural concerted agency from artificial concerted agency. Natural concerted agency is the same as what I have elsewhere called 'teamwork'.[17] In teamwork, each team-member adapts her intentions to the actions and intentions of the others so as to avoid frustrating each other's intentions. But that is not all. Each team member also adds an extra intention, that of contributing to the work of the team as a whole. She intends not only that she (and each of the others) should make their complementary efforts, but that this should also be part of a team effort. So her own intention makes an essential reference to the intention of the team. When it does so, it also helps to constitute the intention of the team. The team is then a further agent distinct from the human beings who go to make it up. It too does things and tries to do things and intends to do things—things that are distinct from, albeit dependent on, the things that its individual members do and try to do and intend to do. In the orchestra, for example, each player intends to play her part. But she also intends that, by all together playing their parts, the orchestra as a whole should play the symphony. That feature turns orchestral performance into teamwork. There may be only 105 human beings but there are at least[18] 106 agents involved in the performance. The 106th is the orchestra itself.

In natural concerted agency (teamwork) there may be norms that assign and regulate leadership and other special roles in the team (eg the role of the orchestra's conductor, its lead violinist, and so on). But in natural concerted agency there is no need for, nor any possibility of, a norm that assigns to anyone the role of *representing* the concerted agent. Nobody in the orchestra, for example, is its representative for the purpose of playing a symphony. The orchestra itself plays the symphony. At the same time somebody in the orchestra (or more likely in its management) is probably its representative for the purpose of booking concerts, hiring musicians, and so on. Such actions of the orchestra belong to the realm of *artificial* concerted agency.

---

[17] 'Reasons for Teamwork', *Legal Theory* 8 (2002), 495.
[18] I say 'at least' because maybe there are some intermediate agents between the individual human beings and the whole orchestra. Possibly the string section is agent 107, the wind section is agent 108, and so on.

Artificial concerted agency is strictly speaking a form of vicarious agency, the possibility of which depends on the existence of norms that empower one agent (eg a chief executive) to act in the name of another (eg a charitable organization). Such norms are needed when a concerted agent needs to (be able to) perform an action (eg entering into a contract or making a promise) that can only be performed by the further action of a single human being (eg by signing a name or shaking a hand). Such single-human-being actions cannot even in principle be performed by teamwork, and so require representation. But norms to empower representation can also be used more widely to enable teams to perform actions that could in principle be performed by teamwork, but only with excessive cost or difficulty. They can also be used to confer a capacity for concerted agency on a bunch of interacting human beings (eg a nation, a local community, a government) whose interactions do not naturally qualify as teamwork because one or both of the intentions required for teamwork is absent.

Modern legislative institutions typically work by a combination of natural and artificial concerted agency. There are officials (and committees and separate legislative chambers and so on) whose actions are treated for certain purposes as actions of the legislature. They may have powers to act in the name of the legislature for some parts of the legislative process. But the institution's ordinary members also work on legislation as a team, in natural concerted agency. Barring the occasional drunken accident, the members intend to participate in the legislative process whenever they do so. They not only intend to vote and to adjust their voting to the votes or intended votes of other members. They also intend that their votes contribute to legislative action or inaction on the part of the institution itself. The constitution of the institution must obviously determine which human beings count as members of the institution for this purpose, and how their votes will be counted, and so on. So the agency of the institution still depends on norms determining who may be part of the team and what roles they will have. Nevertheless there is genuine teamwork. The relevant members act as a team in debating and approving legislation. When they do so, within the rules, it is the institution itself that legislates.

Can there be legislation without any concerted action, either natural or artificial? Of course there can, for in the Great Dictatorship, the Great Dictator legislates all by himself. The live question is only whether there can be legislation *involving multiple human beings* without concerted action, either natural or artificial, on the part of those multiple human beings. The answer is that there cannot. To interpret what one has before one as legislation, one must interpret it as an attempt by someone to effect normative changes expressly. One therefore needs to think of the text (or the word or sentence or paragraph, etc) as having an author who was trying to convey a meaning. One therefore needs to think of its creation as either an individual action or a concerted action. There must have been an action of legislating and hence an agent (an individual agent or a concerted agent) who legislated. Most anxieties about this conclusion come of the thought that the concerted agency in question is a legal fiction. There are two responses to this thought. First, the concerted agency is not completely fictitious; the members of legislative institutions do typically perform much of their work as a team, and in that respect they are to be regarded as natural concerted agents akin to orchestras and football teams. Second, there is nothing wrong with a legal fiction of concerted agency, if by that phrase we mean simply that the law attributes actions by one agent (an official) to another agent (an institution) under norms that make the former a representative of, and hence an agent who acts on behalf of, the latter. For there are artificial concerted agents, and many of them are creatures of law. It does not follow from the fact that they are creatures of law that they do not exist or that they are not agents. On the contrary, it follows from the fact that they can perform actions with legal effect, such as legislating, that they do exist, and that they are agents.

2. Customary law

Legislated law may be influenced by custom. It may also refer to custom, giving it legal recognition, for example by saying that the statutory standard to be applied in judging the conduct of an electrician is the standard of conduct that is customary in the electrical trade. This is not customary law. The customary norm in this case is not, even after its legal recognition, a legal norm. It is merely a legally recognized norm. It is the same situation as obtains when English law refers to some norm of French law in settling some family law problem arising out of a marriage conducted in France. This does not make the norm of French law into a norm of English law. Likewise, a legislative reference to a customary norm does not make the norm into a norm of customary law.[19] Customary law, rather, is made up of customary norms that are *ipso facto* legally binding, that are part of the law without further ado.

Bentham distinguished two different kinds of custom that may constitute customary law: custom *in pays* (the custom of a population of legal subjects) and custom *in foro* (the custom of a population of legal officials).[20] In the complex legal systems that law school professors are used to dealing with, there is little customary law that is made *in pays*. A possible exception is in International Law. In International Law, states constitute the population of legal subjects. Arguably some customs that hold in the relations between states are *ipso facto* part of International Law. But the example is made problematic by doubts about International Law itself. It is an anomalous legal system in which the distinction between officials and subjects is blurred. Arguably this even makes it a borderline case of a legal system.[21] In what follows I will therefore be thinking mainly about legal systems other than International Law, and hence about custom that is unequivocally or unambiguously *in foro*: customary law that is constituted as law by the customs of legal officials such as judges, police officers, and bailiffs. Again I will consider the distinguishing features of this kind of law under three headings, to facilitate a contrast with legislated law. First, customary law is not made by articulating (or otherwise expressing) its content. Second, customary law is not intentionally made. Third, customary law is not made by one agent but by many.

---

[19] Joseph Raz, *Practical Reason and Norms* (London 1975), 152–4.

[20] Jeremy Bentham, *A Comment on the Commentaries and A Fragment on Government* (ed Burns and Hart, London 1977), 182–4.

[21] As Hart argues in *The Concept of Law*, above note 3, Ch 10. See further Chapter 11 following.

SOME TYPES OF LAW 67

Customary law is not expressly made. Customary law is, of course, communicated. It is disseminated by example, and dissemination by example is a kind of communication. However, customary law, unlike legislated law, is not *made* by any acts of communicating it. It is made by acts of conforming to it. It is created and changed, not by what people say is to be done, but by what they actually do. So no formulation of a customary legal norm is ever canonical. Once a legal norm acquires a canonical formulation, any other way of settling its content answers to the canonical formulation in the event of conflicting interpretations of the norm. But where a customary legal norm is concerned, any other way of settling its content (including by formulating it) answers to the behaviour of the relevant population.

Customary law is created and changed, not by what people say is to be done, but by what they do. What kind of doing is required? Is it enough that a population's behaviour converges? Is it enough that mowing the lawn is what people round here do every Sunday morning? Or must the population's behaviour also converge *around a norm,* such that they are attempting to follow the norm when they act? Must it be the case that mowing the lawn is what people round here regard as the done thing on a Sunday morning, and that is why they do it? The first case is that of a social habit. The second case is that of a social norm. Here is a simple argument for thinking that customary law must be constituted by a social norm rather than a social habit. If a custom is to form part of the law, it must be normative in the eyes of the law. It must constitute a legal norm. So there must be someone who, on behalf of the law, regards the custom as normative. That someone could, to be sure, be someone other than the population whose custom it is. It could be, for example, a legislature or a court. But in that case it is the fact that the legislature or the court regards the custom as normative that gives it whatever legal effect it has. This is not customary law. Rather, it is custom that is legally recognized in legislation or case law. This leaves as a case of genuine customary law only the case in which the someone who regards the custom as normative, on behalf of the law, is the very same population whose custom it is. Therefore convergent behaviour across a population is capable of constituting customary law only if the convergence takes place under a social norm. A mere social habit does not suffice.

H.L.A. Hart argued that every legal system must have at least one norm of customary law, which he called a rule of recognition. A rule of recognition of a legal system is a norm that identifies some person or institution as an ultimate (= non-delegated) maker of law.[22] Why must every legal system have such a norm? Hart's argument proceeded from his criticisms of Austin. As well as claiming that all laws are commands, Austin claimed that every legal system has an ultimate legislator (or commander), whom Austin labelled its 'sovereign'. The identification of the sovereign, said Austin, is not a legal matter. There is no law on the subject. For if I make law under a law identifying me as a legislator, there must be someone above me in the system who in turn makes that higher law identifying me as a legislator. In which case I am not, after all, the sovereign: I am not an ultimate, but only a delegated, legislator. It follows that the sovereign cannot be identified by a legal norm.[23] Rather, the sovereign must be identified by conforming behaviour. The sovereign is the person or institution to whose commands people round here habitually conform. Sovereignty is efficacy.[24]

Hart agreed with Austin in holding that a legal system is in force only if it is efficacious.[25] The efficacy condition is met so long as legal subjects largely abide by the laws, but irrespective of whether they know the legal basis on which they do so (ie what makes these laws into laws). Yet, argued Hart, there must be such a legal basis. Within each legal system the identification of the ultimate legislator is itself a legal question. It is a question of constitutional law. How can this be? Austin was right to think that a legislature cannot possibly be identified as an ultimate legislator by further legislation so identifying it. His mistake, thought Hart, was merely to conclude that a legislature therefore cannot be identified as an ultimate legislature by *law* so identifying it. This holds true only if, as Austin thought, all law is legislated.

---

[22] Ibid 92–3.
[23] Austin, *The Province of Jurisprudence Determined*, above note 2, 212, 239.
[24] Austin, *Lectures on Jurisprudence*, (5th ed, London 1885), 220–1.
[25] *The Concept of Law*, above note 3, 100–1.

SOME TYPES OF LAW 69

But in fact it is not. There is also the possibility of customary law. Customary law is capable of identifying a legislator (as it were) from below, not from above. The law identifying the ultimate legislature—the rule of recognition—is constituted by other people's conformity to the legislation.[26] The legislature's power to make law is not delegated by these other people. For these people are *ex hypothesi* not legislators and so they have no legislative powers to delegate. In fact they do not delegate any powers at all. Rather, by their custom they create a legal duty, a legal duty to treat the ultimate legislator's word as law, a law which in turn may create legal powers for others.[27]

Whose custom? Which custom? It is tempting simply to follow Austin and say: the social habit of the wider population of legal subjects. But Hart notices that this answer is not adequate to the task at hand. The task at hand is not only to point to the conforming patterns of behaviour but also to explain how it is that they constitute legal norms. What makes the conforming behaviour normative from the legal point of view? For the law to have a point of view there must be people who represent the law in the identification of norms. These people are legal officials. To be more exact, they are law-applying officials. They not only do what, according to the ultimate legislature, is to be done. They also treat adherence to the word of the ultimate legislature as the done thing. They regard the norms created by the ultimate legislature as norms for them to apply, because there is a norm under which, as officials, they have a duty to apply norms created by the ultimate legislature. So conformity to the word of the ultimate legislature is a social rule among the officials, not just a social habit. For Hart, this social rule is what constitutes the rule of recognition of the legal system. The rule of recognition is therefore an example of customary law *in foro*.[28]

One may quibble with various aspects of Hart's account. Some of his arguments are incomplete. But one major insight cannot be denied. Especially, but not only where a legal system has no

---

[26] Ibid 98–9.

[27] This aspect of the rule of recognition was clarified by Raz in *Practical Reason and Norms*, above note 19, 146.

[28] *The Concept of Law*, above note 3, 113.

canonical constitutional text, it is common to say that ultimate constitutional questions are questions of practice (or *realpolitik*), not questions of law. Hart exposed this as a false contrast.[29] That a question is one of practice does not mean that it is not one of law. For some law is made by what people do, not by what they say. Much constitutional law is made in this way. What Hart calls 'rules of change' and 'rules of adjudication' are often but not always found in customary, as opposed to legislated, constitutional law.[30] But if Hart is right, every legal system has at least one rule—at least one rule of recognition—that is customary rather than legislated. The rule of recognition is unwritten even in legal systems with written constitutions. A rule of recognition may come to be articulated by some legal officials, maybe even in a constitutional document. But the articulation is never canonical. Inasmuch as the norm as articulated departs from the norm as practiced by law-applying officials, the practice of the officials is what fixes the content of the rule of recognition. Do as we do, not as we say.

Customary law is not intentionally made. Unlike legislated law, customary law is not intentionally made. True, the actions by which it is made are almost always intentional actions. The officials who create Hart's rule of recognition, for example, clearly intend to follow (what they take to be) a rule when they do so. What they do not intend to do is to *create* or *change* a rule in the process. Their law-making is usually an accidental by-product of their intended law-applying. For example, by treating an Act of Parliament as valid law—by raising no questions about its validity and interpreting its contents as law—judges contribute to making it the case that Acts of Parliament in general are valid law. They contribute to making the rule of recognition what it is. But that is not what they usually intend to do. What they usually intend to do is to apply a legal norm that, so far as they are concerned, exists quite apart from their action of applying it, because it is a norm found in an Act of Parliament. And in a way they are right. The norm is in the Act and it is part of the law of the land according to a

---

[29] Ibid 108.   [30] Ibid 93–6.

rule of recognition of the legal system, which is a customary norm that no single judge is in a position to change. Moreover, because any change in this rule depends on the usually unforeseeable actions of many other law-applying officials, usually no single judge is in a position to *intend* to change it either.[31] And yet as a law-applying official each single judge is part of the official population whose social rule constitutes the legal rule, and as part of this population he can contribute to changing the rule. It follows that a single judge can readily be an accidental participant, but only rarely an intentional participant, in a change of customary law.

In the scenario just sketched, the intentional application of one legal norm (a legislated norm) potentially makes an accidental contribution to change in another legal norm (a customary norm). In a different scenario, the legal norm that the judge accidentally helps to change is the very same customary legal norm that she intends to apply without changing it. This possibility helps us to see a way forward with an old and tiresome debate. We all know that the law can be changed by the actions of judges. That is what gives the law a history that can be studied by studying judicial decisions. Yet judges almost always talk as if all they are doing is applying the law unchanged. Should we regard this self-presentation as a mere pretence, a spin that judges put on their arguments to shore up their legitimacy? Sometimes, no doubt, we should. But sometimes we should regard it more generously as an innocent slip on the part of the judge. Such slips are particularly easy to make where customary law is concerned, thanks to the indeterminacy of customary norms.

All legal norms have their indeterminacies. In the case of legislated norms these typically include indeterminacies of language and indeterminacies of intention.[32] But customary law is subject to another kind of indeterminacy which comes precisely of the fact that it is neither articulately nor intentionally made. When a new situation emerges that is close to one that is already regulated by a customary norm, what determines whether it is or is not regulated by the norm? In the case of customary norms (or more generally norms that are made by their use) there is

---

[31] See R.A. Duff, *Intention, Agency, and Criminal Liability* (Oxford 1990), 56.
[32] Hart, *The Concept of Law*, above note 3, 124–6.

nothing that determines this except what people do next by way of supposed application of the norm. The norm is indeterminate in its application until actually applied. This makes for a characteristic kind of slip in the application of customary law. Overlooking tiny differences between the present situation and past situations that were admittedly regulated by the norm, it is easy to jump to the conclusion that the norm already regulates the present situation, when in reality it is still indeterminate in respect of its regulation or non-regulation of the present situation. This represents a tiny mistake of law. But such mistakes can contribute gradually to changes in the custom, and hence to changes in the law. Over time the customary law comes into line with its own hitherto mistaken applications. Officials who intended only to apply the norm without changing it contributed accidentally to the change. This, it strikes me, is the usual way in which customary law *in foro* changes.

Customary law is not made by one agent. Again, the next step has been anticipated. The making of customary law requires multiple actions by multiple agents. There must be widespread convergence of actions before we have a custom, and hence before we have customary law. What is not required is any kind of joint agency, any kind of teamwork on the model of an orchestra or Parliament. Joint agency is possible only when the participants in it are aware of each other's actions, and intend their actions to contribute to the same project as the actions of others. In the case of Parliaments, this is how the intention to make law takes shape: the various members and officials of Parliament do not merely happen to go through the lobbies together. They do it in the awareness that others are doing it and intending their actions to contribute, together with the actions of others, to the making of law. Custom is very different. Participants in customs are, as we saw, sometimes acting with the intention to follow a social rule (to do the done thing). But their intentions here are not joint intentions. They are merely intentions in common. They do not require mutual awareness, nor an intention to participate in a common project. And sometimes—when a custom is constituted by social habit—not even an intention in common is needed. It is enough that behaviour converges, never mind the reasons.

A great deal of ink has been spilt on the question of what kind of interaction among law-applying officials is required to constitute Hart's famous rule of recognition. Hart originally took the minimal view described above. Law-applying officials need only regard it as the done thing for law-applying officials like themselves to treat the word of the ultimate legislature (and other authorities of inherent jurisdiction) as law. But under pressure from Ronald Dworkin, Hart later allowed that the rule of recognition is perhaps not just a social rule but a *conventional* social rule.[33] This opened the way to elaborate discussions of Hart's 'conventionalism' about law. In particular, Hart's thinking came to be linked with a body of philosophical literature on convention which gave a highly technical sense to the term, in which conventional rules are only those social rules that serve coordinating social functions.[34] From here it was a surprisingly short step to the idea that the officials whose actions add up to constitute the rule of recognition of each legal system are engaging in something close to teamwork, intentionally coordinating with each other in the manner of an orchestra playing the symphony of law.[35] It seems to me that all this extra baggage is not only misguided and unnecessary but contrary to the tenor of Hart's original proposal.[36] It brings the rule of recognition ever closer to the model of legislated law, a creation of many working as one. But Hart's whole point was that a different kind of law is needed before legislated law is possible. It is needed to create legal institutions of the kind that can pass undelegated legislation. This customary law is not the work of many working as one. It is the work of many acting as

---

[33] *The Concept of Law* (2nd ed, Oxford 1991), 267.

[34] Jules Coleman, *The Practice of Principle* (Oxford, 2001), 92.

[35] Ibid 98. For further work on the idea, see Scott Shapiro, 'Legal Practice and Massively Shared Agency', unpublished manuscript available at: <http://hvrd.me/IC0HVW>, accessed 19 April 2012.

[36] Other doubters: Joseph Raz, 'On the Authority and Interpretation of Constitutions: Some Preliminaries' in Larry Alexander (ed), *Constitutionalism* (Cambridge 1998), 161–2; Leslie Green, 'Positivism and Conventionalism', *Canadian Journal of Law and Jurisprudence* 12 (1999), 35; Julie Dickson. 'Is the Rule of Recognition Really a Conventional Rule?', *Oxford Journal of Legal Studies* 27 (2007), 373.

many. They create new law collectively as an accidental by-product of their individual efforts to follow the law as it is. Each intends in her own case to follow the rule of recognition, not to change it.

3. Case law

It is essential to the nature of law that all legal systems have law-applying officials who make legal rulings. A legal ruling is a legally binding decision on the application of a legal rule to what lawyers call a 'case': to a situation-token rather than a situation-type. In the case of *Barnewall* v *Adolphus*, for example, there may be a legal ruling that Barnewall now owes Adolphus $50. An official who has the power to make such a legal ruling—typically a judge—also has the power to change people's legal positions. He has the power to change Barnewall's legal position and Adolphus's legal position and the legal position of the bailiffs who execute the debt and the legal position of newspapers who report the decision, and so on. But he does not necessarily have the power to change the law itself in the process. He has the power to change the law itself in the process only if, by making the legal ruling, he can also change the legal rule under which he makes it, thereby affecting its application in cases other than the one before him. We have already seen how a judge might contribute to doing this by contributing to a change in official custom. But in some legal systems some judges also have the power to change legal rules *solo*, and instantaneously, by making legal rulings. This is not customary law because no convergence of official behaviour around the new rule is required to make it part of the law. This type of law is known as case law.

Typically judges set about adding to case law by applying existing law; ie by applying law that exists apart from their act of applying it. Typically they argue that a certain ruling, even if not required by existing law, would be consistent with existing law and a sound development of existing law. They proceed in this way because they have a professional moral duty (usually crystallized in their oath of office) to keep faith with whatever existing law there is on any subject on which they make a ruling. But this professional moral duty need not and often does not circumscribe the legal power of judges to make law. In many legal systems, judges with the ability to add to case law do so even if they do so *per incuriam*: even if they ignore and contravene existing law in doing so. When that happens, other judges may have extra powers to overrule the errant decision when it comes to light in later cases. But this confirms, rather than challenges, the claim that the law was changed by the errant decision in the meantime. If the law was not changed, overruling would not be necessary. Such judicial law-making without the support of existing law is in one respect akin to legislating. It is an activity of making law *de novo*. Yet it is not legislating. For legislators do not make law *de novo* by applying law. *Qua* legislators they make legal rules but no legal rulings. Whereas judges, even when they make legal rulings without the support of existing law, always make law by applying it. Whenever they make case law, they make law by the act of applying the very same law that they thereby make.

So case law is neither legislated law nor customary law. It has some features in common with each. To see the similarities and differences more clearly, I will ask the same questions about case law that I asked about legislated law and customary law. Is case law expressly made? Is it intentionally made? Is it made by one agent or by many?

Case law is not expressly made. Case law is a kind of law made by judges. It is to be found in the judgments that judges give when they decide the cases brought before them. These judgments take the form of texts, which (like legislated law) may be either written or oral, which may be expressed in declarative or (rarely) imperative sentences, and which call for interpretation. These latter features may encourage the thought that case law is a kind of legislated law. But a major difference lies in *how* the judgment of a judge creates whatever new law it creates. Case law, unlike legislated law, is not made by being articulated. It is made by being used in argument. In this respect case law, in spite of its delivery in textual form, has more in common with customary law than it has in common with legislated law. Recall that customary law is made by (social) rule-following. Using a rule in argument is also a kind of rule-following, even though the rule in question need not be a social one.

An argument is made up of at least two premises and a conclusion. For simplicity, let's imagine a very simple two-premise legal argument that could be made by a judge.

Rule: Any person who calls another person a liar has a duty to pay $50 to that other person.
Fact: Barnewall (a person) called Adolphus (another person) a liar.
Ruling: Thus, Barnewall has a duty to pay $50 to Adolphus.

To be sure, arguments made by judges are often much more complicated than this. The facts of the case are often much more arcane. There are often subsidiary arguments that bear on the interpretation of the rule, or the interpretation of the facts. And the main argument often runs through a series of interim conclusions which are then used as premises in the next stage of the argument. But none of this makes any difference to the point about case law that concerns us now. So, let's focus on the simple, pared-down case of *Barnewall* v *Adolphus*.

To do her judicial work in the case of *Barnewall* v *Adolphus*, the judge must express at least one legal norm: she must express her ruling. Until she has ruled, she has not judged, and until she has expressed her ruling, she has not ruled.[37] Judging in the sense of making a ruling on a case may be thought of as akin to a legislative act, since the ruling is not only expressed but expressed with the intention of binding the parties legally by that very act of expressing it. But unlike legislation, the ruling by itself does not make new law. The law is made up of legal rules, legal norms that apply to more than one case. Legal rulings are legal norms that apply only to the case in which the ruling is made, and hence do not form part of the law.

So if the judge in *Barnewall* v *Adolphus* does make new law, that law lies not in her ruling but in the rule she uses to make it. Yet she might not attempt to formulate her rule. She might only state the facts and the ruling, leaving the later interpreter of the case to work out the rule that she is using. The rule she is using is one that, combined with the facts of the case, suffices to yield the ruling. So in interpreting the case one begins by working back to

---

[37] As with legislation, this expression is typically in words, but it could be by symbol or gesture (eg a thumbs-down).

SOME TYPES OF LAW 77

the rule from the facts and the ruling. This may be what prompts some people to say that judges decide cases, and hence make case law, by reasoning 'on the facts' rather than by the use of rules.[38] The contrast here is false and the suggestion, taken literally, is baffling. No number of facts can ever yield any legal ruling except in combination with a legal rule which renders those facts legally pertinent. What makes it seem otherwise is merely that, where case law is concerned, the rule being used belongs to what David Lyons aptly calls implicit (or implied) law, as opposed to explicit (or express) law.[39] The rule is implicit because it is made by being used in the case, rather than by being expressed. It is the rule as used rather than the rule as stated.

I said that the rule for which a case stands is one that, combined with the facts of the case, suffices to yield the ruling. But surely, in any given case, there are many possible rules that meet this specification? Surely the rule could always be rendered more general and still combine with the facts to yield the ruling? Perhaps the rule in *Barnewall* v *Adolphus* is not the narrow

Rule 1: Any person who calls another person a liar has a duty to pay $50 to that other person.

Perhaps it is the broader

Rule 2: Any person who calls another person an insulting name has a duty to pay $50 to that other person.

Or perhaps it is the even broader

Rule 3: Any person who calls another person a name has a duty to pay $50 to that other person.

---

[38] See eg Bruce Chapman, 'The Rational and the Reasonable: Social Choice Theory and Adjudication', *University of Chicago Law Review* 61 (1994), 41 at 66–7.

[39] David Lyons, 'Moral Aspects of Legal Theory' in M. Cohen (ed), *Ronald Dworkin and Contemporary Jurisprudence* (London 1984), 49 at 58. The expression 'implicit law' was first used by Lon Fuller in *The Anatomy of Law* (New York 1968), where it was contrasted with 'made law'. Since implication is but one way of making law, Fuller's contrast is unfortunate. Lyons improves upon it by contrasting 'implicit law' with 'explicit law', but strangely still tends to talk as if those who believe that law is made can recognize only explicit law.

Any of these three rules (and countless others) can be combined with the fact as found in *Barnewall* v *Adolphus* to yield the same ruling. So how do we know which of these many rules the case stands for? Which is the *ratio decidendi* of the case? Perhaps there is no answer; in which case we have some seriously indeterminate case law before us. It may be indeterminate which of these three rules (among countless other possibilities) is the rule in *Barnewall* v *Adolphus*. The effect of the case on the law is then arguable, and the case could therefore be relied upon in later cases to support various rival arguments and hence incompatible rulings.

In practice, however, such legal indeterminacies tend to be mitigated in a number of ways. Let me mention four.

First, a legal system that makes extensive use of case law may have closure rules to help render its case law more determinate. There might, for example, be a rule of law according to which (subject to indications to the contrary in the judgment) the *ratio decidendi* of a case is the narrowest rule that suffices, in combination with the facts of the case, to yield the ruling in that case. In which case, all else being equal, rule 1 in would beat rules 2 and 3 to qualify as the rule in *Barnewall* v *Adolphus*.

Second, the rule that a case stands for must be consistent not only with the ruling in that case but also with the rulings in any other cases on which the judge relied in arriving at his ruling (for these rulings too form part of the argument in the case). In legal systems that depend heavily on case law for their development, there are often long lines of cases that combine to lend increasing determinacy to the rule for which the last of them stands. This is the main way in which case law gradually crystallizes over time, sometimes referred to as its 'organic' quality.

Third, the arguments presented by judges often include not only the application of a rule but also a rationale for the rule as applied. If so, this rationale also forms part of the *ratio decidendi* and constrains the range of possible interpretations of the rule in the case. The rule in the case must then be one capable of being supported by its rationale, as well as one capable, in combination with the facts of the case, of yielding the ruling.

Finally, judges often do formulate the rule, or aspects of the rule, for which they regard their case as standing. In such a case, subject to the previous three points, the judicial formulation of the rule helps us to narrow down the range of possible rules for which the case stands. Obviously, the rule so narrowed down must still suffice to yield the ruling in the case—and otherwise be compatible with the argument in the case—or else it is not the rule for which the case stands. In the terms I used before, the argument in the case is still the primary object of interpretation. Interpreting the formulation is merely a way of aiding the interpretation of the argument. This marks a key difference between case law and legislative law. Where legislative law is concerned, as we saw, the legislative formulation is canonical. So long as one is applying the legislation one may not abandon the legislative formulation as an object of interpretation, even if it cannot be reconciled with a certain ruling or a certain rationale. With case law the reverse is true: the rule that a case stands for is a rule that supports the ruling in the case, and is supported by the rationale in the case, even if these cannot be reconciled with the judge's attempted formulation of the rule.

Case law may be intentionally made. Case law differs from customary law in that the act of making it may be intended to make law. But case law differs from statutory law in that the act of making it is not *necessarily* intended to make law. To put it simply: the act of making new case law may be either intentional or accidental. The judge may either mistake the rule he is applying for the existing rule of law, and hence not intend to add anything to the law by applying it, or he may realize that the rule he is applying is a departure from the existing rule of law, and hence intend to change the law by applying the rule he is applying. Which path the judge is taking is rarely apparent from the judge's own arguments. This is because, even when a judge is intentionally changing the law, he or she has a professional moral duty to do so on legal grounds; ie by pointing to existing legal rules that, when soundly developed, would justify a departure from, and hence change in, the particular legal rule that is now under consideration. When she changes the law on legal grounds, the judge often is not sure, and does not need to be sure, whether what she is doing counts as changing the law. It often strikes the judge only as a matter of reconciling two apparently conflicting rules of law. It often does not matter to her whether these rules of law are only apparently conflicting (in which case neither of the rules need be changed in order to reconcile them) or whether they are really conflicting (in which case at least one of the rules needs to be changed in order to reconcile them).

In English law (and in many other legal systems of English descent), judges sometimes have the power to overrule previous judges on points of law, something which cannot be done (knowingly)[40] without intending to change the law. But judges also often have the power to do something more modest, which is to *distinguish* cases decided by earlier judges. One distinguishes a case by narrowing the rule used in an earlier case so that it still yields the original ruling in that case (and is otherwise still consistent with the *ratio decidendi* of that case) but does not regulate the case now being decided, leaving the court in the present case free to rely on a different and apparently conflicting rule. There is no doubt that the judicial power to distinguish is a power to change the law.[41] But is the law changed every time the power to distinguish is ostensibly exercised? Surely not. There are surely many cases in which the rule in a previous case already does not extend to the case at hand and so does not need to be narrowed to secure its non-application. The 'distinguishing' of the case is then a precaution devoid of legal effect, or an explanation by the judge of why the case does not need to be distinguished. It is rare that judges need to know whether they are distinguishing a case (using their power to narrow the rule so as to disapply it) or merely 'distinguishing' it in this inert way (pointing out that it is already narrow enough not to be applicable). So it is rare that judges need to form an intention to change the law when they are engaged in adding to the stock of case law by distinguishing earlier cases.[42] Since a great deal of the stock of case law in England and in

---

[40] So-called 'implied overruling'—where the overruling court is unaware of the case it is countermanding—need not be intended to change the law.

[41] For discussion, see A.W.B. Simpson, 'The *Ratio Decidendi* of a Case and the Doctrine of Binding Precedent', in A.G. Guest (ed), *Oxford Essays in Jurisprudence* (Oxford 1961); Joseph Raz, 'Law and Value in Adjudication' in his *The Authority of Law* (Oxford 1979); Frederick Schauer, 'Precedent', *Stanford Law Review* 39 (1987), 571.

[42] Grant Lamond, 'Do Precedents Create Rules?', *Legal Theory* 11 (2005) 1 at 13–14. Lamond contrasts distinguishing a case with interpreting its *ratio*. But one may do both at once: one may narrow the rule in a case on the ground that the

cognate jurisdictions is furnished by distinguishing, a great deal of case law is likely to have been unintentionally made.

Case law is made by one agent. Like legislators, the makers of case law may be human beings (individual judges) or institutions (courts made up of a number of judges). In some legal systems both individual judges and the courts they belong to are capable of contributing to the stock of case law. Individual judges have a certain authority when they deliver their own judgments. But when they agree with each other in such a way that their judgments add up to the judgment of the court, their authority is augmented and the rules they agree on become harder for later courts to disregard or overrule. To understand this one needs to understand courts as having artificial personalities akin to those of legislatures. There are rules about how the actions of the members of the court come together to constitute actions of the court itself. It matters who is in the majority, and failing that, who is in the plurality, etc. At the same time, many judges (unlike ordinary members of the legislature) have some legal powers as natural persons and can affect the content of the law by what they do and intend to do, even when they are at odds with the decision of their court (for example, when they are dissenters in respect of the judgment of the court, or they are concurrers who arrive at the same ruling as the court but using different rules). One may be tempted to conclude from this that case law can either be made by many agents or by one. But in fact it is always made by one. The agent is either a single human being (a judge) or a single institution (a court populated by judges).

Of course, since the authority of case law may vary, it may be to one's legal advantage to have a lot of case law on one's side. When one cites a long line of cases dating back for centuries, it may seem as if one is really relying on customary law, not case law. But in three ways what one is relying on differs from customary law. First, the authority of the line of cases rests on an aggregation (quite a complex aggregation) of the authority of the courts and judges whose decisions are included in the line.

---

rule in that case was wider than was needed to do justice to the rationale that was given for it in that very same case.

With customary law, by contrast, there is no legal force to these individual decisions until they are aggregated. The second is that the cases need not include any real convergence on the law. Perhaps no two cases in the line apply exactly the same rule. They may instead tell a story of continuous legal change, with a series of acts of distinguishing that gradually and inexorably turn the law in one's favour. The third, implicit perhaps in the second, is that even to the extent that the cases in the line do converge, they need not include any simultaneous convergence. It is part of the nature of custom that there should be a measure of simultaneous convergence. Even two hundred reputable nonconformists do not constitute a custom of nonconformity if there was never more than one nonconformist at a time; if there was at no time a social rule of nonconformity. Whereas two hundred reputable nonconformists on the judicial bench do constitute a huge weight of authority in case law, even if they all engaged in their nonconformity at quite different times, and merely passed the baton of their nonconformity along against a backdrop of completely countervailing custom. Case law, to put it simply, may readily conflict with customary law *in foro*.

The following table summarizes the classification of types of law that we have encountered so far:

	Expressly made?	*Intentionally made?*	*By what kind of agency?*
Legislated law	Express	Intentional	Individual
Customary law	Not express	Unintentional	Multiple
Case law	Not express	Either	Individual

4. Common law

Common law is not another type of law to be added to the above table in addition to legislated law, customary law, and case law. The Common Law (with capital letters) is a legal tradition marked by a number of different and only contingently related features. The tradition is polytypic: most but not all of its distinguishing features are present in each legal system belonging to the tradition. Some of these features do not concern the way the law is made. So, for example, the following are characteristic features of Common Law legal systems:

1. Common Law legal systems employ a distinctive 'adversarial' fact-finding process, of which trial by jury is the epitome.
2. Common Law legal systems embody a distinctive doctrine of the rule of law, according to which officials of the system are, with specific exceptions, subject to the same legal rules as non-officials.
3. Common Law legal systems make use of certain distinctive legal categories, such as trustee, consideration, and estoppel.

When referring to common law without capital letters, however, many lawyers working in the Common Law tradition are referring to only part of the law of their own systems. Often they are drawing a contrast with legislated law. Common law, one may glean, is law that comes into being in a different way from legislated law. But how does it come into being? Is it case law or is it customary law? The founding myths of The Common Law as a legal tradition tend to present it as a system of custom *in pays*.[43] It is law that rises up from the general population, as opposed to statute law which descends upon the population from the King. This founding myth is in many ways ridiculous. The law in question was mostly the work of the King's judges. But even if this were not the case in the twelfth century, it is surely the case now. The common law doctrines in use now are the creatures of judicial use. Yet this leaves open the question: what kind of judicial use? Is it judicial use in one case at a time, constituting case law? Or is it concurrent and convergent judicial use, constituting customary law *in foro*?

It seems to me that common law, as contrasted with legislated law, contains elements of both case law and customary law. In England, where we have an almost entirely unwritten constitution, there is probably more common law that is custom *in foro* than in some legal systems belonging to the Common Law tradition that have a canonical constitutional document. This is because in the English setting, not only the rule of recognition,

---

[43] Postema, 'Philosophy of the Common Law', above note 12, 590–2.

but also many other constitutional rules are made and sustained accidentally by the judicial custom of following them. When at long last these rules are explicitly challenged in court, there is often no previous case law on the point. No pertinent case has ever been argued before any court. And yet many judges and other officials have been quietly following the same rules over hundreds of years. So here we have judicial customary law, as opposed to case law, that is part of the common law of England.

One nice example, in England at least, is the doctrine of *stare decisis*, which regulates the extent to which and the ways in which later courts may overrule earlier courts. In large measure this doctrine entered the common law of England as a kind of judicial custom. But notice that it is not a doctrine concerned with the development of customary law. It is a doctrine concerned with the development of case law. Indeed, comparative lawyers sometimes talk as if only legal systems with a doctrine of *stare decisis* can include case law. This is a mistake. For the decisions of earlier courts may add to the stock of case law even though there is no protection against these decisions being superseded by the decisions of other courts. Where there is no such protection it is tempting to say that there is no 'binding' precedent, but only 'persuasive' precedent. But this is strictly speaking incorrect. Courts may change the law on Tuesday even though other courts may change the law back again on Wednesday. When legislators do such things, we do not deny that the legislated law made on Tuesday is binding, albeit only briefly. After all, if such legislated law were not binding there would be no need for it to be changed back again on Wednesday. Instead it could be disregarded. We should say exactly the same thing with case law. The decision of an earlier court must be binding in law for it to be necessary for a later court to overrule it. So a doctrine of *stare decisis* does not alter the power to make binding law. It only alters the power of later courts to change the binding law that was thereby made. It follows that one may have case law in a legal system without having a doctrine of *stare decisis*. On the other hand, one may not have a doctrine of *stare decisis* without having case law.

In spite of that, the doctrine itself need not be created by case law. It could in principle be created by statute. More to the point it could be created by judicial custom. That is the position, it seems to me, in England. So it would be a mistake to think of common law as case law alone. Common law is probably better thought of as case law combined with judicial customary law concerning the reception and use of case law. In both respects it can usefully be contrasted with legislated law.

Yet the contrast with legislated law is also impure. When common law is contrasted with legislated law it is almost always contrasted with legislated law as developed by case law. Common law, we could say, includes only that part of case law which is not concerned with the interpretation of legislation. True, even in Common Law jurisdictions, there is a great deal of case law concerned with the interpretation of legislation. The point is only that one could equally have a legal system with a great deal of case law but no common law. There would be no common law because all the case law would be case law concerning the interpretation of legislation. Legislation—including the legislation of the written constitution—would be regarded as the primary object of interpretation, with the interpretation of case law required only as part of the process of interpreting the legislation. What seems most special about Common Law jurisdictions is that they have a great deal of case law that is not about the interpretation of legislation. It is only about the interpretation of other case law.

5. Positive law

All three of the types of law I discussed here are types of positive law. They are all made by somebody and we know that they count as law only when we know who made them. Legislated law is made by legislators. Case law is made by judges. Customary law is made by (official or non-official) populations. Case law and customary law—'non-legislated law' for short—is sometimes represented as non-positive law, simply because it is not made expressly or intentionally. Thanks to these features it is easy to make it seem as if non-legislated law is not really made at all. Ronald Dworkin, for example, relied on these features of case law in arguing that at least some of it exists without anyone's ever having made it. The implicit law to be found in the cases exists, according to Dworkin, in virtue of the fact that it provides a sound moral justification for whatever explicit law there might be in those same (and other?) cases. So it can be made without any kind of engagement with it by anyone. It exists even before it is cited or used by anyone.[44] My discussion has suggested that this is a mistake. It is true that case law is implicit law in the sense that it is not made by being expressed. Nor is it always made intentionally. The rule in the case has to be worked out by examining the judge's argument, to see what rule he implicitly, and maybe accidentally, relied upon. Nevertheless, the judge brings the rule into existence by relying on it. So implicit law, like explicit law, is still brought into existence by someone. It is still positive law. For there is no such thing as non-positive law. There are no legal norms that come into existence without being brought into existence by someone. It is merely that there are several ways of bringing them into existence.

As mentioned at the outset, Dworkin errs in thinking of all law-makers as legislators. This leads him to think that any law that is not legislated does not have a law-maker. The error is dramatic. Yet it is readily understandable. For there is a sense in which legislative law-making is paradigmatic law-making. How so? Several times in this chapter I have referred to the *authority* of legal officials. I have also referred to the authority of the law itself; eg the authority of case law. You may understand this to be no more than another way of referring to the positivity of law; ie to the fact that all legal norms are made by someone. But my references to authority suggest a stronger thesis. For, while all exercises of authority are acts of changing the norms that apply to others, not all acts of changing the norms that apply to others are exercises of authority. To exercise authority is to change the norms applicable to others by the very act of attempting to change them. It is an intentional action by definition. So, of the types of law we have identified, only legislative law need be made by an exercise of authority. Case law may but need not be made by an exercise of authority. Customary law, meanwhile, is not made by an exercise of authority at all.

This need not, however, inhibit us from referring to customary law as authoritative. Nor does it stop lawyers from referring to

---

[44] 'Hard Cases', above note 1, 110–18.

cases as authorities even when the only law-making they involve is accidental. The explanation is given by Raz:

> [An analysis of law-making as an exercise of authority] could in principle apply to a legislator and his acts of enactment. But not all law is enacted. Customary rules can be legally binding. Can they be authoritative despite the fact that they are not issued by authority? It is possible to talk directly of the authority of the law itself. A person's authority [is] explained by reference to his utterances: he has authority if his utterances are protected reasons for action, i.e. reasons for taking the action they indicate and for disregarding (certain) conflicting considerations. The law has authority if the existence of a law requiring a certain action is a protected reason for performing that action.[45]

Legislating is the paradigm of law-making because it involves an exercise of authority: an attempt to change another's normative position by that very act of attempting to change it. Customary law, and accidentally made case law, is also authoritative, but only in a derivative sense. It is not made by an exercise of authority. But in respect of its normative force, it is treated as if it were. It is authoritative in reception albeit not in creation. One can understand what it means to receive something as authoritative only by understanding what it means to exercise authority. So, inasmuch as the authority of law is central to its nature, one naturally understands law by working out from legislative law to other types of law. One understands other types of law by grasping how they differ from legislative law.[46]

Why should we think of the authority of law as central to its nature? Here is the answer suggested by Raz himself:

> [To play] a mediating role between ultimate reasons and people's decisions and actions... the law must be, or at least be presented as being, an expression of the judgment of some people or of some institutions on the merits of the actions it requires. Hence, the identification of a rule as a rule of law consists in attributing it to the relevant person as representing their decisions and expressing their judgments.

---

[45] 'The Claims of Law' in Raz, *The Authority of Law* (Oxford 1979), 29.

[46] Compare Jeremy Waldron, 'Legislative Intent and Unintentional Legislation' in his *Law and Disagreement*, above note 14, who unexpectedly sacrifices the paradigmatic status of legislative law by attempting to explain the nature of authority without any mention of intentionality.

Such attribution need not be on the ground that this is what the person or institution explicitly said. It may be based on an implication. But the attribution must establish that the view expressed in the alleged statement is the view of the relevant legal institution. Such attributions can only be based on factual considerations. Moral argument can establish what legal institutions should have said or should have held but not what they did say or hold.[47]

On this view, it is the role that law plays in coordinating and otherwise assisting our rational agency that explains why law must be thought of as authoritative. And it is the need for law to be thought of as authoritative that explains why all law is positive law, why all law needs its law-maker(s). I have not defended this line of thought here. I have limited myself to the more modest task of showing how customary law and case law, no less than legislative law, qualify as types of positive law in spite of distracting features which may lead one to think otherwise.

[47] 'Authority, Law and Morality' in Raz, *Ethics in the Public Domain* (rev ed, Oxford 1995), 210 at 321.

4
Can There Be a Written Constitution?

1. The possibility of an unwritten constitution

Does the United Kingdom have a constitution? Some people doubt it. But there is no room for doubt. A constitution is a conceptual necessity of every legal system. In every legal system there are rules that specify the major institutions and officials of government,[1] and determine which of them is to do what, and how they are to interact, and how their membership or succession is to be determined, and so forth. Without some such rules, as H.L.A. Hart explained in *The Concept of Law*, there is no legal system.[2] These rules without which there would be no legal system (or some of them, invariably in combination with some other rules) make up the constitution of that system. Since the United Kingdom undeniably has some law, and since all law is necessarily the law of one or another legal system, the United Kingdom necessarily has at least one constitution.

I say 'at least' because the United Kingdom has three distinct municipal legal systems (the law of England and Wales, the law of Scotland, and the law of Northern Ireland). Does it correspondingly have three constitutions? And if it has three, doesn't it inevitably have four, for surely there must also be an overarching constitution of the whole union that determines the relations among the other three? Or do the three distinct legal systems share just one constitution between them? Is that a conceptual possibility? Can it be squared with the proper criteria for individuating legal systems? These questions are vigorously debated, and not only by theorists.[3] Some of them are political hot

---

[1] Or perhaps I should say 'governance', to anticipate the objection that only states have governments, but that not all legal systems are state legal systems.
[2] *The Concept of Law* (Oxford 1961), 95–6. (In this chapter, abbreviated as *CL*.)
[3] For a predictably excellent theoretical treatment, see Neil MacCormick, *Questioning Sovereignty* (Oxford 1999), Ch 4. For a similarly excellent discussion of the like problem of the individuation of legal systems in the European

potatoes. For present purposes, however, I will ignore them. At the risk of being hijacked for the unionist cause, I will speak brazenly of 'the United Kingdom constitution' (or 'the UK constitution' for short), for the questions I want to tackle here are unaffected by the possibility that the UK has a cluster of interrelated constitutions. Whether there is one constitution or several, each alike exhibits the feature that causes people to doubt whether the UK has any constitution at all.

The feature that provokes the doubts, notoriously, is that the UK constitution is an unwritten one. When they ask what the constitution of some country or state has to say on some subject, people nowadays typically expect to be directed to a canonical constitutional master-text on the model of the Constitution of the United States of America (complete with its Amendments). Thus the political furore about the proposed 'Constitution for Europe' was not about whether the European Union should have a constitution—as it already has a legal system, necessarily it already has a constitution—but whether it should acquire a canonical constitutional master-text to match.[4]

In the UK, there is no canonical constitutional master-text, and no live proposal to have one. This does not mean, I hasten to add, that there are no rules of the UK constitution that have canonical texts. On the contrary, there are many. To take a few famous examples, there are constitutional provisions in Magna Carta 1297, the Laws in Wales Acts 1535–1542, the Habeas Corpus Act 1679, the Bill of Rights 1689, the Act of Union (with Scotland) 1707, the Act of Union (with Ireland) 1800, the Judicature Acts 1873 and 1875, and the Statute of Westminster 1931. More debatable examples, among many, include the Great Reform Act of 1832 and its successor Representation of the

---

Community, see Julie Dickson, 'How Many Legal Systems? Some Puzzles Regarding the Identity Conditions of, and Relations Between, Legal Systems in the European Union', *Problema* 2 (2008), 9.

[4] For the now-abandoned constitutional text, see *Official Journal of the European Communities* C310/01 (2004). Mads Andenas and I tried to introduce some of the theoretical issues underlying the political debate in 'Can Europe Have a Constitution?', *King's College Law Journal* 12 (2001), 1—in particular the idea of a 'capital-C Constitution', which I will not make use of here.

CAN THERE BE A WRITTEN CONSTITUTION? 91

People Acts, the Parliament Acts 1911 and 1949, and the European Communities Act 1972. But none of these, nor all of them stapled together, is 'the UK constitution', in the sense that many inquirers have in mind. They are only some written fragments of the otherwise unwritten (and so maybe we should say 'uncodified' rather than 'unwritten') UK constitution. This is not altered by the fact that two of them—the Acts of Union—are founding documents in the sense that they establish the UK as a union. For what establishes a union is not necessarily its constitution. A union may be established (as in the case of the UK) by uniting its parts complete with elements of their existing constitutions, and without, in the process, reducing those elements to writing. In that case the founding document of the union only adds another fragment to its constitution.[5]

Notice that all of the constitutional fragments listed above are Acts of Parliament that were passed and promulgated in the ordinary way. Their status as part of the constitution is not determined by some special origin or process of enactment. They do not have 'constitutional' printed or stamped on them at point of issue. Even if they did, it is not clear that this by itself would have any legal effect.[6] The UK constitution does not provide for Parliament to act as a primary legislator other than by passing an Act of Parliament in the ordinary way. Nor is there any other primary legislator constituted by the UK constitution[7] whose enactments bind Parliament.[8] That is one reason why there

---

[5] Contrast Neil MacCormick, 'Does the United Kingdom Have a Constitution? Reflections on *MacCormick* v *Lord Advocate*', *Northern Ireland Legal Quarterly* 29 (1978), 1.

[6] Thus the grandly titled Constitutional Reform Act 2005 has yet to establish its constitutional credentials. Likewise the Constitution Act 1982, which did not have constitutional effect at the time of its enactment but only later: see *Manuel* v *Attorney General* [1983] Ch 77, discussed in note 9 following.

[7] I say 'constituted' rather than 'recognized' because arguably the European Commission, which is constituted by the European Community constitution not the UK constitution, has nevertheless come to be recognized by the UK constitution as a primary legislator whose enactments are capable of binding Parliament. See *Factortame* v *Secretary of State for Transport* [1991] AC 603 at 658–9 per Lord Bridge for a strong judicial statement to that effect.

[8] Which is not to say that no other primary legislator is constituted by the UK constitution. There is also the Privy Council, which makes Orders in Council as a

is no live proposal to have a canonical constitutional master-text in the UK. Even if one were thought desirable, it is far from clear how anyone would set about creating one. The UK constitution includes no procedure for its own deliberate amendment, never mind for its own encapsulation in a canonical master-text.

If the UK constitution contains no procedure for its own deliberate amendment, how do certain Acts of Parliament come to have constitutional effect? Their constitutional effect is not determined by how they are created, but rather by how they are received, by their treatment in either the customs or the decisions of certain law-applying officials, principally the courts. The Acts in question are regarded, usually only some time after enactment, as placing constitutional limits on what various major political institutions, including the courts themselves, can do (ie are empowered or permitted to do) by law. In that sense, even though written, they remain part of an unwritten constitution, for their constitutional status—their entry into the constitution—comes of the unwritten law of the law-applying officials who subsequently treat them as having that status. The debatable cases, meanwhile, are debatable precisely because of a continuing indeterminacy in the way they are treated by the relevant law-applying officials. The indeterminacy may come of official dissensus or official circumspection. Or the issue may never have come up for official determination. This is not to deny, of course, that the Acts in question are determinately recognized as valid Acts of Parliament. It is only their constitutional status that has yet to be put to a decisive test.

When commentators are thinking about what might count as a decisive test, they often focus on whether the Act in question could validly be repealed by a future Parliament. Would a purported repeal of the European Communities Act 1972 be legally

---

primary legislator under (what is left of) the Royal Prerogative: *Council of Civil Service Unions* v *Minister for the Civil Service* [1985] AC 374 at 399, per Lord Fraser of Tullybelton. I say 'what is left of' because these Orders do not bind Parliament. They may be and often have been countermanded and superseded by Acts of Parliament, and with them those parts of the Royal Prerogative to which they pertained. There are also, a separate matter, Orders in Council that serve as delegated legislation *under* Acts of Parliament.

valid, even if it were in breach of the Treaty of Rome? How about a purported repeal of the Statute of Westminster 1931, aimed at recolonizing various former British colonies over the heads of their own constitutions? These are intriguing, although sadly imponderable, questions of law.[9] As tests for the constitutional status of an Act of Parliament, however, they are too strict. Even if a certain Act A could validly be repealed by Parliament in the ordinary way, ie by subsequently passing Act B to repeal it, Act A may meanwhile be recognized as having an effect on the operation of other parts of the UK constitution. Most importantly, without yet being recognized by the UK courts as either repealable or not repealable, Act A may be recognized by the UK courts as immune from the normal doctrine of *implied* repeal. By the normal doctrine of implied repeal, in the event of a conflict between Act A and Act B, the later Act B prevails even if Parliament did not notice, and hence in Act B did not make any provision for resolving, the conflict. This is a rule of the UK constitution. So if Act A is treated by the courts as an exception to it (on the basis that Act A provides for itself to be an exception or for any other reason), Act A is thereby elevated by the courts to a special constitutional status. The European Communities Act 1972, for example, has whatever constitutional status it has in the UK because and to the extent that the courts have held it immune from implied repeal.[10] That it could still be expressly repealed by Parliament, if it could, does not strip it of that constitutional status. It only goes to show that at least some parts of the UK constitution are less deeply entrenched than are at least some parts of, say, the US constitution. They are not immune from the normal process of deliberate legislative change, even though

---

[9] See *Manuel v Attorney General* [1983] Ch 77 at 87–9 per Megarry VC for interesting *obiter* discussion of the second question. At 89, Megarry VC distinguishes what it is possible for Parliament to do 'as a matter of abstract law' from what it is possible to do 'effectively'. One reason why the question is imponderable, however, is that this distinction collapses too quickly. There must be a supporting practice (a measure of effectiveness) among law-applying officials before a legislature can do anything, even as a matter of abstract law. Here, as Hart rather cryptically put it, 'all that succeeds is success': *CL,* 149.

[10] *Thoburn v Sunderland City Council* [2002] QB 151 at 186–7 per Laws LJ; *Jackson v Attorney General* [2006] 1 AC 262.

they are immune from some forms of accidental legislative change.[11]

I have emphasized the courts as principal arbiters of the constitutional status of legislation in the UK. To do so is to invite further political controversy. Richard Bellamy cautions against a 'legal constitutionalism' that presents the courts as the true guardians of the UK constitution. He advocates instead a 'political constitutionalism' according to which 'the constitution is identified with the political rather than the legal system, and in particular with the ways political power is organised and divided'.[12] This, however, is a false contrast. My emphasis on the courts does not prevent me from endorsing Bellamy's view of the constitution. Let me mention just a few reasons why.

(i) I already agreed that constitutions, not just in the UK but everywhere, are concerned with 'the ways political power is organised and divided'. To be exact I said that a constitution, even when thought of as part of a legal system, is the part that specifies the 'major institutions and officials of government' and how they are to function, interact, be appointed, etc.

(ii) As Bellamy seems to agree,[13] the courts themselves are political players. In the UK, as elsewhere, they jockey for power and position no less than the other main political institutions.

---

[11] How does the express/implied distinction relate to the deliberate/accidental one? I am assuming that Parliament always has the ability to say what it means, so that if it intends a certain change not to take place, it may always say so. For further discussion of these distinctions as applied to legislated law, as well as to case law, see Ch 3.

[12] *Political Constitutionalism: A Republican Defence of the Constitutionality of Democracy* (Cambridge 2007), 5. Bellamy's main aim in this book is to defend the UK doctrine of Parliamentary Sovereignty against those who would like there to be a judicial power to invalidate held-to-be-odious provisions of Acts of Parliament. This debate about 'constitutional judicial review' will be of no concern to us here. It is only very indirectly related to the question of how much of the constitution should be legalized. And each of these questions is only very indirectly related to the question of whether the UK could or should have a written constitution. A written constitution is not the same as, and need not include, a bill of rights, let alone one that allows for judicial invalidation of primary legislation. Bellamy seems to mix these questions up.

[13] Ibid 5, citing Martin Shapiro's 'Political Jurisprudence', *Kentucky Law Journal* 52 (1964), 294.

CAN THERE BE A WRITTEN CONSTITUTION? 95

(iii) At the heart of the UK constitution is the doctrine of Parliamentary Sovereignty. As a legal doctrine, this has been developed principally by the courts. Some of the rules that go to make it up (those concerning express and implied repeal) have been sketched above. The doctrine, as we saw, severely restricts the ways in which and the extent to which Parliament can bind its successors, for Act A cannot anticipatorily immunize itself against its repeal by a future Act B (even if sometimes the courts may later grant Act A a limited immunity).[14] But Parliamentary Sovereignty also limits the extent to which Parliament is bound by the courts. As the doctrine is applied today, the courts determine the legal effect of Acts of Parliament but Parliament may always re-legislate to overrule the courts, subject again to the courts' determining the legal effects of the re-legislation. Parliament can always get its way in the end by progressively more definite reiteration. Unless Parliament tires of the process, the courts only get to postpone their own defeat.

(iv) The courts are the principal law-applying institutions that determine the legal effect of Acts of Parliament and other legislation, but they are not the only ones. There are also various tribunals, commissions, regulatory agencies, and quangos that share at least some of the work of the courts. In small pockets, work of this type is also undertaken by the police, immigration staff, planning officers, etc. What distinguishes this work is that it involves *authoritative* applications of the law; ie determinations of legal effect that others are legally bound to follow.[15]

(v) The rule of the courts, such as it is, is dependent on the submission to that rule of numerous others, including other officials, such as police and military commanders, and the

---

[14] A revisionist view of the doctrine, defended by Ivor Jennings in *The Law and the Constitution* (London 1959) and by R.V. Heuston in his *Essays in Constitutional Law* (London 1964), and recently revived by Jeffrey Goldsworthy in *The Sovereignty of Parliament* (Oxford 1999) would have it that sovereignty is partly 'self-embracing': Parliament can bind its successors as to the 'manner and form' of future legislation but not as to its content. I doubt whether UK law draws or ever drew such a distinction, but my formulation of the doctrine here is intended to remain agnostic on the point.

[15] In *Practical Reason and Norms* (London 1975), at 134–7, Joseph Raz calls the relevant law-appliers the 'primary law-applying organs' of the system.

submission to those commanders of ordinary soldiers and police officers, and ultimately the submission to these of the wider population.[16] It also depends on *détente* with other institutions to whom there may be greater official or popular loyalty. The $64,000 question about every constitution is this: in a severe constitutional crisis, whose loyalties will lie where (and who has the weapons and who has the numbers on their side)?[17]

(vi) Finally, the courts and other law-applying institutions are only the guardians of constitutional *law*. No constitution is exhausted by its law. In the UK, for instance, there are also what Dicey dubbed the 'conventions of the constitution': customary constitutional rules which the courts may note, rely upon, and accommodate in applying the law but of which the courts' applications are not authoritative, even for the immediate purposes of the case before them.[18] These extra-legal customs, like any other rules, could be transformed into law by the courts themselves treating them as law. But the courts have many reasons to be self-denying in respect of such a change, including but not limited to the risk of breaking the *détente* mentioned in (v), and thereby occasioning a *coup* against themselves.[19]

[16] In an unfortunately much-quoted passage, Hart boiled all this down to 'a complex... practice of the courts, officials, and private persons' (*CL*, 107). But as he promptly made clear in less-quoted passages (110–11, 113), he was referring to several related practices. We should distinguish (a) the courts' practice of applying certain rules as rules of law; (b) a practice among petty officials of submitting to the rulings of the courts; and (c) a practice of the wider population of submitting to, or at least not defying, those petty officials (whether because they are officials of law or otherwise). If (b) and (c) go, so too does (a): without widespread efficacy, these are no longer the courts, and this is no longer the legal system.

[17] As Dwight Eisenhower famously showed on 24 September 1957 in Little Rock, Arkansas, invoking powers under Article I of the US constitution, together with the might of the 101st Airborne Division, to compel the fidelity of the Arkansas National Guard to the order of a federal judge. A perhaps less heroic example, from UK colonial law and policy, is *Madzimbamuto* v *Lardner-Burke* [1969] 1 AC 645, some of the background of which is discussed in H.H. Marshall, 'The Legal Effects of UDI (based on *Madzimbamuto* v *Lardner-Burke*)', *International and Comparative Law Quarterly* 17 (1968), 1022.

[18] A.V. Dicey, *Introduction to the Study of the Law of the Constitution* (London 1885), 23–4.

[19] *R* v *Secretary of State for the Environment ex parte Nottinghamshire County Council* [1986] AC 240 at 250–1 per Lord Scarman, where this self-denial is itself elevated to the status of convention of the constitution.

CAN THERE BE A WRITTEN CONSTITUTION? 97

When thinking about the constitution of any country, theorists of law are naturally most interested in its constitutional law, which leads them in turn to emphasize the courts as arbiters of constitutionality. It does not follow, as Bellamy seems to assume, that they regard constitutional law as the most socially important, let alone the most socially desirable, part of the constitution.[20] They may even think, as I tend to think, that something is amiss in the public life of a society when constitutional questions often have to be settled in the courtroom. Indeed, one might add, there is something amiss in the public life of a society when questions of any type often have to be settled by the courts. A theorist of law need not be an enthusiast for law, let alone for more of it. With that caveat entered, I will continue here to pursue my interest as a theorist of law. So I will persist in focusing on the legal aspect of constitutions except where otherwise indicated. My talk of 'written constitutions' should be understood accordingly.

2. The puzzle of a written constitution

In the UK, to recap, what determines the status of certain law as constitutional law is its reception into constitutional law by certain law-applying officials, principally the courts. Couldn't this claim be extended to constitutions generally? Couldn't it be argued that, in every jurisdiction and at every time, what really determines the status of something as part of the constitution is how it is received by its official users, principally the courts, never mind whether it has 'constitutional' stamped on it at point of issue? If so the tables are turned. For now the doubts do not hang over the possibility of an unwritten constitution like the UK's. Instead they hang over the possibility of a *written* constitution. On closer inspection, it may seem, it is part of the nature of a constitution that it is unwritten, and that its so-called written parts are only parts of it because of their reception into the unwritten law

---

[20] Or that they regard the constitution as the most socially important, let alone socially desirable, part of public culture. Arguably Bellamy and others with similar views decry excessive legalism about the constitution only to fall into a similar trap at the next level by being excessively constitutionalist about politics, or at the next level still by being excessively political about life.

that is made by the customs and decisions of the courts and other law-applying officials. If that much is true, then 'The Constitution of the United States of America' is a serious misnomer, for inasmuch as it is a name given to a document containing canonical formulations of law, it involves a category mistake. Constitutions cannot be, or be contained in, documents. That, at any rate, is the heretical view that I will be exploring here. Although I will reject it in due course, some aspects of it strike me as salutary. They help us to see the exaggerations of the opposite view according to which a written constitution is somehow a more normal case.

Let me begin the argument in earnest by putting the challenge to the possibility of written constitutions in a slightly more elaborate form. As a student of UK constitutional law I was given to understand—or maybe simply came to understand by myself—that the distinction between questions of constitutional law and questions of ordinary public law (also known as administrative law) lies in the type of institutions that these respective parts of the law regulate. Administrative law regulates institutions whose powers are delegated. Constitutional law regulates those that do the delegating; ie institutions whose powers are not delegated but are, as it is sometimes put, inherent or original.[21] Thus, in the UK, constitutional law regulates Parliament—or the Queen in Parliament as the institution is more accurately known—together with the high offices of the Crown (mainly government ministers), the Privy Council,[22] and the Queen herself in her official capacity. It also regulates the High Court and the judicial bodies known as the Appellate Committee of the House of Lords and the Judicial Committee of the Privy Council.

---

[21] Both these terms also have other meanings. In some contexts, eg in Article III of the Constitution of the United States, 'original jurisdiction' is contrasted with 'appellate jurisdiction'. In the sense intended here, however, an appellate jurisdiction may also be an original one. It is original, or inherent, in being a jurisdiction 'which, as the name indicates, requires no authorizing provision': *R v Forbes ex parte Bevan* (1972) 127 CLR 1 at 7 per Menzies J.

[22] The example of the Privy Council shows that some institutions fall under both headings. Depending on the subject matter, the Privy Council acts either as a constitutional institution, making primary legislation under the Royal Prerogative, or as a delegate institution, making secondary legislation on the Parliamentary authority of the Statutory Instruments Act 1946 (see above note 8).

CAN THERE BE A WRITTEN CONSTITUTION? 99

Constitutional law does not, however, regulate the Court of Appeal, which is a creature of statute.[23] Its judges are constitutional officials only in virtue of the fact that they remain, constitutionally speaking, judges of the High Court even after they have been elevated to the Court of Appeal. Nor does constitutional law regulate the police, the army, local councils, magistrates and their courts, tribunals and public inquiries, quangos or arms-length government agencies, industry-wide regulators, tax inspectors, or other similar institutions and officials.[24] These institutions and officials hold their legal powers by delegation, usually from Parliament although sometimes by Royal Prerogative (ie from the inherent constitutional powers of the Crown, exercised on behalf of the Queen by government ministers or the Privy Council).

It does not follow, of course, that these delegate institutions and officials are untouched by the law of the constitution. Most obviously, they can only have delegated powers in law if the original powers are there to delegate, which means that delegate institutions are subject to whatever restrictions the constitution places on the exercise of the same powers by those who delegated them. Moreover, the constitution may regulate which delegations are to take place, by what means, to whom, under what conditions, and so forth. That a delegate institution is picked out for mention in the constitution in this way does not transform it into a constitutional institution. Consider the armed forces in the UK. Thanks to a provision of the Bill of Rights 1689, the Crown lost its constitutional power to enlist and maintain a standing army in the absence of Parliamentary consent. This is

---

[23] The Court was created from scratch by the Judicature Act 1873. See Lord Justice Cohen, 'Jurisdiction, Practice and Procedure in the Court of Appeal', *Cambridge Law Journal* 11 (1951), 3. A criminal jurisdiction was added by the Criminal Appeal Act 1966, transferring the powers of the Court of Criminal Appeal, itself created by the Criminal Appeals Act 1907: *R v Collins* [1970] 1 QB 710 at 713–14; *R v Shannon* [1975] AC 717 at 745–8 and 756–7.

[24] Here I once again stress that we are talking about constitutional *law*. The humble legal position of the police (which is below the constitutional radar) is counteracted by powerful constitutional conventions (which lend the police a vast constitutional importance). For brilliant analysis, see Geoffrey Marshall, *Constitutional Conventions* (Oxford 1984), Ch 8.

an aspect of the Royal Prerogative of national defence which came under early Parliamentary control[25] and which already puts the army at the centre of an important constitutional relationship. But it does not turn the army into a constitutional institution. The provision regulates the Crown and Parliament, not the army itself, which gets its legal powers, if any, only by Parliamentary or Prerogative delegation.

This 1689 provision also helps to forestall other common misunderstandings. An institution of inherent or original power is sometimes understood to mean an institution that determines its own powers,[26] or (more radically still) an institution with unlimited powers.[27] But these definitions, we can now see, are too demanding. The Crown did not cease to be an institution of inherent power merely because it lost its power unilaterally to maintain a standing army. Nor did the Crown cease to be an institution of inherent power merely because it was Parliament, through the Bill of Rights 1689, that restricted the power of the Crown to maintain a standing army. Nor did Parliament itself cease to be an institution of inherent power merely because it was the courts that gave to the Bill of Rights its constitutional status, and so made it the case that Parliament, by enacting the Bill of Rights, had altered the constitutional powers of the Crown in relation to the maintenance of a standing army. So the point cannot be that institutions of inherent power are not subject to

---

[25] These days the armed forces are predominantly regulated by Act of Parliament. However the power to deploy troops, and to declare war or peace, still belongs to the Royal Prerogative, albeit with an emerging constitutional convention that Parliament's consent is required for deployment: House of Lords Select Committee on the Constitution, *Waging War: Parliament's Role and Responsibility*, vol 1 (HL 236.1, London 2006), 34–5.

[26] *Canada Trust Co* v *Stolzenberg* [1997] 4 All ER 983 per Millett LJ at 989.

[27] John Laws, 'Illegality: The Problem of Jurisdiction' in M. Supperstone and J. Goudie (eds), *Judicial Review* (1st ed, London 1991), 69–70. As Hart shows, using the UK doctrine of Parliamentary Sovereignty to illustrate, there is no such thing as an institution with unlimited powers: *CL*, 145–6. (But note that 'unlimited jurisdiction' is used by many lawyers as a misleading but otherwise innocent synonym for what I am calling inherent or original jurisdiction. See, for example, *R (on the application of Cart et al)* v *The Upper Tribunal et al* [2009] EWHC 3052, per Laws LJ.)

legal limitations imposed by others. The point is only that their powers are not delegated to them by others.

Whether there is a delegation is not to be decided by looking at the history of the institutions in question. Historically, in the UK, both Parliament and the High Court (or at least part of it) had their constitutional powers carved out of the constitutional powers of the monarch. The King or Queen from time to time delegated some of his or her personal powers to them or to their predecessors. But these powers, although they were delegated at the time, are not now to be regarded as delegated powers. The legal position—the position under the UK constitution today—is that both Parliament and the High Court have inherent or original powers. They are not delegates and the Queen cannot, constitutionally, revoke their powers. If the Queen purported to revoke their powers they could, constitutionally, ignore the revocation and continue to sit. They might lose some or all of their powers in some other way—as the 1689 example shows, constitutional institutions are not immune from having their powers restricted by others—but they cannot lose their powers by revocation. This is a hallmark of institutions that fall under constitutional, as opposed to administrative, law.

The constitution, as I said, is what regulates institutions of inherent power. The emerging problem is this. The institutions of inherent power in any legal system are also those that are identified by what H.L.A. Hart called 'rules of recognition'. To be exact, they are identified by the ultimate rules of recognition of that legal system.[28] And the ultimate rules of recognition of a

---

[28] In this formulation I am guarding against two errors. (a) As in Hart's most careful formulations (eg *CL*, 112) I speak of *ultimate* rules of recognition because there are plenty of (here irrelevant) lower-level rules of recognition in every legal system, eg those identifying a police officer as an issuer of legally binding traffic signals, those identifying a local council as the source of legally binding planning decisions, etc. (b) I also speak of ultimate *rules* of recognition (plural). Hart sometimes suggested that each legal system has only one ultimate rule of recognition. Not so. All but the most rudimentary legal systems have several ultimate rules of recognition, the inevitable conflicts between which may well come to a head only on rare occasions when they have implications lower down the system. Hart sometimes suggested that there could be no such conflicts. There must be a transitive ranking of the various validity criteria of each legal system, and hence a single rule providing the ranking: *CL*, 103. However, Hart is not

legal system, as Hart explained, cannot be enacted, or otherwise canonically formulated. They cannot exist in legislation. They can exist only in the practices of officials. Putting it more technically, they can only be customary laws *in foro*.[29] Why? To simplify greatly: any attempt to create an ultimate rule of recognition by legislation requires that there be a superior legislator with the power to confer an original or inherent power. But that is a contradiction. If there is a superior legislator conferring the power, it follows that the power conferred is not original or inherent but delegated. The rule of recognition created is not, in other words, an ultimate rule of recognition. It follows that an ultimate rule of recognition cannot be a legislated rule.[30] And one may conclude from this that a constitution, as the part of the law that regulates institutions of original or inherent power, can't be legislated either. It can't take the form of written law, existing in canonical formulation. All constitutions must therefore be unwritten like the UK one.

Many legal theorists embrace something like this argument. Most take it to be a *reductio*.[31] They regard it as axiomatic that there are written constitutions, such as the US constitution, and therefore treat the argument as casting doubt on what Hart has to say about rules of recognition. Either, *pace* Hart, some legal systems do not have ultimate rules of recognition, or else an ultimate rule of recognition is capable, *pace* Hart, of being a

entirely consistent about this. See *CL*, 92 for talk of a system's 'rules of recognition' in the plural and the concessionary remark that 'provision *may* be made for their possible conflict' (emphasis added). For the purposes of this chapter I will overlook Hart's apparent indecision on this point and talk as if he held the correct pluralist view. However, most of what I say could be adapted to sit no less comfortably with the rival monist view.

[29] Jeremy Bentham, *A Comment on the Commentaries and A Fragment on Government* (ed Burns and Hart, London 1977), 182–4.

[30] *CL*, 103–7.

[31] See eg Laurence H. Tribe, 'Taking Text and Structure Seriously: Reflections on Free-Form Method in Constitutional Interpretation', *Harvard Law Review* 108 (1995), 1221 at 1246–7; Charles Fried, 'Foreward: Revolutions?', *Harvard Law Review* 109 (1996), 13 at 26 n66; Frank I. Michelman, 'Constitutional Authorship' in Larry Alexander (ed), *Constitutionalism: Philosophical Foundations* (Cambridge 1998) at 70–2. For a non-*reductio* use, see Michael Dorf, 'Con Law in 12,008', available at <http://michaeldorf.org/2008/06/con-law-in-12008.html>.

CAN THERE BE A WRITTEN CONSTITUTION? 103

legislated rule. Both of these conclusions are, however, inadequately supported by the argument just sketched. For the argument fails to establish any incompatibility between a Hartian (customary) rule of recognition and a written constitution. It is a faulty argument. Let me focus on three of its faults.

3. The rule of recognition in its place

(1) The rules *identifying* institutions of inherent power do not exhaust the rules that *regulate* those institutions. Indeed some rules that identify institutions of inherent power do not regulate those same institutions at all. Hart occasionally encouraged the view that the ultimate rules of recognition of each legal system are those that confer the system's inherent powers.[32] If this was ever Hart's view it should not have been, for it is incompatible with Hart's own careful enumeration and differentiation of the types of rules on the possession of which the existence of any legal system depends. Hart distinguished rules of recognition from rules of adjudication and rules of change, and argued that every legal system has distinct rules of all three types.[33] Rules of adjudication and of change confer powers to apply the law and to change the law, respectively.[34] In the constitution—where we find the ultimate rules of adjudication and change—they confer inherent powers to apply the law and to change the law. But if the legal system's ultimate rules of recognition have already conferred these powers on the same institutions, why are rules of adjudication and change needed? Aren't they just duplicative?

The answer is that they are needed because a rule of recognition does not confer these or any other legal powers. A rule of recognition is a duty-imposing rule.[35] It imposes a legal duty on law-applying officials. One of the UK's ultimate rules of recognition—

---

[32] See eg *CL*, 95, where Hart spoke of a rule of recognition 'confer[ring] jurisdiction'. For more analysis of this passage, see note 44 below.

[33] *CL*, 95: the 'heart of a legal system' is 'the combination of primary rules of obligation with the secondary rules of recognition, change, and adjudication'.

[34] *CL*, 93 and 94.

[35] Joseph Raz, *The Concept of a Legal System* (Oxford 1970), 198–9; Neil MacCormick, *H.L.A. Hart* (London 1981), 103–6.

Hart's stock example of a rule of recognition—is the rule by which what the Queen in Parliament enacts is law.[36] This rule gives law-applying officials the duty, in law, to apply whatever rules Parliament enacts. Does it impose that duty on Parliament itself? No. Except on a narrow range of matters concerning the privileges of its own members, and leaving aside the anomalous position of the Appellate Committee of the House of Lords as a judicial body sitting within Parliament, Parliament does not make (and has no legal power to make) binding rulings on the legal effect of its own laws. It is not a law-applying institution but only a law-making one, and cannot be bound by the rule of recognition.[37] So just as the army is identified by the 1689 Bill of Rights but not regulated by it, so Parliament is identified by this famous rule of recognition but not regulated by it. It is regulated instead by a counterpart rule of change which confers on it the legal power to pass enactments, in the process imposing, by the rule of recognition, a legal duty on law-applying officials to apply the rules contained in those enactments. So Hart's argument to the effect that the ultimate rules of recognition of a legal system can only be customary rules does not entail that only customary rules regulate institutions of inherent power. It leaves open the possibility that in some legal systems the constitutional rules of adjudication and change—the rules that endow the institutions of inherent power with their inherent powers—could be non-customary. Thus there remains a possible subject-matter for a

---

[36] Kent Greenawalt reports that, in correspondence, Hart confessed to 'a slip' in presenting this as a complete statement of the rule, omitting the further criteria concerning case law, customary law, and other types of primary legislation: Greenawalt, 'The Rule of Recognition and the Constitution', *Michigan Law Review* 85 (1987), 621 at 631 n30. But this was not Hart's slip. He was right to regard this as a complete statement of the rule. He was wrong, however, to regard this rule as the UK's only ultimate rule of recognition, for there are several other rules relating to case law, etc. See note 28 above.

[37] It does not follow that Parliament cannot be bound in its law-making by other duty-imposing laws, including duty-imposing laws of the constitution. However, the only examples I know of are found in European Community Law that is incorporated into UK law, eg the compensation duty in Joined Cases 46/93 & 48/93, *Brasserie du Pêcheur SA* v *Germany* and *R* v *Secretary of State for Transport ex parte Factortame Ltd* (1996) 1 CMLR 889. The situation where Parliament 'binds' its successor Parliaments, if there can be such a situation, is not a case of duties imposed but of powers removed.

written constitution, namely the allocation of inherent legal powers to match the duties imposed by the system's ultimate rules of recognition.

Jeremy Waldron resists the idea that the (duty-imposing) rule of recognition here is genuinely distinct from the (power-conferring) rule of change. 'The idea of a power', he writes,

> *is* the idea of a capacity to change people's duties. So if the rule of change empowers Congress [or, we should add, Parliament] to legislate, it necessarily enables it to do something that will change the duties of other actors in the system.[38]

Waldron is not quite right about the idea of a power. One may have a power, yet no ability to change any duties. One's ability may be limited to changing other powers.[39] But it is true that the powers of Parliament and Congress do include the ability to change legal duties, and that someone who doesn't know this by that token doesn't understand the powers of Parliament or Congress (as the case may be). This does not show, however, that the power-conferring rule is also the duty-imposing one. It shows only that the power-conferring rule presupposes the existence of the duty-imposing one. Actually, we could go further. The duty-imposing rule also presupposes the existence of the power-conferring one. Yet the point remains. Two rules that presuppose each other's existence are not the same rule.

This was one of his several battles with Hans Kelsen that Hart won decisively. The power-conferring rule enabling a court to pass sentence for careless driving is incomplete to the point of unintelligibility unless there is also a duty-imposing rule making careless driving a criminal offence. That is because there being a criminal offence of ϕing is built into the very idea that ϕing is something that attracts a sentence.[40] Conversely, a duty-imposing

---

[38] Waldron, 'Who Needs Rules of Recognition?' in M. Adler and K. Himma (eds), *The Rule of Recognition and the US Constitution* (New York 2009), [20].

[39] Or to granting permissions. Not every grant of permission affects the incidence or force of a duty. Instead it may conflict with a duty. For more discussion of powers to empower and permit, see my 'Justification under Authority', *Canadian Journal of Law and Jurisprudence* 23 (2010), 71.

[40] In Hart's terms, the one idea 'involves' the other: *CL*, 39. At this point Hart is dismantling Kelsen's view, set out in *General Theory of Law and*

rule making it a criminal offence to drive carelessly is incomplete to the point of unintelligibility unless it is joined by a power-conferring rule enabling a court to sentence the offender for committing the offence.[41] That is because there being a power to sentence for ϕing is built into the very idea that ϕing is a criminal offence. Finding just one of these rules in the law, a competent law-applier will hold the other rule to exist by necessary implication (so that, if it does not exist already, he will have to bring it into existence himself, or else put out to pasture the bereft rule that he started with).[42] The fact that there is a necessary implication here does not entail, you can now see, that there is only one rule. In fact it entails the opposite: a relationship of necessary implication between rules can hold only if there are (at least) two rules for it to hold between.

As with the rules in a defectively drafted criminal statute, so too with a legal system's ultimate rules of recognition, change, and adjudication. They cannot but cross-refer, and hence depend on each other for their intelligibility, yet each has its own normative force.[43] Each regulates different actions, or different agents, or the same actions of the same agent in a different way. Each is therefore a distinct rule.[44] So the fact that a legal system's rules of recognition must be customary rules does not show that the system's rules of change and adjudication cannot be legislated rules, laid down, perhaps, in a written constitution.

State (trans Wedberg, Cambridge, Mass. 1945), 53–4, that there is only one legal norm here, and that what looks like a second is merely a fragment of the first.

[41] *CL*, 35–41.

[42] A common mistake is to think that every rule, the existence of which is entailed by a legal rule is also a legal rule. Why is this a mistake? See Raz, 'Legal Rights', *Oxford Journal of Legal Studies* 4 (1984), 1 at 9–12.

[43] See MacCormick, *H.L.A. Hart*, above note 35, 108–11, showing that a search for logical priority between the three types of rules is ill-fated. This led MacCormick to suspect a vicious circularity. But he later came to see that the suspicion was unfounded: see his *H.L.A. Hart* (2nd ed, Stanford 2008), 151.

[44] This returns us to the passage at *CL*, 95 where Hart says that there may be a rule of recognition that is 'also' a rule of adjudication conferring jurisdiction on some law-applying body. This suggests identity, not entailment. However Hart quickly goes on to speak, more carefully, of two 'inseparable' rules, one a rule of recognition, the other a rule of adjudication.

CAN THERE BE A WRITTEN CONSTITUTION? 107

(2) A connected point. Hart is uncertain whether to classify the ultimate rules of recognition of a legal system as themselves legal rules.⁴⁵ He is right to be uncertain. As he says, for some purposes and on some occasions it is harmless and natural to classify them as legal. They are, after all, rules specific to that legal system. They pertain exclusively to it. But do they quite belong to it? For present purposes it is perhaps better to think that they do not. Why? Because in a way they lie beyond the constitution. One needs rules of recognition even in order to identify the rules of the constitution. One needs to know, even of these rules, that they satisfy the ultimate criteria of legal validity for the legal system one is looking at, before one can identify them as the constitutional rules of that system. Putting the point rather paradoxically, one might say that even the constitution needs to be constituted somehow. Is it constituted by law? Kelsen thought that it must be, and ended up facing a new version of the old problem of infinite regress, ended only by what he latterly came to call the 'fiction' of the validity of some historically first legal act.⁴⁶ Hart avoided the same problem by presenting the ultimate rules of recognition of legal systems as borderline cases of legal rules.⁴⁷ They are rules providing what Hart calls the 'criteria' by which law (the law of a particular system) can be recognized as law (the law of that system). But by their nature they need not themselves meet those criteria. They are found in the custom of law-applying officials but it does not follow that they must (although they may) identify the custom of law-applying officials as a source of law. In that sense they are above the law, rather than part of it. This allows us to recognize that there are ultimate rules of recognition that are, so to speak, above the constitution while at the same time agreeing that there is no *law* that is above the constitution. Constitutional law is as high as the law goes. Correspondingly, a written constitution may exist even though there

---

⁴⁵ *CL*, 108.
⁴⁶ Kelsen, *General Theory of Norms* (Oxford 1991), 256. I am not denying that Kelsen's fictitious basic norm might supply a good answer to some other philosophical question. Possibly it helps us to understand the normativity of law even though it fails as an attempt to explain the possibility of legal validity.
⁴⁷ *CL*, 108.

must be a customary rule of recognition above it, one that identifies it as the constitution, and binds the legal system's law-appliers, *qua* law-appliers of that legal system, to follow it.

Hart himself unfortunately casts doubt on this healthy way of thinking about written constitutions when he writes:

> If a constitution specifying the various sources of law is a living reality in the sense that the courts and officials of the system actually identify the law in accordance with the criteria it provides, then the constitution is accepted and actually exists. It seems a needless reduplication to suggest that there is a further rule to the effect that the constitution (or those who laid it down) are to be obeyed.[48]

It is certainly true of legal systems with unwritten constitutions that they lack a rule of recognition with anything like this content. But Hart seems to think that the same could also be true of legal systems with written constitutions, constitutions which are 'laid down'.[49] As Raz says, 'the constitution, in such cases, should presumably be regarded as created both by legislation [*qua* written] and by custom [*qua* rule of recognition], a position which... needs some explaining'.[50] Is it explicable? I doubt it. Of course there are examples, as we saw, of constitutions made up of some written and some unwritten law. Probably most constitutions are like this, albeit in various configurations that allow us to think of some as basically unwritten and others as basically written. But that is beside the point. The picture that Hart seems to be trying to conjure up is of a constitution containing some law that is both written and unwritten—legislated and customary—at the same time. The only picture he succeeded in conjuring up for me, however, is of written law which was displaced, perhaps one step at a time, by unwritten law, so that the formerly legislated constitution lost its force in favour of customary rules with similar content. Hart may have thought that this is what happens when the law of a written constitution is developed over time by the courts. The written constitution eventually becomes a dead letter,

---

[48] *CL*, 246.

[49] He says that it is 'particularly clear' of unwritten constitutions, not that it is particular to them: *CL*, 246.

[50] Raz, *The Concept of a Legal System*, above note 35, 198.

referred to only honorifically. As we will see towards the end of Section 4, however, the 'living reality' of a written constitution calls for a different analysis, one consistent with and indeed conducive to the view that the rule of recognition is indeed a customary rule lying beyond the constitution itself, a rule 'to the effect that the constitution (or those who laid it down) are to be obeyed'. As I just pointed out on Hart's behalf in reply to Waldron, this is not 'needless reduplication' of the rules in the written constitution, but a separate rule of recognition without which there is no written constitution to contain those rules.[51]

(3) Finally, my argument for regarding the UK Parliament and High Court as institutions of inherent rather than delegated power rested in part on the proposition that their powers are not, as the constitutional law of the UK now stands, revocable. The monarch cannot lawfully step back in and reclaim the powers that, in the middle ages, were delegated by her predecessors to Parliament and to (what is now) the High Court. This suggests a possible way of thinking about constitutional powers which is consistent with their having been endowed by another through legislation, and consistent with constitutional law recognizing that endowment as the source of the powers. One may say that it is possible for constitutional institutions to have been endowed with those powers by a higher legislative institution so long as that institution cannot revoke them. The easiest way for that condition to be met is for the institution in question no longer to

---

[51] It is worth remembering that when he writes these words Hart is bending over backwards to distinguish his ultimate rules of recognition from Kelsen's basic norm. He may well be bending too far. He rightly points out that Kelsen's basic norm always has the same content, roughly: 'one should always and only obey the historically first constitution'. Hart is right that, unlike this basic norm, ultimate rules of recognition have diverse content, varying from time to time and from legal system to legal system: *CL*, 245–6. It does not follow, however, that there are no ultimate rules of recognition anywhere with content akin to that of the Kelsenian basic norm. Nor would the redundancy of this content *qua* content of a basic norm entail its redundancy *qua* content of an ultimate rule of recognition, since a Kelsenian basic norm and an ultimate rule of recognition do different jobs and are not rivals for the same explanatory space. See Stanley Paulson, 'Christian Dahlman's Reflections on the Basic Norm', *Archiv für Rechts und Sozialphilosophie* 91 (2005), 96 at 105.

exist. This is indeed standard practice in constitution-building today. A temporary constitutional caucus or assembly is conjured up which then endows constitutional powers upon other institutions designed to be permanent. The law then recognizes that the power was endowed, but adds that the method of endowment is not reusable, within the constitution, as a method of revocation, for the delegating body has wound itself up or has been wound up. The delegation is rendered irrevocable. This suggests a possible revision of my original proposal for determining the scope of constitutional law, as distinct from administrative law. Constitutional law regulates those institutions that, according to the law, have either inherent *or irrevocably delegated* powers. Over time institutions with irrevocably delegated powers may come to be regarded, in law, as having inherent powers. But strictly speaking it need not be so.

The US constitution illustrates that it need not be so. It is a written constitution. It is a piece of legislation. The legislator was a temporary institution, a Convention of delegates (yes, *delegates*) from twelve states meeting at Philadelphia in 1787. With only the ratification of subsidiary ad hoc Conventions in the States, this Convention created the standing governmental institutions of today's federal United States, including notably (but not only) the Presidency, Congress with its twin houses, and the Supreme Court. The powers with which these institutions were endowed were delegated to them by the 1787 Convention, which held itself to hold all the powers of the new Federal legal system that it was creating, including the power to delegate those powers.[52] However, the Convention did not make provision for

---

[52] Although not of course all the powers of the various state legal systems, all of which have their own ultimate rules of recognition and change and adjudication. See Kent Greenawalt, 'The Rule of Recognition and the Constitution', above note 36, at 645–7. Curiously, having explained that state institutions are not delegates of federal institutions, and so enjoy recognitional independence of federal law, Greenawalt goes on to formulate a single list of criteria of recognition for 'the American legal system' as seen from 'someplace within the United States', consolidating federal and state criteria: ibid 659. He also presents these criteria as adding up to a single rule of recognition, so perhaps (like Hart, see above note 28) he resists the idea that there could be conflicts between ultimate rules of recognition; perhaps he also extends that resistance so that it applies not only to the rules of recognition of a

its own future existence. Instead it made alternative provision for later amendments to the constitution, in which the amenders would be institutions created by the constitution itself, operating under special procedures designed for the purpose. Thus all the inherent powers that the Convention took itself to have, and is taken by current federal US law to have had, were delegated away to the new institutions that it created. The Convention itself was wound up, putting an end even to its own legal power to reconvene and hence to revoke the delegation.

Or so one version of the story goes. We are straying into another political minefield with this vignette of US constitutional history. Twin amendment procedures are set out in Article V of (the 1787 enactment now known as) the United States Constitution. The first is the well-known and much-used power of Congress to propose amendments (by a two-thirds majority) which take effect upon ratification by three-quarters of the States. The second is this less well-known one:

The Congress... on the Application of the Legislatures of two thirds of the several States, shall call a Convention for proposing Amendments, which... shall be valid to all Intents and Purposes, as Part of this Constitution, when ratified by the Legislatures of three fourths of the several States or by Conventions in three fourths thereof.

According to some, this is a power to reconvene the original 1787 Convention.[53] It is irrelevant to this claim that an Article V Convention has to be called by Congress on the application of the States, and that its proposals then have to be ratified by the

---

single legal system but also to the rules of recognition of multiple legal systems applicable in the same territory, such as state and federal US law.

[53] The discussion is generally cast as one about the terms of reference of an Article V Convention. Can it be limited as to subject-matter of amendment or must it have a roving brief? If the latter, what stands (constitutionally) in the way of a full Constitutional Convention like that of 1787? For defence of the 'roving brief' view see Charles Black, 'Amending the Constitution: A Letter to a Congressman', *Yale Law Journal* 82 (1972), 189; Walter Dellinger, 'The Recurring Question of the "Limited" Constitutional Convention', *Yale Law Journal* 88 (1979), 1623. As Black says at 199, his view 'does not imply that a "runaway" [Article V] convention is possible, for... no convention can be called that has anything to run away from'. The 1787 Convention lives on!

States. The 1787 Convention was itself called under the old Articles of Confederation by Congress on the application of the States, and its product—the constitutional enactment in which Article V appears—was also ratified by the States before coming into effect. It is of equally scant assistance to note that an Article V Convention is limited to proposing amendments to take effect 'as Part of this Constitution'. These words obviously throw up the classic problem of the identity of wholes with fungible parts, which threatens to render them vacuous.[54] But even if they add something, there is another problem. Does 'this Constitution' refer to the institutional arrangements of the US Constitution or does it refer to their canonical formulation in the 1787 enactment as amended? This is important because the 1787 Convention preserved parts of the institutional set-up from the Articles of Confederation under which it was summoned (eg the existence of Congress, the constitutional recognition of the States as ratifiers). So the 1787 Convention too can be argued to have enacted the new constitution 'as Part of' the old (never mind that the new then took on a life of its own and was held, legally speaking, not to owe its validity to the old). In which case there is nothing in these words to distinguish an Article V Convention from the 1787 Convention.

It is true, of course, that an Article V Convention can only amend—taking 'amendment' to designate a lawful mode of constitutional change—if it acts within its constitutional powers. But that only brings us back to our original question. What are those constitutional powers? Are they delegated powers or are they a continuation of the inherent powers by which the 1787 Convention itself is now regarded as having acted? Does the US

---

[54] Plutarch, *Lives: Volume 1* (trans Perrin, Cambridge, Mass. 1914), 49: 'The ship on which Theseus sailed with the youths and returned in safety... was preserved by the Athenians down to the time of Demetrius Phalereus. They took away the old timbers from time to time, and put new and sound ones in their places, so that the vessel became standing illustration for the philosophers in the mooted question of growth, some declaring that it remained the same, others that it was not the same vessel.' I will not attempt to sample the vast modern literature on this 'mooted question', except to note that it is sometimes recast as the 'problem of constitution': see eg Michael Rea, 'The Problem of Material Constitution', *Philosophical Review* 104 (1995), 525.

CAN THERE BE A WRITTEN CONSTITUTION? 113

constitution recognize and require the continuing existence of its own super-legislator, a legislator which, although dormant, could be stirred back to consciousness by Congress on the application of two-thirds of the States and could validly revoke—and revoke, perhaps, to *tabula rasa* except for its own continuing powers—the various legal powers conferred upon the institutions created at its own previous meeting in 1787?[55]

The answer is nowhere close at hand. If the triggering condition is met—if a valid application is received from the States—it is probably mandatory under Article V for Congress to call a Convention.[56] But whether the triggering condition has ever been met is a matter of some dispute. It depends on how State applications are to be individuated and counted. When States apply severally rather than jointly, perhaps with differently worded and differently scoped applications many years apart, are their various applications to be aggregated until the two-thirds line is reached? Or, as most constitutional lawyers assume, is more co-ordination or convergence among States required before their petitions come together to qualify as an application under Article V? Whatever the answer, Congress has never called an Article V Convention, and the Supreme Court has never ruled on the legality of Congress's not having done so. Nor is it clear that the Supreme Court would rule on this matter if it were petitioned. The Supreme Court has ruled in the past that other Congressional decisions concerning the amendment process under Article V are non-justiciable; ie not subject to the court's authoritative rulings on their constitutionality.[57] Other federal

---

[55] Could it even amend the voting powers of the states in the Senate, a matter explicitly excluded from its amending power by Article V? Why not begin by amending Article V to remove the exclusion? For valuable reflections, see Akhil Reed Amar, 'Popular Sovereignty and Constitutional Amendment' in Sanford Levinson (ed), *Responding to Imperfection: The Theory and Practice of Constitutional Amendment* (Princeton 1995), 90–2. Notice that we are raising here the question of whether the power of a revived 1787 Convention would be 'self-embracing' above note 14. The issue of 'self-embracingness' is not unique to the doctrine of UK Parliamentary Sovereignty but, as Hart said, 'can arise in relation to ultimate criteria of legal validity in any system' (*CL*, 148).

[56] *United States* v *Sprague* 282 US 716 (1931).

[57] *Coleman* v *Miller* 307 US 433 (1939).

courts have extended the same rule to the calling of an Article V Convention.[58] This may mean that constitutional questions about the calling of an Article V Convention are non-legal questions. They are to be settled elsewhere in the political process, regulated not by law but at most by what Dicey might have called the conventions of the US constitution.[59] This leaves us several frustrating steps away from achieving any legal determinacy on the vexed question of whether an Article V Convention, were one to be called, would have the original powers of the 1787 Convention or merely delegated powers conferred by or under the 1787 Convention.

Can't we find the answer to this vexed question in another way? Surely US constitutional law is by now amply determinate in classifying the Presidency, Congress and the Supreme Court as constitutional institutions. If the 1787 Convention were merely sleeping, wouldn't the powers of these institutions have to be reclassified as revocably delegated powers, and hence as non-constitutional, powers? In which case—shock, horror!—these famous institutions would not be constitutional institutions after all. Indeed the 1787 constitution (the document that calls itself 'The Constitution of the United States of America') would no longer qualify as the US constitution, for now it would be merely repealable delegating legislation made under the pre-1787 constitution. And most of what is known in US law schools as 'constitutional law' would be nothing of the kind.

Things are getting out of hand. A power should not be classified as revocable, for our purposes, merely because its revocation is imaginable. Even if Congress and the Supreme Court together control and always conspire to deny access to the only process by which their own powers could imaginably be revoked, then those powers, albeit delegated, are irrevocable enough to

---

[58] *Walker* v *United States*, unreported C00-2125C, US District Court Western District (2001); *Walker* v *Members of Congress*, unreported, US District Court Western District C04-1977RSM (2004); US Court of Appeals 9th Circuit 05-35023 (2005); certiorari denied Supreme Court 06-244 (2006).

[59] On the role of Diceyean conventions in the US Constitution, see H.W. Horwill, *The Usages of the American Constitution* (New York 1925), which in some ways parallels Marshall's work on the UK cited at note 24 above.

qualify as constitutional powers. At this point, attention returns to the questions of loyalty—the loyalty of petty officials and the loyalty of the wider population—which we touched upon in Section 1. Unflinching refusal of Congress and the Supreme Court to grant an application for an Article V Convention could imaginably be overcome, but only by mass defection to rival institutions. If we regard the 1787 constitution—the one headed 'The Constitution of the United States of America'—as the true US Constitution, then that mass defection would qualify as a new American revolution. If, on the other hand, we deny that the 1787 document is the true US Constitution, treating it as a mere delegating act, then such mass defection would arguably be no more than a *coup*.[60] Either way, however, it would be a usurpation of legal powers under the constitution, for on either view it is only by usurpation that the power to call an Article V Convention can be wrestled from the hands of a peristently *refusnik* Congress and Court. And once the possibility of usurpation has been opened up, we are no longer talking about amendment, understood as a lawful mode of constitutional change. We are changing the subject.[61]

We may conclude, with a sigh of relief, that the Presidency, Congress and the Supreme Court are not mere administrative bodies regulated by a jumped up kind of administrative law. They are constitutional bodies and they are constitutional bodies because their powers, although delegated to them and hence not strictly speaking inherent or original, are delegated to them irrevocably by the 1787 constitution, as amended. This turns out to be true irrespective of whether an Article V Convention, if called, would be a reawakening of the 1787 Convention.

We have taken a long detour into the dimmer recesses of the US Constitution. The point was mainly to illustrate a realistic

---

[60] On the problematic distinction between revolutions and *coups*, see J.M. Finnis, 'Revolutions and the Continuity of Law' in A.W.B. Simpson (ed), *Oxford Essays in Jurisprudence: Second Series* (Oxford 1973).

[61] But cf Bruce Ackerman, 'Discovering the Constitution', *Yale Law Journal* 93 (1984), 1013, for doubts about the amendment/usurpation distinction as it applies to the US constitution. Ackerman tends to think that the US Constitution somehow invites or compasses its own overthrow.

possibility. The possibility is that the ultimate rules of recognition of a legal system may identify different institutions from those mentioned in its ultimate rules of adjudication and change. This seems to be the case in the US. The ultimate rules of recognition of the federal US, like all ultimate rules of recognition around the globe and throughout history, are indeterminate in numerous respects.[62] But federal US law is by now entirely determinate in treating the 1787 Constitution, as amended, as its Constitution. This is the custom of the Supreme Court and of all the other federal courts and of other authoritative law-applying agencies. There is little doubt, then, that one of the ultimate rules of recognition of the US says something like: 'Whatever is laid down in the constitution produced by the 1787 Philadelphia Convention, as amended, is law.' Notice that this rule does not mention Congress, the President, or the Supreme Court. They are mentioned for the first time only in the rules of change and adjudication that are *in* the 1787 Constitution.

So constitutional authorities—to go back to our original problem—need not be identified in the system's ultimate rules of recognition, even in that rule of recognition by virtue of which they are constitutional authorities. If the constitution is a written one, only (the author of)[63] the written constitution need be identified in the relevant rule of recognition, while the main constitutional institutions are those identified *in* the written constitution. By this route too we find that a customary rule of recognition can be squared with a written constitution.

4. The written constitution, redux

What I have said so far was designed to fend off a certain set of objections to the idea that constitutions can be written. It did so

---

[62] As Hart explained at length: *CL*, 144–50.

[63] On the parenthetical words, see Greenawalt, 'The Rule of Recognition and the Constitution', see above note 36, 640. Greenawalt leans towards the view that 'the legal authority of ... the original Constitution is established by its continued acceptance', not by its having been validly enacted in 1787. On a rival view, it is the validity of its enactment in 1787 that is now accepted, and that gives the Constitution its legal authority. For the purposes of the argument here the point is not crucial. Hence the parentheses.

by tweaking the scope of constitutional law to cover irrevocably delegated powers as well as inherent or original powers, by distinguishing the rules that identify a constitutional institution from those that regulate it, and by placing the rule of recognition of a legal system outside (above) the constitution itself. Actually, to be more exact, we only placed the rule of recognition above the *law* of the constitution. We should always keep in mind the important warning issued at the end of Section 1 and repeated more than once already. Constitutions are not exhausted by their law. In every country with a constitution, and hence in every country with a legal system, there are also constitutional rules which are distinguished from the rest of the constitution precisely in being rules of which the authoritative law-applying institutions do not get to make authoritative applications. This makes space for there to be actions which are unconstitutional but which are neither illegal nor legally invalid. The role of this fact may vary from legal system to legal system. In the UK it is a fairly prominent aspect of the constitution. In the US it is less prominent, but—as we just saw in Section 2.3—it is certainly not absent.

Is an ultimate rule of recognition one of those rules of which the law-applying institutions do not get to make authoritative applications? Is it in that way (although plainly not in other ways) akin to a Diceyan 'convention of the constitution'? Hart seems to have thought as much.[64] Of course, he insisted that every ultimate rule of recognition is a rule made by the authoritative law-applying institutions of that legal system of which it is a rule of recognition. But he thought that it was made by the customs of the officials of those institutions in the course of exercising their authority over *other* things, not in exercising authority over the ultimate rules of recognition themselves.[65] Authoritative law-applying institutions, typically courts, get to decide cases authoritatively. In all but the most rudimentary legal systems, when they decide cases authoritatively the higher courts (not only and not always courts of inherent jurisdiction) also get to make a kind of law known as case law. This is a kind of unwritten law that is found in the premises of the arguments that higher courts use to

[64] *CL*, 107–8.   [65] *CL*, 99.

arrive at their authoritative decisions. It differs in several ways from their customary law *in foro*.[66] For a start, case law can be made by one law-applying official (or one committee of such officials) in one case—by a single exercise of judicial authority—whereas customary law *in foro* requires for its existence a temporally extended pattern of relevantly convergent behaviour by multiple law-applying officials. Why couldn't an ultimate rule of recognition be made by the case-law method instead of by the customary-law method? Hart did not explain. Maybe he did not appreciate that case law differs from both legislated law and customary law. Certainly he tended to speak of judge-made law, when not customary, as legislated.[67] Subsequent discussion of the issue has been hampered not only by repetition of this error, but also by the tendency (to which, as we saw, Hart also gave some succour) to confuse rules of recognition on the one hand with rules of adjudication and change on the other.

It would take us too far afield to pursue these problems about the rule of recognition here. But our remarks about judge-made law, including judicial contributions to the constitutional rules of adjudication and change, provoke a new question about written constitutions. Perhaps there can be written constitutions—I have just argued that there can—but can there be *entirely* written constitutions? To make the issue less complex I will set aside those parts of the constitution that are not constitutional law (the Diceyan 'conventions of the constitution'), as well as the ultimate rules of recognition of the system. So my question is this: can (the rest of) constitutional law be entirely written? Or must it always also include some customary law or case law?

The answer seems plain enough. On the day it is enacted a new constitution is wholly written law. But that day does not last. As soon as ripe disputes begin to arise that concern the meaning of constitutional provisions, written constitutional law inevitably

---

[66] I explore some of the main differences in Ch 3.

[67] See eg *CL*, 131–2. At 149–50, Hart seems to suggest, collapsing two distinctions that are only very indirectly related, that the ability of the courts to make law is either customary-and-inherent or legislative-and-delegated. But cf 93 and 98, where he distinguishes *both* custom *and* precedent from legislation.

CAN THERE BE A WRITTEN CONSTITUTION? 119

needs to be filled out with case law and/or customary law. What is written in the constitution needs to be invested with more determinate meaning, and by and large this has to be done at the point of its authoritative application, principally by judges. With the passage of time, such judge-made law tends to predominate over the parts of constitutional law that exist apart from it. With the passage of time, one knows an ever-smaller proportion of the law of the constitution—or at any rate an ever-smaller proportion of the material that goes to make up the law of the constitution—simply by reading the constitutional text.

Like other things we have said, this plain answer may strike some as political explosive. It may seem to lead us straight into the big controversies of contemporary US constitutional law. In the red corner, ladies and gentlemen, those who insist that the Constitution is found in what was written and nothing but what was written by the 1787 founders and their authorized legislative amenders. And in the blue corner, those who say that the constitution is a living body of law and should not be regarded as frozen in time at the moment of enactment. Is this the fight we are getting into? No. Nothing I have just said takes sides in this or any other debate about how the US Constitution should be interpreted. I do not doubt, of course, the profound political significance of such debates and—especially when the disputants are Supreme Court judges—their huge potential consequences for the future direction of America. My only point is this: inasmuch as these debates have huge potential consequences for the future direction of America, that is because they have huge potential consequences for the future development of American constitutional law. And they have huge potential consequences for the future development of American constitutional law precisely because, in both corners, we have people with proposals for how American constitutional law should be developed. Both sides are assuming that it will be developed, and that it will be developed by judges. The only question is, how will it be developed? Which way are the judges to take it? Both sides—or since it is not really a two-corner fight, I should really say all sides—must be in agreement that US constitutional law is not just what is contained in the text of the written constitution. For all of them it must also include judge-made law. For if it did not include judge-made law there would be no point in fighting over how judges should make constitutional decisions. The only possible reason for choosing a textualist Supreme Court nominee over a purposivist, or an originalist-textualist over a strict-constructionist-textualist, or a original-intent-originalist over an original-meaning-originalist, or indeed a baggist over a raggist, is that each of them, or at any rate each of them in combination with some like-minded judges, will have the power to change the law of the constitution by giving the constitution a meaning different from the one that it would have under the authority of a judge or a combination of judges from some rival camp.

Aren't there a few elaborate theoretical positions, in these debates over constitutional interpretation, that genuinely include the proposition that judges don't change the law? Doesn't Ronald Dworkin famously say exactly that? At any rate, doesn't he say that when judges get their decisions on points of constitutional law right—when they give 'right answers'—all they are doing is applying the law that is already in the constitution, albeit maybe implicitly rather than explicitly?[68] I doubt whether Dworkin still holds this view.[69] Possibly he never held it.[70] But consider its implications. Its implications include that judges only change the law of the constitution when they get their decisions wrong. It follows that, according to this view, constitutional law may only ever be changed for the worse by judges, for each change necessarily introduces yet another error. Better, then, if the law doesn't change at all. But then if it should never change at all, judges should never have added all the case law that they added during the couple of centuries that they have done so. Better if they had answered each question of law by saying: 'Just use what you already have, it's all there. Don't come bothering us.' On this

---

[68] The least equivocal rendition is Dworkin, 'No Right Answer?' in P.M.S. Hacker and J. Raz (eds), *Law, Morality, and Society* (Oxford 1977). My formulation is most influenced by Hart's famous summary in 'Legal Duty and Obligation' in H.L.A. Hart, *Essays on Bentham* (Oxford 1982), 147–8.

[69] See Dworkin, *Law's Empire* (Cambridge, Mass. 1986), 255–63, where a 'right answer' seems to be relativized to the convictions of each judge.

[70] See Dworkin, *Justice in Robes* (Cambridge, Mass. 2006), 266 n3, where he denies that he has changed his mind about the thesis.

reading of his 'right answer' thesis, Dworkin does not become a mere closet textualist. He departs even from the mainstream textualist view in holding that judges should not develop US constitutional law in either a textualist or an opposing, more innovative, direction. They should not develop US constitutional law at all. At each moment they give the 'right answer' only if they leave the law exactly as it is, complete with all the previous accumulated errors.

This is a crazy view, which explains why I am reluctant to ascribe it to Dworkin. Even if he once held this crazy view, however, it would have been hard for him to deny that (worse luck!) there has been a huge judicial contribution to US constitutional law. Even if the judges should not have added to it, they have added to it. Thanks to them there is a lot more of it now than there was in 1790, or in 1832, or in 1896, or in 1926, or even in 1964. And since judges are fallible human beings like the rest of us, it had to be that way. So even if one says, crazily, that judicial law-making is always erroneous, one cannot avoid reaching the same result: any constitution that provides for authoritative adjudications regarding its own application cannot but be to some extent a living constitution; ie cannot but contain less law at its inception than it comes to contain later.

It is tempting to conclude from all this that a constitution cannot be entirely written. From soon after its birth, it seems, the written constitution must constitute only part of the constitution, the rest being made up of judge-made law.[71] But does that follow? Let me suggest two ways in which it is apt to mislead.

First, possibly the law of the constitution (or constitutional law) should not be thought of as identical with the constitution itself, even if we restrict our attention to the parts of the constitution that form part of the law. We can bear this thought out somewhat by considering two ways of responding to the question 'What does the constitution have to say about this?' One response would be to hand over the document, the canonical text, assuming one is in a country that has one. A rival response would

---

[71] Thus—to take one example from a huge selection—Thomas C. Grey's 'The Uses of an Unwritten Constitution', *Chicago-Kent Law Review* 64 (1988), 211 has as its main topic creative judicial interpretation of the written constitution.

be to mention a case, a judicial decision in constitutional law, which is relevant to the issue. Both are intelligible responses but their rivalry shows that there are, where constitutions are concerned, at least two rival objects of interpretation. There is the constitutional document, the text, as one possible object of interpretation. And then there is constitutional law, the rules, as another possible object of interpretation. They are not the same but they often bear the same name. Many confusions in constitutional theory come of a failure to clarify which object of interpretation is at stake in which debates. I hazard a guess that much of the debate between the different '-isms' of US constitutional interpretation is crippled by such confusions, and would be better abandoned and restarted in entirely different (and I dare to hope, less philosophically pretentious) terms.

Second, one possible link between the two possible objects of interpretation just mentioned—constitutional law and the canonical constitutional text—is that the former may present itself as an interpretation of the latter. In other words, interpreting constitutional law is partly a second-order activity in which one interprets the attempts and claims of others, mainly judges, to be interpreting a canonical text. Interpreting a text is explaining (or exhibiting) some meaning that it has.[72] This truth about interpretation has led some to think that, inasmuch as constitutional case law has interpreted the constitutional text to include norms that are not already part of its meaning, that cannot count as interpretation. But it is no part of the concept of interpretation that the meaning one explains by interpreting must already be part of the text before one so interprets it. One may also interpret a text by giving it some meaning, such that it has that meaning from now on in virtue of one's having given it.[73] There are undoubtedly moral and political questions about how innovative, or how retrievalist, one should be on a certain interpretative occasion, but none of these is settled by the concept of interpretation. This suggests that we can afford to take a more expansive

---

[72] J. Raz, 'Interpretation Without Retrieval' in Andrei Marmor (ed), *Interpretation in Law* (Oxford 1995), 155.

[73] Ibid 169–72, explaining how such meaning-giving is constrained by properties of its object, and hence still qualifies as interpretation.

CAN THERE BE A WRITTEN CONSTITUTION? 123

view of what a written constitution, and written law more generally, is. We can include under the heading of 'written law' both the text and its meaning (for without meaning there is no law in the text) and we should include in its meaning whatever meaning it has, legally speaking. This includes meaning that was authoritatively extracted from it by interpretative retrievers, as well as meaning that was authoritatively attached to it by interpretative innovators.

Of course there may be some meanings that were authoritatively attached to it and then authoritatively removed (by the judicial overruling or distinguishing of an earlier case, or by a change in judicial custom). But until such a removal takes place, all the meaning is there. To the extent that it conflicts, and those conflicts are not resolved by legal rules for ranking the conflicting interpretations (such as rules of *stare decisis*), it leaves the law of the constitution correspondingly indeterminate. The indeterminacy comes not of there being too little constitutional law, but of there being too much. Not only are there inconsistent but co-existing legal rules about judicial review of legislation, constitutional amendment, the domestic recognition of international law, and so on. There are also inconsistent but co-existing legal rules for determining what the constitution says about such things; ie for interpreting the constitution.[74]

Thinking this way puts controversies about interpretative technique in their place. They are straightforward moral and political debates about what judges should do when they

---

[74] In general these rules are permissive, not mandatory. American theorists tend to assume, mistakenly, that the main US rules of legislative and constitutional interpretation must be mandatory rules, such that in cases of dissensus, at least one of the dissentients must be in breach of legal duty (if only we could work out which). British theorists, by contrast, almost universally acknowledge the permissive character of the main UK rules of legislative interpretation: see, eg the classic formulations by Rupert Cross in his *Statutory Interpretation* (London 1976), 43. Such rules conflict only in that, as a user of them, one must sometimes choose between legal permissions that would give rival meanings to the object of interpretation. One makes one's choice on other grounds, usually moral grounds that are local to a particular object of interpretation, ie a particular provision or Act. Thus one need not be predisposed to use the same method in successive cases involving different provisions or Acts. Still less need one have a 'theory' of interpretation, with inevitably monopolistic aspirations.

interpret, debates which concede on all sides that whichever way judges lean—more retrievalist or more innovative—they change the meaning of the text accordingly. For our purposes the most startling implication of this is also a simple one. Where there is a written constitution, there is no logical obstacle to the whole law of the constitution being written law. For there is no logical obstacle to its all being contained in the text, either because it was found there by subsequent judgments of courts or because it was put there by subsequent judgments of courts. Written constitutions, in short, may be entirely written constitutions, for their developments in case law, by way of interpretation, cannot but become part of their meaning *qua* written.[75]

---

[75] I am not suggesting that the US constitution falls into this category. Doubtless some parts of US constitutional law are judge-made, but not by way of interpretation of the canonical text or of previous interpretations of it. They are independent judicial or legislative contributions to constitutional law of the kind that are characteristic of UK constitutional law. For a very illuminating if overstated account, see David Strauss, 'The Irrelevance of Constitutional Amendments', *Harvard Law Review* 114 (2001), 1457. I say 'overstated' because, as his title hints, Strauss sometimes slips into the rival analysis evoked by Hart at *CL*, 246 (see the remarks at the end of Section 3.2 above).

5
How Law Claims, What Law Claims

Many people think that law, wherever it may be found, makes certain characteristic assertions, claims, self-presentations, or promises. In recent times, such an idea has been endorsed and relied upon by writers as otherwise diverse as Drucilla Cornell,[1] John Finnis,[2] Philip Selznick,[3] and Jacques Derrida.[4] But it has come to be particularly associated with the work of Joseph Raz and Robert Alexy. Both Raz and Alexy believe that it is part of the very nature of law that all law makes a moral claim. They disagree about what exactly the content of the moral claim is. Raz says it is a claim to moral authority. Alexy says it is a claim to moral correctness. I will say something shortly about the differences between these views, and their respective attractions. My first objective in this chapter, however, will be to assess the thesis on which Raz and Alexy converge, namely the thesis that the law claims some moral standing for itself. Is this thesis true? Is it even intelligible? I think it is not only intelligible but true. In what follows, I will try to allay various doubts, but also to identify problems with how the thesis has been presented that may have contributed to the spread of those doubts.

1. Law's capacity to claim

A natural first question is this. Is law even capable of making claims? Is it the right kind of thing to do so? A prominent doubter

---

[1] *Beyond Accommodation* (New York 1999), 122. ('To enforce law...is to reinforce the male viewpoint, in spite of law's claim to do the exact opposite.')
[2] 'The Authority of Law in the Predicament of Contemporary Social Theory', *Notre Dame Journal of Law and Public Policy* 1 (1984), 115 at 120. (Law 'presents itself as a seamless web.')
[3] *The Moral Commonwealth* (Berkeley 1992), 444. (Law 'promise[s] justice.')
[4] 'Force of Law: the "Mystical Foundations of Authority"' in Drucilla Cornell (ed), *Deconstruction and the Possibility of Justice* (New York 1992), 22. (Law 'claims to exercise itself in the name of justice'.)

is Ronald Dworkin.⁵ He directs his doubts mainly at Raz's treatment of the topic, although the same doubts could be raised about Alexy's writings. As Dworkin notes, whatever sense we give to Raz's talk of 'law's claims', it must be consistent with Raz's thesis that claiming moral authority is not the same as having moral authority.⁶ A claim, for Raz, has to be capable of being true or false. That is already enough to show that Raz uses the word 'claim' advisedly, intending to invoke at least part of its literal meaning. It is not, for him, a *mere* figure of speech. On the other hand, argues Dworkin, Raz's talk of 'law's claims' must be *partly* a figure of speech. For a claim surely requires a claimant, a person who advances it. And law is not a person. It may be a practice; it may be the set of all norms of a certain type, or all normative systems of a certain type; it may be a mode of social organization; it may be an ideal. But it is plainly not a person, and any personification of it must therefore be figurative. So in Raz's talk of 'law's claims', we can read 'claims' literally only if we read the attribution of claims to law figuratively.

Or can we? Maybe—Dworkin concedes—Raz's attribution of claims to law is not so much figurative as elliptical. For Raz often

---

⁵ Dworkin, 'Thirty Years On', *Harvard Law Review* 115 (2002), 1655 at 1665–8. Similar doubts have been expressed by Kent Greenawalt in 'What Does "the Law" Claim about Trivial and Extremely Broad Legal Norms?', *American Journal of Jurisprudence* 50 (2005), 305 at 307, by Neil MacCormick in 'Why Law Makes No Claims' in George Pavlakos (ed), *Law, Rights, and Discourse* (Oxford 2005), 59 at 62–4, by Carsten Heideman in 'Law's Claim to Correctness' in Sean Coyle and George Pavlakos (eds), *Jurisprudence or Legal Science* (Oxford 2005), 127 at 128–36, and, earliest and best, by Ken Himma in 'Law's Claim of Legitimate Authority' in Jules Coleman (ed), *Hart's Postscript* (Oxford 2001), 271 at 277–9. Himma's treatment is more thorough than Dworkin's, and perhaps more deserving of a detailed response. The two authors differ in various ways (see note 17 below, for an example). However, Himma shares with Dworkin the view that a moral claim is made by or on behalf of the law only if there are persons (legal officials or law-subjects) who have morally favourable attitudes towards the law. So at least the first of my rejoinders to Dworkin below is equally, and equally decisively, a rejoinder to Himma (as well as to Greenawalt). In much the same way the second of my rejoinders to Dworkin doubles as a rejoinder to Heideman (with whom, however, I have less of a disagreement), and the third of my rejoinders to Dworkin doubles as a rejoinder to MacCormick.

⁶ Dworkin, 'Thirty Years On', above note 5, 1666.

puts law's supposed claim to moral authority in the mouth of law-applying officials, who are admittedly persons:

The claims that law makes for itself are evident from the language it adopts and from the opinions expressed by its spokesmen... The law's claim to authority is manifested by the fact that legal institutions are officially designated as 'authorities', by the fact that they regard themselves as having the right to impose obligations on their subjects, by their claims that their subjects owe them allegiance, and that their subjects ought to obey the law as it requires to be obeyed.[7]

So perhaps, when he talks of law's claims, Raz means no more and no less than claims that law-applying officials advance about the legal system of which they are officials. This avoids the personification of law itself. But it faces the new problem, says Dworkin, that not all law-applying officials make the claim that Raz ascribes to all law.[8] Dworkin gives the example of Oliver Wendell Holmes. Holmes, he points out, believed that law is incapable of creating moral obligations. So he could not have believed that law is capable of having moral authority, which is a way of creating moral obligations. So he could not, as a Justice of the Supreme Court, have joined in with the claims that Raz says law-applying officials must make for law. More fundamentally, says Dworkin, there is nothing that unites the 'actual beliefs and attitudes' of law-applying officials such that *any* uniform claim— be it a claim to moral authority or otherwise—is made by them all alike and could be elliptically ascribed to law.[9]

Dworkin makes several mistakes in this argument. I will mention three. His first mistake is to think that what an official claims for the law depends on what 'beliefs and attitudes' the official has about or towards the law.[10] It is true that Raz speaks in the above passage of how officials 'regard' the law. But this is misleading. As Raz makes clear elsewhere, claiming that law has moral authority is consistent with believing that it does not. It is also consistent

---

[7] Raz, 'Authority, Law, and Morality', *The Monist* 68 (1985), 295.
[8] Dworkin, 'Thirty Years On', above note 5, 1666.
[9] Ibid 1667.
[10] Or more generally on what anyone 'think[s]' about law: ibid 1667.

with having no morally favourable attitude towards law.[11] It is consistent with regarding law as a joke or a racket or a scam. That is because, as well as being capable of being true or false, claims are capable of being sincere or insincere. A charity worker and a confidence trickster may equally claim to be helping the poor. Perhaps neither of them actually helps the poor; perhaps both of them make a false claim. But only one of them makes an *insincere* claim. The same cross-cutting distinctions may be drawn where the claims of law-applying officials are concerned. As well as classifying their claims as true or false, we may classify their claims as sincere and insincere.[12] So it is no objection to Raz's view that Holmes doesn't believe that law ever creates moral obligations, or doesn't have a positive moral attitude towards any law. This leaves the possibility that Holmes brazenly (because insincerely) claims otherwise when he sits on the bench. If asked why, he might say: 'That's how they pay me to talk. I'm only doing my job.'

There is a further possibility. Holmes can claim that the law creates moral obligations without even believing that this is what he is claiming, never mind whether he believes that what he is claiming is true. Even if sincere, he may be confused. People often claim things without knowing what they are claiming, because they are not fully aware of the meaning of what they are saying or doing. So one need not believe that Holmes was insincere in order to admit that he made claims for law that were at odds with his beliefs about law (ie claims that attributed to law properties that Holmes believed law not to have).

Dworkin's second mistake is to think that the question of whether law-applying officials make a uniform claim for law can only be an empirical question, so that it could be answered

---

[11] Raz, *Practical Reason and Norms* (London 1975), 147–8; Raz, 'Legal Validity' in his *The Authority of Law* (Oxford 1979), 154–7.

[12] Contrast Postema's statement that, for Raz, 'self-identified participants in legal practice must *believe* that legal norms ... have some sort of moral justification'. G.J. Postema, 'Law's Autonomy and Public Practical Reason' in Robert George (ed), *The Autonomy of Law* (Oxford 1996), 79 at 84 (emphasis added). In the passage relied upon by Postema, Raz is talking about what must be 'adduced', not believed: Raz, 'The Purity of the Pure Theory' in R. Tur and W. Twining (eds), *Essays on Kelsen* (Oxford 1986), 79 at 92.

by a study of the behaviour of law-applying officials (once they have been independently identified as such).[13] Not so. Suppose Dworkin is right that Holmes, in certain of his pronouncements, declined to make moral claims about law. The only conclusion we should draw, according to Raz's analysis, is that, when he made those pronouncements, Holmes was not acting in his capacity as a law-applying official. He was not acting on behalf of the legal system. This chimes with what we know of Holmes. His conceptually revisionist work in the law journals, attempting to debunk the ordinary legal discourse of obligations and rights and so on,[14] did not prevent him from participating fully in the ordinary legal discourse of obligations and rights and so on when he sat in the Supreme Court.[15] In the former role he was not an official and did not speak for the law; in the latter role he was and he did. You may say that the criteria by which we determine this are independent of any claims that Holmes made in the two contexts. If Holmes was not writing in his capacity as a law-applying official when he was debunking law, that is because at the time he was not wearing his robes, or not sitting in his courtroom, or not dealing with a dispute between real people, or not being paid by the US Treasury, or such like. Yet none of these casual indicators of official activity is any more than casual. In principle—and in many legal systems in practice too—a senior judge can exercise her authority on the phone, wearing pyjamas, outside working hours, and in anticipation of a possible future dispute. By what criterion is *this* activity official, now that the casual indicators are gone? Says Raz: by the criterion, *inter alia*, of the official's claims as she acts. And this is a conceptual, not an empirical, proposition, a proposition that no survey could displace (for there is now no independent way to identify the class of behaviour that would need to be surveyed).

Dworkin's third error lies in his thinking that the claims of law-applying officials can be attributed non-elliptically and non-figuratively to law only by an implausible personification of law.

---

[13] 'Thirty Years On', above note 5, at 1667.
[14] Notably 'The Path of the Law', *Harvard Law Review* 10 (1897), 457.
[15] Notably *Abrams* v *US*, 250 US 616 (1919) at 629–31; *Lochner* v *New York* 198 US 45 (1905) at 75–6. See the appendix following for more discussion.

What makes a personification of law implausible, I suggest, is its attribution to law of what I will call 'concerted agency'. There are two types of concerted agents.[16] There are those, such as football teams and symphony orchestras, that come into existence simply by virtue of the mutually responsive actions of their members. And then there are those, such as companies and legislatures, that come into existence by virtue of constituting rules which ascribe actions to them on the occasion of certain of their members' actions (whether those in turn be individual or concerted actions).[17] The hallmark of concerted agency, either way, is that the actions of a concerted agent are a function of the actions of (one or more of) its members, and are intended by its members, yet are not identical with the actions of its members. When a legislature legislates, for example, its doing so is a function of the voting of those of its members who intend the legislature thereby to legislate, but the legislature does not thereby do what its members do. The members vote; the legislature legislates. And when an orchestra plays a symphony, its doing so is a function of the playing of various instrumental parts by its members, who intend the orchestra thereby to play a symphony, but again the orchestra does not do what its members do. The members play their parts; the orchestra as a whole plays the symphony. In the same vein, the CEO signs her name intending that the company should thereby enter into a contract, but it is the company that enters into the contract. And the striker scores a goal intending that his team should thereby win the game, but only the team wins the game. We could capture this point by saying that the

---

[16] I have written about the first type in my 'Reasons for Teamwork', *Legal Theory* 8 (2002), 495. For more about the second type, see Ch 3 in this book.

[17] In 'Law's Claim of Legitimate Authority', above note 5, Himma seems to think that the best prospect for rescuing the idea that law makes claims lies in thinking of it along these lines; ie as an artificial (he says 'fictional') concerted agent. Here he differs from the many who have tried, with considerably less plausibility, to ascribe to the aggregated law-applying officialdom of each legal system a (more or less) orchestral kind of agency. See Jules Coleman, *The Practice of Principle* (Oxford 2001), 96–9; Scott Shapiro, 'Law, Plans, and Practical Reason', *Legal Theory* 8 (2002), 387; Christopher Kutz, 'The Judicial Community', *Philosophical Issues* 11 (2001), 442.

intentional actions of concerted agents are logically, but not materially, autonomous.

Now law as a whole is not a concerted agent. Nor, I would add, is the law of a single jurisdiction. Nor, for that matter, is a single legal system. Yet it is easy to see why one might be tempted to think otherwise. Legal systems do perform logically autonomous actions. For example: a typical modern legal system regulates almost every area of its subjects' lives, even though no legal official regulates almost every area of its subjects' lives. However, such logically autonomous actions of legal systems—often ascribed elliptically to law itself—are not intentional. Like the actions of markets, societies, and other highly complex webs of human activity they are the unintentional byproducts of many actions performed with other (more modest) intentions. So they do not represent any kind of concerted agency.

This point is irrelevant, however, to the truth of Raz's thesis that law claims moral authority. Claiming cannot but be an intentional action (even when one is confused about what exactly one is claiming). But the law's action of claiming moral authority is not autonomous, even logically autonomous, of the actions of law-applying officials. Law makes claims only insofar as law-applying officials make those very same claims at the very same time and place. The claims of law are identical to certain claims of its officials. And these claims must be non-elliptically ascribed to law, not because of any mutual responsiveness among the law's officials, nor because of any constitutional rules that make law itself the agent of anything in virtue of what its officials do. Rather, they must be non-elliptically ascribed to law because the only way to unpack the idea that they are claims made by law-applying officials is as follows. Some people (be they dressed in robes or in pyjamas) make these claims on behalf of law, and making these claims on behalf of law is part of what makes them law-applying officials. It is an irreducible part of this explanation that the claims in question are made on behalf of law. One cannot omit, from any adequate explanation of what a law-applying official is, the fact that law-applying officials serve as law's representatives or spokespeople, identified by law to do law's bidding. So one cannot explain the nature of the action performed by the official without ascribing agency, albeit not autonomous agency, to law itself. I tend to think that persons are agents whose intentional agency is at least logically autonomous, so that ascribing non-autonomous agency to law is not a personification of law at all.[18] But if there is some kind of personification here, it is only a very attenuated and not at all disturbing personification, falling well short of what befits concerted agents such as teams or companies or indeed specific institutions of law (eg legislatures and courts).[19]

2. Law's claims as moral claims

So that, with no more than the barest of personifications, is how law makes claims. Armed with this capacity to make claims, what claims, if any, does law indeed make? The place to begin, nobody doubts, is with the language that law-applying officials use. In explaining the law, they cannot but use the language of obligations, rights, permissions, powers, liabilities, and so on. What they thereby claim—and they cannot say it without claiming it—is that the law imposes obligations, creates rights, grants permissions, confers powers, gives rise to liabilities, and so on. The question is, what do these claims amount to?

Some people hold that the full necessary extent of the claims made by officials who use this language is that there are *legal* obligations, *legal* rights, *legal* permissions, *legal* powers, *legal* liabilities, and so on.[20] Now it is certainly true that there are such things, and that their existence can be and routinely is claimed by law-applying officials. But this claim cannot be law's claim. Why?

---

[18] The connection between personhood and autonomy is, of course, widely discussed, although most discussions focus exclusively on human persons and their material autonomy. A classic example is Harry Frankfurt, 'Freedom of the Will and the Concept of a Person', *Journal of Philosophy* 68 (1971), 5.

[19] Compare Dworkin's own ruminations on the agency of concerted agents, such as legislatures, in *Law's Empire* (Cambridge, Mass. 1986), 169–71. And note his willingness to extend the same 'working personification' to 'communities': ibid at 172–5. Here he helps himself to various moves that he later denies to Raz, including the move of distinguishing 'officials in their official capacity' as 'agents of the community'. If of the community, why not of law?

[20] Stephen Perry attributes this view to John Finnis. See Perry 'Law and Obligation', *American Journal of Jurisprudence* 50 (2005), 263 at 289, relying on scattered remarks in Finnis, *Natural Law and Natural Rights* (Oxford 1979).

Because a legal obligation or right is none other than an obligation or right that exists according to law. And an obligation or right that exists according to law is none other than an obligation or right, the existence of which law claims. So the claim that there is a *legal* obligation or right—whether made by a law-applying official or by anyone else—is a second-order claim, a claim *about* what law claims. Now it is true, of course, that law could make a second-order claim about its own claims. But not this one. For as we already learnt, a claim has to be capable of being true or false. It is not a claim unless there is logical space for its falsity. And it makes no sense to attribute to law a false claim about these legal obligations and rights, for there is no criterion of legal truth and falsity that is independent of law. So an error about, and hence a claim about, what legal rights and obligations there are can only be attributed to a particular law-applying official, not to law itself.[21] I am not suggesting, of course, that the official makes the error in her personal capacity. For in other respects—for example in making law's moral claim—she may continue to represent the law even while she is making her error of law.[22] All I am saying is that her error of law, and her claim about what legal rights and obligations there are, are hers and not the law's, albeit they are an error and a claim that she makes in the course of her work as a law-applying official.

It is against this background that the proposal emerges that law's own claim is a moral one: that when, according to law, there are obligations and rights and so on, law's claim is that these are *moral* obligations and rights and so on, not merely legal ones. Unless accompanied by some clarification, this way of presenting the content of law's claim courts confusion. Notoriously, the sense of the word 'moral' shifts depending on what it is contrasted

---

[21] On related grounds, Scott Shapiro says that the attribution of such a claim to law is 'banal' yet also 'deeply paradoxical': 'On Hart's Way Out', *Legal Theory* 4 (1998), 469 at 469–70.

[22] These considerations, incidentally, begin to reveal what was wrong with the movement in English public law after *Anisminic* v *Foreign Compensation Commission* [1969] 2 AC 147 to treat all errors of law as jurisdictional; ie as taking an official outside her official capacity.

with.[23] Two of its many senses are important here. We sometimes use the word 'moral' in a broad sense simply to draw the contrast already drawn in the previous paragraph. There are obligations and rights, such as legal obligations and rights, or the obligations and rights accorded by tradition or convention, which are merely claimed or supposed obligations and rights. And then there are obligations and rights that are not merely claimed or supposed. They are the very ones that the claimed or supposed ones are claimed or supposed to be. If we use 'moral' to mark out this entire group of NMCS (= not-merely-claimed-or-supposed) considerations, it is an innocent tautology that law claims its obligations and rights, and indeed all other legal considerations, to be moral ones. However, we sometimes use the word 'moral' more narrowly to refer to just *some* of the considerations that qualify as 'moral' in the broader sense just mentioned. We contrast them with other NMCS considerations. We contrast them with aesthetic considerations, say, or with considerations of prudence or self-interest. We may disagree about which considerations qualify as NMCS, and we may doubt the sustainability of some of the familiar contrasts drawn among even what we agree to be NMCS considerations. But we can still agree that it is a familiar use of the word 'moral' to pick out just some of these NMCS considerations, so that the proposition 'law makes moral claims' is no longer tautological.

Or is it? I shifted here from talk of obligations and rights to talk of 'considerations' because otherwise tautology quickly seems to return. Which subset of NMCS considerations are we to designate by the word 'moral'? Here we are faced, no doubt, with a subsidiary fragmentation of the possible senses of 'moral'. But it is tempting to think that, in all the relevant senses of the word 'moral', the subset of NMCS considerations that qualify as moral includes all those considerations that are obligatory, which in turn

---

[23] It is what J.L. Austin calls a 'trouser word'. Compare the word 'real': '[A] definite sense attaches to the assertion that something is real, a real such-and-such, only in the light of a specific way in which it might be, or might have been, *not* real.... I don't know *just* how to take the assertion that it's a real duck unless I know *just* what, on that particular occasion, the speaker has it in mind to exclude.' Austin, *Sense and Sensibilia* (2nd ed, Oxford 1962), 70.

includes all rights-based considerations. There may be self-interested and aesthetic considerations, but there are no self-interested or aesthetic obligations. As soon as we encounter obligations, we are thereby crossing the line into morality. Thus if the law's ultimate concern is with obligations—if the law's concern with permissions and powers and liabilities and rights and so on is ultimately a concern with the obligations to which they give rise—then the law's claims turn out to be tautologically moral, even in the narrower sense of 'moral'. Or so it is tempting to think. In fact the matter is not quite so simple. First, it is not so clear that the law's ultimate concern is only with obligations.[24] Second, there are some NMCS obligations which resist the designation 'moral', such as obligations of etiquette. When we are subdividing the NMCS domain, we usually reserve the title 'moral' for important NMCS obligations, those NMCS obligations, breach of which has important consequences for somebody. So even if we limit our attention to NMCS considerations, 'moral obligation' is not quite a tautology.

It follows that the idea that law claims its obligations to be moral obligations is equally not quite a tautology. Yet we can restore our confidence in the idea that all law makes a moral claim for itself, even in this narrower sense of 'moral', by noting the following. The mere fact of their being embodied in law already lifts what would otherwise be non-moral NMCS obligations—such as obligations of etiquette—from a relatively unimportant to a relatively important position. Advertisement of the law will cause some people to alter their daily pursuits. Enforcement of the law will put some people under stress or cost them money or freedom. Even if the law is not advertised or enforced, this itself raises moral issues about the behaviour of those responsible for advertising or enforcing it. Every legal issue, however superficially

---

[24] Rights can be understood as grounding obligations. Permissions can be understood as cancelling obligations or as cancelling some of their obligatory force. H.L.A. Hart argued that powers, although they are logically distinct from obligations, exist to enable variation of obligations: *The Concept of Law* (Oxford 1961), 78–9. Liabilities, in turn, are best understood in terms of powers. Does all this add up to yield the conclusion that obligations are law's ultimate concern? The obscurity of 'ultimate' makes it hard to be sure.

technical, is a moral issue, for its resolution inevitably has important consequences for someone.

You may wonder why we should be interested in whether law makes a moral claim, in the narrower sense of 'moral'. Here is one suggestion. We use this distinction between moral claims and non-moral claims to distinguish legal systems from, for example, games and recipes. Let me focus on games.[25] Games include such things as obligations, permissions, rights, powers, and liabilities. In *Monopoly*, for instance, there is the right to receive £200 as one passes 'Go', the power to buy an un-owned property when one lands on it, the obligation to pay rent when one lands on an unmortgaged property owned by another player, and the permission to leave jail with a 'Get Out of Jail Free' card. It is a normative system, so far indistinguishable from a legal system. Where it differs is in the claims it makes on its players. It is not that *Monopoly* makes no claims—for it too has a rule-applying official who speaks for it, in the form of the banker—nor that it does not claim to create NMCS considerations. It is merely that these claims are not moral claims, in the narrower sense of 'moral'. For adding an obligation or power or permission or right or liability to *Monopoly* need not have important consequences for anyone (assuming that it does not affect the overall playability of the game). This difference between games and legal systems has important consequences of its own. Since law is not a game, nobody—least of all law-applying officials—should take a playful or light-hearted attitude to it while administering it. As we saw, a law-applying official might conceivably take such an attitude, speaking with apparent earnestness for law but all the time laughing to herself about law's stupidity. This attitude does not stop one from being a law-applying official but it does call into question one's fitness for the role. By contrast, one may be fit for the role of banker in *Monopoly* even though one takes a light-hearted attitude to both the role and the game.

In a way more fundamental, though, is a feature that law shares with *Monopoly*. There are two opposite errors about what is known as the 'normativity' of law that constantly recur in the

---

[25] I discuss recipes in more detail in Ch 6 below.

literature, and it is hard to keep them both at bay at once. On the one hand, there is the error of thinking that legal obligations (and rights and permissions and so on) are themselves one family of NMCS obligations (etc), and hence are not merely claimed to be. Indeed, they are not *even* claimed to be. It cannot be a claim because there is no logical space for it to be false. When the law says 'jump', on this view, one has without further ado a NMCS obligation to jump. It does not even need an argument from the legal to the NMCS obligation; for if there is no NMCS obligation, there is by that token no legal obligation. On the other hand, we find the opposite but sadly even more familiar error of understanding law as the 'gunman situation writ large'.[26] Legal considerations are prudential considerations—threats and other incentives—and inasmuch as law makes claims, the only claim it makes is a claim on the prudential attention of those who are subject to it. If one takes the latter line one must read the law's talk of obligations, rights, permissions, powers, etc as a smokescreen, for such categories have no place in the alternative discourse of threats and incentives.

One might sum up the two polarized alternatives here by saying, as Matthew Kramer does, that 'morality and prudence exhaust the realm of reasons'.[27] If legal obligations, rights, permissions, powers etc. are not moral obligations, rights, permissions, powers, etc. they must, on this view, be dictates of prudence, which are merely *labelled* as 'obligations', 'rights', 'permissions', 'powers', etc, using all this moralistic language in a technical (and, we should add, euphemistic) legal sense.

The way to avoid both errors at once is to understand law to be making a moral claim for itself, in the sense of a claim to be made up of moral obligations, rights, permissions, and so on (ie obligations, rights, permissions, and so on that are not merely claimed or supposed to be such). This interpretation is consistent, as we saw, with individual law-applying officials advancing the law's claims insincerely or in the grip of confusion. Unlike the 'gunman' interpretation, however, this interpretation does not

---

[26] As Hart famously put it, in *The Concept of Law*, above note 24, at 6–7.

[27] Matthew Kramer, 'Requirements, Reasons, and Raz: Legal Positivism and Legal Duties', *Ethics* 109 (1999), 375 at 379.

require insincerity or confusion on the part of law-applying officials when they talk of obligations, rights, permissions, and so on. As a law-applying official, one might also be a sincere and clear-headed moral supporter of the law. And there are numerous options in between. The challenge, as H.L.A. Hart saw, is to explain the following facts about law:

> [A]llegiance to the system may be based on many different considerations: calculations of long-term interest; disinterested interest in others; an unreflecting inherited or traditional attitude; or the mere wish to do as others do.... [Officials] express their sense of [law's] requirements in internal statements couched in the normative language which is common to both law and morals: 'I (You) ought', I (he) must; I (they) have an obligation.' Yet they are not thereby committed to a *moral* judgment that it is morally right to do what the law requires.[28]

How is this possible? Hart experimented fruitlessly with the idea that there is some belief or attitude on the part of officials that makes it possible. He most often characterized it as an attitude of acceptance, which is consistent with moral disapproval.[29] His successors, including Raz and Alexy, have helped us to see the source of the fruitlessness in this line of thought. Legal officials must make a moral claim on behalf of the law, but they need not believe it and it need not reflect their own attitudes to law—even the barest acceptance of law.[30] For legal officials do not, or at any rate need not, speak for themselves. Librarians advocate literacy but they may be TV-loving philistines. Recycling officers agitate to reduce waste but they may be gas-guzzling slobs. Judges make moral claims for law but they may be anarchist subversives who are trying to bring law down from the inside. Or, less racily, they may just be people who need to hold down their jobs to pay their overambitious mortgages. When they speak of the law as being made up of obligations, rights, permissions, powers, and so on, they speak as officials of law and it is the moral claim of law that

---

[28] *The Concept of Law*, above note 24, 198–9.
[29] Ibid at eg 57, 113.
[30] See Raz, 'Legal Validity', above note 11, 155: officials 'normally' accept the law but—be that as it may—they cannot but claim to endorse it.

they express, whether or not it is a claim that they themselves believe or even so much as accept.

3. Correctness, justice, authority

Raz and Alexy, as I said, converge on the thesis that law makes a moral claim. Alexy defends his version of this thesis with two famous examples, each of which is said to reveal the impossibility of law without its distinctive claim. The first example is that of a constitutional provision according to which 'X is a sovereign, federal, and unjust republic'.[31] The second is that of a judge who rules: 'the accused is sentenced to life imprisonment, which is an incorrect interpretation of prevailing law'.[32] We can all see that these statements are awkward. Alexy argues that they are also conceptually incoherent because they defy law's claim.

But do they? The claim that is defied—or rather the counter-claim that is made—by the judge in the second example is a claim about what the law has to say on a certain point, about what legal powers and obligations the judge has in sentencing an offender. As we saw already, claims to the effect that such-and-such is the law (that it is a legal power or is a legal obligation or a legal right or such like) are not law's claims. Why? Because a legal power or obligation or right is no more and no less than what the law claims to be a power or obligation or right. The judge in Alexy's second example is not making a first-order claim on behalf of the law but making his own second-order claim about whatever it is that the law independently claims. It is, of course, an interesting further question whether judges and other law-applying officials necessarily claim to be applying the law, or at least (a weaker requirement) to be not defying the law in their official activities. In my view, the answer is no. Personally I find a pragmatic but not a conceptual problem in the judicial utterance in Alexy's second example. But that is irrelevant to our topic here. For the claim in the second example is not law's claim and does not help to show the content of law's claim.

---

[31] Robert Alexy, *The Argument from Injustice: A Reply to Legal Positivism* (trans Paulson and Paulson; Oxford 2002), 36.
[32] Ibid 38.

Alexy's first example is different.[33] It includes not a claim about legal obligations and so on but a claim about their moral standing. They are claimed to be unjust. Is it intelligible for such a claim to be made on behalf of law? Alexy thinks not. He says that law necessarily claims to be just and so cannot claim to be unjust.[34] He also thinks that law necessarily claims to be morally correct, and the example is also supposed to support that view. How are these two theses about the content of law's claims supposed to be related? They are certainly not equivalent. It is possible for something to be morally correct yet unjust, or *vice versa*. This is because, although all considerations of justice are moral considerations, not all moral considerations are considerations of justice. Not even all moral *obligations* are considerations of justice. There are also moral obligations of humanity, mercy, honesty, prudence, tolerance, etc. It follows that a certain rule or ruling found in the law, or indeed a whole legal system, may be morally correct but unjust, or just but morally incorrect. This being so, the law may claim to be unjust without claiming to be morally incorrect, or claim to be just without claiming to be morally correct. Indeed, the constitution imagined by Alexy may continue: '...for injustice is the price we rightly pay for our tolerant, humane and merciful civilization'. Would this, according to

---

[33] Or is it? Sometimes Alexy explains law's claim as a claim to correctness *simpliciter*, not as a claim to legal correctness coupled with a claim to moral correctness. The problem with this suggestion is that all claims, or at least all claims with a propositional content, are necessarily claims to correctness. 'I claim that P is correct' means the same as 'I claim that P' in much the same way that 'I assert that P is true' means the same as 'I assert that P'. Thus ascribing to law a bare claim to correctness leaves us none the wiser regarding the *content* of the claim—the relevant P—except that it is propositional. I am assuming in the text that Alexy is interested in explaining something about the content of law's claim(s). Cf. Joseph Raz, 'The Argument from Justice, or How Not to Reply to Legal Positivism' in George Pavlakos (ed), *Law, Rights, and Justice: The Legal Philosophy of Robert Alexy* (Oxford 2007), 17 at 29–30. Raz goes further than I do and suggests that all intentional actions trivially include the generalized claim to correctness.

[34] Another writer who believes that law claims to be just is Philip Soper. See his 'Law's Normative Claims' in George (ed), *The Autonomy of Law*, above note 12, 215 at 247. Soper also criticizes Raz's alternative proposal.

Alexy, be conceptually incoherent? It would not, after all, defy the claim to be morally correct.[35]

Possibly, according to Alexy, justice is the special kind of moral correctness suited to legal systems, so that, according to Alexy, a claim to moral correctness on the part of a legal system must resolve into a claim to justice. I think Alexy would be wrong to embrace this line of thought. The connection between law and justice is more complex.[36] Even law-applying officials should sometimes sacrifice justice to mercy or prudence, and do so in the name of the law. But be that as it may, law does not make either of the moral claims that Alexy ascribes to it—either the claim to be just or the claim to be morally correct—and so it is unnecessary to consider in any detail how it could be thought to make both claims together. To illustrate, let's compare Alexy's first example with the following, a real-life judicial comment of a kind not unfamiliar in common law systems:

I feel... that I would be lacking in candour if I were to conceal my unhappiness about the conclusion which I feel compelled to reach. In my opinion, although of course the courts of this country are bound by the doctrine of precedent, sensibly interpreted, nevertheless it would be irresponsible for judges to act as automatons, rigidly applying authorities without regard to consequences. Where therefore it appears at first sight that authority compels a judge to reach a conclusion which he senses to be unjust or inappropriate, he is, I consider, under a positive duty to examine the relevant authorities with scrupulous care to ascertain whether he can, within the limits imposed by the doctrine of precedent (always sensibly interpreted), legitimately interpret or qualify the principle expressed in the authorities to achieve the result which he perceives to be just or appropriate in the particular case. I do not disguise the fact that I have sought to perform this function in the present case.... I have considered anxiously whether there is any other interpretation which the court could legitimately place on Lord Diplock's statement of principle in *Caldwell*, which would lead to the conclusion which I would prefer to reach, that the respondent was not reckless whether the shed and contents would be

---

[35] A similar objection is raised by Mark Murphy in 'Defect and Deviance in Natural Law Jurisprudence', in Matthias Klatt (ed), *Institutionalized Reason: The Jurisprudence of Robert Alexy* (Oxford 2012).

[36] Some aspects of it are discussed in Ch 10 below.

destroyed by fire. I have discovered none which would not involve what I would regard as constituting, in relation to the relevant offence, an illegitimate departure from that statement of principle.[37]

What does Goff LJ claim here? He does not claim that the law is just or that it is morally correct. Indeed, he expressly says that he finds the law either 'unjust or inappropriate' in its application to the case before him. He does not make clear which. Maybe both. But this does not matter, for he does not need to claim that the law is unjust in order to avoid claiming that it is just; nor does he need to claim that the law is morally incorrect to avoid claiming that it is morally correct. To avoid making the positive claims it is sufficient for him to claim, as he does, that the law is either unjust or morally incorrect. Is this claim inconsistent with his acting as a law-applying official? Is he a secret follower of the extrajudicial Holmes, denying the moral obligatoriness of the law?

No. For Goff LJ expressly holds himself to the standards of interpretative 'legitimacy' which, in his view, the law places upon him. He regards the rule previously set out by Lord Diplock as constraining him, and not merely as claiming to constrain him. In other words, he does not merely report what he takes to be his legal obligations, but holds these out as his moral obligations too. Does he really believe that they are his moral obligations? Is he a morally committed judge? Nothing in the passage tells us either way. All that we can discover from the passage are his claims. And they clearly include a moral claim on behalf of the law, viz. a claim that the law is morally binding whether or not it is just and whether or not it is morally correct. He claims that it would be 'illegitimate' for him to attempt to render the law just or morally correct because, as he puts it in an adjoining passage, he is 'constrained [not] to do so by authority'.[38]

So we can see at once why Raz renders the moral claim of law as a claim to moral *authority*, not a claim to moral correctness or a claim to justice. It is because legal officials often speak as Goff LJ speaks, and accept that they are morally bound by some prior exercise of the law's authority—a statute or a previous judicial

---

[37] *Elliott* v *C* [1983] 2 All ER 1005 at 1010 and 1012.
[38] Ibid at 1010.

decision—while challenging the justice or other moral merit of the exercise of authority in question. There is a sense, of course, in which a claim to moral authority always incorporates a claim to moral correctness. It always incorporates a claim that those subject to the authority would be acting morally correctly if they were to submit to the authority and do its bidding. Thus Goff LJ naturally represents himself as acting with moral correctness in following Lord Diplock's rule. This, however, is a red herring in the present context. For it is consistent with Goff LJ's denying that Lord Diplock acted with moral correctness in *creating* the rule. In other words it is consistent with denying the moral correctness of the law itself, and hence denying law's claim to correctness. Indeed, that is the point: moral authority is such that abiding by it is morally correct even though the exercise of it was morally incorrect. Authority may bind one morally to do certain things that one should never have become morally bound to do, for of any moral power it is true that its valid exercise does not depend entirely upon its correct exercise.[39]

This may lead us to return our attention to Alexy's first example. Why would it seem conceptually challenging, as it certainly seems to me, for a constitution to announce the moral incorrectness of the legal order that it constitutes? The answer is not that law makes a claim to moral correctness. The answer is that law makes a claim to moral authority. But the constitution, of course, contains those rules of the legal system that allocate ultimate (non-delegated, or if delegated then irrevocably delegated) authority. So a confession of law's moral incorrectness in the provisions of the constitution is quite different from a confession of law's moral incorrectness in, for example, the decision of Goff LJ. A confession of moral incorrectness in the provisions of the constitution, unlike a confession of moral incorrectness in Goff LJ's decision, contradicts law's claim to moral authority. And that, it seems to me, is its only conceptual problem. For law makes a

---

[39] The moral power to promise illustrates the same point. A promise to do something positively immoral is not morally binding. But a promise to do something stupid or vapid usually is morally binding, even though it is not only an act that should never have been done apart from the promise, but also an act, the doing of which should never have been promised.

claim to moral authority, but law makes no claim to moral correctness or to justice.

4. A necessary connection

That law makes a moral claim, Raz and Alexy agree, constitutes a necessary connection between law and morality. No surprise there, since there are numerous necessary connections between law and morality. Nobody has ever got close to defending the view that there are none. Alexy seems to regard 'legal positivism' as defending this view. But inasmuch as anyone, 'legal positivist' or otherwise, ever set out their view in this way, they always had to introduce caveats and provisos. In particular, they always had to point to ways in which law and morality are related in order to get enough purchase for meaningful distinctions to be drawn between law and morality. Central to this endeavour, and of common concern to 'legal positivists' and their opponents alike, has been the fact that the law shares a core conceptual, or at least linguistic, apparatus with morality, the apparatus of obligations, rights, powers, and so on. This already marks a necessary connection between law and morality. The question is, how do we interpret it? Interpreting it as the making of a moral claim by law is one attractive way to make sense of it.

In two ways this interpretation of the law's apparatus is conducive to the historic project of so-called 'legal positivists'. First, on this interpretation of legal discourse there can be immoral laws. The law claims to be moral, so it must be the case that the law can fail to be moral, for nothing is claimed unless there is logical space for it to be false. Second, for something to make claims it must, minimally, be capable of making claims. It must be a person or at least have persons ('officials') who act and speak on its behalf. If law is like this, that is another respect in which it differs from morality at large. Morality has no officials and cannot make claims. It is no accident that Dworkin, whose main mission is to strike out against the 'legal positivist' tradition, also opposes the thesis that law makes moral claims. What is not so clear is why Alexy regards this thesis as pointing in the opposite direction. He makes it part of 'A Reply to Legal Positivism' when, in reality, it

HOW LAW CLAIMS, WHAT LAW CLAIMS   145

is much more comfortably understood as part of legal positivism's reply to him.

Appendix: On Holmes' claims

In a previous discussion of Dworkin's views on the claims of law, I issued the warning, repeated above, that the beliefs of Oliver Wendell Holmes, the noted legal intellectual, should not be confused with the claims of Justice Holmes, the celebrated judge who sat on the United States Supreme Court.[40] Dworkin rebuked me on that occasion for not citing any of the relevant judicial writings. And he ventured a guess that, were I to have cited any, they would have confirmed Holmes' adherence, even on the bench, to his famous extrajudicial stance as a sceptic about moral obligation, or at least about the moral obligatoriness of law.[41] I must confess that my failure to cite came of the belief that Holmes' judicial work is universally well-known, and that just about any example of it taken at random would have borne out my point. But Dworkin's view that, on the contrary, I could not have borne my point out by any example of Holmes' judicial work makes me wonder whether Holmes' judicial work really is as well-known as I supposed. So to bear my point out in some detail, I propose we consider the following sample passages, from two of Holmes' best-known dissents:

In this case, sentences of twenty years' imprisonment have been imposed for the publishing of two leaflets that I believe the defendants had as much right to publish as the Government has to publish the Constitution of the United States now vainly invoked by them. [...] *Only the emergency that makes it immediately dangerous to leave the correction of evil counsels to time warrants making any exception* to the sweeping command, 'Congress shall make no law ... abridging the freedom of speech'. Of course, I am speaking only of expressions of opinion and exhortations, which were all that were uttered here, but I regret that I cannot put into more impressive words my belief that, in their conviction upon this indictment, *the defendants were deprived of their rights under the Constitution of the United States.*[42]

This case is decided upon an economic theory which a large part of the country does not entertain. If it were a question whether I agreed with that theory, I should desire to study it further and long before making up my mind.

---

[40] Gardner, 'Law's Aims in *Law's Empire*' in Scott Hershovitz (ed), *Exploring Law's Empire: The Jurisprudence of Ronald Dworkin* (Oxford 2006), 207 at 215.
[41] Dworkin, 'Response' in ibid 291 at 306. Note that once again Dworkin presents the question as being one about Holmes' 'attitudes', not his claims.
[42] Holmes J in *Abrams v US*, 250 US 616 (1919) at 629–31. Emphasis mine.

But *I do not conceive that to be my duty, because I strongly believe that my agreement or disagreement has nothing to do with the right of a majority to embody their opinions in law.* [. . .] Every opinion tends to become a law. I think that *the word liberty in the Fourteenth Amendment is perverted when it is held to prevent the natural outcome of a dominant opinion, unless it can be said that a rational and fair man necessarily would admit that the statute proposed would infringe fundamental principles as they have been understood by the traditions of our people and our law.* It does not need research to show that no such sweeping condemnation can be passed upon the statute before us.[43]

Throughout these twin passages Holmes speaks of rights and obligations (aka duties), his own and other people's. Some of them he explictly presents as rights and obligations conferred or imposed by law (see the second italicized remark in the first passage). Others he does not (see the first italicized remark in the second passage). One might insist that even when he does not explicitly present them thus, he is still referring only to legal rights and obligations, and makes no claims for them other than that they are legal rights and obligations—in particular, no moral claims for them. But this interpretation sits ill with the way in which Holmes integrates the claimed legal rights and obligations into his lines of argument. For he uses moral lines of argument in support of these claimed legal rights and obligations. Consider, for example, the first italicized remark in the first passage and the second italicized remark in the second passage. In the former, Holmes relies on the 'danger' of some things and the 'evil' of others to make out his argument for the scope of the legal right to free speech under the First Amendment. In the latter, he relies on the imagined judgments of a 'rational and fair man' about 'fundamental principles' to defend his interpretation of the scope of the right to due process of law in respect of deprivations of liberty under the Fourteenth Amendment.

Some, including Dworkin in other works, read argumentative moves of this kind as breaking down the distinction between legal rights and obligations on the one hand and moral rights and obligations on the other.[44] But this radical reconstruction goes far beyond what is needed to make sense of what Holmes is saying. It is possible to be faithful to exactly what Holmes says while preserving the possibility that Holmes is legally correct about these rights and obligations while morally

---

[43] Holmes J in *Lochner* v *New York* 198 US 45 (1905) at 75–6. Emphasis mine.

[44] This was an implication of Dworkin's very first argument against Hart in 'The Model of Rules', *University of Chicago Law Review* 35 (1967), 14. The argument was designed to establish that there is no test (and we must therefore assume, no criterion) for distinguishing legal norms from non-legal norms.

misguided about them or morally correct while legally misguided. Perhaps he is wrong about what the law of the Constitution says but right about what it would say if only it were morally upstanding. Or perhaps, more salient to our present purposes, he is right about what the law of the Constitution says but wrong to endow it, as he does, with moral credibility. Objections of both these types might intelligibly be advanced by a judge who sides with the majority against Holmes' dissent. To keep these objections intelligible we should understand Holmes as making only a moral *claim* for the law as he presents it. He is claiming that the said legal rights and obligations (as he claims them to be) also have moral standing, that they are moral rights and obligations too. The 'also' and the 'too' here presuppose, rather than eliminating, the distinction between legal rights and obligations and their moral counterparts. They presuppose that at least some legal rights and obligations could fail to be moral rights and obligations, for (as we saw) nothing is a claim unless there is logical space for its falsity.

For completeness, we should note which moral claim it is that Holmes makes; ie what content he gives to the claim. Like Goff LJ, he clearly does not claim law's moral correctness. He claims only law's moral authority. He argues that his 'agreement or disagreement has nothing to do with the right of a majority to embody their opinions in law'. Or to put it another way: where law has moral authority— perhaps because of its democratic credentials—it has the ability to create moral obligations whether or not it took the morally correct path in doing so. Of course, Holmes reserves his own right, working with his fellow judges, to issue a 'sweeping condemnation' of the democratically created law and thereby to remove it from the law. Judges often do this, although different legal systems give them different scope to do it. Alexy, like Dworkin, tends to read this kind of judicial remark as a sign that grossly immoral rules cannot form part of the law.[45] But that is not what such remarks signify. Here, as elsewhere, the remark is a sign that Holmes claims the moral authority of the Supreme Court, speaking on behalf of law itself, to review the moral authority of a democratically elected legislature. How do we know that this is what Holmes claims? We can be fairly confident about it because we can be fairly confident that even if Holmes had felt able to issue the 'sweeping condemnation' called for by the final sentence of the second passage, he would not have regarded this condemnation as having legal effect—as determining the

---

[45] Alexy, *The Argument from Injustice*, above note 31, at 28. I have not dwelled on this thesis of Alexy's, which I regard as conflicting with his other views.

rights and obligations of the parties to the case, let alone of other courts in the United States in similar or related cases—unless his condemnation were an operative part of the ruling of a *majority* on the Supreme Court—unless, as well as being a sweeping moral condemnation of the law, it also met the conditions for itself being a binding authority.

6
Nearly Natural Law

1. Humanity, rationality, morality

We human beings are rational beings. We have a highly developed capacity to respond to reasons. This is an important aspect of our nature. It does not follow that there can be no case of a human being whose capacity to respond to reasons is limited or missing. It only follows that such a rationally deprived human being is not the central case or paradigm of a human being. In explaining what a human being is, it would be profoundly misleading, for example, to present someone in a permanent vegetative state as a first illustration. For she lacks altogether the natural human capacity to respond to reasons. This may tempt some to say that she is not human, and hence that she lacks human dignity or human rights or such like.[1] But this goes much too far. Even in her permanent vegetative state she is still human in various other respects. She still has, for example, a human biology and a human physiognomy. These too are important aspects of human nature. Why are they important? Here is one reason why. That someone in a permanent vegetative state is still human in these other respects is the primary reason why we care about her being deprived of her human capacity to respond to reasons. We care because, as a human being, she ought to be rational. If she were not a human being, but literally a vegetable, her lack of rational capacities would not worry us. For it is not part of the nature of a vegetable to be rational.

Our highly developed capacity to respond to reasons includes the capacity to use *norms* to guide our actions and beliefs and feelings and desires and so on. A norm is the same thing as a standard. Some norms apply to us inescapably just because we are rational beings. These include, most obviously, the norms of rationality itself, such as the norm by which one should believe

---

[1] See Michael Tooley, 'Abortion and Infanticide', *Philosophy and Public Affairs* 2 (1972), 37 (discussing persons rather than human beings, and neonates rather than permanent vegetative state patients, but following the same pattern of thought).

or act only for an undefeated reason. They also include the norms of logic, such as the principle of non-contradiction, conformity to which makes it possible for us to engage in reasoning. They also include moral norms. Being subject to morality is an inescapable part of being rational in much the same way that being subject to logic is an inescapable part of being rational. And being rational, to repeat, is part of being human.

It follows that any human being who asks the question 'Why should I be moral?' has already misunderstood either human nature or the nature of morality.[2] To ask this question is to suggest that one has some rationally intelligible alternative to being engaged with morality. But one has no such alternative. It is part of human nature to be engaged with morality; a being with little or no responsiveness to moral norms, even if otherwise highly responsive to reasons, is rationally deprived. If we are explaining what a human being is, this one, like the human being in a permanent vegetative state, is not a suitable example. To hold him up as not only an example but indeed a model is the basic error of modern economics. It is no answer for economists to say that *homo economicus* does respond to moral norms whenever it is rational for him to do so. For this response uses a debased notion of the rational according to which morality is something from which one could rationally disengage, and hence for engaging with which one needs further (non-moral) reasons. In fact, being responsive to morality is an integral part of being rational, and so needs no (further) rational explanation.

Let's give this thesis a name—the 'inescapable morality thesis' or '(IM)' for short—and a canonical formulation:

(IM) Engagement with moral norms is an inescapable part of rational, and hence human, nature.

Three lines of thought, all fallacious, have tended to fuel doubts about the truth of (IM).

---

[2] For discussion see John Hospers, *Human Conduct* (New York 1961); Bernard Williams, *Morality* (New York 1972), 17–27; Michael Smith, *The Moral Problem* (Oxford 1994); Thomas Nagel, 'The Value of Inviolability', *Revue de Métaphysique et de Morale* 99 (1994), 149; Joseph Raz, 'The Amoralist', in G. Cullity and B. Gaut (eds), *Ethics and Practical Reason* (Oxford 1997) 369.

The first and most obvious source of doubt is that human beings perpetrate, and always have perpetrated, a great deal of immorality. It hardly needs saying that widespread failure to conform to moral norms does not by itself suggest that (IM) is false, since the explanation for much of the failure might be that human beings are prone to make moral mistakes just as they are prone to make other kinds of rational mistakes. The offenders in question are not disengaged from morality but merely misunderstand or misapply its norms. This explanation is consistent with, and indeed supportive of, (IM). So the immoralities emphasized by those who doubt (IM) must be different. They must be *knowing* or *indifferent* failures to conform to moral norms. Personally I doubt whether there is very much moral indifference in the world. In my experience even the basest people tend to kid themselves as well as others that what they do is morally acceptable. Even the torturer and the gun runner and the ethnic cleanser cloak themselves in pathetically inadequate moral self-justifications (eg 'if I didn't do it someone else would' or 'Nothing personal, it's only business' or 'They deserved it'). There is no general reason to suspect that these self-justifications are uttered insincerely. So long as they are sincere, even if self-deceptive, then this is not moral indifference but moral mistake, and it remains consistent with, and indeed supportive of, (IM). As for knowing failures to conform to moral norms, these are equally reconcilable with (IM). (IM) is not the thesis that, for a rational being, nothing can conflict with moral norms, nor is it the thesis that moral norms override everything with which they conflict. Human beings almost always have their reasons, often nakedly self-interested reasons, for their knowing failures to conform to moral norms. That human beings are prone to allow moral norms to be too easily defeated in conflicts with naked self-interest, and hence often need incentives to improve their moral conformity, does not show that their engagement with morality is rationally escapable. Once again, it shows nothing more than a tendency for rational agents to make rational mistakes, this time mistakes about the relative importance of their own profit. And once again this diagnosis is consistent with, and indeed supportive of, (IM).

Beyond all this there is the more general point that (IM) cannot be called into question by pointing to the existence of any number of human beings who lack moral engagement. For these supposed counter-examples may only go to show that, so far as the moral aspect of human nature is concerned, many or even most human beings are non-central cases. When we study the nature of human beings (or the nature of anything) there is not only the question of which things are included in and which things are excluded from the category at the limits, but also which of those included are members of the category par excellence, and should be used as examples to shed light on the rest. One single counter-example suffices to show that a proposed explanation of the nature of something is mistaken at the limits. But no number of supposed counter-examples can show that a proposed paradigm is not a paradigm. That is because a paradigm or central case is simply the case that shows how the other cases—including those supposed counter-examples—ought to be. It is part of the very idea of a central case that there might be cases (even statistically preponderant cases) that do not exhibit all the features that make the central case a central case.

So much for the first source of doubt about (IM). Here is a second source. Every proposed moral norm calls for justification. Actually, every proposed norm, moral or otherwise, calls for justification. But with moral norms the stakes are particularly high. Moral norms are among those that stand or fall on their justification. If the norm does not turn out to be justified (ie if those to whom it applies are not justified in using it) then it is not a moral norm. Surely this is enough to vindicate the economist's insistence that we need further reasons for acting morally, and hence to rehabilitate the scorned question 'Why should I be moral?' For this question, surely, is only a generalization of the sensible question 'Why should I do that?', asked by someone who wants to hear the justification for a proposed moral norm. Or is it? On closer inspection, the questions are very different. Those who ask the second question are already caring about, and hence engaging with, morality, in defiance of the sceptical tenor of the first question. They are asking whether this is what morality really expects of them precisely because, if it does, there will be nowhere rationally to hide from the expectation. So they are affirming, rather than casting doubt on, (IM). The economist who points out that *homo economicus* does respond to moral norms whenever it is rational for him to do so may seem only to be asserting the innocent truth that moral norms stand or fall on their justifications. But that would be true only if the economist allowed moral justifications to count without insisting on the need for a further non-moral justification for rational beings to take an interest in the moral justification in question.

The third source of doubt about (IM) is that it seems to assimilate morality to invariant bodies of norms like the norms of logic. While there are arguably some timeless and placeless moral norms, to regard morality as wholly comprising these is to limit morality to too narrow a range of subject-matters. The norms that forbid race discrimination, for example, are sensitive to various historical and social contingencies, but it would be a mistake to conclude from this that race discrimination is not immoral. Yet doesn't (IM) entail that it is not? This challenge is closely related to the previous one and involves a similar misreading of (IM). (IM) has nothing to say about the content or scope of morality. It concerns only morality's hold over us as rational beings. Whatever subject-matters morality may regulate and with whatever sensitivity to changing circumstances, a rational being cannot but be concerned with its norms in all the cases to which those norms apply. To know a moral norm as moral, to put it another way, is to be committed to using it as a guide to action (albeit one that may be defeated by countervailing considerations). This is perfectly consistent with the idea that morality adapts itself to changing circumstances and thereby remains justified at all times and places. So, for example, some of the moral norms that apply in situations of dire emergency may be different from those that apply otherwise. Yet even in emergencies, moral norms— those moral norms that are applicable in the circumstances— remain rationally inescapable and (IM) continues to hold. There is no room for the response 'It's an emergency so morality doesn't apply' because morality, by its nature, already adapts itself to the emergency.[3]

---

[3] By the same token there is no room for David Gauthier's view, in his *Morals by Agreement* (Oxford 1986) at 84, that perfectly competitive markets, if any existed, would be a 'morally-free zone'. If under certain conditions there is no moral objection to pursuit of profit at another's expense, that is not because under

2. Norm and normativity

(IM) implicitly contrasts moral norms with at least some other norms, norms from which rational beings might in principle disengage, and hence with which they need a (further) reason to engage. Yet the very idea of such a norm is puzzling. If a norm is such that its existence doesn't already entail that we have reason enough to engage with it, in what sense is it a norm? The simple answer is that something is a norm if it can be used as a norm. And not everything that can be used as a norm is such that, rationally, one cannot but use it as a norm. As a rational being I can, for example, use Marcella Hazan's recipe for *ossobuco* or I can use Anna del Conte's recipe for *ossobuco*. I can also take no interest at all in any recipe for *ossobuco*, or indeed in any recipe at all. Engagement with the norms contained in cookery books is not inescapable for rational beings. And yet they are undoubtedly norms. The Hazan and del Conte recipes cannot be used except normatively; ie in guiding and appraising one's attempts to cook *ossobuco*. The same is true of, for example, the platinum-iridium bar that was once kept by the French Academy of Sciences to provide an authoritative measurement of one metre in space. The markings on this bar were normative; ie available for use as norms of measurement. Yet engagement with these markings was never inescapable for rational beings, who might always have decided to measure space in yards or cubits instead.

You may say that parallel examples exist in morality. For example, friends are subject to norms of friendship. But there is no rational requirement to have friends. Friendless people may be missing out on one of the good things in life, but so (you may say) are people who don't try Marcella Hazan's recipe for *ossobuco*, or even people who prefer yards to metres. So it seems that the norms of friendship are, in the relevant sense, escapable: they are not such that one cannot but use them as norms. Doesn't this falsify (IM)? Or at any rate isn't the only way to rescue (IM) in the face of this counter-example to deny, in desperation, that the norms of friendship are moral norms? Not quite. The supposed

---

those conditions morality does not apply, but because under those conditions morality permits what would otherwise be immorality.

resemblance here between the moral norms of friendship and the norms contained in Marcella Hazan's recipe for *ossobuco* is superficial and deceptive. The best way to see this is to think about the two sets of norms as they might be invoked by an observer or adviser. While preparing for a dinner party, let's suppose, Alan asks Beth, his partner, for advice concerning his (Alan's) friendship with Colin: 'Should I avoid mentioning this dinner party to Colin in case he is hurt at not having been invited?' Never mind what Beth replies. The point that matters here is that if Beth regards her reply as dictated by a moral norm of friendship, or indeed any other moral norm, then she cannot but be committed to this norm as a guide to Alan's action (and to her own action of judging Alan's actions). She cannot intelligibly say: 'Morally you should certainly tell him, but I wouldn't give any credence to that norm if I were you.'[4] But things might be very different if, later in the same conversation, Alan asks Beth for advice concerning his (Alan's) culinary efforts. 'Should I put the meat in the oven now?', asks Alan. Beth may reply, citing a norm from the cookbook lying open on the table: 'According to Marcella Hazan, you should wait until the oven is at 180°C.' At this point Alan may intelligibly continue: 'So that's what I should do, right?' And Beth may intelligibly reply: 'No, I wouldn't give any credence to that norm if I were you. Hazan is wrong.' In other

---

[4] I mean she cannot intelligibly say this if she regards her reply as dictated by a genuine moral norm. I do not mean to deny that she could intelligibly say it to convey some other meaning. In particular, the word 'moral' and its cognates are sometimes used in scare-quotation marks (or in a special tone of voice, or with a capital letter, etc) to refer to some sectional moral outlook such as that of the bourgeoisie or one's parents or the Church or social convention, etc. In this parasitic usage a reference to 'morality' may be scathing and not at all committed. Consider, for example, Hans Kelsen's portrayal of 'moralities' as sectional normative systems in his *General Theory of Law and State* (trans Wedberg, New York 1945), 374–5. I find that many of my students follow Kelsen, putting scare-quotation marks (visible or invisible) around references to 'morality', and listing as 'moral' various norms that they clearly find ridiculous or worse. This is one of the tendencies that Bernard Williams rightly derides when he derides the modern reinvention of morality as a 'peculiar institution' in *Ethics and the Limits of Philosophy* (London 1985). Unfortunately, Williams shows little backbone in the face of this tendency. He decides to rebrand (genuine) morality as 'ethics', which makes for more and worse confusion.

words it is open to Beth to cite a norm from the cookbook—unlike a moral norm—without being committed to this norm as a guide to Alan's, or anyone else's, action. She can cite it as a norm in what Joseph Raz usefully calls a *detached* way.[5]

Of course, Beth may also have her own norms for cooking *ossobuco*, to which she is committed. She may (for all we know) be a believer in the Anna del Conte recipe. So the suggestion is not that one can *only* relate to culinary norms in a detached way. The suggestion is that one can relate to culinary norms in either a committed or a detached way, whereas moral norms (norms that one recognizes to be moral norms) are among those that one cannot but relate to in a committed way. It is irrelevant to the last point that many moral norms apply only in certain situations (eg only between friends, only in emergencies) and that one can in principle avoid being in these situations. Moral norms are all inescapable in the sense relevant to (IM), even though there is clearly a different sense in which some of them remain escapable (in that one can avoid getting oneself into the situations in which one would inescapably be engaged with them). This is just another way to make the point I already made once: the contrast implicitly drawn in (IM) between norms with which a rational being is inescapably engaged and those from which she may instead be disengaged is not the same as the contrast between norms that apply invariantly (irrespective of circumstance) and those that have a narrower scope of application.

Nor is the contrast implicitly drawn in (IM) to be confused with the contrast between norms of obligation (or duty) and other norms. Norms vary in respect of their normative force. Some are obligation-imposing, some are permission-granting, some are power-conferring. It is tempting to say that the difference between the moral norms of friendship and the norms found in a Marcella Hazan recipe is that the former are (or include) obligation-imposing norms and the latter are (or do) not. This is a mistake.[6] Except where she makes space for variations, the norms in Marcella Hazan's recipe for *ossobuco* are straightforwardly obligatory. If one is to follow the recipe one

---

[5] Raz, 'Legal Validity' in his *The Authority of Law* (Oxford 1979), 153–7.

[6] For a recent example of this mistake see Sophie Delacroix, *Legal Norms and Normativity* (Oxford 2006), xi–xii.

must take these specified steps whether one likes it or not. It is no answer to say that one has no obligation to follow the recipe in the first place, or to keep following it. For it is equally true that one has no obligation to make friends, or to stay friends with them, and yet the norms of friendship clearly include obligation-imposing norms. Whether a norm is obligation-imposing does not depend on whether the activity or relationship it helps to structure is itself obligatory. Still less does it depend on whether the norm is such that engagement with it is rationally inescapable: one can recognize a norm as obligation-imposing without thinking it remotely worth using as a guide to action.

If the cookbook case does not convince you, consider this case instead. Barring special situations, nobody has an obligation to play *Monopoly*, nor (if they do play *Monopoly*) to assume the role of 'banker' in the game. Yet under the rules of *Monopoly*, whoever does assume the role of banker has to pay out £200 from the bank to each player whenever that player's token passes 'Go'. This is the banker's obligation. She must do it whether she likes it or not. In respect of normative force there is no difference between this norm of *Monopoly* and the norm of friendship according to which, when a friend is in trouble, one must give the friend's needs priority over the no less urgent needs of strangers. What strikes some as a difference in respect of normative force here is in fact the difference, identified by (IM), between moral norms and some other norms. Both norms are obligation-imposing, but it is possible to cite the *Monopoly* obligation in a detached way—while, for example, deriding the playing of *Monopoly* as a total waste of time ('as this daft obligation owed by the banker only goes to show!'). Whereas recognizing the obligation of friendship as an obligation of friendship (and hence a moral obligation) entails being committed to it as a guide to the action of those who have friends, and to the judgment of those who judge them.

H.L.A. Hart famously struggled, in *The Concept of Law*, to explain the nature of obligations in such a way that one could still regard a norm as obligation-imposing while remaining non-committal about whether to engage with it as a guide to action. Solving this problem was important to his explanation of the nature of law. For him it brought to a head the wider problem of the normativity of law. How, wondered Hart, is it possible that the law is made up of norms even though these norms do not exhibit the property picked out in (IM); ie even though it is not the case that engagement with legal norms is rationally inescapable? Hart's progress towards a solution of this problem was inhibited by his failure to keep apart two questions.[7] One is the question of whether it is possible to use a norm in the sense of *following* it without being committed to it as a guide to anyone's behaviour. The other is the question of whether it is possible to use a norm in the sense of *applying* it without being committed to it as a guide to anyone's behaviour. You may say that applying a norm is just another way of following it. But the case of Alan and Beth above shows that it need not be. Beth uses the norm from Marcella Hazan's cookbook *qua* norm-applier (she applies it to the case of Alan's *ossobuco*), but she does not use it *qua* norm-follower nor does she commit herself to its being so used by Alan or by anyone else. She applies it only to say that it should not be followed.

Hart failed to register this distinction in his famous and otherwise highly illuminating treatment of what he called the 'internal aspect' of rules.[8] The consequences for his attempt to explain law's normativity were severe. Thinking only of those who use legal norms by following them, he found it impossible to explain how a legal norm could be used except by those who were committed to it. He correctly stressed that this commitment on the part of legal norm-users—their 'internal point of view'—need not be a moral commitment. It could be a commitment out of fear, for the sake of a quiet life, to subvert the system from within, etc. In other words it could be the kind of half-hearted commitment that he often designated by the word 'acceptance'.[9] But however he rephrased this point the basic problem re-emerged that, when we focus on norm-use as norm-following, there is no room for legal norms to be used as norms, and hence to qualify as norms in the first place, except for one who is (to the relevant degree) committed to their use as a guide to action. From this we may be tempted to

---

[7] A failure previously pointed out by Neil MacCormick in *Legal Reasoning and Legal Theory* (Oxford 1978), 292.
[8] Hart, *The Concept of Law* (Oxford 1961), 55.
[9] Ibid 112–13, read with 198–9.

conclude that there is no normativity without commitment. If this is true, then (IM) can be generalized to all norms, including legal norms, the norms of games, the norms in recipes, etc. Hart knew full well that this was the wrong answer.[10] But having missed the distinction between the two modes of norm-use, Hart could not see where his handling of the problem had gone wrong.

The 'problem of normativity' with which Hart was struggling is the same puzzle with which we started this section: how can there be norms, engagement with which is not an inescapable part of rational, and hence human, nature? How can it be the case that grasping (for example) legal norms, *qua* legal norms, does not commit one to their use as guides to action? I will call this 'Hart's problem of normativity'. This is the very opposite of the 'problem of normativity' that is emphasized by some recent moral philosophers in the Kantian tradition, led by Christine Korsgaard.[11] These neo-Kantians wonder: 'How can there be norms, engagement with which is an inescapable part of rational, and hence human, nature? How can it be the case that merely grasping (for example) moral norms, *qua* moral norms, commits one to their use as a guide to action?' I will call this 'Korsgaard's problem of normativity'. One may be troubled by both of these problems of normativity. But in a way they are rival problems. One must treat one of the two problems of normativity as solved or dissolved in order to see the other as a problem. Hart's problem of normativity becomes a problem only when one tends to think of a norm as a kind of reason, and hence as inescapably engaging the attention of any rational being without further ado. Korsgaard's problem of normativity, by contrast, becomes a problem only when one thinks of a norm, not as a reason in itself, but as something which rational beings might or might not have a reason to use. I hope I have made my own position on this rivalry tolerably clear. I think of a norm as a kind of reason. So the real problem of normativity, for me, is Hart's problem of normativity: if a norm is such that its existence doesn't already entail that we have reason enough to engage

---

[10] See the entry in his diary reported by Nicola Lacey in *A Life of H.L.A. Hart: The Nightmare and the Noble Dream* (Oxford 2004), 228.
[11] See Christine Korsgaard, *The Sources of Normativity* (Cambridge 1996), 10–16.

with it, in what sense is it a norm? Fortunately there is a solution at hand. The simple solution, as I said, is that something is a norm if it can be used as a norm. But this simple solution conceals much complexity. For what does it mean to use a norm? The answer is that one can use something as a norm by applying it as a norm, and since one can apply some norms in a detached way (witness Beth), there can be norms, the existence of which does not entail that we have reason enough to engage with them.

3. Law and its central case

To repeat: even though his explanation of how this is possible failed, Hart believed that legal norms belong to the latter class of norms—the class of norms, the existence of which does not entail that we have reason enough to engage with them. He believed the 'escapable law thesis', or '(EL)' for short:

> (EL) Engagement with legal norms is not an inescapable part of rational, and hence human, nature.

Is (EL) true? You may think it is not true if, as some believe, law is necessary for human beings, or human societies, to flourish.[12] Of course, this proposal does not have much plausibility when applied to small groups of human beings living in isolated circumstances. At the very least it needs to be qualified to apply only to more complex civilizations and mobile populations. Perhaps, even its proponents may admit, there are relatively few contexts in which it applies with full stringency. But never mind that. In those contexts in which it does apply—where law is humanly necessary—isn't it the case that engagement with legal norms is humanly inescapable, contrary to (EL)?

Not so fast. True, the necessity to have law, if and when there is such a necessity, might sometimes be a reason for me to obey the law (eg where my breaking the law would contribute to law's breakdown). It might even yield, on occasions, a moral obligation for me to obey the law. But this consideration points in favour of

---

[12] I am thinking of the position taken by Tony Honoré in 'Must we Obey? Necessity as a Ground of Obligation', *Virginia Law Review* 67 (1981), 39.

(EL), not against it. The same is true, indeed, of all other arguments in support of the existence of a moral obligation to obey the law. After all, believers in the existence of a moral obligation to obey the law offer the moral obligation to obey the law as part of their answer to the question 'Why should I obey, or otherwise engage with, the law?' And that question is a good one precisely because law (unlike morality) is something that one needs (further) reasons to obey, or indeed to engage with. Legal norms answer to rationality. Unlike moral norms, they do not form an inescapable part of rationality. An unjustified moral norm is an oxymoron; an unjustified legal norm is always a live possibility. It follows that law is humanly escapable in the relevant sense (even if it is also humanly necessary).

So in this respect—in respect of the property picked out in (EL)—legal norms are unlike moral norms and like the norms of a game or a recipe. Their existence as norms leaves open the question of whether they (or some of them) are worth using as guides to action. Thus one may cite them as norms in a detached way. One may intelligibly say 'That's the law, but I wouldn't give it much credence if I were you', in much the same way that one might dismiss a recipe for *ossobuco* or a game of *Monopoly*.

Yet law is neither a recipe nor a game. There are numerous differences.[13] I will emphasize just one. Legal norms, unlike the norms of games or recipes, inevitably have moral consequences. To change the law is inevitably to change the position of some people in morally important ways. Advertisement of the law will cause some people to alter their daily pursuits. Enforcement of the law will put some people under stress or cost them money or freedom. Even if the law is not advertised or enforced, this itself raises moral issues about the behaviour of those responsible for advertising or enforcing it. Every legal issue, however superficially technical, is a moral issue, for its resolution inevitably has morally important consequences for someone. This is not true of every issue addressed in a cookbook or in the rules of a game. These are made morally important only by the addition of special circumstances (eg we are cooking for people with dangerous

---

[13] For some of the most important differences, see Raz, *Practical Reason and Norms* (London 1975), 150–4.

allergies or we are playing for the last place on the lifeboat). Another way to put this is to say that every legal norm, unlike every norm in a cookbook or in a game, is a putative (or purported or supposed) moral norm: it is a proposal, on the part of the law, for tackling and resolving one or more moral problems. If the legal norm does that job well, then in the process it is absorbed into morality. It becomes a moral norm as well as a legal one. And those who see it as such cannot but be committed to it as a guide to action: they cannot but be committed to it *qua* moral even though *qua* legal it was open to them to raise doubts about its hold over them.

John Finnis famously argues that understanding this feature of law is essential to understanding the nature of law. '[A]ctions, practices, etc.,' he writes, 'can be fully understood only by understanding their point, that is to say their objective.'[14] And unlike a game or recipe, he adds, law has, by its nature, a moral point or objective (viz. the solution of moral problems). This fact is said by Finnis to have the following implications:

> If there is a point of view in which legal obligation is treated as at least presumptively a moral obligation ... a viewpoint in which the establishment and maintenance of legal as distinct from discretionary or statistically customary order is regarded as a moral ideal ... then such a viewpoint will constitute the central case of the legal viewpoint. For only in such a viewpoint it is a matter of overriding importance that law as distinct from other forms of social order should come into being, and become an object of the theorists' description.[15]

One may wonder why Finnis contrasts law here with 'other forms of social order', and not with games or recipes. For surely all 'forms of social order' share law's predicament—their operations cannot but affect people in morally significant ways—and hence, by Finnis's logic, they must equally have as their central case the case in which they are morally successful? Yes indeed, and that is part of Finnis's message. Law's moral objective, he supposes, suffices to distinguish law from a game or a recipe. But it does not suffice to distinguish law from various non-legal ways

---

[14] Finnis, *Natural Law and Natural Rights* (Oxford 1980), 3.
[15] Ibid 14–25.

of organizing society. What suffices to distinguish law from various non-legal ways of organizing society is the distinctive (Finnis might be tempted to say 'superior') way in which law serves (when it does serve, as it does in its central case) the moral objective that it shares with them. To understand the nature of law we have to understand this distinctiveness in law's mode of service, and that, says Finnis, requires first an understanding of the moral objective that is being served. There is much to say about this last claim: about the claim that we need to know about law's objective(s) in order to understand law's distinctive mode of service to whatever objectives it may have. However, we are not concerned here with trying to understand law's distinctive mode of service.[16] Our interest is only in the thesis that law has by its nature a moral objective, and the thesis about law's central case that is said by Finnis to follow from it.

Strictly speaking, of course, Finnis does not speak of *law's* central case in the passage just quoted.[17] He speaks of the central case of the 'legal viewpoint'. That is because he is reacting to Hart's discussion of the 'internal point of view' of legal officials and other law-followers. He is reacting, first and foremost, to Hart's suggestion that those who accept the law as a guide to action may do so for reasons of many kinds, including non-moral as well as moral reasons. True enough, replies Finnis, but the law-follower who complies because he regards legal norms as morally binding is a more central case of a law-follower than is the one who does so for other reasons; eg out of fear for his job or wish to subvert the regime.[18] For the law-follower who complies because he regards legal norms as morally binding is the one who complies with law on law's own terms, as a solver of moral problems. By the same token, law that merits such compliance—morally successful law—is a more central case of law than law that does not. So it is a mistake for those studying the nature of law to be indifferent, in their selection of examples, as between moral and immoral legal systems or as between moral and immoral laws. In explaining what a legal system or a law is, says Finnis, it would be deeply misleading to present (say) the Nazi legal system or a

---

[16] See Ch 8.
[17] He does so later in the same book. Ibid at 276ff.   [18] Ibid 13–14.

South African apartheid law as one's basic illustration of law. Such legal systems and laws are, in a sense, not true to law's nature. They are 'deviant' cases of law.[19]

This claim that morally successful law is the central case of law is sometimes taken to mean that immoral law is only doubtfully or questionably law. It occupies a grey area, or sits on a borderline, between law and non-law.[20] Now there is no doubt that there are borderline cases of law, for there are borderline cases of everything. There is probably also a grey area between law and non-law, into which emerging and crumbling legal systems temporarily fall.[21] But Finnis cannot mean to consign immoral law to such an indeterminate status. For the failure of immoral law is, according to Finnis, a failure to be what law should be—a failure of law *qua* law—and that failure is troubling precisely because what we are dealing with is indeed a case of law. Recall the same point as it arose in connection with human nature. Human beings that lack characteristically human rational capacities, such as those in permanent vegetative states, are not non-human or doubtfully human. It is the fact that they are human beings that makes their lack of characteristically human rational capacities troubling. It is because they are indeed human beings that they ought to be as human beings ought to be, viz. rational beings. And likewise it is because immoral law is indeed law that it ought to be as law ought to be, viz. morally successful in whatever way counts as moral success for law.

Finnis has been known to say that he does not much care whether Nazi law or South African apartheid law is law, that the matter strikes him as philosophically inconsequential, that the important thing is to focus our attention on the central case of law.[22] But this is an unsustainable stance. For, as I said before, it is part of the very idea of a central case that there might be cases

---

[19] Ibid 14.

[20] Finnis encourages this reading at ibid 10, when (explaining the distinction between central and non-central cases) he quotes a remark about borderline cases from Raz's *Practical Reason and Norms*, above note 13, 150.

[21] A prominent theme of Hart's stylized discussion of the emergence of law in *The Concept of Law*, above note 8, Ch 5. See Ch 11 following.

[22] Finnis, 'On Reason and Authority in *Law's Empire*', *Law and Philosophy* 6 (1987), 357 at 376; similarly, 'Natural Law Theories' in Edward N. Zalta (ed),

(even statistically preponderant cases) that do not exhibit all the features that make the central case a central case. And it is possession of the *other* features, and hence membership of the class of things that is under investigation, that makes the limit cases eligible to be compared with the central case, and found wanting relative to the central case. So we need to ask what those other features are. Studying the central case of something can therefore only be part of the task of studying the nature of that thing. Finnis criticizes some 'legal positivists' for focusing all their attention on the limit cases of law at the expense of attention to the central case, and thereby offering incomplete theories of law.[23] But the criticism can be turned on its head and aimed back at Finnis himself. There can be nothing resembling a theory of law—a complete explanation of law's nature—that includes only treatment of law's central case and shows no parallel interest in what Raz calls 'the limits of law',[24] a topic raising no less intriguing philosophical questions.

But perhaps there is a question of priority as between the two topics. Does Finnis mean that we should begin our explanation of law's nature with an explanation of law's central case, and only then move out to the limit cases? One ambitious version of this proposal, associated with Ronald Dworkin, would have it that the point or objective of law, as realized in the central case, explains all the other defining features of law, including all those that obtain in the limit cases where the point or objective is not realized. How law is depends entirely on how it ought to be. Law is comprehensively tailored to its purpose.[25] As a general approach to the study of the nature of things, this is wildly implausible. Take human nature. Human beings are rational beings: they have a highly developed capacity to respond to reasons. They are also embodied beings: they have a human

---

The Stanford Encyclopaedia of Philosophy (Spring 2007 edition), available at <http://plato.stanford.edu/entries/natural-law-theories/> at §3.1.

[23] And in their incompleteness, 'incoherence': see 'The Incoherence of Legal Positivism', *Notre Dame Law Review* 75 (2000), 1597.

[24] Raz, 'Legal Principles and the Limits of Law', *Yale Law Review* 81 (1972), 823.

[25] Dworkin, *Law's Empire* (Cambridge, Mass. 1986), 92–5.

biology and a human physiognomy. They are embodied even in limit cases.[26] But their capacity to respond to reasons varies, and its most highly developed version marks the central case of humanity. Should we conclude that human embodiment is explained by human rationality? I see no reason to think so. Rationality and embodiment are relatively independent aspects of human nature. Even inasmuch as they are connected, there is no general explanatory priority as between them. It is not the case that the truth of 'human beings are embodied by nature' is explained by the truth of 'human beings are rational by nature', nor *vice versa*. Indeed these two propositions do not admit of explanation at all, in the sense that Dworkin has in mind. They admit of elucidation ('How do you mean?') but not justification ('Why is that the case?'). They are simply given by the concept of a human being, and there is no further question of why they are so given, in virtue of what they are so given, or such like.

The concept of law is no different. To present it as different, Dworkin has to present the concept of law as belonging to a special class of concepts (called 'interpretive concepts') of which it is true that the (other) criteria for the correct use of the concept answer to the point or objective of the thing of which it is the concept.[27] But a moment's thought shows that one already needs at least some other relatively independent criteria to identify the thing in question, such that one can begin to discuss *its* (that very

---

[26] I simplify. There are various limit cases. One may equally be a limit case of a human being in virtue of lacking a human physiognomy, even though one has a fully human rationality. The proper treatment to be accorded such a human being is the theme of the famous story of Joseph Merrick, played by John Hurt in David Lynch's 1980 film *The Elephant Man*, and sensitively discussed in Ashley Montagu, *The Elephant Man: A Study in Human Dignity* (London 1972). The case of a being that lacks a human biology but possesses both human rationality and human physiognomy is in a way more troubling. The proper treatment of such imaginary beings has been the subject of much science fiction. In the central case of humanity, human rationality, human physiognomy, human biology, and various other features converge. At the limits, one or more of them is lacking while others remain. Similar points can be made about the central and limit cases of law and legal system. The central case of law is not only morally successful but includes a division between officials and subjects, a system of courts, etc. There are various limit cases in which one or other of these features is lacking, while others remain.

[27] *Law's Empire*, above note 25, 410.

thing's) point or objective. Our conclusion should not be that these other criteria have explanatory priority over the study of law's point or objective.[28] Our conclusion should be that study of the nature of law, or indeed of the nature of anything, is like the mid-ocean reconstruction of Neurath's boat. As each aspect of the nature of law is elucidated, other aspects need to be held constant in the background to orientate the investigation; one can in principle begin one's investigations with any aspect of the nature of law so long as one does not attempt to open up everything else at the same time; one cannot dismantle the whole ship and rebuild it from one plank, as Dworkin's radical proposal would have us do.

There is, however, a more modest and more plausible version of the idea that we should begin our explanation of law's nature with an explanation of law's central case. If the central case of law is, as Finnis says, a case of law that is successful relative to a certain distinctively legal point or objective, then we need to understand what counts as successful law in order to understand law that fails. That is simply an application of the more general truth that one cannot understand failed endeavour except by understanding what it fails to be, viz. successful endeavour. One cannot understand what attempted murder is without first understanding what murder is. One cannot understand what it would be to fail in one's plan to buy a house without first understanding what counts as buying a house. Similarly, if law by its nature has a moral objective, one cannot understand what immoral law is without first understanding what morally successful law is. For if law has a moral point or objective, then immoral law is a failed attempt at morally successful law. Immoral law is, in that sense, a deviant case, and its study is logically parasitic on the study of its paradigmatic (morally successful) counterpart.[29]

---

[28] In an earlier version of Ch 2 above ('Legal Positivism: 5½ Myths', *American Journal of Jurisprudence* 46 (2001), 199 at 226) I said that the study of the conditions of legal validity has 'logical priority' over the study of law's point or objective. John Finnis rightly took me to task over this remark in 'Law and What I Truly Should Decide', *American Journal of Jurisprudence* 48 (2003), 107 at 129. I was much closer to the truth when I wrote, earlier in '5½ Myths', of these as 'relatively independent questions' (ibid 224). I have corrected the error in Ch 2 in this book.

[29] This reading bears out Finnis's claim (*Natural Law and Natural Rights*, above note 14, at 20) that what he calls the 'central case' is the same thing that Aristotle

If this is what Finnis means by insisting on the priority of the central case in the study of the nature of law, then our attention inevitably turns to the question of whether law does indeed have, by its nature, a moral point or objective. Now the point or objective of law can only be the point or objective of those human beings who represent the law.[30] Law cannot act apart from the acts of its human agents, viz. its officials. So we need to know whether the law's officials, acting *qua* officials, cannot but act with a moral point or objective. The obvious and fatal objection to this proposal, admitted by Finnis himself, is that some officials only pretend to act with a moral point or objective when they act on behalf of the law. They present the law as morally binding but their reasons for doing so are (say) nakedly self-interested or capricious.[31] They think of their position as a business opportunity or a game. It is no answer to say that this makes them deviant cases of legal officials. For Finnis's thesis that morally successful law is the central case of law is based on the claim that, even in the deviant cases, law still has a moral point or objective. Since there are admittedly some deviant cases where it does not have that objective, because those who represent it and give it its objective do not, Finnis's argument seems to fail at the first step. Or does it?

Not quite. For Finnis's line of thought, if we are interpreting it correctly, can readily be extended. Just as one needs to understand success in order to understand the corresponding failure, so one needs to understand a true proposition (ie what would count as its being true) in order to understand its false counterpart. Just as morally successful law is the central case of law with a moral point or objective, so law with a moral point or objective is the central case of law with a supposed or claimed moral point or objective. It follows that, even when we acknowledge the existence of the

explains at *Eudemian Ethics* 1236^{a}16–20, and which Aristotelian scholars have come to call 'focal meaning' (following G.E.L. Owen, 'Logic and Metaphysics in Some Earlier Works of Aristotle' in I. Düring and G.E.L. Owen (eds), *Aristotle and Plato in the Mid-Fourth Century* (Gothenburg 1960).)

[30] I discussed this constraint in more detail in 'Law's Aim in *Law's Empire*' in Scott Hershovitz (ed), *Exploring Law's Empire* (Oxford 2006) and in Chapter 5 above.

[31] *Natural Law and Natural Rights*, above note 14, at 13–14.

official who merely pretends to act with a moral objective, the central case of law remains the case of morally successful law. And it remains the case that the deviant case can only be understood as a deviation from the central case. We need to understand what counts as successful law in order to understand law that fails in the attempt, and we need to understand what is being attempted in order to understand the false claim to be attempting it. In this way morally successful law remains the model relative to which all other kinds of law fall to be understood. Finnis is right to insist, then, that law has a moral nature. We need to understand law's moral claim—the moral quality that it presents itself as having—in order to understand even the most immoral of laws.

Although I have presented this line of thought as a development of Finnis's position, it also has powerful echoes in the work of Hart and Raz. It was incipient (although no more) in Hart's early attempt to explain the defeasibility of the criteria for the correct use of certain concepts of interest to lawyers.[32] Hart rightly saw that a full analysis of some concepts (including the concept of law) requires sensitivity to negative as well as positive criteria. But he botched the important point that the negative criteria, or at least some of them, *qualify* rather than *deny* the application of the concept to a particular case, and do so by relegating that case to non-paradigmatic status: 'Yes, it's a law, but an immoral one'; 'Yes, she's a human being, but she's not fully in command of her faculties'; 'Yes, it was a promise, but it was extracted under duress'; and so forth. Raz develops the same line of thought in much greater detail as applied to law. He explains that law always claims legitimate authority, even though it does not always enjoy such authority. One cannot understand law without understanding this claim, which is a claim to be morally binding. Thus one cannot understand law that is not morally binding except as a deviation from the central case in which law is morally binding.[33] More generally, says Raz, one cannot understand detached normative statements except by understanding their committed counterparts, for detached normative statements are parasitic statements made

---

[32] Hart, 'The Ascription of Responsibility and Rights', *Proceedings of the Aristotelian Society* 49 (1948), 171 at 172–82.
[33] Raz, 'Legitimate Authority' in his *The Authority of Law*, above note 5, 8.

from the imagined point of view of one who is committed to them.[34] These thoughts are consonant with Finnis's. They show that any criticism that Finnis has to make of 'legal positivists' for their supposed reluctance to see law through the lens of its central case is exaggerated.[35] Both Hart and Raz espouse versions of the 'central case' approach and both can find room within that approach to recognize law's distinctively moral nature without abandoning their interest in the other features that all law (including the limit case of immoral law) has in common, some of which are independent of its moral nature (for they are also held in common with games, recipes, etc).

4. Laws as presumptively morally obligatory

Recall that the central case of the 'legal viewpoint', for Finnis, is the 'point of view in which legal obligation is treated as at least presumptively a moral obligation'. Why 'presumptively'? If law that is presumptively morally binding is a more central case of law than law that is not morally binding, then law that is morally binding without qualification is a more central case of law than law that is merely presumptively morally binding. The completely central case of law, to put it another way, is the case of law that is completely morally successful. It has precisely the moral implications that it purports to have: absolute legal obligations are absolute moral obligations, unconditional legal obligations are unconditional moral obligations, universal legal obligations are universal moral obligations, and so on. For an unqualified legal obligation to count as a qualified (merely presumptive) moral obligation represents, by these lights, a kind of failure, and hence a less than perfectly central case of law.

Which leads us to the next question: what is a 'presumptive' moral obligation anyway? Is it one that only appears to be a moral obligation, but may still turn out on closer inspection not to be a moral obligation at all? Or is it a moral obligation that is real enough, yet is capable of being overridden by countervailing considerations? The two ideas are often run together, but they

---

[34] Ibid 159.   [35] *Natural Law and Natural Rights*, above note 14, 357.

are not the same. An obligation that is merely apparent does not need to be, and cannot be, overridden by countervailing considerations, for there is, on closer inspection, nothing there to override.[36] Discussions of the 'prima facie moral obligation to obey the law' usually take 'prima facie' to mean 'overridable', rather than 'apparent', but it is not clear that Finnis follows suit. It is not clear, indeed, that Finnis believes in the logical possibility of overridable moral obligations. He may hold that where others see overridden moral obligations there are, on closer inspection, no moral obligations at all.[37]

Be that as it may: in what follows I will attempt to remain equivocal between the epistemic interpretation of 'presumptive' as apparent and the practical interpretation of 'presumptive' as over-ridable, for nothing turns here on the difference between the two. For simplicity's sake I will also ignore the doubts I have expressed about law's being, in its central case, presumptively morally obligatory rather than morally obligatory *tout court*.

So let's agree, with all quibbles set aside, that the central case of the 'legal viewpoint' is indeed the 'point of view in which legal obligation is treated as at least presumptively a moral obligation'. It is tempting to draw the conclusion, without further ado, that legal obligations *are* presumptively moral obligations. One can see what is tempting about this line of thought by returning to Hart's idea of 'defeasibility'. It is a short step from the thought that law is *defeasibly* morally binding to the thought that law is *presumptively* morally binding. A short step, but a fallacious one. The first of the two thoughts, as sketched in Section 3 above, is a thought about concepts.[38] Its implication is that a legal norm that is not also a

---

[36] John Searle, '*Prima Facie* Obligations' in J. Raz (ed), *Practical Reasoning* (Oxford 1978), 81.

[37] See Finnis, 'Some Professorial Fallacies about Rights', *Adelaide Law Review* 4 (1972), 377 at 387. What Finnis says on this page about rights must be applicable, *mutatis mutandis*, to the corresponding obligations.

[38] See G.F. Baker, 'Defeasibility and Meaning' in P.M.S. Hacker and J. Raz (eds), *Law, Morality, and Society* (Oxford 1977). I am not attempting to monopolize the word 'defeasible' to express a thought about concepts. It can also conveniently be used to express the thought that a certain reason is subject to being overridden by others. Hart himself confused these two thoughts from time to time in 'The Ascription of Responsibility and Rights', above note 32. I am merely

moral norm is not a central but a deviant case of law. But this tells us nothing about how many cases of law are central and how many are deviant, and nor does it suggest, as the second thought does, that one should be disposed to regard or treat each case of law that one encounters as a central case of law. It is perfectly compatible with the first thought to conclude that all or most of the law that exists in a given legal system, and indeed in the world, is deviant law, and should be treated with contempt, or should be treated with contempt unless special considerations apply. One can readily hold that law is morally binding in its central case while all the time maintaining epistemic and practical dispositions according to which law is rarely morally binding, and requires special considerations to make it so in particular contexts or particular cases. Law is defeasibly morally binding, in the conceptual sense of 'defeasibly', but it is not presumptively moral binding, in either the epistemic or the practical sense of 'presumptively'.

That law is defeasibly morally obligatory (ie that immoral law is law only in a deviant sense) is part of the nature of law, a conceptual truth. That law is presumptively morally obligatory (ie that we should be disposed to regard or treat whatever law we encounter as morally obligatory) is no part of law's nature. It is a proposition that needs to be defended by moral arguments. I am not suggesting that Finnis makes no moral arguments in favour of law's presumptive moral obligatoriness. On the contrary, he makes a moral argument at some length. To boil it down, he argues that law's distinctive mode of contribution to its moral objective lies in its co-ordination of the conduct of those whom it regulates, and that this co-ordinative contribution can be made only to the extent that legal norms are treated as morally binding by virtue of their membership in a legal system, even when they would not qualify as morally binding taken one at a time.[39] The success or failure of this argument is not our concern here. Our concern is with the extent to which it may garner accidental and

---

trying to avoid perpetuating this confusion by using 'defeasible' consistently and univocally to express a thought about concepts.

[39] Ibid 319 and nearby. The argument is elaborated further in Finnis's 'The Authority of Law in the Predicament of Contemporary Social Theory' in *Notre Dame Journal of Law, Ethics and Public Policy* 1 (1984), 115.

unwarranted support from Finnis's remarks about law's central case. On the one hand it is possible to read parts of Finnis's discussion of the moral obligation to obey the law as bearing on the moral obligation to obey the law *only in the central case of law*. But reading the discussion in this way makes it a foregone conclusion that there is a presumptive moral obligation to obey the law, for it is part of the very specification of the central case of law that a legal obligation in the central case is 'at least presumptively a moral obligation'. A moral argument to establish this is redundant. On the other hand a moral argument is essential if the discussion is read as a discussion of the moral obligation to obey the law more generally; ie not limited to law's central case, but including its deviant cases. Since Finnis does make a moral argument at length, and since he includes extensive discussion of cases in which the presumption of moral obligatoriness is displaced by the immorality of particular laws, we must assume that he means the discussion to be understood as a discussion of the latter topic; ie of law more generally, including its deviant cases. But some of his readers may understand it to be a discussion of the former topic, and so may allow themselves to be swayed in favour of Finnis's conclusion (that the law is presumptively morally obligatory) by the fact that, in its central case, law is presumptively morally obligatory by its very nature. In general, Finnis does not help to forestall this potential confusion. His tolerance of continuing and unresolved ambiguity in the meaning of the word 'law' means that it is extremely hard to keep track of whether, in particular contexts, he is speaking of the central case of law only or the whole gamut of law all the way out to the limit cases.

There is a corresponding, and correspondingly disorienting, toleration of ambiguity in Finnis's use of normative language more generally. At times he allows that there can be normativity that does not entail commitment on the part of the norm-user; ie that there can be norms, including norms of obligation, the existence of which does not entail that we have reason enough to engage with them.[40] On other occasions he seems to deny such

---

[40] This is the stance of the passage from *Natural Law and Natural Rights* quoted in the text at note 14 above, where even legal obligations that are not morally obligatory are nevertheless classified as obligations (without quotation marks).

things the standing of norms. They are merely 'regarded and treated and enforced' as norms, and their being regarded and treated and enforced as norms does not mean that they are norms.[41] This returns us to (EL). Does Finnis endorse it? Does he accept that laws which are not morally binding—and indeed which we have no reason to follow—are nevertheless norms? It seems clear to me that he needs to accept (EL) and the corresponding idea of normativity. For the idea that we have an obligation to obey the law (and hence the question of whether we do have such an obligation) makes sense only on the footing that the law is made up of norms, things which are capable of being obeyed or violated. Moreover it is only if laws are norms that it makes sense to hold them up for scrutiny as norms and to find them wanting ('deviant') if they are not good (morally acceptable) norms. Finnis clearly needs both of these ideas to make sense. It is open to him to say, with Hart and Raz, that the central case of a norm (and hence of normativity) is the case of a norm that we are justified in following. But he cannot, consistently with his own arguments, deny that there are other norms as well, disappointing though they may be.

5. Natural law for legal positivists

These remarks, if sound, show the affinity between Finnis's thesis according to which morally successful law is the central case of law and the central concerns of the 'legal positivist' tradition.[42] Legal positivists are those who have reminded us, time and again, that (EL) is true: that law is rationally escapable. There is always an intelligible question of whether one should obey the law, and that (the positivists rightly insist) is because law is a human creation and therefore exhibits the familiar and pervasive human capacity for moral error. By that route one could understand the main thrust of this paper as a defence of legal positivism.

---

[41] Finnis, 'Natural Law: the Classical Tradition' in Jules Coleman and Scott Shapiro (eds), *The Oxford Handbook of Jurisprudence and Philosophy of Law* (Oxford 2002), 1 at 23.

[42] An affinity which Finnis readily concedes in spite of his many other criticisms of the legal positivist tradition. See his 'The Truth in Legal Positivism' in R. George (ed), *The Autonomy of Law* (Oxford 1996).

In mounting this defence, nevertheless, I have espoused a number of doctrines (and tackled a number of issues) more often associated with the so-called 'natural law' tradition in jurisprudence. The name of that tradition is in various ways misleading. In particular it encourages a search for some elusive kind of naturalness in the existence of human laws and legal systems. There may be some sense in which human laws and legal systems are natural, but they are certainly not natural in the sense in which morality is natural. Morality is natural in the sense given by (IM): engagement with moral norms is an inescapable part of human nature. By this criterion, law is decidedly unnatural. As (EL) says, engagement with legal norms is *not* an inescapable part of human nature. Concerning legal norms the question always arises, as it does not concerning moral norms, of why I should obey them. Contrary to the impression given by its name, this is acknowledged and indeed emphasized in the natural law tradition. Natural law, in the tradition of that name, is not the same thing as human law. Natural law is the same thing as morality. It is the higher thing to which human law answers. We may regret that members of the tradition seem to feel a need to present morality as a kind of law, which it is not. For a start, morality is not a system (and is not made up of systems) and nor does it make claims, pursue aims, or have institutions or officials, all of which features are essential to the nature of law. Nevertheless, even as we resist the idea that morality is a kind of law, we should endorse the idea that morality is entirely natural. It binds us by our nature as human beings, while law binds us, to the extent that it does, only by the grace of morality.

Next I explored and endorsed the thesis, also associated with the natural law tradition, that law's answerability to morality is part of the very nature of law. I explained how the study of the nature of law can and must begin, in a certain sense, with the central case of law as morally successful law. For one must understand the non-central cases, the deviant cases, as deviations from that model of morally successful law. Nevertheless, I insisted, one must understand the deviant (or limit) cases too: the philosophically fruitful study of the nature of law is not exhausted by the study of law's central case. For law's other features, found in the limit cases, make the limit cases eligible to be compared with the central case, and found inadequate according to the standards captured in the central case. Inasmuch as those who belong to the natural law tradition have eschewed detailed philosophical work at the limits of law in favour of a predominant focus on law's central case, they have provided only a partial account of their subject, in much the same way that they have sometimes accused legal positivists of doing by labouring away at the limits of law without attending adequately to the moral success that marks law's central case.

Finally I turned my attention to the supposed moral obligation to obey the law. The natural law tradition has sometimes been associated with the view that there is such an obligation, at least presumptively. I have not rejected that view here. But I have warned against a possible inference from the view that the central case of law is the case of presumptively obligatory law to the view that law (more generally) is presumptively obligatory. This, I warned, is a fallacious move.

7
The Legality of Law

'Philosophy is not lexicography', as Joseph Raz reminds us.[1] An explanation of the nature of law is not an explanation of the meaning (let alone a definition) of the word 'law', nor of any of its cognates. We speak of laws of nature and laws of logic. We speak of legal moves in chess and illegal operations by computer programmes. There is nothing suspect or misleading about these usages. They are not, for example, mere figures of speech. Yet we should not expect a philosopher of law to account for them. It is no objection to an explanation of the nature of law that according to it the laws of logic are not laws, or that according to it a computer programme cannot act illegally. Whereas it is an objection to an explanation of the nature of law that according to it the laws of Sweden are not laws, or that according to it the US Government cannot act illegally. This shows that there are non-verbal criteria involved in settling what falls inside, and what falls outside, our enterprise as philosophers of law.

Nevertheless, some recent work in the philosophy of law has been insufficiently sensitive to ambiguities. In this chapter I will briefly compare and contrast some different senses of 'law' and 'legal', all of which must be accounted for in a complete explanation of the nature of law. Because of the complex relationships among these different senses, proposals like 'law is made up of laws' and 'all laws are legal' are not as tautologous as they look. Behind their simple truths they harbour complex untruths. In getting at the complexity I will mainly be drawing on H.L.A. Hart's work. Hart showed great sensitivity to the ambiguities I have in mind, and thereby avoided many confusions. No doubt this helps to explain why he is sometimes accused, unfairly, of confusing philosophy with lexicography.

---

[1] Raz, 'The Problem about the Nature of Law' in his *Ethics in the Public Domain* (rev ed, Oxford 1995), 198.

1. The genre and its artefacts

It was once thought—notably by Austin and Kelsen—that the best way to approach the question 'What is law?' is to begin with the more humble question 'What is *a* law?' Laws, it was thought, must have some properties in common with each other that distinguish them as laws even when they are taken in isolation from other laws. Thus, said Austin, a law is a command of the sovereign backed up by the threat of a sanction. No, said Kelsen, a law is a norm directing an official to exact a sanction under specified conditions. Of course, both agreed, laws relate to each other in interesting ways—notably, in adding up to legal *systems*—and to explain the nature of law one must explain not only what laws are but also these interesting ways they have of relating to each other. But already having an explanation of the nature of a law, it would be a good deal easier to explain how laws relate to each other. For Austin, a legal system is that set of laws issued by one and the same sovereign. For Kelsen it is the set of laws ultimately authorized by one and the same constitution. Either way, legal systems are sets of appropriately related laws, the nature of laws having been independently explained.

In *The Concept of Law*, H.L.A Hart explored two difficulties with this traditional order of inquiry.[2] The first was also spotted by Kelsen.[3] All laws are legal norms but not all legal norms are laws. Laws are only those legal norms that are capable of being applied to a succession of different fact-situations. 'Tortfeasors are liable to pay reparative damages to those whom they tortiously injure' is a possible law. 'Jones is liable to pay Smith $50 in reparative damages', by contrast, is a possible legal norm but not a possible law. So legal systems are not simply systems of laws. They are systems of laws (or legal rules) and binding applications of those laws (or legal rulings).[4] Here Kelsen and Hart agreed. But they disagreed on a second and more important point. Kelsen defended the traditional order of inquiry thus:

---

[2] Oxford 1961.
[3] *General Theory of Law and State* (trans Wedburg, New York 1945), 37.
[4] *The Concept of Law*, above note 2, 94–5.

This dynamic concept differs from the concept of law defined as a coercive norm. According to this [dynamic] concept, law is something that is created by a certain process, and everything created this way is law. This dynamic concept, however, is only apparently a concept of law. It contains no answer to the question of what is the essence of law, what is the criterion by which law can be distinguished from other social norms. This dynamic concept furnishes an answer only to the question whether or not and why a certain norm belongs to a system of valid legal norms, forms a part of a certain legal order.[5]

Exposing the fallacy in Kelsen's thinking here, Hart showed how it is possible that legal norms have no 'essence', nothing that makes them distinctively legal, except that they are norms belonging to one legal system or another. And Hart argued, I think successfully, that this is not only possible but true. One needs to begin by asking what property or set of properties all legal systems have in common that distinguish them from non-legal systems. Only when armed with that information can one identify legal norms (including laws) as legal norms. One distinguishes laws and other legal norms as norms belonging to legal systems. *Pace* Kelsen, one does not distinguish legal systems as systems made up of laws and other legal norms.[6]

Hart himself emphasized various intriguing features as the distinguishing features of legal systems. Notably: (a) legal systems are systems of norms, not systems of (say) predictions, incentives, commands, or beliefs;[7] (b) the norms of any legal system are all made (whether accidentally or deliberately and whether by delegation or by inherent jurisdiction) by human agents acting individually or collectively (Hart calls them 'officials');[8] (c) each legal system contains a 'rule of recognition' that identifies its officials of inherent jurisdiction (of whom all other officials are delegates) and

---

[5] *General Theory of Law and State*, above note 3, 122.
[6] *The Concept of Law*, above note 2, 77ff.
[7] Ibid 79–88.
[8] Ibid 92–3. Note that Hart's espousal of 'soft' positivism (ibid 199) does not compromise this thesis. In Hart's view, the demerits of a norm can invalidate it legally if the rule of recognition so provides, without any further invalidating act. But invalidation is one thing and making is another. Hart gives no reason to think that the rule of recognition or any of the norms made under it is thereby exempt from the requirement of being made by someone.

specifies by which actions which of these officials of inherent jurisdiction can make legal norms;[9] (d) each legal system has some officials of inherent jurisdiction who at least sometimes make legal norms by applying other legal norms;[10] and (e) in each legal system the rule of recognition is a legal norm that is made by the norm-applying actions of these latter officials, insofar as they add up to a practice of treating certain agents (including themselves) as officials of inherent jurisdiction who make legal norms.[11]

This is not the end of Hart's list of features. He adds quite a few more. But features (a) to (e) are enough to illustrate the difference between Hart's views and those of Austin and Kelsen. For Hart, one knows that one is dealing with a legal norm only if one knows something about the norm taken on its own—that it possesses feature (b)—together with something about the normative system to which it belongs, which must possess features (c), (d), and (e). Kelsen had also noticed feature (c), or something like it, and hence had rejected the famous Austinian thesis that officials of inherent jurisdiction are not regulated by the legal system of which they are officials. Unfortunately, Kelsen relegated feature (c) to what he called the 'dynamic' aspect of law. He agreed with Austin that one can already identify legal norms as legal norms 'statically', ie without mentioning feature (c). Hart put them both right.

In spite of this disagreement, Hart shared with Austin and Kelsen a more elementary commitment that he never stopped to explore in any detail. He thought that 'law', the abstract noun, at least sometimes identifies a genre of artefacts, just like the abstract nouns 'sculpture' and 'poetry'. Thesis (b), to slightly narrower versions of which Austin and Kelsen also subscribed, has it that laws (plural) are artefacts. And Austin, Kelsen, and Hart all agreed that law is the genre to which these artefacts belong. But can we conversely assume that all the artefacts that belong to the genre law are laws, in much the same way that all the artefacts that belong to the genre sculpture are sculptures and all the artefacts that belong to the genre poetry are poems? No we

[9] Ibid 97–107.   [10] Ibid 98–9.   [11] Ibid.

cannot. And the most important difference is this. Having distinguished poems and sculptures, one distinguishes poetry books as books containing poems, and sculpture gardens as gardens containing sculptures. But, as Hart showed, things are different with law. One cannot begin by distinguishing laws and then distinguish legal systems afterwards as systems containing laws. One needs to distinguish legal systems in order to distinguish laws.

This has the following pay-off: whereas a sculpture garden, unlike the sculptures in it, does not belong to the genre sculpture, and a poetry book, unlike the poems in it, does not belong to genre poetry, both laws and legal systems belong to the genre law. Law, understood as a genre of artefacts, is a genre made up of systems of norms together with the norms that belong to those systems. Of course, Kelsen and Austin did not deny that legal systems belong to the genre law. They both agreed with Hart that all laws necessarily belong to legal systems. That is enough by itself to distinguish the relationship between laws and legal systems from the relationship between sculptures and sculpture gardens. But it is not enough to establish that legal systems and laws alike belong to the genre law. Hart's arguments establish that extra point. They establish that legal systems are the basic units of law, and laws are essential (but not the only) sub-units.

One may think of Hart's list of features (a) to (e), together with the others he mentions, as a set of proposed *criteria* for determining which artefacts belong to the genre law. In criterion (c), Hart claims that every legal system has a rule of recognition. Such a rule obviously sets further criteria, namely criteria for determining—in a particular system—who can make laws and how. Thinking of laws as sub-units of legal systems, it is tempting to think of these further criteria set by the rule of recognition as sub-criteria for determining which artefacts belong to the genre law. Criterion (c), the thinking goes, can on closer inspection be unpacked into sub-criteria $(c_1), (c_2) \ldots (c_n)$.

This is the rendition of Hart's position that Ronald Dworkin uses against him in *Law's Empire*.[12] In his earliest work Dworkin had launched his criticisms of Hart's work by focusing on

---

[12] Dworkin, *Law's Empire* (Cambridge, Mass. 1986).

criterion (b). Some legal norms, he had argued, exist solely by virtue of the moral support they provide for other legal norms, and so are not made by anyone. These supporting legal norms, dubbed 'principles', are not artefacts.[13] Dworkin originally mounted a critique of Hart's criterion (c) by relying on this inventive critique of criterion (b).[14] But by the time of *Law's Empire* Dworkin has refined his criticisms of criterion (c) so as to render them independent of his criticisms of criterion (b). We know that the two criticisms are now to be regarded as independent because in making his new case against criterion (c) Dworkin repeatedly relies on analogies between legal norms and works of art and literature. He does not deny that the latter are all of them artefacts with authors. On the contrary, he assumes that they are artefacts with authors.[15] What he denies is that the *meaning* of a work of art or literature can be settled by reference only to the actions of its author. And carrying the same point over to law, he denies that the meaning of legal norms can be settled by reference only to the actions of those who made them. This he takes to be fatal to Hart's proposed criterion (c) for determining what belongs to the genre law.

I believe that this argument against Hart's criterion (c) fails, because Hart's criterion (c) already allows that the meaning of a legal norm could depend on things other than the action of those who made it.[16] But our interest here is not in the success or failure of Dworkin's argument. Our interest is in the radical pay-off that Dworkin ascribes to it in *Law's Empire*. If there are at least some legal systems in which there are no such criteria as those laid down by Hart's rule of recognition, thinks Dworkin, then that has wider repercussions for Hart's enterprise. For it means that there are no criteria that 'supply the ... meaning' of the word 'law'.[17] Hart's attempt to enumerate such criteria—what I listed as (a) to (e) above—is therefore doomed. It is not enough, says Dworkin, for Hart to abandon criterion (c). He must abandon the search for criteria altogether.

---

[13] Dworkin, *Taking Rights Seriously* (London 1977), 40–1, 66.
[14] Ibid 43–4.   [15] *Law's Empire*, above note 12, 50.
[16] See Ch 2.   [17] *Law's Empire*, above note 12, 31.

Dworkin offers no argument to explain why he thinks this radical conclusion follows from the supposed error of Hart's criterion (c). Instead, he begins *Law's Empire* by simply merging the question of whether criterion (c) is correct with the question of whether there are any criteria such as those I labelled (a) to (e). He merges both into the single question: 'What are "the grounds of law"?'[18] He is wrong to do so. The question of whether there are criteria such as those provided by a rule of recognition is quite distinct from the question of whether there are criteria such as those I labelled (a) to (e). The criteria set by rules of recognition necessarily vary from legal system to legal system. So they cannot possibly be among the features that legal systems or legal norms have in common that distinguish them as belonging to the genre law. So they are not eligible to join the list (a) to (e). They cannot be thought of as sub-criteria (c_1), (c_2) ... (c_n). The misconception that they can comes of the sound thought that something that was not made by an official identified in the rule of recognition, or by some direct or indirect delegate of such an official, is not a legal norm. Since it is not a legal norm, and obviously it is not a legal system, surely it can't belong to the genre law? That is true but misleading. Because the genre law is made up of legal systems together with the norms that belong to them, there are two different possible explanations of why some artefact doesn't count as a legal norm. One possible explanation points to the non-fulfilment of one of the (universal) criteria for determining which artefacts belong to the genre. But a different possible explanation points to the non-fulfilment of any legal system's (parochial) criteria for a norm to be part of it.

Hart, in *The Concept of Law*, was interested only in the first class of explanations. He left the second class of explanations to lawyers (not quite anticipating the philosophical ingenuity that Dworkin would later bring to their aid). It is true that, by exploring or problematizing the parochial criteria, one might reasonably hope to show that Hart has one or more of the universal criteria wrong. One might hope to expose a parochial counter-example to Hart's supposedly universal criterion (b), or

---

[18] Ibid 4.

Hart's supposedly universal criterion (c), etc. This is what Dworkin quite reasonably set out to do in his early work. But his criticisms of some of Hart's proposed universal criteria do not even begin to suggest that there are no universal criteria. On the contrary: Dworkin's arguments by parochial counter-example depend for their success on there being such universal criteria. There can only be a counter-example to Hart's proposed criteria for determining what belongs to the genre law if there are rival criteria such that the counter-example meets them and therefore counts as an example of law, ie a legal artefact. If it does not count as a legal artefact, it obviously cannot be a counter-example to the proposed criterion for determining what counts as a legal artefact and so cannot serve to undermine the proposed criterion. A successful critique of Hart's criterion (c) therefore depends on abjuring a larger critique of Hart's whole enterprise in seeking criteria like (a) to (e).

As these remarks suggest, Dworkin had different concerns that only overlapped to a limited extent with Hart's. Dworkin was and remains much more of a lawyer than Hart. Lawyers are experts on *the* law, meaning the particular norms of a particular legal system (whether unique to that system or shared with some others). They study legal artefacts in all their parochial glory. Hart, by contrast, aimed to study law without its definite article, the genre to which such artefacts belong.[19] What Dworkin argued is that the identification of *the* law, in at least some legal systems, is more complicated than Hart's proposed universal criteria (b) and (c) seem to allow. If Dworkin is right that the complications are incompatible with one or more of Hart's proposed universal criteria for identifying law (without the definite article), then the offending criteria on Hart's list clearly have to be modified or replaced with others. Maybe Hart still didn't get his list of features (a) to (e) and so on quite right. But this is just the same kind of criticism that Hart directed at Kelsen and Austin, and Kelsen directed at Austin, and so on. It is not, as Dworkin fancifully maintains, a new 'interpretive' approach to the philosophy of law that casts doubt on the humble Austin–Kelsen–Hart

---

[19] John Finnis, 'Reason and Authority in Law's Empire', *Law and Philosophy* 6 (1987), 357 at 367ff.

enterprise of isolating the distinguishing features that artefacts of the genre law have in common by virtue of which they are artefacts of that genre and not of some other.

2. From genre to practice

In *Law's Empire* Dworkin obscures the important differences between questions about law and questions about *the* law. He relies on expressions that are ambiguous between the two to help him obscure these differences. But he also neglects another ambiguity to which Hart was highly attentive. The abstract noun 'law' can be used to refer to a practice as well as genre of artefacts. The abstract nouns 'poetry' and 'sculpture' have the same ambiguity. Sculpture is the genre to which sculptures belong but it is also (differently) what sculptors do. Law, likewise, is the genre to which legal systems and legal norms belong but it is also (differently) what lawyers and legal officials do. Dworkin does not respect the difference.[20] But it is an important difference. A practice is made up not of artefacts, but of actions and activities. Many practices are practices of engaging with a certain, often eponymous, genre of artefacts. Often the engagement is one of production. Sculpture is the practice of producing sculptures. With law, however, things are a bit more complicated. Law is not the practice of producing legal norms (law-making). It is the practice of *using* legal norms (law-applying). Yet its central and most distinctive activity is a combination of the two: the production of legal norms by the use of legal norms (law-making by law-applying).

Hart's explanation of law as a genre emphasizes this central activity, paving the way for an integrated explanation of both the genre and the practice. Recall that according to Hart's thesis (d), in every legal system there are officials of inherent jurisdiction who at least sometimes make legal norms by applying other legal norms. So far as modern municipal legal systems are concerned,

---

[20] See his discussion of interpretation in the arts (*Law's Empire*, above note 12, 55–65), where remarks about the interpretation of artistic practices are treated as applying without further argument to the interpretation of works of art, and *vice versa*.

the officials that Hart has in mind are mainly judges. And the ways that he imagines them making legal norms by applying other legal norms are two. We have already noticed them both.

(1) Officials sometimes make new legal norms by applying, as legal norms, other norms that would not have been legal norms but for those very actions of applying them. This, according to Hart's thesis (e), is the way that a rule of recognition is made and changed. In every legal system there is a legal norm designating certain agents as makers of legal norms. This norm is in turn made by an official practice of applying, as legal norms, norms made by the agents that it designates. Here one legal norm (the rule of recognition) is made by applying—usually as an accidental by-product of applying—other norms as legal norms (norms made by the agents designated in the rule of recognition).

(2) By contrast, officials sometimes make new legal norms by applying *existing* legal norms. The simplest and most everyday examples are those in which courts make legal rulings (legal norms applicable to one case only) by applying legal rules (legal norms applicable to a succession of cases). The ruling is always a new legal norm, even though the case is already regulated by the rule. Why? The making of the ruling has legal consequences: it changes the application of other (not yet mentioned) legal norms. Not until the ruling has been made in his favour, for example, can Smith lawfully enlist petty officials who will auction Jones's property, or attach Jones's earnings. This shows that the ruling is a legal norm even where it is merely a judicial application of the legal rule that already applies to the case.

In examples of type (2), but not examples of type (1), we find our first examples of legal *arguments*. In a legal argument, an existing legal norm is a major premise and a new legal norm is the conclusion. The legal arguments in everyday type (2) examples are, of course, very simple. They go something like this:

> Tortfeasors are liable to pay full reparative damages to those whom they tortiously injure;
> Jones tortiously injured Smith to the tune of $50;
> therefore, Jones is liable to pay Smith $50 in reparative damages.

Many legal arguments are a lot more complex than this. Even this one could be made a lot more complex. In the simple variant, we can imagine that the $50 quantification is agreed. But now let's suppose that Jones and Smith disagree about the quantification. In *Smith v Jones (No 2)* we can imagine Smith demanding $100, and we can imagine Jones offering, and the court accepting, the following counter-argument:

> Tortfeasors are liable to pay full reparative damages to those whom they tortiously injure;
> Jones tortiously injured Smith to the tune of $100;
> but the tort was also the breach of a contract between Jones and Smith;
> the contract provided for maximum reparative damages of $50 for any breach;
> contracts and the limits on damages they set are legally binding as between the parties to the contract;
> and it is unjust to let someone avoid a legally binding contractual limit on damages by instead suing the other contracting party in tort;
> therefore, Jones is liable to pay Smith only $50 in reparative damages.

In this argument, several additional norms are relied upon to justify a departure from the existing legal rule. Two of these norms (the norm which Jones breached when he breached his contract, and the norm in the contract providing for a maximum $50 damages for its breach) are legally recognized norms but not legal norms.[21] They are contractual norms that have legal effect thanks to the third additional norm, which is a legal norm giving legal effect to contractual norms. The fourth additional norm relied upon in the argument is a moral norm of justice.

We can imagine a legal system in which the idea of using the law of tort to circumvent the disadvantages of contractual terms has already been frowned upon and ruled against by some officials with the ability to make laws. In such a legal system the final additional norm in the argument might be an existing law. But in the legal system I have in mind here we are not yet at that stage.

---

[21] Raz, *Practical Reason and Norms* (London 1974), 152–4.

This is the first case in which this circumvention tactic or anything like it has been tried and the first time it has been considered a possibility by any legal official. The reason why this court frowns on it is not that the law already frowns on it, but simply *that it is unjust*, never mind what the law already says. Of course, this court may be one with the legal power not only to depart from existing legal rules in its rulings, but also to make new legal rules by doing so. In which case, future courts inherit a new legal rule, something like: tortfeasors are liable to pay full reparative damages to those whom they tortiously injure, except where the tort is also a breach of contract and awarding full reparative damages for the tort would allow their recipient to circumvent a legally binding contractual limit on damages for the breach of contract. The ruling in *Smith* v *Jones (No 2)* is the application of such a rule, but it is not a legal rule until that ruling makes it so by applying it as a legal rule.

In this explanation I have taken for granted Hart's thesis (b): that the norms of legal systems are all made by human agents. From this it follows that a moral norm, such as a norm of justice, does not become a legal norm until it is made into a legal norm by a human agent, such as a court. What does not follow is that an argument relying on such a norm is not a legal argument. It is a legal argument if it is an argument about what to do (eg what ruling to make) in which at least some legal norms figure among the major premises. In our argument, there are two such legal norms: the legal norm that tortfeasors are to pay full reparative damages to those whom they tortiously injure, and the legal norm that contracts and the limits on damages they set are legally binding as between the parties to the contract. The moral norm of justice is called upon to help resolve a local conflict between these two legal norms. It is a legal argument because only the question of how to apply the two norms—and in particular which of them to depart from—makes the moral norm argumentatively relevant. Without the legal norms that make it argumentatively relevant the moral norm that makes it unjust to let someone avoid a legally binding contractual limit on damages by instead suing the other contracting party in tort would be entirely irrelevant to whether Smith should receive $100, or $50, or anything at all from Jones. That is why the argument remains a legal one even though not all of the norms that figure in its premises are legal norms. Not all sound legal arguments show that a certain legal ruling is required by existing legal norms. So being committed to Hart's thesis (b) does not commit one to the view that legal argument is non-moral argument.[22]

Should we think of the role of moral norms in legal arguments as akin to the role of contractual norms in legal arguments? Should we suppose that moral norms of justice are relevant to a legal argument like that in *Smith* v *Jones (No 2)* only because of some (undisclosed) legal norm according to which moral norms, or moral norms of justice, are legally binding or at any rate admissible in legal argument? Of course not. This turns the world upside down. The main puzzle about law, as a practice, is not the problem of how legal practitioners, including judges, come to be *legally* permitted or required to apply *moral* norms. It is the problem of how legal practitioners come to be *morally* permitted or required to apply *legal* norms. Legal practitioners, including judges, should act morally in their work for the same reason that doctors and soldiers should: because their work affects people's lives in morally significant ways. There is no further problem of why they should act morally. Whereas there is a further problem—a moral problem—of why they should defer to legal norms when they do so.

In *The Concept of Law*, Hart tried to answer this question by arguing that rule-following—and hence the resort to laws—has some generalized trace of moral value independent of whether the rules in question are (otherwise) morally acceptable, lending the same generalized trace of moral value to the law-applying work of lawyers and judges as such.[23] I think this was a mistake. There is no such value. Any generalized allegiance that legal practitioners owe to the legal norms of the system in which they practice is normally owed to the moral bindingness of their oaths and undertakings, their contracts with their clients, and other voluntary and semi-voluntary incidents of their profession. By and large these oaths, etc, do not bind lawyers only to apply the

---

[22] Raz, 'Legal Rights' and 'On the Autonomy of Legal Reasoning', both in his *Ethics in the Public Domain*, above note 1.
[23] *The Concept of Law*, above note 2, 202.

existing law. By and large they bind them to do much more complicated things, including making legal arguments, advising on the use of legal arguments, making rulings on the basis of legal arguments, etc. Legal arguments are arguments in which existing legal norms are used to create (or to advocate or defend the creation of) new legal norms, either rulings or rules, and such arguments often need moral premises, whether or not the legal norms themselves authorize such a resort to moral premises.

There is another lesson here apart from the lesson about legal argument. Contrary to what Dworkin assumed in his earliest critique of Hart's work, not all the norms of legal practice—the norms that apply to legal practitioners because they are legal practitioners—are legal norms.[24] They cannot possibly be. The norms of legal practice must also include moral norms governing the relationships that legal practitioners have, as legal practitioners, with the legal norms that they make and apply. The practice of law therefore extends its normative horizons in at least three ways beyond the genre of law and its legal artefacts. First, legal norms often require or permit the application of non-legal norms (norms made by non-officials), such as norms created in contracts or conveyances. Second, even when legal norms are silent on the matter, sound legal arguments often involve the application of non-legal as well as legal norms, and in particular the application of moral norms which are made relevant just by virtue of the fact that legal arguments affect people in morally significant ways. Finally, legal practitioners are bound by the moral norms of their professions which regulate, among other things, how legal and moral norms should be treated in their work, including their legal arguments.

3. Legality as an ideal

That there are moral ideals of legal practice is already entailed by the fact that there are moral norms governing its conduct. The moral ideals in question are ideals of conformity with the relevant moral norms. Some of these moral norms are, of course, the same

---

[24] Cf *Taking Rights Seriously*, above note 13, 35.

moral norms that apply to everyone. But others are special moral norms that apply only to legal practitioners, or to certain groups of legal practitioners, such as judges. These in turn can be subdivided into those that are tied to a particular legal system or legal tradition (eg those that come of a certain judicial oath or professional code of conduct), and those, subjection to which comes of the very nature of the job, such that a beginner who doesn't grasp the norms doesn't grasp what line of work it is she is launching herself into. An example of the latter kind of norm—what we could call a constitutive professional norm—is the norm that judges should put norms of justice ahead of other moral norms (such as those of kindness or prudence) in their applications of legal norms. Out of such constitutive professional norms, stylized universal ideals of the great judge, or great lawyer, can be constructed.

As well as moral ideals for law as a practice, there are moral ideals for laws and legal systems—for artefacts of the genre law. Of course, strictly speaking it is not the artefacts that are regulated by the moral norms that constitute these ideals. Artefacts are not directly regulated by moral norms; moral norms regulate actions and activities. So the moral norms that regulate laws and legal systems as artefacts strictly speaking regulate the actions of certain agents, namely the officials who make or contribute to the making of the artefacts. This may make it tempting to think that these norms are the same moral norms that regulate the practice of law. But they are not. Firstly, not all legal officials need be legal practitioners, nor *vice versa* (even though judges are both). Secondly, and more importantly, the moral ideals for laws and legal systems regulate the actions of law-making officials not only according to how they make legal norms, but also according to what legal norms they make. It is common to confuse the two. A common error is to think, for example, that since judges should put norms of justice ahead of other moral norms in their applications of legal norms (this is a constitutive moral norm of judicial practice) it follows that laws and legal systems should be just above all. But that does not follow at all. It could be a *disadvantage* of judge-dominated legal systems that the more morally upstanding the activities of the judges as law-appliers, the more morally skewed the laws of the system. The judges, whose law-applying activities ought to be just above all, in the process skew *laws* towards being just above all, when as laws it is no less important that they be kind, prudent, etc.

I give away my own view here, about which I have plenty more to say.[25] It is not the case that laws and legal systems should be just above all. Whereas judges should first and foremost administer justice, law-makers should not give priority to norms of justice over other moral norms (those of kindness, prudence, etc) in determining what laws to make. This often puts judges in situations of moral conflict: they would often be making a rule that is all things considered bad (it is just, but unkind, imprudent, etc) by making a good (just) ruling.

There is a long tradition—of which Dworkin is the most prominent contemporary representative—of trying to carve out a distinct ideal of legality as an ideal comprised of moral norms to which legal systems should conform above all others.[26] But there are no such moral norms. Law answers to all moral norms in proportion to their ordinary moral importance. What do exist are *additional* moral norms that laws and legal systems should conform to only because they are laws and legal systems, norms which add up to constitute a distinctive ideal of legality, also known as the rule of law. They are norms requiring that laws be made clear, prospective, open, general, etc. These norms do not take any priority over the many other non-specialized moral norms by which laws and legal systems may be judged. There is no reason to think that laws and legal systems should live up to the ideal of legality—should be clear, open, prospective, etc—above all else. Nevertheless laws and legal systems should live up to this ideal of legality *inter alia*, in a way that other arrangements need not. It is no bad reflection on me as a friend that I do not announce or clarify the rules of our friendship. On the contrary, it would normally be a bad reflection on me as your friend, or at least a sign that something has gone wrong in our friendship, if I did. But it *is* a bad reflection on me as a law-maker that the legal norms I make

---

[25] See Ch 10 for a full account.

[26] Dworkin's originally calls his ideal 'integrity' (*Law's Empire*, above note 12, Ch 6) but he later spells out, if it was not clear already, that this is his rendition of the ideal of legality: 'Hart's Postscript and the Character of Political Philosophy' *Oxford Journal of Legal Studies* 24 (2004), 1 at 29ff.

are not announced or clarified to those whose actions they purport to regulate. It is a bad reflection because the various functions that legal norms exist to serve, which serve to justify their existence, are by and large better served to the extent that those whose actions the legal norms purport to regulate are able to resort to those legal norms for guidance in advance. It is a *morally* bad reflection because legal norms typically have morally significant implications for those whose actions they purport to regulate, and being able to resort to these norms for guidance in advance typically enables these people to control the implications (normally, by avoiding actions that would fall foul of the norms). This is not the same mistaken claim that Hart made when he claimed that rules by their very nature have some residual moral value in virtue of their generality. The ideal of legality regulates rulings as well as rules, and it is an ideal that rules as well as rulings can fail to live up to. Norms may be genuine rules (susceptible of application to more than one case) and yet lack the rule-of-law qualities of openness, clarity, certainty, prospectivity, and even (all but the most trivial and morally unredeeming) generality.[27]

This is not the place for a study or defence of the ideal of the rule of law.[28] It is, however, the place to observe that the existence of this ideal makes fully intelligible the superficially oxymoronic proposition that some laws are illegal. They are, of course, laws—artefacts of the genre law—and in that respect they are necessarily legal. But they may still fail to live up to the moral ideal of legality that artefacts of that genre should by their nature live up to. Sensitive as ever to ambiguity, Hart brought this point out very vividly in a neglected passage towards the end of *The Concept of Law*.[29] He claimed that there are two concepts of law, captured in many European languages by distinct words: '*lex*', '*Gesetz*', '*loi*', and '*legge*' (capturing the genre that he had been trying to explain in the rest of the book), and '*ius*', '*Recht*', '*droit*', '*diritto*' (capturing a 'narrower' genre, the genre of law that lives up to whatever moral ideal law should live up to). One may doubt whether Hart's foreign-language lexicography is up to scratch here. But as he himself says, that is not the point;

---

[27] See Ch 2.   [28] See Ch 8 for a study (with only hints of defence).
[29] *The Concept of Law*, above note 2, 202ff.

philosophy, after all, is not lexicography. The point is that, however the distinction is marked in language, there is law and then there is *legal* law. Should we say, with Hart himself, that 'legal law'—law that lives up to the ideal of legality—is a second *concept* of law? Probably that is too dramatic, drawing us into orthogonal debates about the individuation of concepts. Perhaps it is better to say that there are specialized moral norms that are partly constitutive of law as a genre. Anyone who hasn't picked up that legal norms ought to be open, prospective, clear, etc hasn't fully understood the genre. For they haven't understood what Lon Fuller aptly called 'the inner morality of law',[30] a phrase which Hart himself endorsed as suitable to convey this point, and as marking a necessary connection between law and morality that he too could readily accept.[31]

---

[30] Lon Fuller, *The Morality of Law* (New Haven 1964), Ch 2.
[31] *The Concept of Law,* above note 2, 202.

8
The Supposed Formality of the Rule of Law

1. The internal morality of law

General, open, prospective, clear, consistent, stable, capable of being obeyed, and upheld by officials. So must the laws of a legal system be, according to Lon Fuller, if the system is to live up to the ideal known as the rule of law.[1] Of course, as Fuller well knows, there is more to the ideal of the rule of law than just these eight desiderata. As its name suggests, the ideal of the rule of law is the ideal according to which it is the law that rules. In its widest interpretation it is the ideal according to which people, including but not limited to officials, are to use the law for guidance and thereby to avoid breaking it. Fuller's eight desiderata tell us only what, in his view, the law itself must be like if this state of affairs is to obtain. Obviously, the law can't do all the work in securing the rule of law, interpreted in this wide way. The rest of us must also do our bit by using the law when it is available for use.

Fuller's main interest, however, was in the law's contribution to maintaining the rule of law. For this reason among others he generally spoke, not of the eight desiderata of the rule of law, but of the eight desiderata of the 'internal morality of law'.[2] He included the word 'internal' (or sometimes 'inner')[3] to make clear that law is not exempt from the rest of morality (which he sometimes called 'external morality').[4] His point was always that, in addition to doing the right thing by the ordinary moral standards that apply to it, the law has some distinctive or specialized moral work of its own to do under the heading of the rule of law. Law can fail in many ways, and failing to live up to the desiderata of the rule of law is only the most distinctive (law-specific) way it has

---

[1] Fuller, *The Morality of Law* (revised ed, New Haven 1969), 46–91. (In this chapter, abbreviated *ML*.)
[2] *ML*, 4.   [3] eg *ML*, 43 and 154.   [4] eg *ML*, 44 and 153.

of failing. It is not necessarily the most important (serious, immoral, iniquitous) way of doing so.[5]

Fuller's interpretation of the ideal of the rule of law (as it applies to the law) belongs to a family of interpretations that have sometimes been described as 'legalistic'.[6] But what should an interpretation of the rule of law (aka the ideal of legality) be if not legalistic? Legalistic as opposed to what? It is true, as Judith Shklar famously argued, that there is a pernicious ideology, 'legalism', which prevails in many law school classrooms, afflicts some lawyers and bureaucrats, and to some extent enters wider political culture.[7] Legalists overstate the importance of the rule of law (or of everyone's 'playing by the rules', as their deceptively chummy expression has it) as compared with other moral and political ideals. For some, indeed, the rule of law is the be-all-and-end-all of sound government, the one and only valid political ideal. That is, for example, Friedrich Hayek's view.[8] But it is not Fuller's. As already noted, Fuller holds the law answerable not only to law's internal morality but to the rest of morality as well. He says that often legal systems are 'condemned to steer a wavering middle course' between living up to the ideal of the rule of law and pursuing other moral ideals,[9] and that often, therefore, 'with respect to the demands of legality... the most we can expect from constitutions and courts is that they save us

---

[5] I am leaving aside here Fuller's much-discussed ambivalence on the subject of whether legal systems can fail, or radically fail, to live up to their inner morality. I will say only this: it is a necessary truth about standards (norms, principles, rules, rulings, etc) that whoever is subject to them can conceivably fail to live up to them. It follows that, to the extent that law cannot conceivably fail to be clear, open, prospective, general, etc, these are not standards for law, and can be no part of law's inner morality. It follows that, however he connects them (and connect them he should), Fuller cannot avoid having two distinct topics of discussion: (1) Which things are instances of law?; and (2) once we know that, what standards should we set for them *qua* law? In Section 3 below the connection between these two topics will loom large.

[6] Anton-Hermann Chroust, 'Law: Reason, Legalism, And The Judicial Process', *Ethics* 74 (1963), 1; N.W. Barber, 'Must Legalistic Conceptions of the Rule of Law Have a Social Dimension?', *Ratio Juris* 17 (2004), 474.

[7] Judith Shklar, *Legalism* (Cambridge, Mass. 1964).

[8] Friedrich Hayek, *Law, Legislation, and Liberty vol 2: The Mirage of Social Justice* (Chicago 1976), 1–5 (especially the endorsement of Harrington's remark at 2).

[9] *ML*, 44–5.

THE SUPPOSED FORMALITY OF THE RULE OF LAW 197

from the abyss'.[10] These are hardly the remarks of an uncompromising rule-of-law fanatic. Indeed, any legalism in the immediate neighbourhood seems to be mainly that of Fuller's critics, who think that his interpretation of the rule of law makes it too anaemic to do all the important work that has to be done by it. Who says that all this important work has to be done by the rule of law? Not Fuller. He would be quick to correct the legalistic misconception of those who think that the rule of law is so uniquely important that other ideals (democracy, respect for human rights, the eradication of poverty, 'life, liberty, and the pursuit of happiness,' solidarity, cultural diversity, etc) had better be part of it, or else be condemned to unimportance, at any rate to unimportance in the life and work of the law.

So 'legalistic' is a mysterious charge to lay against Fuller. A still more mysterious charge is that his interpretation of the rule of law is 'formal' or 'formalistic'. I call this a 'charge' because 'formalist' has become, in some parts of the legal academy, a crass playground insult.[11] Even among those who do not use it simply for name-calling, it has vaguely pejorative overtones. When Fuller himself uses the word 'formal', it is usually to denote what he regards as a surface feature of legal experience, a veneer which may need to be stripped away to arrive at the deeper truth.[12] Yet the word's use in characterizing the Fullerian interpretation of the rule of law, and others like it, is not confined to detractors. Although Fuller himself did not to the best of my knowledge characterize his interpretation of the ideal as a formal one, Joseph Raz, building consciously on Fuller's work,[13] says:

---

[10] ML, 44.

[11] I like to imagine Captain Haddock, in Hergé's *The Crab with the Golden Claws* (London 1958), shouting: 'Troglodyte! ectoplasm! formalist!' Like other playground insults, 'formalist' can also become a badge of pride to those who want to parade their sturdy resistance to fashion and peer pressure. Hence Ernest Wenrib's appropriation of the title 'formalism' to designate his own contrarian views on various topics, sold as a package deal (a 'comprehensive theoretical position': Weinrib, 'Why Legal Formalism?' in Robert George (ed), *Natural Law Theory* (Oxford 1992), 341 at 352). There is little to connect Weinrib's 'formalism' with any of the concerns of this chapter.

[12] *ML*, eg at 104, 116, 137, 142.

[13] Raz, 'The Rule of Law and its Virtue' in *The Authority of Law* (Oxford 1979), 218 n7.

'It is evident that this conception of the rule of law is a formal one.'[14] Jeremy Waldron says, in a sympathetic treatment, that Fuller emphasizes 'the formal side of the ideal'.[15] And a new attempt to revitalize and defend Fuller's thinking is to be entitled *Forms Liberate*, and promises to show how Fuller explores 'the ways in which the form of law introduces meaningful limits to lawgiving power'.[16] In what sense, we may wonder, is Fuller interested in the *form* of law, and what makes his interpretation of the ideal of the rule of law correspondingly a *formal* one?

2. Formality: two false starts

(a) Form v content. Here is the first part of Paul Craig's widely cited attempt to explain how a conception of the ideal of the rule of law qualifies as a formal one:

Formal conceptions of the rule of law address the manner in which the law was promulgated (was it by a properly authorised person, in a properly authorised manner, etc.); the clarity of the ensuing norm (was it sufficiently clear to guide an individual's conduct so as to enable a person to plan his or her life, etc.); and the temporal dimension of the enacted norm (was it prospective or retrospective, etc.). Formal conceptions of the rule of law do not however seek to pass judgment upon the actual content of the law itself.[17]

The topics that are said by Craig to be 'addressed' by a formal conception are a miscellany. What makes it qualify as a formal conception, it seems, is what the conception does *not* address, viz. 'the actual content of the law itself'. So now we want to know,

---

[14] Ibid 214.
[15] Waldron, 'The Concept and the Rule of Law', *Georgia Law Review* 43 (2008), 1 at 8.
[16] Kristen Rundle, *Forms Liberate: Reclaiming the Jurisprudence of Lon L Fuller* (Oxford 2012). The title of her book is lifted, explains Rundle, from a cryptic note found among Fuller's private papers.
[17] Paul Craig, 'Formal and Substantive Conceptions of the Rule of Law: an Analytical Framework', *Public Law* [1997], 467 at 467. I should say that Craig does not discuss Fuller's ideas directly, but only their development by Raz. What he says about Raz indicates, however, that he would regard Fuller's interpretation of the rule of law, perhaps *a fortiori*, as a formal one.

what does that mean? Does it simply mean 'the content of the law'? That seems a reasonable interpretation. The form of something is often quite naturally contrasted with its content. The content of a cake is one thing (sponge, jam, etc) and its form another (cylindrical, tiered, etc). The content of a book is one thing (jokes, short stories, etc) and its form (hardback, e-book, etc) is another. Likewise, presumably, there may be questions about the form of law as well as about its content. The problem is that in terms of this contrast there is not much that is 'formal' about Fuller's interpretation of the rule of law, or others (such as Raz's) that are built on it. For most of Fuller's desiderata of the rule of law *do* 'pass judgment' on the content of the law.

True, a law that goes unpromulgated (ie that is kept secret) need not have different content from its open counterpart. All else being equal, however, a law that it is impossible for people to obey needs to have its content changed if it is to become possible for people to obey it. Likewise, all else being equal, at least one of two mutually inconsistent laws needs to have its content changed if they are to be rendered consistent with each other. What is more, a retrospective law that regulates ϕing necessarily has different content from its prospective counterpart, in that it regulates ϕing in the past as well as ϕing in the future. Stability and generality in a law are also none other than stability and generality in that law's content; ie in what is regulated by it and what is not. A more general law regulating ϕing is one that regulates more cases of ϕing than its less general counterpart. A more stable law regulating ϕing is one that varies less over time, in respect of which cases of ϕing it regulates, than does its less stable counterpart. All of these Fullerian desiderata pass judgment on the content of the law, and indeed on nothing else.

Although it is a bit harder to see at first, even legal clarity is primarily a matter of the law's content. Lawyers thinking about clarity may be tempted to jump straight to the question of how the law is formulated; ie the linguistic clarity of legislation and other sources containing authoritative statements of the law. But as Fuller emphasizes, the desideratum of clarity that he has in mind is not, or not only, oriented towards linguistic clarity, nor only towards authoritative statements of the law. There may also be 'clear standards of decision [that] emerge from a case-by-case treatment of controversies as they arise'.[18] Here we have law that is made clear other than by being clearly stated. Quite possibly it is made without being stated at all. So the Fullerian question of clarity is not a question about clarity of legal language. Indeed it is not even the question of how clearly the legal standard is conveyed to those who are held subject to it (a question that might more naturally be treated under the heading of 'openness' rather than 'clarity'). No: the question is about the clarity of the standard itself. To what extent is it afflicted by indeterminacy, or in other words by what are often known as 'grey areas'?

Here we are right back at the law's content. A more determinate law that regulates φing has content different from that of a less determinate counterpart. When the law is more determinate, there are more cases of φing of which it is true that the law either does or does not regulate them, and fewer of which it is true that the law neither does nor does not regulate them.[19] Whether the greater determinacy in question is achieved by lucid drafting in legislation or by rigorous reasoning in leading cases or by an established 'body of...practice and...principles shared by a community'[20] of law-users: now *that* could naturally be described as a question of the law's 'form' (legislated law v case law v customary law) as opposed to its content. But the determinacy itself, which may well be constant from one form to the next, can only be determinacy in the law's content.

Where clarity is concerned, as with most of the other desiderata he lists, the content of the law is what Fuller's 'internal morality of law' mainly regulates. It has little to say about which form of law is the best choice for giving the law that content. That, says Fuller, 'depends on the nature of the problem' that a particular law exists to tackle.[21] So Hayek is no less wrong to think that the rule of law comprehensively favours case law and custom than Bentham is to think that it comprehensively

---

[18] *ML*, 65.

[19] On this understanding of 'simple indeterminacy', see Raz, 'Legal Reasons, Sources, and Gaps' in his *The Authority of Law*, above note 13, 72–4.

[20] *ML*, 64.

[21] *ML*, 64.

favours codification.[22] Legislation may be better for some problems, customary law better for others, and case law better for yet others. The rule of law has no general guidance to give regarding law's form. This puts paid to Craig's first attempt to explain what makes a Fullerian conception of the rule of law 'formal'.

Unless, maybe, when he speaks of 'the actual content of the law itself', Craig means something more than or other than 'the content of the law'? It is hard to know what else Craig may mean by this phrase. Unless, maybe, he means the following...

(b) Form v substance. Hot on the heels of his first attempt, Craig makes what appears to be a second attempt to differentiate 'formal' conceptions of the rule of law from the rest, which he now calls 'substantive' conceptions:

Those who espouse substantive conceptions of the rule of law... accept that the rule of law has the formal attributes mentioned above, but they wish to take the doctrine further. Certain substantive rights are said to be based on, or derived from, the rule of law.[23]

Once again, what counts as a 'formal conception' of the rule of law is explained negatively, by telling us what such a conception does not do. According to this new explanation, a formal conception is one that does not regard the rule of law as giving rise to 'substantive rights'. So now we need to know more about what that might mean. What is a 'substantive right', and is it true that Fuller's 'internal morality of law' doesn't confer any?

The word 'substantive' is notoriously unhelpful. It has many incompatible meanings. No less than the word 'formal', its use for classificatory purposes cries out for explanation. 'Substantive' as opposed to what? If the answer is 'substantive' as opposed to 'formal', we are back where we started, none the wiser. Craig does not, however, leave us so completely in the dark. Among lawyers, 'substantive' is usually contrasted with 'procedural', and Craig seems to want to preserve and deploy that contrast. Indeed

---

[22] Hayek, *Law, Legislation, and Liberty 1: Rules and Order* (Chicago 1973), 72ff; compare Bentham's views as reconstructed from manuscripts in Gerald J. Postema, *Bentham and the Common Law Tradition* (Oxford 1986), 267ff.

[23] Craig, 'Formal and Substantive Conceptions', above note 17, at 467.

he speaks at one point of 'procedure or form as opposed to substance', thereby giving the impression that 'formal', for him, is a synonym for 'procedural'.[24] If that is so, we can start to give some meaning to what he says. In legal thought a procedural rule (or right, requirement, etc) is one that regulates the steps that are taken to establish some conclusion, often the conclusion that another rule (or right, requirement, etc) applies. The latter rule then qualifies, relative to the former, as a 'substantive' rule.

The words 'relative to' are important here. The substance-procedure distinction, as used by lawyers, has a shifting baseline. In a lawsuit against the police (say, for unlawful imprisonment) the court and the parties are subject to all the usual procedural rules about the issuing of a claim, the advance disclosure of evidence, the right to be heard and represented, the calling and questioning of witnesses, and so forth. These regulate the steps that must be taken to establish whether the claimant was unlawfully imprisoned, which is the substantive question in the case. But of course that question may in turn resolve into a procedural one. Possibly the imprisonment was unlawful if and only if the police did not follow the proper procedures for the arrest, detention, and questioning of a suspect (with a view to determining whether to lay charges). The rules governing these police procedures are procedural rules, and yet they are also substantive rules relative to certain other procedural rules (viz. the ones governing how to sue for false imprisonment). This faces us with a preliminary challenge in applying Craig's distinction. Is the right to a fair trial, we might well ask, a 'substantive right' in the sense that he has in mind? There can be litigation about whether it has been violated, in which the rules that constitute the right are both procedurally and substantively in play. They regulate how the litigation is conducted but also provide the subject-matter of the litigation. The substantive question for trial, indeed, is whether there were procedural violations in other proceedings. So the rules (and rights) at issue in the case are simultaneously procedural and substantive.

Maybe this is not a very serious problem for Craig. It entails an extensive grey area in his distinction between 'substantive' and

---

[24] Ibid 485.

THE SUPPOSED FORMALITY OF THE RULE OF LAW 203

'formal/procedural'[25] conceptions of the rule of law, but that may well be consistent with, or even conducive to, his larger classificatory project, according to which there is a spectrum of possible interpretations of the rule of law arrayed from 'formal' to 'substantive'. More serious is the problem that (even allowing for grey areas) Fuller does not regard the rule of law as primarily, or even extensively, a procedural ideal.[26] Laws can be general, open, prospective, clear, consistent, stable, and capable of being obeyed irrespective, or largely irrespective, of the procedures for creating them, applying them, improving them, and enforcing them. Fuller's illustrations of his desiderata at work range freely across the law and amply illustrate this point. His objection to strict liability in his discussion of the 'obeyability' desideratum is a particularly sharp illustration. The objection is patently to strict liability itself and not to the procedures by which it is imposed.[27]

It is only when Fuller begins to discuss the final desideratum on his list—the one that I summarized at the outset by saying that the law must be 'upheld by officials'—that he begins to consider whether the ideal of the rule of law places any specifically procedural demands on the law. This desideratum, he says, is 'the most complex of all'.[28] It concerns 'preventing a discrepancy between the law as [promulgated] and the law as actually administered'.[29] We may include under it, he says,

> most of the elements of 'procedural due process' such as the right to representation by counsel and the right of cross-examining adverse witnesses. We may also include as being in part directed towards the

---

[25] Ibid 481.

[26] One procedural desideratum that Fuller conspicuously does *not* include on his list is the one mentioned by Craig, ibid 467, viz. that the law be made 'by a properly authorised person, in a properly authorised manner, etc'. Presumably Fuller leaves this off because, confused though he sometimes is between the conditions for something to be a law and the conditions for it to conform to the inner morality of law, even Fuller realizes that something that was not made 'by a properly authorised person, in a properly authorised manner, etc'. is not a law and hence is not subject to law's inner morality.

[27] ML, 74–8.

[28] ML, 81.

[29] ML, 81. Fuller says 'declared' but in view of his important reminder that not all law is legislated, I have substituted the wider 'promulgated'.

same objective habeas corpus and the right to appeal an adverse decision to a higher tribunal. Even the question of 'standing' to raise constitutional issues is relevant in this connection.[30]

One might wonder, as Raz does, whether Fuller is right to try and squeeze all of this into (or out of) his final desideratum, or whether instead it should be disaggregated and treated as a set of further desiderata to add to his list. But be that as it may, it shows as clearly as can be that Fuller's is not a 'formal' conception of the rule of law according to Craig's second criterion.

How does it show that? Because the procedural implications of the rule of law are, for Fuller, mainly implications of just the last of his eight desiderata. Since 'substantive' apparently means 'non-procedural', the other Fullerian desiderata must have primarily substantive implications, in Craig's sense. Of course, it does not quite follow that they ever give rise to 'substantive rights'. But it seems very likely that they do. Even though there is no right that there be no secret laws, probably there is a right, derived from the openness desideratum, not to be prosecuted, convicted, or punished under a secret law. And even though there is no right that there be no non-general laws, such as Bills of Attainder, almost certainly there is a right not to be on the receiving end of one. And even though there is no right that there be no strict liability offences, if Fuller is thinking straight there may very well be a right not to be held strictly liable.[31] In any event, there is nothing in Fuller's account to suggest that such 'substantive rights are [not] based on, or derived from, the rule of law'. So there is nothing to suggest that Fuller's interpretation of the rule of law, or others based on it, should be classified by Craig as 'formal', or towards the formal end of his spectrum. In fact, it is very hard to imagine anyone embracing a conception of the rule of law that is largely 'formal' according to Craig's second criterion of formality (any more that his first).

---

[30] *ML*, 81.

[31] I add 'if Fuller is thinking straight' because he seems to confuse the question of whether it is impossible to conform to a law with the question of whether a law is impossible to control whether one is conforming to it. In 'Legal Responsibility and Excuses' in his *Punishment and Responsibility* (Oxford 1968), 43–50 Hart runs (essentially) a version of Fuller's argument from which this confusion has been eradicated.

3. Not formal but modal

Here is something that Fuller himself says that may have helped to send Craig down this blind alley. Fuller says:

> As a convenient (though not wholly satisfactory) way of describing the distinction being taken [between the internal and external moralities of law] we may speak of a procedural, as distinguished from a substantive natural law. What I have called the internal morality of law is in this sense a procedural version of natural law, *though to avoid misunderstanding the word 'procedural' should be assigned a special and expanded sense so that it would include, for example, a substantive accord between official action and enacted law*. The term 'procedural' is, however, broadly appropriate as indicating that we are concerned, not with the substantive aims of legal rules, but with the ways in which a system of rules for governing human conduct must be constructed and administered if it is to be efficacious [*qua* system of rules].[32]

Let us leave aside the traps that Fuller sets by using the expression 'natural law' in connection with his ideas.[33] For present purposes the important trap, the one into which Craig falls, is the other one that Fuller sets. Fuller mentions the distinction between substance and procedure only to confirm, in his characteristically circumspect way, that this is not the distinction that interests him. What interests him is the distinction between ends and means, between the 'aims of legal rules' on the one hand, and how to go about serving those aims by the use of legal rules on the other. The word 'substantive' has to be put in front of 'aims of legal rules' only as a way of alerting us to the fact that the means–end distinction is another one with a shifting baseline. All means are capable of serving as subsidiary ends, as intermediate destinations on the way to our destination. That the law lives up to its internal morality may, of course, be treated as a subsidiary end, and in that sense an ideal for law. But Fuller is warning us (again) not to fall into the legalistic trap, not to mistake the subsidiary end for the

---

[32] *ML*, 96–7, emphasis added.
[33] As he says (*ML*, 97), it is pretty obscure what connection exists between his work and 'the natural law tradition', not least (I would add) because it is pretty obscure what unites the tradition itself. I have attempted to run through various possibilities in Ch 6 above.

end to which it is subsidiary, not to think that we need have no aims for legal systems other than that they conform to the rule of law. Law's inner morality is only the morality of *how*, not the morality of *why*. If there were no external morality applicable to law we wouldn't have anything worthwhile to do with law in the first place and there wouldn't be any intelligible role for an internal morality of law.

Knowing that this is how Fuller understands the internal morality of law (as governing the means, not the ends) helps us to interpret some of the elusive things he says about the very nature of law. Fuller says, quoting one of his own catchphrases, 'that law, viewed as a direction of purposive human effort, consists in "the enterprise of subjecting human conduct to the governance of rules"'.[34] This is rendered by some, and occasionally by Fuller himself, as the thesis that law has the defining purpose of subjecting human conduct to the governance of rules. But that may be an elliptical and uncharitable rendition. Fuller says that law is a *direction* of purposive human effort, and he does not commit himself on what the purpose or purposes towards which the effort is directed might be. When he does say, elsewhere, that his catchphrase is designed to capture law's 'modest and sober' defining purpose, he makes clear that it is a purpose subsidiary to 'objectives ... of the most diverse nature'.[35] No doubt he would want to include all the obvious candidates on any list of these diverse objectives that he might draw up: reducing undesirable behaviour, co-ordinating desirable behaviour, enabling people to give effect to their reasonable wishes, helping to resolve disputes, and so on. Clearly, however, 'subjecting human conduct to the governance of rules' does not, on any credible view, belong on the same list. 'Subjecting human conduct to the governance of rules' is, rather, the enterprise's way of serving whatever diverse purposes (ends, objectives) the enterprise may serve.

If that interpretation is right, Fuller joins Kelsen and Hart in thinking that law is a modal, as opposed to a functional, kind.[36]

---

[34] *ML*, 130.   [35] *ML*, 146.

[36] The terminology is Leslie Green's, from 'The Concept of Law Revisited' *Michigan Law Review* 94 (1996), 1687 at 1709.

THE SUPPOSED FORMALITY OF THE RULE OF LAW 207

That is not to say, obviously, that law has no functions. Of course it has functions; as Fuller's self-quotation implies, there is nothing to be said for 'subjecting human conduct to the governance of rules' unless one does it as a 'direction of purposive human effort'; ie as a means to some end. No, to say that law is a modal as opposed to functional kind is merely to say that law is not *distinguished* by its functions—by the purposes it is capable of serving.[37] It is distinguished rather by the distinctive means that it provides for serving whatever ends it serves. Law is what Kelsen memorably called a 'specific social technique'.[38]

Fuller's suggestion that law is the specific social technique of 'subjecting human conduct to the governance of rules' is, however, nowhere near specific enough (unless 'subjecting' or 'governance' bears some hidden technical meaning). Patently, not all rules are legal rules.[39] We nag our children to share their toys, to get to bed by bedtime, and to take turns with the chores ('You know the rules, kids!'). We publish recipe books, yoga videos, and checklists for successful dating ('Follow these six simple rules to keep your man/build your six-pack/make delicious desserts!'). We play games of poker, football, hide-and-seek, and ludo ('Let's play by the Texan/Australian/traditional rules today!'). We make New Year's resolutions to work less or get more exercise or cut down on chocolate ('Four days a week, that's my rule for 2012!'). We have our personal rules for organizing our computer files, for combining shoes with clothes or drinks with food, or for allocating household expenditure. Not every 'subjecting [of] human conduct to the governance of rules', not even every 'enterprise' of

---

[37] Notice that I understand a function of something to be a possible purpose of it, a purpose to which it could be put even if that was not the purpose for which it was made, and even if it was not made for any purpose at all. This is important in nuancing what Fuller says because not all law is made with a purpose (some is made accidentally) and, even when made with a purpose, not all law is later used to serve the purpose for which it was made.

[38] Hans Kelsen, 'The Law as a Specific Social Technique', *University of Chicago Law Review* 9 (1941), 75.

[39] Fuller notes this and relishes the implication that the inner morality of law is not only that of law, but of many other law-like normative systems besides: *ML*, 124–9. He may be right, but he should add that other law-like systems are subject to law's inner morality only to the extent that they are law-like. So we still need to know more exactly what law is.

doing so, is law. Law is not so much the specific social technique *of* subjecting human conduct to the governance of rules as a specific social technique *for* subjecting human conduct to the governance of rules.

That formulation helps us to see why some people might think of 'subjecting human conduct to the governance of rules' as the defining purpose of the legal enterprise. As the means to which law is a more specific means, it naturally invites re-description as an end. But like other subsidiary ends, it has to be pursued with an eye to whether it will help us reach the further ends to which it is subsidiary. No point in using law to implement rules, only to find that the rules we implement serve no further purpose. No point, analogously, in flying to LAX tomorrow if that still won't get me to Auckland in time for my lecture on Thursday. That I have just set off for LAX doesn't suggest that getting to LAX is anything other than a way of getting to Auckland. That we have, in law, a specific social technique for subjecting human conduct to the governance of rules likewise doesn't suggest that subjecting human conduct to the governance of rules is anything more than a technique available to serve some further purpose or purposes.

Fuller, to repeat, does not spell out all of the specifics of the specific social technique that is law. But he does take one or two of them for granted in his account of the internal morality of law. While there is (he rightly asserts) no legal system without rules, there is also (he rightly takes for granted) no legal system without *rulings*, meaning authoritative official decisions in particular cases that purport to be applications of the law's rules. Notice that the rulings need only *purport to be* applications of the law. Here we see one way in which there may arise (in Fuller's words) 'a discrepancy between the law as [promulgated] and the law as actually administered'.[40] The problem, I hasten to add, is not that of judges changing the rules, or creating new rules, in the process of applying them. Done right, as Fuller says, 'a case-by-case treatment of controversies as they arise', gradually developing a legal rule at the point of its application, is consistent with the

---

[40] ML, 81.

internal morality of law.[41] No, the Fullerian discrepancy problem is that of judges and other officials, such as police officers and tax inspectors, not applying the legal rules at all (even those rules that they lawfully make or could make in the process) when they make their rulings. This makes their behaviour contrary to law. Yet it does not follow that they stop being officials of the law when they engage in it, and it does not follow that their decisions are not legally binding in the case at hand.[42] Thus they may still make valid legal rulings, albeit contrary to the applicable legal rules.[43] Fuller describes the problem, aptly enough, as that of (official) 'fidelity to law'[44] but his characterization of law as 'the enterprise of subjecting human conduct to the governance of rules' does nothing to disclose how the nature of law sows the seeds of the problem. We can see that only when we see that law is, more specifically, the enterprise of subjecting human conduct to the governance of rules *and rulings*. Law exists only when there are law-applying officials with the authority to rule on particular matters in purported application of the legal rules.

If this is right, then the internal morality of law is not simply, as Fuller sometimes presents it, the internal morality of rules.[45] It is not enough that the law's rules be clear, open, prospective, etc.

---

[41] *ML*, 65.

[42] As Hart explains, the question of the validity of what people (including officials) do can and often does come apart from the question of its lawfulness. A court may well have the legal power to make rulings that it also has a legal duty not to make, or no legal permission to make. The long-standing debate in administrative law over whether there can be errors of law that are not jurisdictional errors is a debate about this point. Answer: yes there can. Hart, *The Concept of Law* (Oxford 1961), 68. The problem can also be unpacked in the way explained by Joseph Raz in 'Legal Rights' in Raz, *Ethics in the Public Domain* (rev ed, Oxford 1995): there can be content-independent justification for legal statements even when content-dependent ones are lacking.

[43] Indeed, they qualify as having authority in law-application precisely because at least some of their rulings have legal effect even if erroneous in law. See Raz, 'The Argument from Justice, or How Not to Reply to Legal Positivism' in George Pavlakos (ed), *Law, Rights, and Discourse: Themes from the Legal Philosophy of Robert Alexy* (Oxford 2007), 17 at 32.

[44] Fuller, 'Positivism and Fidelity to Law: a Reply to Professor Hart', *Harvard Law Review* 71 (1958), 630.

[45] Or as Leslie Green, puts it 'the rule of law is not merely the rule of rules, it is the excellence of a particular mode of governance by rules'. See his 'Globalization,

Sound institutional arrangements for upholding the rules at the point of their purported official application must also be in place. This thought is what lies behind Raz's well-known development of Fuller's ideas, and especially his more careful unpacking, enumeration, and foregrounding of so much that is crammed awkwardly and cursorily into Fuller's final desideratum (what I called the 'upheld by officials' desideratum).[46]

The rule of law, as Raz explains, does not only require clear, open, stable, and prospective general rules that are capable of being followed. It also requires a robustly independent judiciary that does not shy away from decision, together with affordable and easy access to the courts for plaintiffs and defendants alike, effective provision for judicial review of executive action as well as appeals from lower courts, dispassionate professionalism among police, prosecutors, and other enforcement officials, and a strong culture of respect for procedural propriety (*audi alterem partem*, *nemo in sua causa iudex*, the giving of reasons for decisions, etc) across the executive and judicial branches alike. And under the heading of 'generality' it requires not only that the law regulate by rules capable of regulating an indeterminate class of people and cases, but also that rulings against particular people in particular cases be made according to those rules (sometimes, according to rules made in the making of the rulings). It is a violation of the requirements of the rule of law for a judge to separate the rule from the ruling by declaring what the rule is (or will henceforth be) while declining to apply it;[47] or likewise by denying that there is a rule (in other words, claiming that the case under decision is being decided only 'on its particular facts').[48]

Disobedience and the Rule of Law', working paper available at <http://www.iilj.org/courses/documents/Green.Globalization.pdf> (accessed 29 December 2011).

[46] In Raz, 'The Rule of Law and its Virtue', above note 13, 214–19.

[47] This includes what is sometimes known as 'prospective overruling', of which the House of Lords rightly took a dim view in *National Westminster Bank PLC v Spectrum Plus Ltd* [2005] UKHL 41.

[48] The Court of Appeal strayed dangerously close to this kind of behaviour in *Re A (children)* [2000] EWCA Civ 254. The tension that Ward LJ felt between his moral sensibilities and his rule of law responsibilities was pathetically brought out in his description of the case as 'very unique'.

Do these further desiderata, or some of them, add 'social' elements to an otherwise 'legalistic' conception of the rule of law?[49] Are they 'substantive' additions to an otherwise 'procedural' ideal?[50] Do they turn our attention from the form of the law to its content? The questions are muddled. They reflect deep misunderstandings of the reason why the rule of law, as an ideal for law, takes the shape that it does. The rule of law is a modal ideal because law is a modal kind. One needs to grasp law's distinctive modality in order to grasp law's distinctive morality. Fuller, noting that law is a system of rules, emphasizes the qualities that make for a rule that is in good shape, just *qua* rule. Raz, noting that law is (more specifically) an institutionalized system of rules and rulings, emphasizes the qualities that make for a rule that is in good shape, just *qua* rule, together with those that make for an institutional arrangement that is in good shape for upholding those rules via rulings, just *qua* institutional arrangement oriented to that purpose. But note that the 'purpose' here can only be a subsidiary purpose, an intermediate destination; the true purposes of law are the further various purposes of the various rules that are upheld, regulated by external morality. If law were a functional kind, distinguished by the purposes it is capable of serving, then the list of desiderata for law's internal morality would also naturally pass judgment on law's ends. But law is not a functional kind, and the evaluation of its ends is therefore left to ordinary, unspecialized, external morality, the same morality that binds us all.

4. A valid moral ideal?

If you are convinced, as I am, by this broadly Fullerian analysis then you are pushed towards a disturbing conclusion: the rule of law, in its widest interpretation, is not a valid moral ideal. By 'its widest interpretation' I mean the interpretation with which we started, according to which we live under the rule of law if and only if people, including but not limited to officials, use the law for guidance and thereby avoid breaking it. Morally speaking, there is

---

[49] As Barber suggests in 'Legalistic Conceptions', above note 6, 478.
[50] Barber, ibid, calls them 'strangely substantive' additions.

nothing to be said for such universal reliance on the law. The law is no more than a means and we should welcome reliance upon it only to the extent that reliance upon it serves some worthwhile end. Sometimes reliance on the law does serve such an end and sometimes it doesn't. There are a lot of pointless laws about, and not only laws that are pointless because they go unfollowed (although there are a lot of those about too) but also laws that remain pointless even when followed. No doubt the makers of such laws had their purposes, but their purposes were not served, or are no longer served, by their laws, or else their purposes were not, or are no longer, worth serving, and no alternative worthwhile purposes for the law can be found.

There are probably some legal systems where such pointless laws predominate. In such legal systems we should be glad that the law is widely ignored, that people have enough sense not to 'play by the rules'. This deceptively chummy expression, as I called it before, makes law sound like a game, maybe a game of cat and mouse as portrayed in some charming Ealing Comedy. But law is not a game. There is no point in following one of the rules of a game (*qua* game) unless one follows all of them.[51] By contrast, the mere fact that one does not follow all the rules of a legal system does not in itself affect the appeal, one way or the other, of following each of those rules. True, helping to maintain and uphold a worthwhile rule is a possible purpose, on occasions, for going along even with a worthless one. Sometimes otherwise unobjectionable actions set bad examples (because their unobjectionability is overgeneralized by later agents). But that fact counts in favour of, not against, the point I am making. It confirms rather than denies that before one 'plays by the rules' there had better be some further purpose in doing so (which may, on occasions, be the further purpose of not setting a bad example). Presenting 'playing by the rules' as *itself* the purpose is mistaking the means for the end, a classic legalist mistake. It follows, I think, that the rule of law cannot be interpreted this way (as a matter of

---

[51] See Raz, *Practical Reason and Norms* (London 1974), 113–23. Strictly speaking this applies only to what Raz calls 'continuity rules' of the game, but the qualification need not detain us here.

everyone's being guided by the law) except at the price of no longer qualifying as a valid moral ideal.

However, it does not follow that the rule of law as interpreted more narrowly by Fuller and Raz is not a valid moral ideal. In their interpretation, the rule of law (aka the internal morality of law, the ideal of legality) is the ideal according to which the law of each legal system should be such that people *can* use it for guidance and thereby avoid breaking it, irrespective of whether they actually do so. On this narrower interpretation, contrary to the claims of 'law-and-order' types, the mere fact that Molotoff cocktails are thrown in Syntagma Square or Khao San Road does not signal or constitute an assault on the rule of law. If there is an assault on the rule of law, it will be found entirely in how officialdom responds to the rioting. If the relevant populations are lucky enough to live under the rule of law, the rioters should be able to find out, before and afterwards, what the law has to say about their actions, and the law should be such that, once they know what it says, they can judge when they are violating it and find a way to avoid doing so. They should be able to rely on what the law has to say to predict and plan for the official response. And they should be able to use the same law to challenge—with public funding and official support if needed—any illegality by police, magistrates, government ministers, and so on.

The rule of law entails, in other words, an unequal struggle between officialdom and the rest of us. It places burdens on the law and on its officials that it does not place on ordinary folk. We need not be on the right side of the law ourselves to be able to insist, under the heading of the rule of law, that the law and its administrators and enforcers stay on the right side of the law, and indeed give us every assistance in using the law against them when they do not. They, on the other hand, promptly jeopardize their moral standing to use the law against us every time their handling of the situation slips below the standards that the rule of law sets, including when they resort to illegality in their own actions. I will call this the 'asymmetrical interpretation' of the ideal of the rule of law. It has the implication that judges and other officials are often morally bound to uphold the law in their dealings with us (including, for example, in punishing us for its breach) even though, as they well know, we were not and are not morally bound by the same law ourselves. Some people find this implication uncomfortable. I, on the other hand, regard it as an independently attractive conclusion, and count the yielding of it as a point in favour of the asymmetrical interpretation.[52]

A number of more or less distinct moral arguments can be made in defence of the rule of law, asymmetrically interpreted. Some are more universal in their reach than others. Some lend more importance to the ideal than others. Here, mainly for the sake of focus, I will mention just one of them. It is an argument tailored to the conditions of life in industrial and post-industrial societies, and succeeds in making the asymmetrically interpreted ideal of the rule of law a particularly important (but still not uniformly overriding) moral ideal for law and government under those conditions. Here is Fuller's rather tendentious rendition of the argument I have in mind:

> The directives issued in a managerial context are applied by the subordinate in order to serve a purpose set by his superior. The law-abiding citizen, on the other hand, does not apply legal rules to serve specific ends set by the lawgiver, but rather follows them in the conduct of his own affairs.... [I]f the law is intended to permit a man to conduct his own affairs subject to an obligation to observe certain restraints imposed by superior authority, this implies that he will not be told at each turn what to do; law furnishes a baseline for self-directed action, not... instructions for accomplishing specific objectives.[53]

In reading this passage we must remember that Fuller is using 'law' in an idealized sense, to mean 'law that complies with the rule of law' or 'law that lives up to its inner morality'. The 'if' at the beginning of the third quoted sentence gives this away: depending on the regime, the law may or may not be intended, or indeed function, to 'permit a man to conduct his own affairs'. Yet if the rule of law is upheld, according to Fuller, there is some

---

[52] I have explored some aspects of it in 'Relations of Responsibility' in Rowan Cruft, Matthew Kramer and Mark Reiff (eds), *Crime, Punishment, and Responsibility: The Jurisprudence of Antony Duff* (Oxford 2011) and 'Criminals in Uniform' in Antony Duff, Lindsay Farmer, Sandra Marshall, and Victor Tadros (eds), *The Constitution of Criminal Law* (Oxford, forthcoming).

[53] *ML*, 207.

benefit, as compared with the 'managerial' alternative, in respect of what he calls 'self-determination'.[54] As Hart puts the same point, a good deal more clearly and less tendentiously:

> Consider the law not as a system of stimuli but as what might be termed a choosing system, in which individuals can find out, in general terms at least, the costs they have to pay if they act in certain ways. This done, let us ask what value this system would have in social life and why we should regret its absence. I do not of course mean to suggest that it is a matter of indifference whether we obey the law or break it and pay the penalty. Punishment is different from a mere 'tax on a course of conduct'. What I do mean is that the conception of the law simply as goading individuals into desired courses of behaviour is inadequate and misleading; what a legal system that [lives up to the ideal of the rule of law] does is to guide individuals' choices as to behaviour by presenting them with reasons for exercising choice in the direction of obedience, but leaving them to choose.[55]

Call this the 'liberal' argument for the rule of law, asymmetrically interpreted. As Raz points out, the liberal argument is not that the rule of law makes people free, or that 'forms liberate', or anything so far-reaching as that. Rather it is the argument that the rule of law helps to protect people against certain *specific* threats to their freedom to which law otherwise gives rise (Fuller's 'managerial directives', Hart's 'goading').[56] It follows that the argument can't show an advantage, even a potential advantage, in having a legal system. The point is only that *if* one is going to have a legal system, it had better be a rule-of-law legal system, for the sake (in Hart's words) of 'maximiz[ing] individual freedom

---

[54] *ML*, 162. Fuller mentions self-determination in the course of a slightly different argument in favour of the inner morality of law, which is also worthy of attention but which will not detain us here.

[55] Hart, 'Legal Responsibility and Excuses', above note 31, 44. My square-bracketed insertion replaces the very different words 'makes liability generally depend on excusing conditions'. I give lengthy justification for translating this into 'lives up to the ideal of the rule of law' in my introduction to the second edition of Hart's *Punishment and Responsibility* (Oxford 2008), at xxxiv–xliv.

[56] Raz, 'The Rule of Law and its Virtue' above note 13, 224. Raz says that conformity to the rule of law combats 'an evil that could only have been caused by the law itself' but 'only' strikes me as too strong. I have toned it down in my paraphrase.

within [= as against] the coercive framework of law'.[57] That this is a conditional imperative doesn't prevent it from being a moral one.[58] It is a moral imperative that applies to legal systems—an internal morality of law—so necessarily it applies only on condition that there is a legal system for it to apply to. Perhaps there is also a liberal argument for having a legal system to begin with, but that would have to be a different argument; Hart and Fuller, like Raz, say nothing here to support it.

I sketch out the argument not in order to add myself to the long list of liberal defenders of the rule of law (although I am one), but rather in order to scotch two further false rumours about Fuller's interpretation of the ideal, and those based on it.

First, it is sometimes presented as a matter of dispute among those who share a broadly Fullerian interpretation of the ideal, whether the ideal is a moral one. Fuller himself takes Hart to be doubting it, but this is not exactly what Hart doubts. Hart doubts (a) whether the rule of law should be called *a* morality (inner or otherwise), since on any plausible view (including Fuller's) moral success does not come to the law by adherence to the desiderata of the rule of law alone;[59] and (b) whether the mere fact that law is a 'purposive enterprise' with its own native ('inner') desiderata of success is enough to show that those desiderata are moral ones, since the same may well be true of poisoning, torture, etc.[60] None of this suggests that, for Hart, there is no moral merit in the law's living up to Fuller's desiderata. Indeed, Hart clearly and committally designates Fuller's desiderata as 'requirements of justice',[61] where justice 'constitutes one segment of morality'.[62]

Raz too says that adherence to the rule of law 'is one among many moral virtues that the law should possess', although wisely he does not follow Hart in assimilating it to the virtue of justice, and he adds that it is 'not merely a moral virtue [but also] a necessary condition for the law to be serving directly any good

---

[57] Hart, 'Legal Responsibility and Excuses', above note 31, 23.
[58] Or, as Hart puts it, a matter of 'moral preference': ibid 44.
[59] Hart, *The Concept of Law*, above note 42, 202.
[60] Hart, 'Review of *The Morality of Law*', *Harvard Law Review* 78 (1965), 1281 at 1286.
[61] Hart, *The Concept of Law*, above note 42, 207. [62] Ibid 167.

purpose at all'.[63] True, Hart and Raz are not sure that Fuller has correctly grasped, since he has not consistently represented, that the rule of law is a modal ideal for a modal kind. They suspect him of functionalism.[64] But they agree that a modal ideal can also be a moral one. Indeed for liberals, they think, it has to be a moral one: the means as well as the ends of government can clearly be more friendly, or more hostile, to freedom; and freedom is liberal morality's distinctive preoccupation.

Second, the rule of law on its Fullerian interpretation is sometimes said to be, or to be regarded by its supporters as being, 'more neutral or less controversial' than some other ideals.[65] It is true that (where the same verdict can be reached either way) Fuller commends to judges the tactic of deciding cases on internal morality grounds, rather than making 'unnecessary' forays into external morality.[66] Every law student learns that trick early: capitalize when you can on others' misplaced allegiance to the ideology of legalism; as a lawyer, try to avoid forays into the controversies that the ideology so helpfully conceals. Because it comes as such an early lesson, some law students forget that this is a trick, and legalism becomes their creed too; they proudly testify that *all they are doing* is standing up for the rule of law, as if they were exempt, as lawyers, from all other moral concerns.

As we already know, however, that is not Fuller's position. He knows and insists repeatedly that the rule of law is not the only moral ideal applicable to law and lawyering, and that it is also not a neutral ideal, meaning a morally neutral or non-ideological one. How could an *ideal*, a *morality* indeed, be thought to be morally neutral or non-ideological? As Fuller says, the ideal as he sees it 'cannot be neutral in its view of man himself'.[67] And it only *seems* (but is not) 'ethically neutral'.[68] Commitment to it may well be compatible with a range of other moral commitments, not all of which are compatible with each other; but there's nothing special about that. All valid moral ideals meet that specification. And it

---

[63] Raz, 'The Rule of Law and its Virtue', above note 13, 225.
[64] Hart, 'Review', above note 60, 1284; Raz, 'The Functions of Law' in his *The Authority of Law,* above note 13, 164.
[65] Craig, 'Formal and Substantive Conceptions' above note 17, at 478 n24.
[66] *ML,* 105.   [67] *ML,* 162.   [68] *ML,* 157 and 159.

may be true, of course, that the rule of law is less publicly controversial than some other moral ideals with the same value base, but that could just be a sign of how accomplished lawyers are at pulling the wool over people's eyes. It certainly isn't a reason to regard it as a valid moral ideal for law. Why would the fact that a moral ideal is uncontroversial count as a reason to regard it as valid, still less the fact that a moral ideal is controversial count as a reason to regard it as invalid? Often lack of controversy bespeaks widespread acquiescence in easy falsehoods. I do not think that regarding the rule of law as a valid moral ideal is an easy falsehood, but its value being uncontroversial does nothing to reassure me of that.

5. Compatible with very great iniquity?

Hart and Fuller do have a genuine dispute about a much more specific neutrality that might be claimed for the rule of law as both of them understand it. Hart asserts, and Fuller denies, that Fuller's desiderata are 'neutral *so far as the external aims of law are concerned*'.[69] The issue is not whether Fuller's desiderata have a closer ideological affinity with some aims (purposes, objectives, ends) than with others. Clearly they do. Clearly a regime with a moral commitment to the rule of law based on the liberal argument sketched earlier might reasonably be expected also to take liberal positions on the external morality of law, favouring (for example) the use of law to support freedom of speech, freedom of religion, and freedom of association. However, not every regime that respects or attempts to respect the rule of law does so on moral grounds, let alone liberal ones. Doing so may also be a way of attracting inward investment or qualifying for international aid or building a tourism industry; it may help to deflect criticism of other policies, maintain political alliances, gain recognition in the international arena, or wrong-foot bullies with adventurist ambitions in the region; it may even make the legal system itself an attractive export commodity, a haven for shell corporations and ships flying flags of convenience.

---

[69] *ML*, 157, emphasis added.

THE SUPPOSED FORMALITY OF THE RULE OF LAW 219

This possibility of (as it were) a *realpolitik* adherence to the rule of law gives rise to the question on which Hart and Fuller differ. Does a regime that respects the rule of law (for one or more of these *realpolitik* reasons) thereby inhibit its own pursuit of immoral ends through the law? Does conformity to law's internal morality tend to serve the cause of conformity with external morality too? Hart argues that Fuller's desiderata can just as readily be put to evil ends as to good ones, and in that narrow respect—note: in that narrow respect *only*—are neutral principles.[70] Fuller demurs: he denies that conforming with the internal morality of law is, in Hart's words, 'compatible with very great iniquity'.[71] Or at any rate he denies that conforming with the internal morality of law is just as conducive to external moral failure as it is to external moral success.

Hart is quick and right to point out, in reply, that *some* external moral failures are indeed inhibited, *some* 'iniquitous moral aim[s]' are indeed rendered harder to achieve, by conformity with the rule of law.[72] Nevertheless, thinks Hart, one can make use of the rule of law just as readily to maintain as to destroy, say, an immoral system of racial apartheid of the kind that obtained in South Africa between 1948 and 1994.[73] Fuller thinks that the example cuts the other way. He thinks that the openly discriminatory laws of that regime fell foul of the clarity desideratum, and moreover that this was no coincidence: such immoral purposes are ill-served by clarity, prospectivity, openness, and so forth.[74] Hart insists that, on the contrary, they can also be well-served, that any rule-of-law deficiencies in the South African system were largely coincidental to its evil aims.[75]

There are several empirical questions lurking here, which, like Hart and Fuller, I am in no position to tackle. Nevertheless my instincts run with Hart's. If the apartheid laws were any less clear (prospective, open, etc) than their morally upstanding counterparts, that was largely a coincidence. It only goes to show that the

---

[70] Hart, 'Review', above note 60, 1287.
[71] *ML*, 159ff, quoting Hart, *The Concept of Law*, above note 42, 202.
[72] Hart, 'Review', above note 60, 1288.   [73] Ibid 1287.
[74] *ML*, 160.   [75] Hart, 'Review', above note 60, 1287.

government and parliamentary lawyers in apartheid South Africa did not quite do their jobs. It did not go to show that, consistently with the rule of law, their jobs could not be done, or could not be done so readily as those of similarly placed lawyers in less odious regimes. Immoral lawyering, even immoral lawyering that stands up for the rule of law, is always a live possibility and lawyers, like other professionals, need to guard against it and not hide behind the mask of their profession when moral trouble hits. Just as Josef Mengele could pervert his medical expertise, including no doubt his fine bedside manner and keen grasp of hygiene, to serve the causes of extermination and experimentation on humans,[76] so lawyers and even judges in oppressive regimes can pervert their legal expertise, including their special role of upholding the rule of law, to aid the regime's oppression. Fuller is no legalist but he is surely, on this front, a bit of a quietist. He encourages lawyers to think that they are already doing their bit, *qua* lawyers, to save us from the abyss so long as they are upholding the rule of law. But there is always more, and sometimes more important, work to do.

---

[76] The analogy is inexact since medicine, unlike law, is a functional kind. The inexactitude of the analogy does not, however, affect the use to which I am putting it here.

9
Hart on Legality, Justice, and Morality

1. 'No necessary connection'

Many people associate H.L.A. Hart with the transparently false thesis that there is no necessary connection between law and morality. That is not surprising, perhaps, since Hart sometimes said 'there is no necessary connection between law and morality', or similar things, in bungled attempts to formulate other theses that he did endorse.[1] But it seems most unlikely that he endorsed the thesis itself. Not only is its falsity transparent enough that a thinker of Hart's acuity could scarcely have failed to notice it; there are also important passages in which Hart appears to have gone to some lengths to draw attention to its falsity.

Best-known of these is the long section at the end of Chapter 9 of *The Concept of Law*,[2] where Hart reviews various suggested necessary connections between law and morality. He complains that the suggestions, as presented in the literature, are often unclear or confusing.[3] But he does not brand them all as false. A number of them, indeed, he attempts to rescue from their lack of clarity or confusion. His main aim in doing so, it seems to me, is to cut them down to size. The suggestions may be true—they may point to authentic necessary connections between law and morality—but they do not have the large implications that are often hoped for and gestured towards by their originators. None

---

[1] 'Positivism and the Separation of Law and Morals', *Harvard Law Review* 71 (1958), 593 at 601 n25; 'Commands and Authoritative Legal Reasons', in his *Essays on Bentham* (Oxford 1982) at 264; and 'Introduction', in his *Essays in Jurisprudence and Philosophy* (Oxford 1983) at 8. In all of these passages, the context suggests that what he was really trying to say was 'there are no moral standards for law which are such that law automatically satisfies them', which is a very much more specific claim, and one that is analytically true (not because of anything special about law, but just by the nature of a standard).

[2] *The Concept of Law* (Oxford 1961) (In this chapter, abbreviated *CL*.).

[3] *CL*, 198.

of them, in particular, suffices to rule out the possibility, or indeed the very widespread reality, of gravely immoral laws that add up, in some cases, to yield gravely immoral legal systems.

That fact in itself reveals a necessary connection between law and morality. It reveals that law is the kind of thing that can be judged by moral standards and found wanting. (Compare fish, arthritis, colour, gravity, and spelling, all of which can be judged by standards, but not by moral ones.) Do we have here an unimportant necessary connection between law and morality? No. If we deny it, all moral debates about law become unintelligible. Not surprisingly, then, all the other supposed necessary connections between law and morality reviewed by Hart presuppose this one. And Hart endorses it. Some important moral ideals, says he, have 'obvious relevance in the criticism of law'.[4] This is already enough to show, without further ado, that Hart did not embrace the 'no necessary connection' thesis.

One moral ideal relevant in the criticism of law and considered by Hart in Chapter 9 is the ideal of the rule of law, made up (as Hart puts it) of 'the requirements of justice which lawyers term principles of legality'.[5] Lon Fuller had famously claimed that nothing could qualify as a legal system except by (largely) meeting these requirements. Hart quite rightly denied this in an earlier exchange with Fuller,[6] and he continues to deny it in *The Concept of Law*. But Hart had always agreed with Fuller, again quite rightly, that there are such requirements for law to meet, and in his Chapter 9 survey he reaffirms the point:

If social control of [the law's] sort is to function, the rules must satisfy certain conditions: they must be intelligible and within the capacity of most to obey, and in general they must not be retrospective, though exceptionally they may be. This means that, for the most part, those who are eventually punished for breach of the rules will have had the ability and opportunity to obey.... [O]ne critic of positivism [sc.

---

[4] *CL*, 201. As he says on the same page, '[s]ome may regard this as an obvious truism; but it is not a tautology'.

[5] *CL*, 202.

[6] Hart, 'Positivism and the Separation of Law and Morals', above note 1, to which Fuller responded in 'Positivism and Fidelity to Law—a Reply to Professor Hart', *Harvard Law Review* 71 (1958), 630.

Fuller] has seen in these aspects of control by rules, something amounting to a necessary connection between law and morality, and suggested that they be called 'the inner morality of law'.... [I]f this is what the necessary connection of law and morality means, we may accept it. It is unfortunately compatible with very great iniquity.[7]

Trying to maintain Hart's association with the 'no necessary connection' thesis, and thereby to pit his own ideas in opposition to Hart's, Nigel Simmonds has argued that this passage should be given what he calls an 'ironic reading'. According to this reading, the passage does not assert the necessary connection between law and morality that it seems to assert at the end.[8] Instead, the passage merely reports Fuller's pallid use of the word 'morality' to do work that Hart himself would not dignify with that name. Simmonds contrasts this with a 'concession reading' in which the passage is held to embrace the Fullerian usage, pallid though it may be, and hence to assert the same necessary connection between law and morality that Fuller asserted (while continuing to cast doubt on several of the larger implications that Fuller saw in it).[9] He attributes the concession reading to me.[10]

There is a significant textual obstacle to the ironic reading, and it is found in the already-quoted words with which Hart introduces the brief reminder of his quarrel with Fuller. He says, to repeat, that this quarrel concerns 'the requirements of justice which lawyers term principles of legality'. While one could see implicit scare-quotation marks around 'principles of legality' in this remark, there is no credible way of placing them around 'requirements of justice'. What are principles of legality according to lawyers are requirements of justice according to Hart himself. If they are requirements of justice, are they not by that token also moral requirements? Isn't justice part of morality? And if they are also the same requirements 'which lawyers term principles of legality' are they not in turn necessarily (because conceptually[11])

---

[7] CL, 202.
[8] Simmonds, *Law as a Moral Idea* (Oxford 2007), 74.
[9] Ibid 70.
[10] Citing the original version of what is now Ch 2 of this book.
[11] I will be restricting my attention to conceptually necessary connections. I should stress, however, that this is only part of Hart's topic in Ch 9 of *CL*. He also discusses, earlier in the chapter, various possible connections which are humanly

connected to law? If these questions are as rhetorical as they seem, there is the following chain of necessary (because conceptual) connection between law and morality:

> law ↔ the ideal of legality or the rule of law ↔ justice ↔ morality

Where, in interpreting Hart, are we to break the chain to make room for the ironic reading? Are we to say that, according to Hart, there is no conceptual connection between law and legality? Or, in spite of the already quoted remark, no conceptual connection between the ideal of legality and justice? Or no conceptual connection between justice and morality? I will be considering all three possibilities in turn.

2. From law to legality

Hart's views about the connection between law and the ideal of legality are made a little harder to unpack because of his conspicuous distaste for that particular way of branding the ideal, well illustrated in the remark just quoted in which he attributes that way of talking to 'lawyers'. It is tolerably clear what gives rise to his distaste. Hart fears that people will assume that legality is a property necessarily possessed by all law, and hence that, if legality is an ideal, all law necessarily lives up to it. That is the confusion that Hart plausibly attributes to Fuller. In spite of Hart's resulting drive for terminological hygiene, it is a confusion that has since been perpetuated in, for example, the work of Ronald Dworkin. In Dworkin's view it would be

nonsense to suppose that though the law, properly understood, grants [P] a right to recovery, the value of legality argues against it. Or that though the law, properly understood, denies her a right to recovery, legality would nevertheless be served by making [D] pay.[12]

---

rather than conceptually necessary; ie which are inevitable given only some inevitable aspects of the human predicament. He rightly concludes (eg in his famous commitment to a 'minimum content of natural law' at *CL*, 188–9) that there are some necessary connections under this heading too.

[12] Dworkin, 'Hart's Postscript and the Character of Political Philosophy', *Oxford Journal of Legal Studies* 24 (2004), 1 at 25.

There is a way to read Dworkin as dishing up a mere tautology here, by deeming the expression 'properly understood' to mean 'understood to conform to the value of legality'. Inasmuch as a proposition is tautological it is of course nonsensical to deny it. But if 'properly understood' is seen for the distracting verbiage it more probably is, the tautology disappears and with it goes the nonsense. It is not nonsense to suppose that there is such a thing as illegal law. It is law that fails to live up to the ideal of the rule of law and there is, as Hart potently argued against Fuller, plenty of conceptual space for it. Seeing the ease with which Dworkin occludes that space, however, we should not be surprised that Hart shied away from using the word 'legality' to explain it.

It has to be admitted, though, that Hart himself contributed to the same occlusion at some points in his work. In Chapter 5 of *The Concept of Law*, for example, Hart tells his brilliant and seminal fable of the emergence of a legal system (differentiated by its secondary rules of recognition, adjudication, and change) from an imagined pre-legal or proto-legal arrangement of customary primary rules alone. As a way of making such a development rationally intelligible, his narrative emphasizes the gains in efficiency and predictability that these secondary norms bring with them. Unfortunately, to the lasting confusion of many readers, he thereby makes it sound like he is extolling the virtues of the transformation from proto-law to law. Not surprisingly, he is therefore taken to task by some critics for attempting to smuggle in a political ideology under cover of his supposedly ideologically neutral explanation of the nature of law.[13] And that political ideology seems to many, not implausibly, to be none other than the ideology of the rule of law. That is why it is so easy for Dworkin to represent Hart's Chapter 5 elucidation of certain aspects of the nature of law instead as a defence of a certain version of the ideal of legality (a 'conventionalist' version of which, as is well known, Dworkin disapproves).[14]

---

[13] See eg Malcolm Wood, 'Rule, Rules and Law' in Philip Leith and Peter Ingram (eds), *The Jurisprudence of Orthodoxy* (London 1988), 27 at 30–1; Peter Fitzpatrick, *The Mythology of Modern Law* (London 1992), Ch 6; Roger Cotterrell, *The Politics of Jurisprudence* (2nd ed, London 2003), 94–5.

[14] Dworkin, 'Hart's Postscript', above note 12, at 28, summarizing a position staked out at length in *Law's Empire* (Cambridge, Mass. 2006). Hart does not help

For all its brilliance, then, Hart's fable is afflicted by severe and damaging presentational flaws. The secondary rules, Hart should have made clear, do not automatically bring with them the rule of law and, even for believers in the rule of law, their arrival is not necessarily to be welcomed. For life without any law at all might well be better than life with law but without the rule of law. The arrival of a legal system makes some forms of oppression possible, and others easier, and there is a further step to be taken to help protect people against such law-enabled and law-facilitated oppression, namely the step from merely having a legal system to having a legal system under the rule of law. That there are two steps here, and not just one, is essential to the success of Hart's critique of Fuller. If there were only one step, then Fuller would be right that nothing qualifies as a legal system except by largely conforming to what he calls 'the inner morality of law', which is what Hart repeatedly and rightly denies.

That Hart does not identify having a legal system with living under the rule of law should not lead us to suppose, however, that he sees no conceptual connection between the two. How could he? As the previous comments show, although it is possible for there to be a legal system without the rule of law, it is not possible for there to be the rule of law without a legal system. And it is not possible because the rule of law is, at its simplest, the ideal of being ruled by law, and (as Hart emphasized) there is no law, ruling or otherwise, where there is no legal system. So what we have here is already a conceptual connection between law and legality, which explains the naming of the ideal. Hart was aware of this connection: his objection to Fuller was only that law is insufficient for legality, not that it is unnecessary.

That is not all. In what is perhaps a more striking concession to Fuller, Hart draws attention to a second conceptual connection between law and the ideal of legality. The connection is hinted at in the Chapter 9 passage quoted above. According to Hart, recall, the rule of law is needed '[i]f social control of the [law's] sort is to

to dispel Dworkin's confusion with his own confused response to the *Law's Empire* critique in his posthumously published 'Postscript': Hart, *The Concept of Law* (2nd ed, Oxford 1994), 249–50.

function'. What is the relevant 'sort' of social control? Hart says it is 'control by rule', which

consists primarily of general standards of conduct communicated to classes of persons, who are then expected to understand and conform to the rules without further official direction.[15]

Now laws, as Hart explains, are rules. This much is determined by the nature of law. But there is more than one way for laws to function as instruments of social control, and not all involve laws functioning *as* rules. Laws need not be used to guide; they can also be used to subdue, intimidate, overwhelm, or more generally, as Hart puts it in *Punishment and Responsibility*, to 'goad' those who are subject to them.[16] We live under the rule of law, for Hart, to the extent that law is used to guide us, not to goad us, and this condition is not met in all legal systems. In some legal systems, as Hart explains at length in Chapter 6 of *The Concept of Law*,[17] the law only guides, and maybe is only set up to guide, a small elite of officials; the ordinary folk are then (legally) at the mercy of those officials and inhabit what Hart calls, in *Punishment and Responsibility*, 'an economy of threats'.[18] Here there is law, to be sure, but without the rule of law. It is in that respect (although perhaps not in all respects) degenerate law. The rules are not, in Aristotelian terms, fulfilling their *telos* as rules, which is to guide—to *rule*— those who are subject to them.

So here we have a second conceptual connection between law and the rule of law that Hart concedes and indeed emphasizes in the passage under scrutiny: the nature of legal systems (as systems of rules) brings with it a properly legal way of functioning (as a source of guidance) which nevertheless some legal systems may abjectly fail to realize. In such systems there may be lots of law and yet a conspicuous shortage of legality.

This already suggests the existence of a third conceptual connection between law and legality. Perhaps one does not fully

---
[15] *CL*, 202.
[16] Hart, 'Legal Responsibility and Excuses', in *Punishment and Responsibility* (Oxford 1968), 44.
[17] *CL*, 108–14.
[18] 'Legal Responsibility and Excuses', above note 16, 40.

master the concept of law until one grasps the properly legal way of functioning, and in particular until one grasps the *telos* of rules, which is to rule. Perhaps, to put it another way, it is part of the very nature of law that law should live up to the ideal of the rule of law (even though it depressingly often fails to do so). I think this much is true, but it is doubtful whether Hart agrees. He continues his Chapter 9 discussion by reflecting on the distinction (drawn in many European languages other than English) between *ius*, *Recht*, *diritto*, *derecho*, or *droit* on the one hand and *lex*, *Gesetz*, *legge*, *ley*, or *loi* on the other. The former terms for law, Hart says, 'are laden with the theory of Natural Law';[19] they carry, as we might put it in less sectarian terms, an implication of conformity to (at least) the ideal of legality. He continues:

[W]hat is really at stake is the comparative merit of a wider [*lex*] and a narrower [*ius*] concept or way of classifying rules, which belong to a system of rules generally effective in social life.... The wider of these two rival concepts of law includes the narrower.[20]

So Hart holds that there are 'two rival concepts of law' in play here whereas I hold, under the influence of subsequent work by John Finnis[21] and Joseph Raz,[22] that there is just one concept of law, but with central cases (*ius*) as well as limit cases (*lex* that is not *ius*).[23] And it seems to me, but apparently not to Hart, that one doesn't fully grasp *lex* at the limit unless one understands that it ought, by its nature as *lex*, to be *ius*. In other words, a full mastery of the concept of law requires an understanding of law complete with its built-in aspiration of legality, just as, for example, a full mastery of the concept of football or cricket requires an understanding of football or cricket complete with its built-in aspiration to sportsmanship (however rarely that aspiration may be realized in actual games of football or cricket).

So here, perhaps, is a conceptual connection between law and the ideal of legality that Hart denies. Where I see a single concept

---

[19] *CL*, 203.
[20] *CL*, 204.
[21] *Natural Law and Natural Rights* (Oxford 1980), Ch 1.
[22] 'Legitimate Authority', in *The Authority of Law* (Oxford 1979).
[23] On this point Dworkin has lately, and quite amazingly, sided with Hart. See his *Justice in Robes* (Cambridge, Mass. 2006), Ch 8.

with limit cases and central cases, he seems to see a 'wider' concept extending to (what I would call) the limit cases and another 'narrower' concept extending only to (what I would call) the central cases. Or does he? There is some conflicting evidence in *Punishment and Responsibility* where he accuses those who miss law's aspiration to legality of holding a 'conception of the law' that is 'inadequate and misleading'.[24] He may have held different views on this point at different times. But this does not affect what appears to be a more consistent commitment, on his part, to the following two conceptual connections between law and the ideal of legality that we noted earlier in this section. First, to live up to the ideal of legality—to live under the rule of law—a society must, by conceptual necessity, have a legal system. Second, the ideal of legality or the rule of law is an ideal for law because there is a conceptually necessary feature of a legal system, namely that it is a system of rules, which entails that it has a proper way of functioning as a legal system, namely by guiding or (as we also put it) by *ruling* those who are subject to it.

3. From legality to justice

Hart, as we know, regarded the principles of legality, the ones that go to make up the ideal of legality, as 'requirements of justice'. This may at first seem surprising, since he also regarded them as requirements of legal efficiency, or legal functioning. Efficiency is sometimes contrasted with justice. But there is no reason to doubt that principles of efficiency can also be principles of justice. In *Punishment and Responsibility* Hart explains how, in his view, the two can come together. A principle of justice, Hart claims, is simply a principle 'concerned with the adjustment of claims between a multiplicity of persons'.[25] Legal efficiency, meanwhile, is efficiency at guiding people, or efficiency (as he also puts it) in a 'choosing system'.[26] People can only be guided by the law, says Hart, if they have 'the normal capacities, physical

---

[24] 'Legal Responsibility and Excuses', above note 16, 44.
[25] 'Prolegomenon to the Principles of Punishment', in Hart, *Punishment and Responsibility*, above note 16, 21.
[26] 'Legal Responsibility and Excuses', above note 16, 44, 49.

and mental, for doing what the law requires and abstaining from what it forbids, and a fair opportunity to exercise these capacities'.[27] And this in turn yields the principle that they should not be held in breach of the law, and so not subjected to the legal consequences of such a breach, if they lack those capacities and opportunities. That principle, says Hart, is a 'principle[ ] of Justice which restrict[s] the extent to which general social aims may be pursued at the cost of individuals'.[28] In this light,

[r]ecognition of excusing conditions [by the law] is . . . seen as a matter of protection of the individual against the claims of society for the highest measure of protection from crime that can be obtained from a system of threats. In this way the criminal law respects the claims of the individual as such, or at least as a choosing being, and distributes its coercive sanctions in a way that reflects this respect for the individual. This surely is very central in the notion of justice.[29]

All of this belongs to the 'notion of justice' because it concerns the adjustment of claims between a multiplicity of persons (viz. between each one of us and the rest). And it belongs to the ideal of legality because it contributes to the law's properly legal way of functioning (viz. functioning as a guide, not a goad).

Hart did not get all of this exactly right. For a start, it is not exactly right to say that all principles of justice are 'concerned with the adjustment of claims between a multiplicity of persons'. It is true that all principles of justice are principles of allocation. But not all allocate as between people with rival claims, as Hart's formulation suggests. There are also principles of justice with no competitive, and hence no inevitably interpersonal, dimension.[30] Probably (*pace* Hart) the principles of criminal excuse are better accommodated under that heading. Hart was right, on the other hand, to think that all principles 'concerned with the adjustment of claims between a multiplicity of persons' are principles of justice. And he was right to notice a particular implication of

[27] 'Negligence, Mens Rea, and Criminal Rsponsibility, in Hart, *Punishment and Responsibility*, above note 16, 152.
[28] 'Prolegomenon', above note 25, 17.
[29] 'Legal Responsibility and Excuses', above note 16, 49.
[30] See Joel Feinberg, 'Noncomparative Justice', *Philosophical Review* 83 (1974), 297; Jeremy Waldron, 'The Primacy of Justice', *Legal Theory* 9 (2003), 269 at 286.

this proposition. Principles of justice may be justified instrumentally, by pointing exclusively to the good consequences of having them, following them, or conforming to them. In the case of the principles of justice making up the ideal of legality, thought Hart, the relevant good consequences are consequences for human freedom. Legality 'maximizes individual freedom within the coercive framework of law'.[31] People are better able to steer their lives so as to avoid unwelcome collisions with the law (punishments, taxes, etc) and so as to make use of the law's helpful devices (contract, marriage, etc) when it suits them to do so. To reprise a point that we already encountered, conformity with the rule of law, on this Hartian view, helps to protect people against law-enabled and law-facilitated oppression, against the various modes of unfreedom (such as heavy-handed policing, show trials, and the use of influence to get above the law) that the existence of a legal system otherwise tends to open up and encourage.

Here is another thing that Hart did not get entirely right. In talking of 'the requirements of justice which lawyers term principles of legality', he suggests that the principles of the rule of law are all of them principles of justice. This is not true. The principles of natural justice (*audi alterem partem, nemo in sua causa iudex*) clearly belong to the ideal of the rule of law (as Hart explains) and are equally clearly principles of justice.[32] But compliance with the rule-of-law requirements of stability, prospectivity, generality, and clarity is a public good which does not or at least need not constitute an 'adjustment of [anyone's] claims'. It is plausible to think that breach of these requirements can *give rise to* injustice, but not that it *constitutes* injustice. It is more plausible to think, in other words, that there are further principles of justice (lying outside the ideal of legality) that may tend to be breached when these principles of legality are breached. To that extent, the link between justice and legality is partly a conceptual contingency, rather than a conceptual necessity. But in other respects it is, to repeat, a conceptual necessity. And Hart, whose views we are considering here, plainly thought and repeatedly asserted that it is

---

[31] 'Legal Responsibility and Excuses', above note 16, 48.
[32] *CL*, 156.

a conceptual necessity across the board; ie that all the principles of the rule of law are alike in being principles of justice.

One reason why Hart may have thought it a conceptual necessity across the board is because of his well-known view that 'we have, in the bare notion of applying a general rule of law, the germ at least of justice'.[33] Why does he hold this view? Because that bare notion, to his mind, already entails 'the precept "Treat like cases alike"', which, to his mind, belongs distinctively to 'the structure of the idea of justice'.[34] So for Hart '[t]he connection between this aspect of justice and the very notion of proceeding by rule is obviously very close'.[35] If this connection between law and justice exists, it is a conceptual one, and it short-circuits the more convoluted conceptual connection via the ideal of legality that we have been exploring.

However, the more direct connection does not exist. Hart's argument to the effect that it does is scarred by multiple fallacies.[36] Hart's attachment to the idea[37] would, however, help to explain his thought that the principles of the rule of law are all of them principles of justice. For they are all principles governing what he calls 'the administration of the law' and for Hart this administration necessarily—by virtue of the mere fact that laws are rules—invites an evaluation in terms of justice. This shows that in some ways, contrary to the tenor of Simmonds' discussion, Hart took the conceptual connections among law, legality, and justice to be more tightly woven than they really are. As well as holding (rightly) that law is connected to justice *via* its connection to legality, he held (wrongly) that law is connected to legality *via* its independent connection to justice.[38]

---

[33] *CL*, 202.   [34] *CL*, 156.   [35] *CL*.

[36] See Ch 10 in this book, and Leslie Green, 'The Germ of Justice', working paper available at <http://ssrn.com/abstract=1703008> (accessed 13 February 2012). These both build on David Lyons' classic critique of Hart in 'On Formal Justice', *Cornell Law Review* 58 (1973), 833 at 848ff.

[37] It is introduced in 'Positivism and the Separation of Law and Morals', above note 1, and reiterated twice in *CL* (155–7, 202). However, by the time of his 1983 'Introduction', above note 1, at 18, Hart was 'clear that [the] claim requires considerable modification' in the light of criticisms by Lyons.

[38] There is an independent connection between law and justice, but not the one that Hart thought there was. See Ch 10 of this book.

4. From justice to morality

Hart thought that law is conceptually connected to legality, and that legality is conceptually connected to justice. We are left with the last link in the chain. Did he also think that justice is conceptually connected to morality? Here the evidence is more confusing and in some ways more surprising.

To be sure, one could hardly imagine a clearer statement than the one that introduces the topic in Chapter 8 of *The Concept of Law*. 'Justice' writes Hart, 'constitutes one segment of morality.'[39] He goes on to point out that not all moral criticism of the law is 'made in the name of justice'[40] even though, for him, 'justice [has] special relevance in the criticism of law'.[41]

Elsewhere, however, Hart's thinking on the matter seems to go in a quite different direction. In his 1965 critical notice of Fuller's *The Morality of Law*, Hart complains:

> The difference between [Fuller] and those he criticizes in this matter is that the activity of controlling men by rules and the principles designed to maximise its efficiency are not valued by the latter for their own sake, and are not dignified by them with the title of 'a morality'. They are valued only insofar as they contribute to human happiness or other moral substantive aims of the law.[42]

Among those Fuller criticizes, Hart lists himself. So presumably Hart is among those who would not dignify the principles of the rule of law, Fuller's 'inner morality of law', with the title of 'a morality'. And presumably this is for the reason stated, viz. that the principles of the rule of law 'are not valued [by Hart]... for their own sake'. That Hart does not value them for their own sake we already know. He values them as instruments of maximal freedom against what would otherwise be the oppressive might of the law. And that—maximal freedom—counts as a 'moral aim' because freedom, unlike the rule of law, is presumably something that Hart does indeed value 'for [its] own sake'. These ideas hang nicely together. But they do not hang together at all with what Hart says in *The Concept of Law*. For one startling implication of

---

[39] *CL*, 163.   [40] *CL*.   [41] *CL*.
[42] 'Review' [of Lon L. Fuller, *The Morality of Law* (New Haven 1964)], *Harvard Law Review* 78 (1965), 1281 at 1291.

them is that at least some principles of justice are not moral principles. So justice can't be 'one segment of morality' after all. Recall that the principles of the rule of law are also, for Hart, principles of justice. If they should not be dignified with the title of moral principles *qua* principles of the rule of law, nor should they be dignified with that title *qua* principles of justice.

This result seems odd to say the least.[43] Is there any way to avoid it? Maybe we can read what Hart says in his review of Fuller a bit more charitably. Maybe he is not saying that the Fullerian principles do not qualify as moral principles at all, but rather that they qualify as moral principles only when they serve moral aims. Unfortunately, this doesn't help to explain Hart's thinking. For Hart agrees that the Fullerian principles, the principles of the rule of law, always do serve moral aims. Even when the law is otherwise immoral, argues Hart, the fact that the rule of law is observed helps us to preserve some freedom in the face of the law's immorality, and that is an invariant contribution that observance of the rule of law makes to the moral aim of maximizing freedom. This *leitmotif* from *Punishment and Responsibility* is perfectly consistent with the point, of which Hart makes so much in his review of Fuller, that observance of the rule of law may also help a regime to achieve (other) immoral aims through the law. The lesson of all this is simply that the rule of law is a moral ideal that can be subverted. Even as it bestows its blessings, it may also be used to smooth the path of evil. This is true of moral ideals in general. (Consider the general problem of 'moral hazard' much discussed by economists.) So it couldn't possibly explain Hart's refusal, in the passage just quoted, to classify legality's admitted blessings as moral ones.

Or maybe that is not quite what he is doing. Maybe he is granting that the rule of law is a moral ideal, bestowing its own moral blessings, while declining to classify it, by that token alone, as a morality, even a morality of law. Notice that Hart's scare-quotation marks, in the passage above, surround the word 'a' as well as the word 'morality'. Maybe he is only saying that the rule of law is at most *part* of a morality of law. There must, for Hart, be further moral principles, requirements, aims, or ideals that

---

[43] Although it has one brave defender in the form of Matthew Kramer. See his 'Justice as Constancy', *Law and Philosophy* 16 (1997), 561.

make up the rest. Why must there be? Because the law can be used to pursue (almost) any aim. The rule of law is an ideal that limits only how it does so. Before there can be or needs to be adherence to the rule of law, there needs to be some law, used to pursue some aims apart from that of the rule of law. These are the aims that Hart (I think unhelpfully[44]) calls 'substantive' aims. Why must these 'substantive' aims be moral aims? Actually, they need not be. Law can be used with the sole aim of making the emperor rich or shoring up the privileges of the ruling class. But, as Hart notices, the aims of the law *can* be moral aims. They can include the minimization of suffering or the maximization of freedom or the punishment of the deserving,[45] etc. It follows that there is more to a (complete) morality of law than the ideal of the rule of law. For a complete morality of law also determines which 'substantive' moral aims law is to have. (Note that such a morality of law may mention freedom twice: once as constituting a moral aim for law in its own right and again as setting moral limits on the means by which that aim, or others, are to be pursued by law.)

I tend to think that this is the thought, or the main thought, that Hart is trying to convey in his review of Fuller. If so, then we may be inclined towards a partly ironic reading of Hart's remarks about Fuller in Chapter 9 of *The Concept of Law*. Hart is upbraiding Fuller for conjuring up the fancy label 'the inner morality of law'. This is not, however, because Hart denies that the rule of law is a moral ideal. Rather it is because he denies that it is a moral ideal self-sufficient enough to be regarded as a (let alone *the*) morality of law. The twist in the tale, however, is that Fuller never claimed differently. It was Dworkin who tried to persuade us, much later, that law's inner morality (viz. the ideal of legality) is its *whole* morality. Fuller, by contrast, thought that law is also subject to the rest of morality, the same morality that binds the rest of us. He regarded the law's 'inner' morality as an addition to, not a replacement for, the long list of ordinary moral requirements, principles, aims, and ideals to which the law is also answerable. We know that Fuller thought this because he famously claimed that a

---

[44] Why 'unhelpfully'? See Ch 8 of this book.

[45] In spite of Hart's own doubts about the soundness of this particular aim, he admits it as a *possible* moral aim for the law in 'Prolegomenon', above note 25, 8–9.

failure by a legal system to observe the principles of law's inner morality would tend to bring with it other moral failures on the part of that legal system, and *vice versa*.[46] This claim is implausible. As Hart insisted, law's inner morality can also smooth the path of evil. Implausible or not, however, the Fullerian claim shows that Fuller regarded law as subject to moral requirements, principles, aims, and ideals beyond those of its inner morality. A failure by a legal system to observe the principles of law's inner morality cannot possibly bring with it other moral failures on the part of that legal system unless other moral failures on the part of legal systems are possible, and other moral failures on the part of legal systems are possible only if law answers to some moral standards apart from those of its inner morality. So calling the rule of law 'the inner morality of law' clearly isn't intended by Fuller to suggest that it is anything like a complete morality of law. If Hart is being ironic, in *The Concept of Law*, about the inflation of the moral ideal of legality to a whole morality of law, he has the wrong opponent in his sights, for on this (as on so many other issues) he and Fuller are quite clearly on the same side.

So perhaps—to make the irony bite—we have to return to the proposal that Hart really does not regard legality as a moral ideal. That proposal would incontrovertibly drive a wedge between Hart and Fuller. But the only way to sustain it, as we saw, is to read Hart as advancing the peculiar thesis against Fuller that sound principles of justice, which by Hart's own admission include the principles of legality, need not be moral principles. If we go with this reading, then we plainly have to attribute to Hart a great deal of ambivalence about the nature of morality. For on this reading he makes justice officially part of morality in Chapter 8 but puts some of it outside morality in Chapter 9. That degree of ambivalence would not be a surprise, since Hart is plagued by a wide range of anxieties and doubts about the nature of morality. Indeed, it would not be an overstatement to say that Hart's treatment of morality—by stark contrast with his treatment of law—is a mess. But that should only make us wonder why we would attach such interpretative weight as

---

[46] *The Morality of Law*, above note 42, 153–5.

Simmonds attaches to Hart's 'no necessary connection' remarks. If Hart was ambivalent about the very nature of morality then these remarks are not to be trusted, because they touch an idiosyncratically and obscurely Hartian nerve. ('When I hear the word "morality"', Hart might have been tempted to joke in an echo of Hanns Johst, 'I reach for my revolver'.)

So I suppose we can accept, with Simmonds, an ironic reading of Hart's remark about Fuller in Chapter 9. But why would we want to? Isn't it enough, to put an end to any significant disagreement between Hart and Simmonds, that Hart found multiple necessary connections between law and justice, never mind that it was somehow stressful for him to classify these as necessary connections between law and morality? Simmonds himself seems entirely content to treat justice as a department of morality. He says, for example, that in a 'moral inquiry' we might 'deepen our understanding of values such as justice'.[47] And he speaks, to take a second example at random, of 'substantive moral reflection upon law's justice'.[48] If Hart were to come out and say, as his views clearly commit him to saying, that there are various necessary connections between law and justice, would Simmonds still be able to present Hart as a philosophical foil? I think not. So we still need to know what issue, leaving aside issues about the connotations of the word 'morality' and its cognates, Simmonds finds between himself and Hart under the heading of 'necessary connections between law and morality'.

'The main focus of this book', writes Simmonds in the introduction to *Law as a Moral Idea*, is

upon contemporary legal theory, and in particular upon the work of H.L.A. Hart, who played such a large part in establishing the basic categories and assumptions in terms of which jurisprudential debate is now generally constructed.... My object is not to change the subject by 'changing the subject', so to speak, but to undermine a current orthodoxy by direct opposition.[49]

Yet he fails to show that the so-called orthodoxy he sets out to undermine—that there is no necessary connection between law and morality—is subscribed to by anyone, least of all by Hart.

---

[47] *Law as a Moral Idea*, above note 8, 6.
[48] Ibid 57.   [49] Ibid 4.

10

The Virtue of Justice and the Character of Law

1. Why justice?

The idea that law is intertwined with justice lies so deep in our consciousness that it barely attracts critical attention. Few eyebrows are raised at the fact that we know our judges as Mrs Justice so-and-so and Lord Justice such-and-such. When an Act of Parliament is labelled as an Administration of Justice Act it does not take a lawyer to work out that the Act is about the workings of the legal system. In many countries the government office charged with oversight of the working of the legal system is known as the Ministry of Justice or the Department of Justice. Wherever there is mention of laws and legal systems, invocations of justice are unlikely to be far behind.

When I say that this fact attracts little critical attention I don't mean, of course, that legal systems are widely regarded as paragons of justice. On the contrary, much ink is spilt, and sometimes blood too, over injustices allegedly perpetrated by and through the legal system. The rebranding of Criminal Justice Acts as Criminal Injustice Acts, or Ministries of Justice as Ministries of Injustice, is grist to the mill of campaigners and headline writers. Some critics even doubt whether legal systems really have it in them to live up to the aspiration that they should be just, and accordingly they treat the law's continual invocations of justice as a kind of tragi-comic conceit. But in all this disagreement the assumption generally remains unshakeable on all sides that justice is indeed the correct aspiration for the law, so that a law or legal system which fails to be just is a law or legal system which fails in a respect fundamental to its worthiness as a legal system. In every impassioned denial that the law is just there lurks, in other words, an equally impassioned re-confirmation that just is what it ought to be. That is why the ink, and the blood, is apt to be spilt over the alleged injustices.

To be on the safe side, perhaps we should leave room for the possibility that some particularly cynical types are not really objecting to the injustices as such. Perhaps they don't take a view on whether legal systems should be just; they just take the view that legal systems should not be hypocritical. Legal systems, they say, should live up to their own advertised aims, whatever those aims happen to be. Such critics hold the law up to the light of justice only because that is the same light which the law holds *itself* up to, with all its talk of Mrs Justice so-and-so and Lord Justice such-and such, with all its criminal justice this and civil justice that. But whatever the force of this 'hypocrisy' critique—it leaves me cold—it does not bypass the question we have set ourselves. For it simply reframes that question as the question of why the law would choose the light of justice as the right one to hold itself up to. If the answer is that this is a light which will lend it an aura of public legitimacy, then the same question arises again, in a new guise, as the question of why the light of justice might be publicly regarded as the light most apt to lend it that aura. And so on. Unless we are prepared to say that the association between the law and justice is ultimately arbitrary—hard to square with its endurance and ubiquity—the question cannot be avoided forever. Why should law be thought (by its defenders, by its critics, by itself, by the public, by anyone at all) to be the sort of thing which ought to be just?

One way of reading this question admittedly makes it a silly one to ask. Justice is a moral virtue and it is part of the nature of a moral virtue that anything that has the capacity for moral agency should exhibit it. That capacity for moral agency is not only a capacity of adult human beings but also of the institutions which they create and inhabit. The institutions of law—such as legislatures, courts and tribunals, police forces, and of course law firms—count among those human institutions. And some subset of such legal institutions add up to constitute a legal system.[1] From this it follows, without further ado, that a legal system ought to be just. But so far as it goes this argument entails only that a legal system ought to be just *inter alia*. By the very same

---

[1] For more on the agency of the legal system and its institutions, see Chs 3 and 5.

token it ought to possess all the other moral virtues too. It ought equally to be honest, loyal, trustworthy, humane, temperate, considerate, courageous, charitable, diligent, public-spirited, prudent, and so on. Yet somehow a campaign against the law's inconsiderateness or imprudence wouldn't have quite the same ring to it as a campaign against the law's injustice. And while philosophers have long debated whether an unjust law is really a law, there is no debate about whether an intemperate law or an uncharitable law really is a law. Moreover, the titles Mr Loyalty so-and-so and Lord Courage such-and-such don't sound much like judges' titles (a butler and an admiral, respectively?) and whatever the Ministry of Diligence or the Ministry of Trustworthiness might exist to supervise, it seems unlikely that either exists to supervise the workings of legal system (maybe industrial output and financial services, respectively?)

The point I am making with these transparently daft proposals for renaming is that law is very commonly held to be subject to some *special* imperative to be just beyond that which binds it to exhibit other moral virtues. The puzzle before us is not, therefore, the question of why we should expect and demand of the law that it be just *inter alia*. It is the question of why we should expect and demand of the law that it be just *above all*, just *in particular*, just *as opposed to* morally virtuous in other ways. Given all the other moral virtues that it might possess, and *ceteris paribus* ought to possess, why is the moral virtue of justice so widely seen as the apotheosis of the law's success, and injustice, accordingly, as the most damaging kind of legal failure?

2. Moral virtues and their horizons

To pursue this question, we need to know a bit more about moral virtues and how to differentiate them from each other. The basic answer (although in a longer discussion it would call for some refinement) is that each moral virtue is differentiated from other moral virtues by the distinctive rational horizons of those who exhibit it. By this I mean that people and institutions with different moral virtues are animated by different rationally significant features of actions—not only their own actions but also the actions of others. The main implication is that what strikes, say, an honest person as sufficient reason to perform some action may strike a loyal person as being an insufficient reason to perform that same action, and *vice versa*. Sometimes, accordingly, the honest person and the loyal person may agree on the action to be performed, but disagree about *why* it falls to be performed, since it has more than one rationally significant feature in its favour. The same action is required, let's suppose, both to avoid deceit (which the honest person is keen to avoid) and to avoid betrayal (which the loyal person is keen to avoid). So both the honest person and the loyal person lean, on this occasion, in favour of the same action. On other occasions, by contrast, their disagreement about the whys and wherefores of the available actions may lead the honest person and the loyal person to favour different, even diametrically opposed, actions. All else being equal, the honest person is inclined to betray to avoid deceiving, while the loyal person is disposed the other way. And the disposition in such cases is not only a disposition regarding their own actions. They also apply it to each other. The honest person will see the loyal person as too quick to resort to deceit, while the loyal person will think the honest person too quick to betray.

On a certain view of how reasons for action work this already creates a problem. Surely these two characters can't both be right at once? Surely a given reason is either a sufficient reason to perform a given action or it isn't? So, looking at the honest person and the loyal person, surely on any given occasion on which their rational horizons diverge, and they take against one another's priorities, at least one of them can't really be exhibiting a moral virtue at all, for he or she must be deluded, must have the relative importance of the reasons back to front, must have mistaken priorities? This line of thought led some moral philosophers of the modern age to try and isolate one single trait of character which is the only true moral virtue, being the one which consistently sets up the uniquely correct rational horizons for any moral agent. To fill this role, the utilitarians often alighted on a rather austere kind of public-spiritedness which is sometimes known as 'impartial benevolence';[2] Kant and his followers,

---

[2] For a particularly interesting study of this complex character trait see William Frankena, 'Beneficence/Benevolence', *Social Philosophy and Policy* 4 (1987), 1.

meanwhile, opted for variations on the rather different, but no less austere, theme of diligence or conscientiousness. These instincts to find one true path of moral virtue were based on the assumption that it could not conceivably be rational to be selective in one's attention to reasons; ie that rationality requires sensitivity to all reasons in proportion only to their independent rational force. A more classical view, which is the one I will endorse here, assumes the opposite. It assumes that, while reasons do have an independent rational force and that sometimes, accordingly, there is only one rationally acceptable way to go for a moral agent—which would indeed be the way chosen by all morally virtuous people and institutions—more often the independent force of reasons fails to provide any such closure. In such cases rationality itself leaves various alternative rationally acceptable ways for a moral agent to react to and prioritize the various competing reasons that are thrown up by the practical situation he is in. In such cases people and institutions with different moral virtues tend to react to the reasons and prioritize them in different ways, sometime leading them to different, even mutually antagonistic, actions.

3. The horizons of justice

What, then, are the distinctive priorities of the just person? What sets her rational horizons apart from those of other virtuous people? Aristotle says, a bit obscurely, that the just person has a special concern with *proportionality*.[3] He can't mean just any kind of proportionality. The just person is not preoccupied with keeping windows in proportion to doors, or keeping means in proportion to ends, or keeping reactions in proportion to actions, etc—although she may incidentally care about these things too. Her distinctive concern *qua* just is a concern with proportionality in *allocation*, with whether the right goods and ills are assigned to the right people and on the right grounds.[4]

---

[3] 'The just, then, is a species of the proportionate', *Nicomachean Ethics (NE)*, 1131^{a}29.

[4] Herself included. The just person acts to secure or maintain proportion 'either between himself and another or between two others', *NE*, 1134^{a}2.

There is more than one type of allocative proportionality, as Aristotle points out, and so the just person's distinctive concerns come in more than one guise.[5] On the one hand, the just person has *distributive* concerns which are concerns about securing or maintaining *geometric* proportionality between people. Under this heading the just person asks whether some good or ill—be it pleasure or suffering, love or resentment, consumption or production, truth or falsehood, honour or shame, etc—is divided up in the proper way among those who are, on a given occasion, candidates for receiving it. *Corrective* concerns, by contrast, are concerns about *arithmetic* proportionality between people's allocations of goods and ills. Under this heading the just person would have it that some good or ill regrettably transferred between two parties should be transferred back, so that the *status quo ante* or *status quo alter* may be restored. Roughly, distributive justice is the justice of division, while corrective justice is the justice of subtraction. These two *forms* of justice, as they are sometimes known, are cross-cutting. They do not co-exist harmoniously on the just person's rational horizons. Sometimes a just person may have reasons of corrective justice to effect a transfer which her distributive concerns put her under severe rational pressure not to effect (say, to return the money she just found to its spoilt and ungrateful owner). There is nothing surprising about this. Sometimes, by the same token, reasons of distributive justice may be at war among themselves ('to each according to his need' often conflicts, for instance, with 'from each according to his ability'), and the same is true of reasons of corrective justice (the restitution of wrongful gains famously tends to misalign with the compensation of wrongful losses).[6] A virtuous life is not immune from the experience of moral conflict. What is distinctive about the life of the just person is that moral conflicts for her, *qua* just, are

---

[5] See *NE*, 1130^{a}30ff.

[6] Around *NE*, 1132^{a}12 Aristotle talks as if he denies this; but luckily for his reputation as a sensible thinker he makes clear that in talking of the gain and the loss as coextensive he is using 'gain' in a special technical sense which is widely employed in corrective contexts 'even if it be not a term appropriate to certain cases'.

allocative conflicts. They are conflicts about who gets how much of what and why.

To see the distinctiveness of these rational horizons, try comparing the just person with the humane person.[7] These two characters might well converge on some pursuits. They might well converge, for example, on a campaign for the cancellation of the debts of poor countries in the developing world. It does not follow that they both see the problem in the same light. The humane campaigner cares about the alleviation of suffering. Of course, her concern about the alleviation of suffering is not completely indiscriminate. She baulks, for example, at the intentional infliction of fresh suffering merely in order to prevent greater suffering to other people or on other occasions.[8] But this is not because she focuses on how suffering is allocated as between different people or groups. It is because, *qua* humane, she regards the intentional infliction of suffering as the worst evil irrespective of how it is allocated, and the non-alleviation of suffering—again irrespective of how it is allocated—as the next-worst.[9] The just campaigner, by contrast, foregrounds the allocative questions, the questions about who is suffering, and in what measure, and by comparison with whom, and why, etc. She stresses, perhaps, the fact that the suffering in question is so unevenly spread across the globe, or the fact that it is the fault of fat-cat bankers in the developed world who should accordingly be the ones charged with putting it right, or the fact that current

---

[7] This contrast was first brought to life for me by Tom Campbell's important article 'Humanity before Justice', *British Journal of Political Science* 4 (1974), 1. However, my explanation of the contrast differs from Campbell's. Indeed, I ally myself with some of the views he criticizes.

[8] Herein lies one of my disagreements with Campbell. Allying the humane person with a version of utilitarianism (ibid at 6), he holds that the humane person cares to minimize suffering, rather than to allocate it. But in my view she cares neither to minimize nor to allocate suffering. She cares first that it not be intentionally inflicted and subject to that, second, that it be alleviated. For allied doubts about the utilitarian take on the virtue of humanity, see Brian Barry 'Humanity and Justice in Global Perspective', *Nomos* 24 (1982), 219.

[9] Which is not to say that *no* amount of alleviation of suffering could, in the eyes of the humane person, justify its intentional infliction. Her priorities need not yield an absolute constraint, let alone an agent-relative absolute constraint of the type sometimes called a side-constraint.

anti-poverty measures are not ensuring that each person or group of people in the suffering constituency gets the appropriate share of the remedy, etc. For the humane person these various distributive and corrective concerns all seem like distractions from the real business of alleviating suffering (other than by intentionally inflicting it). For the just person, by contrast, they *are* the real business of relieving suffering; there is no other acceptable way to think about this business, complains the just person, except as a problem of who gets how much of what and why. To which the humane person replies that of course what she does has allocative *consequences* but it is myopic to be fixated with this, when the more important fact about what she does is that it alleviates a great deal of suffering but not by intentionally inflicting any. And so on. Naturally, this difference of *Weltanschauung* can lead to disagreement between the two campaigners about the details of their campaign; eg about whether the debt should be cancelled before we start worrying about who ends up funding the cancellation, or about what should be done about poverty in the meantime.

From the inside of this disagreement—for the campaigners themselves—it may seem that only one of the ways forward can be the correct way. But as I already indicated, the nature of morality is such that there could be two incompatible correct ways forward—in this case, the just way and the humane way. For those of us who possess a modicum of both virtues, this incompatibility surfaces as ambivalence. We are ambivalent about how to go about relieving the suffering which debt brings to poor countries. Are we in favour of sending out food lorries to famine zones, or do we reject this as shoring up the fundamental iniquity of global capitalism, deflecting responsibility from those really to blame, letting ourselves off the hook by a token gesture instead of really making a proportionate sacrifice of our own creature comforts, etc? We are similarly ambivalent about the trial of ageing and frail alleged war criminals, about the misery of investors who were bankrupted by their own money-spinning gamble, about the future of a National Health Service that may be getting better at prioritization of cases but in the process treats patients with less warmth and fellow-feeling, etc. In other words, we experience not only the many conflicts within justice and humanity respectively, but also the conflicts between them, since we are less morally single-minded than the campaigners just portrayed. Unlike them we notice that sometimes we are compromising our humanity in being more just, or alternatively compromising our justice in being more humane.

The contrast between the single-mindedly just campaigner and the single-mindedly humane campaigner helps, however, to illuminate the Aristotelian idea that reasons of justice are distinguished by their 'form'. It helps us to see that, unlike some other moral virtues, the virtue of justice has no special subject-matter of its own, no special goods and ills over which it presides and which fill its horizons.[10] The humane person is distinguished from many others—eg from the honest person and the loyal person—by the evils she is especially concerned about, namely those evils defined by their connection with suffering. Not so the just person. She deals in many goods and ills, including, but not limited to, the infliction and non-alleviation of suffering. She also cares about the goods and ills which animate honest and loyal people, respectively. She is distinguished from all of them, not by *which* goods and ills she cares about, but by *how* she cares about them, namely as possible objects of allocation, whether geometric or arithmetic. Her distinctive concerns are distinguished, in that sense only, by their form.[11]

4. The myth of 'formal justice'

This Aristotelian idea is widely misunderstood. I have often seen it suggested that Aristotle espouses principles of 'formal justice' as opposed to principles of 'substantive justice'.[12] But Aristotle

---

[10] In some people's work this role is filled by the good of equality. I am among those who believe that there is no such good (even though I often support the policy proposals of those who say that there is). I was persuaded by Joseph Raz, *The Morality of Freedom* (Oxford 1986), Ch 9.

[11] Alas, Aristotle doesn't quite stand firm on this point. He is occasionally tempted to associate justice with certain distinctive goods and ills. On which see Bernard Williams, 'Justice as a Virtue' in A.O. Rorty (ed), *Essays on Aristotle's Ethics* (Berkeley 1981).

[12] Eg Patricia Smith, 'On Equality: Justice, Discrimination, and Equal Treatment' in Smith (ed), *Feminist Jurisprudence* (Oxford 1993), 17; Sandra Fredman, *Women and the Law* (Oxford 1997), 15 and 349; *Andrews v Law Society of British*

espouses nothing that could conceivably be called a principle of formal justice. He never says, as he is sometimes accused of saying, that people act justly whenever they act to restore people's relative positions to the *status quo ante*, or whenever they treat like people alike and unalike people unalike, or whenever they secure or restore some kind of proportion, etc. He never claims, in other words, that the just person is merely one whose principles take the correct form. In fact he explicitly denies this. He argues at some length that there are unsound principles of justice as well as sound ones, on both the distributive front and the corrective front.[13] The just person, it goes without saying, is the person who is animated only by *sound* principles of justice. To act on unsound principles of justice—such as 'give black people fewer benefits than white people' or 'an eye for an eye, a tooth for a tooth'—is to be an *un*just person; it is to possess, not the virtue, but the corresponding vice. But sound principles of justice and unsound principles of justice, as you can see from these examples, take the same distinctive forms. By isolating these forms Aristotle is not, therefore, attempting to distinguish the just from the unjust. He is attempting to distinguish the just and the unjust together on the one hand from, on the other hand, the generous and the mean, the honest and the dishonest, the courageous and the cowardly, etc. The form of some principles, in other words, makes them principles of justice. It does not make them *sound* principles of justice.

It follows that, for Aristotle, any principles which merely have the right form and nothing else—these so-called principles of 'formal justice'—are not, and cannot be, sound ones. The only sound principles of justice are (in the language commonly used by participants in this debate) 'substantive' ones; ie ones that have healthy flesh on their allocative bones, ones that tend to allocate the *right* goods and ills to the *right* people on the *right* grounds. There may, of course, be several right grounds and they may

---

Columbia [1989] 1 SCR 143 at 166 per McIntyre J. I will continue to use the terminology of 'formal' and 'substantive', with stipulated meanings, even though I find it very slippery (see Ch 8).

[13] This is the main point of his attack on 'the Pythagoreans' from *NE* $1132^b 22$ onwards.

conflict in what they identify as the right allocations for the right people. But it does not follow that any old ground for any old allocation is right. On the contrary, *some* must be mistaken or there is no such thing as the vice of injustice.

The claim here that the only sound principles of justice are substantive ones rather than formal ones should not be mistaken, as a lawyer might well mistake it, for the claim that there are no sound principles of *procedural* justice.[14] Arguably Aristotle's typology of forms of justice is incomplete in its omission of procedural justice. Arguably considerations of procedural justice are neither distributive nor corrective in form. They are concerned with the interpersonal allocation of goods and ills, but not so much with what would *count as* a sound allocation—whether geometrically or arithmetically—as with *how to go about making* a sound allocation. This need not, of course, be an entirely separate question. There may be an interplay. The fact that it was approached in the right way might turn out, for example, to be one of the factors contributing to making a certain allocation count as correctively or distributively just. Perhaps the fact that the doctrines of *audi alterem partem* and *nemo iudex in parte sua* were observed not only made it more likely that a just settlement of a dispute would be arrived at, but also made whatever settlement of the dispute was arrived at more just than it would have been had it been arrived at by other means.[15] So perhaps it would be a

---

[14] Collapsing the formal and the procedural: Patricia Smith, 'On Equality', above note 12, 17; Matthew Kramer, 'Justice as Constancy', *Law and Philosophy* 16 (1997), 56.

[15] John Rawls famously distinguished principles of 'perfect procedural justice' (which ensure that an independently specified just distribution or correction will emerge from the procedure) from principles of 'pure procedural justice' (which *entail* that a just distribution or correction will emerge, because whatever distribution or correction emerges from the procedure counts as just by definition). See Rawls, *A Theory of Justice* (Cambridge, Mass. 1971), 84–5. Rawls did not consider the possibility of hybrid 'part-perfect, part-pure' principles of procedural justice which partly constitute the justice of an allocation but also partly contribute to its being just according to other independent principles of justice. A classic example of such a hybrid principle is the principle that justice is not done unless it is seen to be done, which turns one aspect of due process—viz. the openness of the decision-making—into a logically necessary but not logically sufficient condition of a just outcome.

mistake to list procedural justice as simply another quite distinct form of justice alongside the corrective and distributive forms. Perhaps, indeed, the relationships among all the forms of justice are more complex that at first it appeared. But be that as it may, any principles of procedural justice that may turn out to exist are identical to principles of corrective and distributive justice in at least one respect. They cannot be valid principles on account of their form alone. Of all the possible ways in which one might go about making allocations of goods and ills between people, some are sound ways and others are unsound ways. The just person uses only the sound ways. She uses only sound principles of procedural justice and leaves unsound ones—like 'when in doubt, follow your prejudices'—to the unjust person. So even the just person's principles of *procedural* justice, if she has any, have healthy flesh on their allocative bones. Even they are principles of substantive justice as opposed to principles of formal justice, even though (using the treacherous word 'substantive' in a different sense) they are, *ex hypothesi*, principles of procedural justice, rather than principles of substantive justice.

5. The forms of justice and the forms of law

In the valuable Aristotelian insight that the concerns of the just person are distinguished from those of other morally virtuous people by their form, we find, at long last, our first serious proposal for linking justice to law. Maybe the form of justice, or one of the forms of justice, is also the form of law. In the hands of some legal scholars, sometimes known as legal formalists, this idea was built up into the self-congratulatory doctrine that law, so long as it remains true to its own distinctive form, cannot but be just.[16] For it is then *formally* just. Alas, as I pointed out a moment

---

[16] Or in one respect just, even though possibly unjust in other respects. This much less self-congratulatory (but still too self-congratulatory) variation is the one ventured by H.L.A. Hart in *The Concept of Law* (Oxford 1961) at 155–7 and at 202, and usefully classified as 'moderate formalism' by David Lyons in 'On Formal Justice', *Cornell Law Review* 58 (1973), 833. For a sophisticated contemporary rewriting of the more radical legal formalist position, see Ernest Weinrib *The Idea of Private Law* (Cambridge, Mass. 1995).

ago, there can be no justice at all in so-called formal justice.[17] The forms of justice are also, by the same token, the forms of injustice. So the mere fact that law has a certain form and remains true to it can't ensure that it is in any way just. But maybe it *can* explain, all the same, why law is the kind of thing that *ought* to be just. Maybe the form of law matches the form of justice (or one of the forms of justice) and that is why law necessarily holds itself out for evaluation specifically in the dimension of justice and injustice. Whatever takes justice's form, you may say, stands or falls by justice's lights, for necessarily—by its very form—it purports to be just.

So what is the form of law? The first problem with this question is that it is not clear what it means. Are we talking about the form that individual laws take, or the form of whole legal systems, or the form of legal arguments, or the form of legal institutions? All of these things are labelled, on occasions, by the abstract noun 'law'. For the moment I will assume that we are interested in the form that individual laws take, on the simple ground that we can at least imagine these figuring on someone's rational horizons, as reasons for and against action. But then we have another problem. The next problem is that there is not really much of any interest to say about the form that individual laws take. The most important step forward in twentieth-century jurisprudence came, after all, with H.L.A. Hart's dawning realization that individual laws do not really have much in the way of a distinctive form. Many of his predecessors had laboured long and hard to squeeze all laws into a single form (eg 'commands of

---

[17] A recent attempt to resurrect the idea that being formally just is a distinct way of being just is Matthew Kramer's in 'Justice as Constancy', above note 14. Kramer pays an excessive price for this attempt. It forces him to the conclusion that being just is not necessarily a way of being good; ie a moral virtue. (I should add that I may be misunderstanding the aim of Kramer's article. As mentioned above, he is one of those who speak interchangeably of formal justice and *procedural* justice. If he is defending the idea that being *procedurally* just is a distinct way of being just, then fine. But in that case he has no warrant for his conclusion that being just is not necessarily a way of being good, for there *is* moral virtue in following sound principles of procedural justice. This is true of sound principles of procedural justice belonging to all the categories enumerated above in note 15.)

the sovereign backed up by the threat of a sanction' or 'directives to officials to apply sanctions if certain conditions are met') in the hope that by their form alone some things might give themselves away as laws. Hart showed us why any such hope is a vain one: laws come in diverse forms and share those diverse forms with many things that are not laws.[18] Probably the most one can say of the form of laws, as such, is that all of them take the form of rules.[19] If some consideration is mentioned in legal argument or legal thinking which is not a rule, that does not stop it from being legally relevant, of course, but it does stop it from being a law. It is in the nature of all laws to be rules—in other words, to hold themselves out as settling what is to be done on more than one occasion—and it is therefore in the nature of legal systems, as Hart said, to be systems of rules.[20]

You may say that there is little here for legal formalists and their friends to get their teeth into, little that could serve to associate law with justice. But some have found enough. Some, including Hart himself, have thought that the mere fact that all laws are rules is enough to associate laws with justice.[21] The thinking goes something like this. Whenever there are rules, there are considerations which hold themselves out as settling what is to be done on more than one occasion. This means that each rule potentially applies to more than one person. This means in turn that, when rules are used, people can always compare how the rules were applied to them with how they were applied to other people. They can ask whether the benefits and burdens of the rule were correctly allocated among those who were affected by the rule. And this is surely a question of distributive justice, for it is a question of whether certain goods and ills were correctly divided up among various candidates. Thus whenever a rule is in play, a question of justice is necessarily in play, and since all laws are rules, the same necessarily applies to laws. The very form of laws is accordingly a form of justice. True enough, it doesn't follow from this that merely by being a system of rules; ie merely by being what it necessarily is, a legal system exhibits any modicum of justice. Perhaps, as I suggested above, that would indeed

---

[18] *The Concept of Law*, above note 16, 26ff.   [19] Ibid 77–8.
[20] Ibid 95–6.   [21] Ibid 156–7.

be too self-congratulatory a conclusion. What does follow, however, is that if the law's rules are sound then the law is just, and, more importantly, that *it is in the name of justice that the law should aim to have sound rules*. For while one-off decisions and actions may exhibit many other moral virtues, justice is the special virtue of the rule-user. And this in turn makes justice the special virtue—the first virtue, if you like—of the law and its institutions.

This line of thought harbours many interlaced confusions and non-sequiturs. The most important, for our purposes, are these. First, it does not follow from the fact that rules apply on more than one occasion that they apply to more than one person. I have a rule not to drink alcohol (let us suppose) and it is a rule that applies, and moreover purports to apply, to nobody but me. This is a rule not of justice but of temperance—one designed specifically for me with my distinctive set of inclinations towards overindulgence. Although legal rules are typically of broader application than this, they need not be. The rule that Queen Elizabeth II is to reside at Windsor Castle for the duration of her reign is a possible legal rule—and it is one designed specifically for her. Secondly, there is no reason to suppose that the benefits and burdens of a rule, even when it does apply to more than one person, need to be divided up at all. Why assume that they are in short supply? If I have a rule that instructs me to tell no lies, then I comply with it by telling no lies. Normally I have an inexhaustible stock of lies not to tell, so my not telling one to you doesn't use up a non-lie that I might have saved for someone else. So I don't need to divide up the benefit of my rule, or allocate it according to some other kind of proportion. The only situation in which this is not true is the special situation in which I must lie to avoid my telling another lie. If the two lies will be to two different people, then admittedly a question may arise—and if it does arise it is admittedly a question of distributive justice—of who is to be lied to. But this question does not arise because I have a rule. It arises because I have a one-off decision to make in the face of a moral conflict. It just happens, incidentally, to be a conflict involving a rule. The rule itself is one, not of justice, but of honesty.

What is true is that people may *interpret* any rule purporting to apply to more than one person as if it were a ground of allocation between those people. It does not follow that this is what it is.

What rule it is depends on how it figures on the rational horizon of the rule-user. If I betray a friend and not another, then the first may wonder what he did to deserve it, why he was picked out for bad treatment, etc. But the answer may be: nothing, nothing at all. When I betrayed him I wasn't distributing the benefits and burdens of the rule 'Don't betray your friends'. I wasn't distributing anything. I was just plain violating the rule, and if the friend I betrayed wants to complain about this, it is my disloyalty he should begin by complaining about, for the rule I violated is a rule of loyalty. If he thinks there is an added insult—ie an injustice— in the fact that I didn't betray my other friend instead, or as well, then he judges me by his rules, not mine. I am simply an ordinary moderately loyal soul aiming not to betray anyone, and occasionally failing. Whereas my aggrieved friend who complains of injustice mistakes me for some kind of allocation fanatic who spends time deciding whom he should betray, given that he is going to betray someone.

Do some people perhaps read law in this rather bizarre way? Do they interpret a legal system as a kind of allocation fanatic in respect of its own rules, always covertly dividing up the benefits and burdens of those rules as between different people in different cases when, taken at face value, the rules mention no such rationing? Is adherence to the rules of precedent, in the view of some, secretly capped at a certain quota, so that whenever the law says to the Court of Appeal 'follow the decisions of the House of Lords' and I lose a case in the Court of Appeal *per incuriam* I should not only complain about the judicial infidelity to law, but also point to someone else in another case properly decided who somehow got my share of judicial fidelity as well as her own? It sounds like a childish reaction, the reaction of somebody who has grasped the forms of justice but hasn't yet grasped the substance.[22] Perhaps some people do interpret all legal rules this way. But if they do, and they do it only with law and not with (say) their friends and colleagues, it must be because there is

---

[22] Cf Jean Piaget's famous study *The Moral Judgment of the Child* (New York 1965), which explains how children develop an ability to frame problems as problems of justice, ie as allocative problems, before they come to be able to distinguish sound allocations from unsound ones.

something else about law apart from the fact that laws are rules that leads people to interpret those rules automatically as rules of justice. So this line of inquiry simply leads us back, by a circuitous route, to the original question of why law should be held up to the light of justice, rather than some other moral light. The answer cannot be that laws are rules, for there can be rules of honesty, loyalty, trustworthiness, temperance, etc, as well as rules of justice. We still want to know why sound legal rules couldn't equally belong to these other categories of rules,[23] but must somehow always be interpreted as purporting to be *just*.

6. Equity as justice's rebellion against law

The foregoing remarks told against the proposal that every act of following a rule, even if it is a sound rule, is a manifestation of justice. But the false association of justice with rules, and hence with laws, also needs to be broken in the other direction. Not every manifestation of justice is an act of following a sound rule. For some, just rulings are not governed by nor capable of being elevated to any sound rule of justice. They are based on a weighing of allocative considerations in their raw, unruly form. Solomon's justice was justice ad hoc. Likewise the justice of a modern-day arbitrator who, unlike a judge in a court of law, looks at the merits of a case before him without being bound to explain how his decision in this case has been or would be generalized to dictate a decision in another case.

On this point it is worth returning to some cautionary remarks of Aristotle's. He argues that the very nature of laws—what we might call their 'ruliness'—makes them prone to over-generality, and hence injustice. 'The reason', he says,

is that all law is universal but about some things it is not possible to make a universal statement which is correct. In those cases, then, in which it is necessary to speak universally, but not possible to do so correctly, the law takes the usual case, though it is not ignorant of the possibility of error.[24]

---

[23] Cf. *NE*, 1129^{b}19ff, in which Aristotle observes that the law enforces rules of courage, temperance, even-temperedness, etc.

[24] *NE*, 1137^{b}12–17.

THE VIRTUE OF JUSTICE AND THE CHARACTER OF LAW 255

The result is that laws inevitably call, on occasions, for adjustment at their point of application to remove the error. And this, says Aristotle,

> is the nature of the equitable, a correction of law where it is defective owing to its universality.... It is plain, then, what the equitable is, and that it is just and is better than one kind of justice [viz. legal justice]. It is evident also from this who the equitable man is; the man who chooses and does such acts, and is no stickler for his rights in a bad sense but tends to take less than his share though he has law on his side, is equitable, and this state of character is equity, which is a sort of justice and not a different state of character.[25]

These remarks confirm my earlier point that, for Aristotle, there is no such thing as a principle of formal justice. Some principles that are of the correct form to be principles of justice are nevertheless unsound (eg the principle that one should always take the share which one has a legal right to take, the following of which makes one 'a stickler for one's rights in a bad sense') and these principles would not, therefore, be relied upon by a just person. But we also need to note another important implication of this Aristotelian view. It is very commonly thought, and not only among lawyers, that it is justice which puts pressure on the law to be 'ruly'; ie to rule on further cases whenever it rules on one case. If Aristotle is right, as I think he is, then the pressure is mainly, although not exclusively, in the opposite direction. It is law which mainly puts pressure on justice to be of general application, and this pressure is a pressure which justice sometimes finds uncomfortable, and thus occasionally rebels against. There are some just rulings, to put it another way, which are not amenable to being rendered as rules; but legal systems, being systems of rules, will tend to insist on trying to render them as rules all the same, a tendency which, for the sake of justice itself, sometimes needs to have its wings clipped. That, as Aristotle says, is where equity comes into play. So not only does the fact that legal systems are systems of rules fail to explain why they ought to be just; the fact that they ought to be just also tells *against* legal

---

[25] *NE*, 1137b26–1138ª2.

systems being too true to their 'ruly' natures, i.e. insisting on generalizing everything all the time.

7. Justice in adjudication

You may say that we are not much further forward. We have heard of some unsuccessful attempts to link law with justice but, so far, nothing very hopeful has emerged. But this is not quite true. For our critique of the view that the law's ruliness is what holds it up to the light of justice also revealed a few more promising ideas. Of these, the most promising is this. It is that laws, like other rules, are forced into the forms of justice only at the point at which their benefits and burdens fall to be *rationed*, and not before. At this point, it seems, questions of interpersonal allocation, and hence questions of justice, cannot but enter into the horizons of the rule user. For the most part the benefits and burdens of legal rules do not have to be rationed at all. I don't have a quota of contracts to make and break this week, so the legal rules to the effect that I am empowered to make contracts but forbidden from breaking them have no built-in allocative dimension. They are basic rules of trustworthiness. But they do come to have a secondary allocative dimension, or secondary allocative implications, whenever a case for breach of contract comes before the courts. For at this point the court cannot but face up to the question of who is to bear the costs of the alleged breach, and in what proportions, and on what grounds, etc. It is now a situation in which there are no winners without losers, no gains without losses, and questions of how to allocate these gains and losses cannot but arise. Some of these questions may be corrective questions about whether and how to restore the parties to some *status quo ante* or *status quo alter*; some may be distributive questions about how to divide up the costs, or how to scale the penalties, in the event of multiple wrongdoers or multiple contributions to wrongdoing; some may be procedural questions about how to go about deciding any or all of these things; eg by rearranging the burdens of proof. All of these are questions of justice. They do not arise because there are rules involved. Questions of justice arise equally whether there are applicable rules or not. They arise, in other words, irrespective of whether we are

THE VIRTUE OF JUSTICE AND THE CHARACTER OF LAW 257

judges or arbitrators, irrespective of whether we decide in the name of the law or without reference to the law, irrespective of whether our approach to the decision is rule-based or ad hoc. The reason they arise is not that laws are involved but that *adjudication* is involved.

The connection of justice to law, on this view, is indirect and non-exclusive. It comes of the combination of two facts: first, that adjudicative institutions should be just above all; second, that adjudicative institutions are, in a sense, the lynchpin of all legal systems. Recall Hart's discovery that individual laws have nothing much in the way of a distinctive form. This was famously coupled with his no less important discovery that *legal systems* have a great deal in the way of a distinctive form. Each is a system of rules created and applied by people and institutions that are themselves also subject to the rules of the system. And for the system to be a legal system, at least some of those institutions need, as Hart explained, to be adjudicative institutions.[26] It is no legal system if there are no institutions that are charged with resolving disputes that arise from the non-observance of the rules, or from the incompleteness or obscurity of the rules. Indeed, as Hart didn't spell out but others have added, the presence of courts turns out to be more crucial to the existence of a legal system than the presence of any other legal institutions.[27] One may have a legal system with no legislature and no police force and no legal professions—that is to say a purely customary legal system—but one has no legal system at all until one has courts; ie adjudicative institutions charged with administering a system of rules by which they themselves are bound (and indeed, as Hart also said, constituted).

The fact that these adjudicative institutions are bound and constituted by rules is by no means irrelevant, I should stress, to what they should do in order to be just. One effect of the fact that courts are adjudicating problems arising under a system of rules is

---

[26] *The Concept of Law*, above note 16, 94–5.
[27] Raz, 'The Institutional Nature of Law' in his *The Authority of Law* (Oxford 1979), 103 at 105ff. Something like this thought also provides Dworkin with his starting point in *Law's Empire* (Cambridge, Mass. 1986), at 14–15, although he would not express it as I do. Dworkin goes on, in my view, to exaggerate its implications.

that, among the many goods and ills that they have to allocate between litigating parties, there are the extra goods and ills of fulfilled and frustrated legitimate expectations, these legitimate expectations having been forged by the rules themselves. This means that the fact that a certain institution is a court of law, and not a mere arbitrator, does sometimes make a difference to what answer it should give to questions of justice. Perhaps the underlying mistake of some 'legal formalists' is to think that the *only* goods and ills that have to be allocated between litigating parties are the goods and ills of fulfilled and frustrated expectations, so that so long as the law doesn't frustrate any of the expectations it creates, but fulfils them all by sticking to the rules, it cannot but be just. There are three mistakes here. The first mistake is the neglect of the other things that must still be allocated apart from the frustrated and fulfilled expectations (such as the losses and the penalties). The second mistake is the mistake of thinking that justice would always be in favour of *minimizing* frustrated expectations on both sides when in fact, were the expectations morally abhorrent ones, justice might be in favour of *maximizing* frustrated expectations on both sides. The third mistake is to think that whatever expectations the law itself creates cannot but be legitimate ones, even when they are immoral ones. We should not slip into any of these mistakes. Thus while the fact that courts of law are administering a system of rules may make some difference to how they ought to answer questions of justice, this fact can't be relied upon to make *all* the difference. If they are to be just, the courts should still not surrender to a rule that cannot be justly applied; in that case, justice would have the courts either change the rule (by distinguishing or overruling) or depart from the rule in favour of a conclusion that would be just on its raw unruly merits (by resort to equity, or *in extremis* by civil disobedience).[28]

---

[28] Of course, the judicial obligation of fidelity to law may sometimes militate against the courts taking either of these routes. But this only goes to show that occasionally judges are not morally well placed to fulfil their definitive adjudicative mission to be just. In such cases—as Lord Denning's remarkable judicial *oeuvre* illustrates—there is always a temptation for judges to behave like arbitrators, to emphasize the first part of their oath at the expense of the second, to dispense '*justice* according to law', rather than 'justice *according to law*'. The

But beyond all these mistakes there lurks the biggest mistake of all. The fact that legal systems are systems of rules can admittedly make a difference to what answer courts should give to questions of justice. But the fact that courts invariably have to face questions of justice in the first place has little to do with the fact that legal systems are systems of rules. It has everything to do with the fact that courts are adjudicative institutions. Any adjudicative institution, whether or not it is administering a system of rules, ought to be just above all. In this respect, courts are in exactly the same position as arbitrators.

8. Extending the priority of justice

Those who want to see justice prioritized by other institutions— for example, by legislatures and regulatory bodies—are saying, in effect, that they want these institutions to adopt the ethos of adjudicative institutions. They want them to develop rational horizons in which every problem is seen first and foremost as an allocative (be that either distributive or corrective) problem. This ambition acquired contemporary philosophical currency in the Rawlsian claim that 'justice is the first virtue of social institutions'.[29] For Rawls the whole problem of social organization fell to be constructed, first and foremost, as a problem of who gets how much of what and why. Recall that the question confronted by our cypher-like representatives in Rawls' original position is the question of how much of everything each of them will end up getting once the veil of ignorance is lifted and they are released into the real world. Some critics of Rawls, often known as 'communitarians', portrayed the main failing of this mechanism as its individualistic conceptualization.[30] People were represented, in the original position, as atomistic individuals concerned only to look after themselves, free of any attachments to each other and devoid of any joint pursuits. No doubt this is a problem

---

formalists, of course, underestimate the extent to which the two parts of this oath may be in tension with each other.

[29] *A Theory of Justice*, above note 15, at 3.

[30] For the most measured critique of the 'communitarian' critique, see Stephen Mulhall and Adam Swift, *Liberals and Communitarians* (2nd ed, Oxford 1996).

for the Rawlsian project, but it is easily remedied by allowing groups, communities, social classes, nations, etc, to be represented in their own right in the original position. This would instantly eradicate the individualism. But it would not eradicate another aspect of the Rawlsian scheme, which some critics seem to confuse with its individualistic conceptualization.[31] This is its preoccupation with allocation. The original position is an adjudicative environment, a kind of grand court of social design, and the society it designs, it designs in its own image. It sets up social institutions on the assumption that all of them must exist first and foremost to judge or to arbitrate in social conflict. It may be conflict between competing individuals or between competing groups, communities, etc—in other words, it may be a more individualistic or a more 'communitarian' conflict—but the decisions to be faced are all to be faced as responses to actual or potential disputes between rival contenders, in which every winner has a corresponding loser, and the question before each institution is accordingly which shall win and which shall lose. As faced by social institutions, according to this Rawlsian view, all moral conflicts are to be interpreted primarily as allocative conflicts calling for adjudication.

There are many opacities in Rawls' explanation of this view. In particular, he never makes it clear which institutions are supposed to count as social institutions in the relevant sense. Is Marks and Spencer or British Telecom a social institution? How about the Methodist Church or the Daily Telegraph? Or well-known charities like the Children's Society and the Royal National Institute of Blind People?[32] That justice is the first virtue of all these institutions may well seem counter-intuitive. In particular, isn't

---

[31] eg Michael Sandel, *Liberalism and the Limits of Justice* (Cambridge 1982), 168–73.

[32] We are not helped much by a restriction Rawls adds to the effect that his own proposed principles of justice are those that apply to the institutions making up the 'basic structure' of a society (*A Theory of Justice*, above note 15, 7–8). This is not supposed to qualify the thesis that justice is the first virtue of social institutions, but merely to leave open the possibility that social institutions outside 'the basic structure' should be animated by *different principles* of justice. Besides, if one believes—as I do—that voluntary organizations play a social role of constitutional importance, then the lack of clarity in the notion of a 'social institution' is echoed as an lack of clarity in the notion of 'the basic structure'.

charity a more natural candidate to be the first virtue of charities? The problem is tricky and cannot be discussed here.[33] To reduce complications, I will leave non-governmental social institutions on one side for present purposes and read the Rawlsian claim as intended to apply principally to the institutions of government, including but not limited to those with law-making powers. Rawls' reason for regarding justice as the first virtue of *these* institutions seems to be that all of them find themselves in what he calls 'the circumstances of justice'.[34] In particular, all of them preside over scarce public resources and all must therefore put at the centre of their attention the question of who is going to get how much of what and why. It is all very well for an institution to be generous, or loyal, or temperate, or courageous (it may be said) when they have plenty of goods to go round and no expense need be spared in the eradication of ills. But the same doesn't hold when whatever one does must have losers as well as winners. Then justice necessarily comes first. One is inevitably in a Solomonic position, and one must inevitably think adjudicatively. Wasn't this, indeed, just what I said in the previous section? Didn't I say that justice must be the first virtue of the courts precisely because once we get to court there cannot be winners without losers? In which case isn't Rawls right to think that the same point applies more generally across the affairs of government? And in particular doesn't it apply to law-making bodies other than the courts—eg to the whole gamut of legislatures and regulators—whose law-making activities cannot but be conducted within the limits of scarce public resources? In which case isn't it indeed the case that we should read every legal rule as an allocative rule, or a purportedly allocative rule, and hold it up to the light of justice in judging it?

9. First response: accidental allocation

One answer to this question is snappy but ultimately unsatisfying. The answer is that the best way for scarce resources to be

---

[33] I discuss it further in 'The Virtue of Charity and its Foils' in Charles Mitchell and Sue Moody (eds), *Foundations of Charity* (Oxford 2000).

[34] *A Theory of Justice*, above note 15, 126ff.

institutionally allocated is not necessarily for the relevant institutions to have predominantly allocative rational horizons. With courts and arbitrators we have no logical option. It is part of their nature to decide who wins and who loses *by asking who wins and who loses*. That is the very question that confronts them, and the fact that they are confronted by this question—not the mere fact that the question can be asked—is what makes them adjudicative institutions. But with other governmental institutions it is logically open to us to conceal from them, or at least to downplay, the allocative character of their activities. A court stops being a court if it stops being confronted with the question of who wins and who loses, but a hospital does not, under the same conditions, stop being a hospital. For much of its history the National Health Service included rather few explicit adjudicative mechanisms. Rationing of medical treatment was real enough, but it was often the more or less accidental outcome of bureaucratic mechanisms and professional interventions which did not directly confront the relative positions of winners and losers. The rules (legal and otherwise) had allocative consequences but did not manifest themselves as allocative rules on the rational horizons of the NHS's own rule-users. Possibly this meant that many of the allocations were unjust ones. But not necessarily. As with all other practical problems, an indirect strategy of allocating without attempting to allocate might have a better hit rate, and this means a better hit rate *even by the standards of justice itself*. Surely the same may hold of legislatures, regulators, government departments, and other public authorities?

This response merits at least three rejoinders. The first is that it mainly serves to postpone the moment of truth. We still want to know whether the standards of justice are the most important standards by which to judge the actions of the NHS and its ilk. It may be true—although the matter is morally problematic—that a wedge sometimes needs to be driven between the standards we should use in evaluating the actions of certain people and institutions and the standards they themselves should use in acting.[35] But be that as it may, the question remains of whether rules of

---

[35] The most important contemporary study of this type of asymmetry is Derek Parfit's *Reasons and Persons* (Oxford 1984), especially Chs 1–3.

justice are the right ones for *anyone* to prioritize so far as the activities of the NHS are concerned. To say that sometimes less injustice will be inflicted by the NHS if the NHS has other rational horizons than those of justice simply concedes, for the sake of argument, that the answer is yes.

And besides, to move onto the second rejoinder, there is a particular difficulty in driving the relevant wedge in the case of justice. We already mentioned that at least some rules of procedural justice are arguably such that they affect constitutively, and not merely instrumentally, the justice of the resulting allocation. This makes it more difficult to conceive of an action that has accidentally just results, for the idea of an accidentally just procedure has a paradoxical air about it. Can we imagine a case in which *audi alterem partem*, for instance, is unintentionally complied with?

Finally, and most straightforwardly, one may doubt whether (even apart from any constitutive contribution that needs to be made by just procedure) an accidental allocation—one not being deliberately adjusted for allocative results at any level in the organization—really is very likely to be a just one under today's cultural conditions. In the face of rapid technological change, ever-widening social pluralism, and constantly changing public expectations, practices that might once have served to allocate justly—assuming for a moment that this is indeed the object of the exercise—are apt to call for constant reappraisal if just allocations are not to rapidly descend into being unjust ones. This is the main purpose of the rules against 'indirect discrimination' familiar from British anti-discrimination law. They are needed to tackle the accidentally discriminatory effects of actions and practices undertaken without discriminatory intentions, and indeed—in some cases—without any allocative intentions at all. We may sometimes regret the extent to which these rules insinuate allocative preoccupations into the work of institutions like the NHS, but if we do regret this it surely cannot be because such institutions really allocate better when they do not have allocative preoccupations. The undeniable moral force of many indirect discrimination claims shows that often enough they do not.[36]

---

[36] It is not for nothing that the phenomenon of indirect discrimination, or at least a version of it, is sometimes known as 'institutional discrimination'. For

Rather, our regret must come of the fact that allocating is not the only job they have to do, and that allocative preoccupations sometimes seem to distract them from other objectives they should serve and other horizons, accordingly, that they should cultivate.

10. Second response: non-scarce and non-allocable goods

This brings us to a second and more fruitful response to the Rawlsian view. This response amounts to a denial that all governmental activity genuinely takes place under 'the circumstances of justice' as described by Rawls. The suggestion is not that the government is failing to take advantage of resources that, if deployed, would put an end to some of the alleged scarcity (although probably this suggestion has some truth to it). The suggestion, rather, is that not all the goods over which the government presides are, in the relevant sense, 'resources'. Not all, to put it another way, are scarce goods amenable to allocation. There are two kinds of counter-examples. First, even among goods that are amenable to allocation, some are not scarce. Just as there is an unlimited number of lies that it is open to me not to tell, so there is an unlimited number of lies that it is open to the Department of Trade and Industry not to tell. In the same vein, there is no quota of official abstention from torture which needs to be distributed by the police or the army. There is in principle an infinite amount of official abstention from torture to go round. If the police and army have legal duties not to torture people it is begging the question in favour of the Rawlsian view to interpret these as duties of justice; ie allocative duties. Barring special features which give them an allocative dimension they are straightforward duties of humanity, duties not intentionally to inflict suffering. Secondly, even among those goods which are admittedly scarce, some are not amenable to allocation. Some public bodies preside over non-excludable public goods like the cultivation of the arts, the development of an attractive built environment, the cleanliness of the air, the prevention of

further discussion see Christopher McCrudden, 'Institutional Discrimination', *Oxford Journal of Legal Studies* 2 (1982), 303.

epidemics, or the elimination of intolerance. In a Rawlsian vein one may think that planning authorities, to take but one example, should be concerned first and foremost with the resolution of conflicts between developers and local objectors, so that their duties to consider objections are mainly allocative duties. Who should get how much natural light? Who should bear the costs of providing for increased car use in the neighbourhood? And so on. But perhaps planning authorities should sometimes put questions of this type in second place behind the question of how to bring about the most spectacular cityscape, never mind who gets how much out of it. Perhaps planning authorities should be visionary or creative as well as, or even as opposed to, being just, in which case they should think in non-allocative as well as, or rather than, allocative terms. For apart from the private goods that they allocate among applicants and objectors there are also public goods over which they preside, and among those public goods are some inexcludable public goods which are goods all round, not (or not only) goods for any person or group in particular. That London be more spectacular is one example of such a good.

What is true, of course, is that the governmental activities I just mentioned as non-allocative inevitably have allocative *consequences*, and so can always be given an allocative spin in terms of those consequences. The rule against police torture can be interpreted as a ranking of the interests of suspected terrorists above the interests of those they may be about to kill or maim. The practice of favouring spectacular cityscapes can be read as feeding the appetites of an aesthetic elite at the expense of providing habitable homes for ordinary folk. These interpretations focus on distributive proportionality. But the question is not whether we *can* interpret the activities of such social institutions in this allocative way. The question is whether we *should* do so. One objection to this way of conceiving all activities of government— and the one which strikes me as most significant—is that it is a reductive way of conceiving the values thereby implicated. Goods that are not scarce or not allocable are revalued in terms of goods that are both scarce and allocable in order to make an allocative issue of them. Police torture is reduced to a mere quantum of suffering (or something like that) in order to be traded off against the suffering of other people thereby avoided;

the argument that a humane person or institution does not deliberately inflict suffering even in order to prevent greater suffering then cuts no ice. Beautiful environments are regarded as mere vehicles for pleasure, say, so that the pleasure taken in them by some people can be compared with the lack of pleasure they give to others, or with the greater pleasure others might get from other uses of the same resources. The NHS, in the same vein, has to be regarded as a *mere* service, so that the amount of service each person gets can be compared with the amount that other people get, never mind that the price of this way of looking at the health service is that other goods—such as the inexcludable public good of spontaneous public compassion—cannot any longer thrive within its walls. And so on. Such reductivism is central to the Rawlsian project. All goods over which social institutions preside are reduced to 'social primary goods', understood as allocable scarce resources.[37] The avoidance of torture, the cultivation of spectacular cityscapes, the provision of compassionate health services, and so on, are not themselves primary goods but rather further 'secondary' goods to be bought or transacted, and hence held up for allocation, in terms of primary goods. Hence they are not to be approached by government under their own native descriptions but under other descriptions, as the preoccupations of sectional interest groups vying for a bigger share of scarce public expenditure or a larger share of civil liberties, etc. They are brought under the circumstances of justice artificially by converting them into other things which are both scarce and amenable to allocation. I know of no general reason to think that this reductive Rawlsian move, this enforced governmental obliviousness to goods that are not allocable and/or not scarce, is either necessary or desirable. I know of no general reason to think, in other words, that the rational horizons of governmental institutions ought to be manipulated to conceal (or consign to the background) the wealth of non-allocative moral

---

[37] *A Theory of Justice*, above note 15, 54–5. The exception is the social primary good of self-respect, which is not an allocable scarce resource, for it is not a resource at all. My own view is that once Rawls admits self-respect to the list of social primary goods his whole edifice comes tumbling down. So it is not surprising that he postpones consideration of it to the end of the book.

considerations, so that it cannot but be the case that justice becomes their first virtue.

This response to the Rawlsian view, although important and revealing, harbours one quite serious exaggeration.[38] Scarcity is one reason why an allocable good might have to be confronted allocatively. But it is not the only reason. Some allocable goods and ills are, as we might put it, *essentially* allocative. It is impossible to think about punishing or rewarding, for example, non-allocatively. It is part of their nature that they are meted out *for* something, and as soon as one asks 'For what?' one implicitly asks 'To whom?' So we should concede that the 'circumstances of justice' are a bit more pervasive than the preceding paragraphs suggested. Questions of justice are forced upon us whenever an allocable good or ill is *either* in short supply *or* essentially allocative. One way to explain the Rawlsian error is to say that he made everything (even punishment and its absence) seem to be in short supply, so that he no longer needed to say anything about essentially allocative goods and ills. An opposite error would be to make every good or ill seem essentially allocative, so that it would never be necessary to mention scarcity in order to force a question of justice onto the table.[39] In whichever of these directions one errs, however, one still errs in forcing questions of justice onto the table too often.

11. The virtues of law

Let me end by bringing the discussion back to the law. When some people say that justice is the proper aspiration for the law, its first virtue, they are maybe just saying in an abbreviated way that justice is the proper ambition for the administration of the law by courts, tribunals, and so on (ie for legal adjudication). In that case I have no quarrel with them. This conclusion is sound, and is already enough by itself to explain why judges are known as Mrs Justice such-and-such and Lord Justice so-and-so, why a statute

---

[38] I am grateful to Leslie Green for pointing this out in comments on the orginal essay on which this chapter is based. See his 'The Germ of Justice', working paper, available at <http://ssrn.com/abstract=1703008> (at 7 November 2011).

[39] This error blights Michael Walzer's *Spheres of Justice* (New York 1977).

bearing on the workings of the courts and their officers might be called the Administration of Justice Act, and so on. But some people baulk at the idea that the quest for justice is limited to the administration of the law in the courts. No, they say, we want *just laws too*, not merely justly administered laws. If you are tempted to say this, you may be missing the point.

When I say that it is the administration of the law that should be just I don't mean that the law itself should be *less* than just. I mean it should be *more* than just. Naturally the law should be just, but it should also be honest, humane, considerate, charitable, courageous, prudent, temperate, trustworthy, and so on, and when these virtues cannot all be manifested together it should not be regarded as a foregone conclusion that any one of them has a general priority. Through its doctrines and institutions the law should, to put it another way, exhibit all the moral virtues that befit the many very different things that it does. Some of the things it does—eg the regulation of discrimination—call for a specifically just response.[40] But not all are like this. In regulating charities, for instance, the law itself should be charitable enough to understand and accommodate (in their own terms) the actions of charitable people. In regulating healthcare it should be compassionate enough to understand and accommodate (in their own terms) the compassionate actions of healthcare workers. And so on. It is only when these various worthwhile endeavours have broken down or gone awry to the extent that adjudication is needed that the priority of justice swings in automatically, for at this point, with a dispute underway, the problem cannot but become an allocative one.[41] Either there is a zero-sum situation— no winner without loser—that makes the situation one of scarcity, or there is an essentially allocative good or ill that has to be meted out, such as punishment. Sometimes both. But only once we get to the point of adjudication. To prioritize justice earlier in the story is, in my view, a counsel of despair. For justice is the first virtue of

---

[40] I have argued for this view in 'Discrimination as Injustice', *Oxford Journal of Legal Studies* 16 (1996), 353.

[41] John Finnis draws much the same conclusion much more quickly in *Natural Law and Natural Rights* (Oxford 1980), 179: 'the act of adjudication itself is always a matter for distributive justice'.

those institutions—adjudicative institutions—whose job it is to mop up when things have already gone wrong. Not only corrective justice, but justice *tout court*, is in a way a remedial virtue.[42] It is a virtue for dispute-resolvers and dispute-anticipators. The law, on the other hand, has many roles to play in getting things to go right in the first place, in guiding and facilitating people's worthwhile actions. It aims too low if it always conceives all these worthwhile activities in advance as potential sources of dispute, in need of adjudication, and hence fails to exhibit the other virtues needed to regulate a well-rounded society.

[42] Here I echo Sandel, *Liberalism and the Limits of Justice*, above note 31, at 30–2 and 171–2, although I obviously reject his assumption that the only alternative to a public culture in which justice takes priority is a public culture in which some kind of solidarity takes priority. Why are we looking for a *first* virtue at all? Sandel's quickly becomes the 'one true path' all over again.

II

Law in General

1. Dworkin's 'sociological question'

Is there anything both interesting and true to say about law in general, law as such, law wherever it may be found? If you have read as far as this final chapter then you may well be one of those who thinks, like me, that there is. You may even think, as I do, that some of the true and interesting things to be said about law in general bear on the very nature of law. They are things which must be true of something if it is to qualify as law, and hence if it is properly to be included in the data set when making either empirical or evaluative observations about law. That is what it means for such observations to be *about* law.

Ronald Dworkin warns that what I am calling the problem of the nature of law, the problem about what qualifies as law, conceals at least two different problems. He invites philosophers of law to focus on one of them and to forget the other:

We must take care to distinguish two questions, both of which might be described as questions about the nature of law. The first is sociological: what makes a particular structure of governance a legal system rather than some other form of social control, such as morality, religion, force, or terror? The second is doctrinal: what makes a statement of what the law of some jurisdiction requires or permits true? The two questions are interconnected but their differences are of capital importance. The sociological question has neither much practical nor much philosophical interest. The doctrinal question, on the contrary, is a question of enormous practical and considerable philosophical significance.[1]

It is an understatement to say that the two questions framed by Dworkin here are 'interconnected'. The second question openly presupposes that the law is divided into 'jurisdictions', and that

---

[1] Dworkin, 'Hart and the Concepts of Law', *Harvard Law Review Forum* 119 (2006), 95.

some things that are true of law in one jurisdiction are false of it in another. Rather obviously, these jurisdiction-specific truths are among the things that are not true of law in general. One of the major tasks of the philosophy of law, on any credible view, is to explain how such jurisdiction-specificity is possible. How can law be such that something that is true of it at Phuntsholing is not true of it at Jaigaon, or that something that is true of it at Haparanda is not true of it at Tornio? Do 'morality, religion, force, [and] terror' cleave to any analogous boundaries? If not— and it seems to me that they do not—then we are immediately thrust into the kind of puzzle about law that Dworkin sets aside as 'sociological'. Yet this is surely, even by Dworkin's lights, a puzzle of 'enormous practical and considerable philosophical significance'. Without understanding how law can vary from jurisdiction to jurisdiction we cannot begin to tackle the ensuing 'doctrinal' question about what the law of any given jurisdiction says on any given topic, and how it can possibly come to say it. When Question 2 can only be answered on the back of an answer to Question 1, Question 1 surely must have at least all the 'practical... and philosophical significance' of Question 2.

Nor is this the only point at which an answer to Dworkin's 'doctrinal' question piggybacks on an answer to his 'sociological' one. His 'doctrinal' question openly presupposes that 'the law of [a] jurisdiction requires [and] permits' things. We may well wonder, how does the law of anywhere get to do that? For that matter, how does the law of anywhere get to do *anything*? By whose agency? Once we get to that question it is not long before we are wondering: do 'morality, religion, force, [and] terror' get to do things too, and if so do they get to do the same things as law does, such as requiring and permitting, or different things? Hot on the heels of these questions we begin to ask ourselves—now clearly reaching the heart of the 'sociological' question—whether it is helpful to compare law with 'morality, religion, force, [and] terror', and in particular whether something slippery is going on when a legal system is classified, with these other things, as a 'structure of governance' or a 'form of social control'. Is there really any single genus, captured in either of these expressions, to which the apparently diverse species 'morality, religion, force, [and] terror', along with law, all belong? Is force a structure? Is terror governance? Is religion a form of control? Is morality social? And is law social, controlling, structured, or governing in the same sense as any, let alone all, of these? Dworkin's denial of 'much philosophical interest' in these questions puts a veneer of intellectual respectability on what may well by now be regarded, less flatteringly, as a refusal to subject his own principal assumptions to open-minded critical testing before embarking on an enquiry that presupposes their truth.

We may be put in mind here of Martin Krygier's complaint about H.L.A. Hart's repeated but unanalysed classification of law, in much the same vein, as a 'method of social control':

[I]t is a pity that, like many sociologists, [Hart] does not tell us what he means by social control. For it is an extremely murky concept, whether used by sociologists, as it so often is, or by analytical jurists. If ever a concept stood in need of clarification and dissection, this one does: it does not make clear what or who controls or what or who is controlled, and it invites a host of ontological problems when any attempt to clarify it is made.[2]

Like Krygier, I doubt whether law in general can helpfully be classified as a method of social control. As Krygier says, it was Hart himself who showed us why. Hart argued compellingly that law, by its nature, is capable of serving a wide range of social functions. He mentioned several, but emphasized two: getting people to do or avoid doing things 'irrespective of their wishes' and, by contrast, 'providing individuals with facilities for realizing their wishes'.[3] Although he is not entirely clear on the point, it seems that Hart intended 'social control' to serve as his umbrella expression for both of these (and indeed all other) possible social functions of law. But if so, as Krygier says, he was using the expression in a very wide and unrevealing (Krygier goes so far as to say 'vapid'[4]) way. He seemingly meant it to cover the cases in which people make use of the law to control aspects of their own

---

[2] Martin Krygier, 'The Concept of Law and Social Theory', Oxford Journal of Legal Studies 2 (1982), 155. See also Brian Tamanaha, Realistic Socio-Legal Theory: Pragmatism and a Social Theory of Law (Oxford 1997), 109.

[3] Hart, The Concept of Law (Oxford 1961), 27. (In this chapter, abbreviated CL.)

[4] Krygier, 'The Concept of Law', above note 2, 163.

lives.⁵ But it gives the opposite impression (and has been used by many writers before and since to give the opposite impression) of people and their lives being controlled through the law by others, or being controlled by the law itself. Since such a broadly Austinian picture of law's nature (as a controlling imposition) was the main one that Hart set out to destabilize in *The Concept of Law*, his choice of 'social control' as the umbrella expression for the diverse social functions that law is capable of serving could scarcely have been more unfortunate. He should rather have said: 'Law is often used as a method of social control, and an account of law's nature must explain how this use of it is possible, maybe even likely. But it is no part of law's nature that it must be so used.'

Maybe Dworkin uses the expression 'social control' in Hart's wide and unrevealing ('vapid') sense. Dworkin's inclusion of 'morality' and 'religion' on the list of other forms of social control suggests, to my ears, that this is indeed how he is using the expression. His inclusion of 'terror' and 'force' on the list, on the other hand, tends to draw our attention back to social control in the ordinary narrow sense of that expression. If that is the sense in which he is using it, he is implicitly rejecting Hart's views about the nature of law, and standing up for something more like the Austinian view that Hart was trying to destabilize. That would not be surprising. For all of its deficiencies, a broadly Austinian view of law's nature continues to appeal to many lawyers, impatient as they are to put aside nice theoretical issues and get on with what they regard as the 'practicalities'. As Dworkin's formulation of and focus on the 'doctrinal' question shows, he tends towards a lawyer's idea of what counts as a 'practicality' and shares the lawyer's impatience with everything else. So he may also be drawn, in formulating the 'sociological' question, to a broadly Austinian view of the nature of law.⁶

---

⁵ *CL*, 39.

⁶ He certainly treats it as a working axiom that law, by its nature as law, has a special connection with coercion by the state: Dworkin, *Law's Empire* (Cambridge, Mass. 1986), 93. Both aspects of this connection (law-coercion and law-state) are sidelined by Hart as he dismantles Austin's views. So the axiom is not, as Dworkin hopes, 'sufficiently... uncontroversial to provide, at least provisionally, the structure we seek'. It is an Austinian throwback.

As I say, that would not be surprising. But what remains surprising, even after all these years, is Dworkin's continued denial that there could be any serious philosophical interest in knowing whether this is indeed the view of the nature of law that he holds. If one is not to dismiss this denial as disingenuous gamesmanship, one must conclude that he is a man of narrow interests. Or, putting it less provocatively, that he has a narrow view of the interests that a philosopher should have.[7] Although he thinks it a worthy task for philosophers to provide a service to appellate judges looking for argumentative inspiration, he does not think it a worthy task for philosophers to provide a service to sociologists, anthropologists, historians, psychologists, and so on, by holding their assumptions about the nature of law, perhaps indeed the nature of anything, up to rigorous critical scrutiny. Little wonder Dworkin finds the history of sociological jurisprudence 'depressing'.[8] The main problem is not, as Tony Honoré jokes, that 'the Sociologists have never learnt the rules' for debating the nature of law with philosophers.[9] The main problem, for Dworkin, is that the sociologists do not have a topic worthy of philosophical attention to start with.

2. Hart's 'descriptive sociology'

H.L.A. Hart felt differently about the relationship between philosophy and sociology, or at any rate he did in 1961. He famously billed *The Concept of Law* as doing double intellectual duty. It is both 'an essay in analytical jurisprudence' and 'an essay in

---

[7] Hence my teasing remark to him in 2003: 'Don't you see, Ronnie? That's your trouble. You expect everything to be "interesting".' Dworkin reports the remark in 'Hart's Postscript and the Character of Political Philosophy', *Oxford Journal of Legal Studies* 24 (2004), 1 at 36. But he does not interpret it correctly. The remark was in reply to Dworkin's dismissal of a very interesting problem (on which one of my students was working) as uninteresting, on the ground that solving it had no practical consequences. I was teasing him by helping myself (in imagined scare-quotation marks, which I thought were evident from my intonation) to his narrow view of what is interesting.

[8] Dworkin, *Law's Empire*, above note 6, 75.

[9] Tony Honoré, 'Groups, Laws and Obedience' in A.W.B. Simpson (ed), *Oxford Essays in Jurisprudence: Second Series* (Oxford 1973), 1.

descriptive sociology'.[10] Nicola Lacey records that Hart later came to regret the second characterization. Writing in his notebooks, he wished that he had claimed more cautiously that the book explained some 'normative concepts required for a descriptive sociology'.[11] Yet in the posthumously published postscript to *The Concept of Law* he continued to insist on the characterization of the main claims in the book as 'descriptive', maintaining against Dworkin that 'description may still be description, even when what is described is an evaluation'.[12] This insistence strongly suggests that what Hart came to regret about his 1961 characterization was not the 'descriptive' bit but the 'sociology' bit. He was perfectly happy to regard his work as a descriptive prolegomenon to sociology, but not to regard it, on that basis, as a descriptive work *of* sociology.

This strikes me as the wrong way out for Hart. He should have held on to his claim to be working at the intersection of philosophy and sociology, while jettisoning the misleading characterization of his work as 'descriptive'. True, if 'descriptive' means 'non-evaluative', a special meaning given to the word by some philosophers and echoed by Hart in the postscript,[13] then Hart's work in *The Concept of Law* is for the most part descriptive. For the most part he abstains from any defence or critique of law (indeed any defence or critique of anything at all, except for the work of other philosophers). But 'descriptive' can also be taken to mean 'empirical'. And Hart's account of the nature of law in *The Concept of Law* is clearly not empirical any more than it is evaluative. It cannot possibly be, for as I pointed out at the start of this chapter, one must already know what counts as law before one can make either empirical or evaluative observations about it

---

[10] CL, v.

[11] Nicola Lacey, 'Analytical Jurisprudence Versus Descriptive Sociology Revisited', *Texas Law Review* 84 (2006), 944 at 949, citing an entry in Hart's notebooks which Lacey dates to the 'late 1980s'.

[12] Hart, *The Concept of Law* (2nd ed, Oxford 1994), 244 (hereafter *CL2e*).

[13] *CL2e*, 240: 'My account is *descriptive* in that it is morally neutral and has no justificatory aims: it does not seek to justify or commend on moral or other grounds the forms and structures which appear in my general account of law, though a clear understanding of these is, I think, an important preliminary to any useful moral criticism of law.'

qua law. Naturally one may still make empirical or evaluative observations about a particular example of law under various other headings; eg as an example of a form of social control, or as an example of a structure of governance. But as we noted, this is not making observations about it *qua* law unless by its nature law is a form of social control or a structure of governance. And whether that is what law is, is neither an empirical nor an evaluative question. It is a question of a third type, a classificatory (sometimes also known as 'conceptual') question.[14]

None of this is to deny that once we know more about what counts as a law, we need to ask subsidiary empirical or evaluative questions in applying what we have learnt to particular candidates for the status of law, to see if law is indeed what they are. Many people think that no system qualifies as a legal one, for example, unless it is in some measure effective across a general (non-official) population. Some people think, meanwhile, that no system qualifies as a legal one unless it is in some respect morally valuable. Whether these thoughts are true is plainly not an empirical or an evaluative question. But to work out whether the criteria that they set for a system to be a legal one are satisfied in any given case, we need to ask not only many further conceptual questions (What is effectiveness? What constitutes a population? What makes a certain value a moral one?) but also some empirical and evaluative ones. We have to observe the relevant population to establish whether the relevant kind of effectiveness prevails across it. We have to work out whether the system exhibits the relevant kind of moral value (which is an evaluative question that may itself raise further empirical ones). Some people think that all the classificatory questions before us eventually reduce out, and we

---

[14] The label 'conceptual' may give the unhappy impression that the object of study is the concept, rather than the thing of which the concept is the concept, in this case law. Notwithstanding the title of his book, which consciously echoed Gilbert Ryle's *The Concept of Mind* (Chicago 1949), Hart made clear in his original 1961 preface that his ultimate interest was in classifying 'social situation[s] or relationships', not the concepts of them: *CL*, v. On what difference this makes, see Joseph Raz, 'Can There be a Theory of Law?' in Martin Golding and William Edmundson (eds), *The Blackwell Guide to Philosophy of Law and Legal Theory* (Malden, Mass. 2005), 324 (and see also the final pages of this chapter).

are left with only empirical and evaluative ones. I think, by contrast, that every empirical or evaluative question raised by a classificatory question raises (usually numerous) further classificatory questions, and that this process continues ad infinitum.[15] But that is consistent with thinking, and indeed it presupposes, that empirical and evaluative questions can also be raised by classificatory ones.

Possibly Hart thought of his explanation of the nature of law as 'descriptive' because, in applying it to particular candidates for the status of law, he thought that we would have to ask a variety of empirical questions about those candidates (Is there such-and-such a practice here? Does anyone here have such-and-such an attitude? Are there institutions here of such-and-such a type?) and relatively few, or perhaps no, evaluative ones (Is the practice doing any good? Is the attitude desirable? Are the institutions just?). But none of this suggests that Hart's enterprise—that of clarifying the nature of law—is itself an empirical one. For none of these are empirical questions *about law*. They are all empirical questions about candidates for the status of law, correct answers to which will help to determine whether they do indeed qualify as law. The question of what it *takes* to qualify, Hart's main question, is a classificatory one. Thus Hart did not go, clipboard in hand, to Nunavut or to Badakhshan or to the Ogaden, to see whether there were practices or attitudes or institutions there meeting the specifications set out in his book. He left such work to others with training in fieldwork. He merely advised on the practices and attitudes and institutions that the clipboard-bearers should look for, if perchance they were looking for law. If there were no such practices or attitudes or institutions to be found, that would be no skin off Hart's nose. For him it would only go to show that in some places and at some times life goes on without law (for better or worse or quite possibly both).

Are sociologists restricted to the clipboard-bearing role in this division of labour? Are their questions only the empirical ones

---

[15] What we can hope to offer as philosophers is perspicuity (ie elucidation of more complex ideas by their relationship with less complex ones), although sometimes, inevitably, the puzzles get worse before they get better: *CL*, 15.

that arise in applying classifications provided by others, perhaps philosophers? It is hard to see how this could be so. It would expel from the sociological canon the most celebrated work of such major figures of the discipline as Durkheim, Tönnies, Weber, and Mauss, arch-classifiers all four. That being so, it is hard to make sense of Nicola Lacey's main critique of Hart, according to which (descriptive or not) his work did not live up to the promise that it would be genuinely sociological:

> Certainly, positivist theorists... have occasionally ventured into the terrain of postulating the varied social functions of law and, to some extent, the institutional structures needed to realize them. But the terrain is more usually occupied by sociological jurists and anthropologists of law, and perhaps for good reason. For the richer the characterization of law's social basis—its institutional forms, its various types of rules, its role, and its functions—the less plausible is any theoretical claim to universality. Hart wanted to maintain the claim to universality as well as descriptiveness.... [He overlooked or underestimated the] capacity of a fuller articulation of the institutional dimensions of law to compromise universality.[16]

There is a well-known problem with Hart's explanation of the nature of law, viz. that it is much too inclusive. The features he enumerates do not yet suffice to distinguish legal systems from many other institutionalized normative systems, such as those regulating universities and trade associations and some competitive games and sports. Hart originally failed to notice the importance, for example, of every legal system's claim to be supreme among all institutionalized normative systems (including but not limited to other legal systems).[17] In that respect, his characterization of law could certainly have been a good deal richer.[18] But that does not seem to be Lacey's point. Indeed, it seems to be almost the opposite of her point. She is not worried that Hart has made too few generalizations about law to capture its distinctiveness. She is worried that he has made too many such generalizations to

---

[16] Lacey, 'Analytical Jurisprudence', above note 11, at 957–8.
[17] He later acknowledged it in response to Raz's: *CL2e*, 249.
[18] Joseph Raz, *Practical Reason and Norms* (London 1974), 146 (Hart's is an explanation of institutional normative systems in general) and 149–54 (extra features that distinguish law from other institutional normative systems).

accommodate its diversity. In fact she seems to think that reflection on law's diversity should have led Hart to recognize that law defies all generalization. So nothing is true of law in general, law as such, law wherever it may be found.

If sound, this objection would put paid to all scholarly work on law. If there is nothing to be said about law in general, then there is also nothing to be said about particular instances of law *qua* law. If law is not a valid classification, then nor is Cheyenne law, international law, Scots law, shari'a law, or Roman law. If there is no general jurisprudence, to put it in terms that Lacey favours, then there is also no special jurisprudence. That being so, no amount of close attention to the amazing variety of laws, or of legal institutions, or of legal systems, or of any other aspects of law, could possibly render less plausible the 'theoretical claim to universality' of Hart's *The Concept of Law*. For as Hart saw more clearly than any of his forebears, the first problem of the nature of law is the problem of how law is *capable* of all this variety.[19] How can law be such that so much variety is nevertheless all of it the variety *of law*? That question, though not a descriptive (empirical) one, is of urgent interest for sociologists of law. They too need to classify some things as law and others as non-law in order to explore law's variety. Is this classification, for them, wholly arbitrary, without rhyme or reason? If so, the classification 'law's variety' is equally arbitrary, and the sociology of law evaporates. But if not, then sociologists like Weber and philosophers like Hart have a shared project, namely the project of getting the classification right. If there is such a classificatory part of sociology, there is no unprejudiced reason for Hart to deny himself, or to be denied, the title of sociologist (even if only *honoris causa*, since he was trained as a philosopher).

3. How social is law?

In one respect, however, this line of thought is already making a philosophical leap. We are assuming that law is a social form, or a social technique, or a social something, and hence a suitable focus

---

[19] *CL*, 2–3; *CL2e*, 239–40.

for sociological (as distinct from, say, neurological or theological or psychological or meteorological) attention.[20] Lacey treats it as a truism that law—and here, *malgré elle*, she presumably means law in general, law as such—has a 'social basis'.[21] Hart did not regard this as a truism. He took it to be one of his main tasks, now necessarily reaching beyond sociology and into its presuppositions, to discover whether and how it is true. In what sense, if any, does law have a 'social basis' such that, *qua* law, it can properly engage sociological attention?

The answer favoured by Hart relied on the idea of a 'social rule'. He famously argued that each legal system has at least one social rule, namely an 'ultimate rule of recognition' that determines which other rules (which need not themselves be social rules) belong to that system, and hence qualify as rules of law. In saying this Hart was also offering a solution to the philosophical puzzle that Dworkin so blithely sidelined as uninteresting. How can there be 'jurisdictions' with their own laws? How is it possible that one law ends at San Diego and another begins at Tijuana? Hart's answer relied upon the simple idea that different social rules prevail at different times and in different places. If what is recognized as law necessarily depends on social rules, then the law may vary as the social rules vary, viz. along spatio-temporal lines. So anyone interested in jurisdictional boundaries should begin their investigations by thinking about social boundaries (rather than, say, geophysical or chromosomal or technological or climatic or territorial ones).

Isn't that all rather obvious? Isn't it truistic; philosophically uninteresting? Not at all. That we have come to see it that way only goes to show how stunningly successful Hart was in explaining the nature of law, and how much we now take his explanatory achievement for granted. For the received wisdoms before *The Concept of Law* were markedly otherwise. As Hart explained,

---

[20] I don't mean, of course, *to the exclusion* of such attention. In Ch 1 above, I pointed to an area in which the study of the nature of law intersects with the study of the nature of God.

[21] Lacey, 'Analytical Jurisprudence' above note 11, at 957. See also Roger Cotterrell, 'Why Must Legal Ideas be Interptered Sociologically?', *Journal of Law and Society* 25 (1998), 171.

there was the Austinian wisdom according to which the possibility of divergence in legal content as between any two legal systems comes of the possibility of social divergence, but only divergence in social habit, not in social rule.[22] And then there was the Kelsenian wisdom according to which the possibility of divergence in legal content as between any two legal systems comes of the possibility of divergence in their ultimate rules of recognition,[23] but without any thought that the rules might be, let alone need be, social ones. The challenge to which Hart rose was to rescue the element of truth from each of these views and to combine them felicitously; ie to explain how the 'basis' of law in the relevant sense—what explains the possibility of such radical variety among legal systems—could be simultaneously social and a rule, in other words a social rule.

We may, to repeat, have come to see much of this as truistic. But is it also true? Is law as social as all that? Brian Tamanaha sketches the largest challenge to those who think that it is:

The notion of society serves as shorthand for a discrete group or community unified in certain essential respects, usually including language, culture, politics, geography, tied at the broadest level to the state ... [I]ts boundaries are tied to groups. Intra-group and trans-group relations, which are essential to any attempt to understand law, are not easily taken account of within a study that centres upon societies.[24]

With such an idea of 'society' in mind, the legal system of the European Communities, later the European Union, has sometimes been wheeled out against Hart, as a supposed counter-example to, or at any rate a problem case for, his views about the nature of law. Hart's explanation of the nature of law, it is said, 'sits uneasily with various forms of regional law (eg European Community

---

[22] CL, 54ff.
[23] Or their 'first constitutions' as Kelsen's historicized but de-socialized rendition has it. Kelsen, *General Theory of Law and State* (Cambridge, Mass. 1945), 115–16. Note that I am not repeating here the familiar error of regarding Kelsen's *Grundnorm* as a rule of recognition or as somehow equivalent to one. The *Grundnorm* is a further norm presupposed by jurists, according to Kelsen, whenever they treat the rule of recognition (the first constitution) as binding.
[24] Brian Tamanaha, *A General Jurisprudence of Law and Society* (Oxford 2001), 206.

Law);'[25] it 'fits most comfortably with a centralized state legal order',[26] or 'one overarching hierarchical system',[27] a model to which EU law does not conform. More generally, it is said, Hart's thinking has somehow been wrong-footed or exposed as too narrow by today's 'globalized'[28] or 'post-sovereign'[29] world, in which national boundaries allegedly count for much less than they did in the supposedly still 'Westphalian'[30] world of 1961, and in which legal life has become more 'polycentric'.[31] But if the national legal system is indeed Hart's comfort zone, isn't that only because his work 'centres upon societies'; ie portrays legal systems as socially constituted? And if that is a problem for Hart, then isn't it a problem *a fortiori* for 'sociological jurists' who are setting out to provide 'a more socially grounded theory of law'?[32]

It is hard to know whether sociological jurists have a problem here. As Tamanaha says, the word 'social', with its meaning left unstipulated, is too vague to be 'serviceable as an analytical device'.[33] Lacey and others (including Tamanaha himself) who call for 'a more socially grounded theory of law' than Hart had to offer rarely say enough about what would qualify, for them, as a distinctively social grounding, or why we should concede, in advance of finding out more about law's nature, that this is the right kind of grounding for a theory of law to have. Hart, by contrast, was pretty clear about what he meant by 'social' and he took great pains to show why every legal system must have as its basis a rule that is social in the relevant sense. He used 'social rules'

---

[25] William Twining, *General Jurisprudence: Understanding Law from a Global Perspective* (Cambridge 2009), 12.

[26] Lacey, 'Analytical Jurisprudence', above note 11, at 957–8.

[27] Sionaidh Douglas-Scott, *Constitutional Law of the European Union* (Harlow 2002), 279.

[28] Boaventura De Sousa Santos, 'State, Law and Community in the World System: an Introduction', *Social and Legal Studies* 1 (1992), 131.

[29] Amy Swiffen, 'Law without a Lawgiver: Legal Authority after Sovereignty', *Law, Culture, and the Humanities* 7 (2011), 66.

[30] William Twining, *General Jurisprudence: Understanding Law from a Global Perspective* (Cambridge 2009), 5.

[31] Brendan Edgeworth, *Law, Modernity, Postmodernity: Legal Change in the Contracting State* (Aldershot 2003), 265.

[32] Lacey, 'Analytical Jurisprudence', above note 11, at 982.

[33] Tamanaha, *A General Jurisprudence*, above note 24, 206.

interchangeably with 'customary rules'.[34] He argued that the ultimate rule of recognition of each legal system is made by the cumulative attempts of officials of the system, or at any rate some of them,[35] to follow that same rule.[36] The relevant officials each follow what they take to be the rule that the others are following. Thereby they contribute to making it the rule, and to making themselves the officials under the rule. It is a customary rule because it is made (a) by the officials collectively, and (b) in large measure accidentally, by contributory actions that are intended only to follow the rule and not to make it.

But notice that the relevant custom, the one that makes the rule what it is, is not the custom of a population that can be identified independently of it. There is no wider population, beyond the official users, who participate in making the rule by their cumulative attempts to follow it. Under some legal systems at some times, a wider population may also follow or attempt to follow the rule but that does not alter what the rule says and (more importantly for present purposes) it is neither necessary nor sufficient to make the rule the ultimate rule of recognition of the legal system. If Hart's labelling of it as a 'social rule' led one to envisage, romantically, an ultimate rule of recognition for each legal system made and used by a population identifiable independently of the rule (say, by ordinary folk bound together by such things as 'language, culture, politics, geography') then one is bound to be disappointed. That is not what Hart meant by 'social rule' and he was pretty clear in saying so.[37]

---

[34] *CL2e*, 256.

[35] His emphasis was usually on the judiciary; other officials participate in creating and maintaining the rule of recognition, it seems, mainly parasitically, by helping to establish who count as the judiciary. See *CL*, 98–9. And see *CL2e*, 256, for Hart's later affirmation that the ultimate rule of recognition of a legal system is 'in effect a form of judicial customary rule existing only if it is accepted and practiced in the law-identifying and law-applying operations of the courts'. I discuss the issue in Ch 4 above (see especially note 15).

[36] Hart often spoke (eg *CL*, 103) as if there were only one ultimate rule of recognition per legal system, and for simplicity I will follow this practice here. It is, however, a mistaken view, as Hart made clear at *CL*, 95, and as Raz later went on to argue at greater length (Raz, *Practical Reason and Norms*, above note 18, at 147–8).

[37] *CL*, 110–14. Also *CL2e*, 256.

This does not mean, of course, that Hart did not regard the existence of a legal system as also depending, in a different way, on the behaviour of a wider population. On the contrary, Hart shared with both Austin and Kelsen the view that no system qualifies as a legal one unless, in large measure, it is effective across a general (non-official) population. But he was also clear that the kind of effectiveness required for this purpose is relatively easy to come by. It does not require the population in question to know about, let alone to use, the ultimate rule of recognition that is used (and thereby created) by the officials of the system. The wider population need not even engage with the legal system as a system of rules.[38] The bulk of them might just think of the legal system as a 'gunman... writ large'[39] issuing a slew of demands and associated threats. True, even for Hart, it can't be sheer coincidence that the general population in question stays, by and large, on the right side of the law. Some explanatory link between their conformity and the legal rules is required. Those who hold themselves out to be the officials of the legal system must be able to affect non-official behaviour by changing or applying the rules, or else they are not officials of the legal system. But the capacity of officials to do this can be very indirect, via a long chain of intermediaries. The constitutional court, for example, may be able to affect the behaviour of appellate courts, who affect the behaviour of magistrates, who affect the behaviour of police officers and other petty officials, who in turn affect wider public behaviour thanks to proxy rules such as 'never argue with a police officer (since they are likely to have, or be able to get, the law on their side)'.

Notice that a population using such a proxy rule might not even be aware that they have just lived through a revolution, in which the legal system was overthrown. They might not realize, for example, that the police of their native San Theodoros, with whom it is always a bad idea to argue, are this morning no longer submitting to the writs of the Grand Court of Tapioca (although it still 'sits' and vainly issues 'rulings' into thin air). The police and other petty officials, knowing what side their bread is buttered

---

[38] *CL*, 59, 110–11.   [39] *CL*, 7.

on, have overnight switched allegiance to the Supreme Court of Alcazar, which has already opened for business under the new revolutionary constitution, the rules of which it is already invoking freely. On the streets nothing has changed. Nor will it ever. Yet the old ultimate rule of recognition has gone, and with it the old legal system, to be replaced by a new one the content of which (apart from the new constitution treated by law-applying officials as valid, and thereby validated, under the new rule of recognition) is indistinguishable from the old. Same old decrepit laws, same old mix of apathetic and corrupt policing, same old slow, inaccessible, unreliable judicial process, same old weary public keeping their heads down to avoid coming to the attention of the powers-that-be.[40]

This example shows just how little 'social basis' a system of rules needs, in Hart's view, in order to qualify as a legal system. It also points the way to a more-than-adequate Hartian explanation of how EU law qualifies as law. EU law has its own ultimate rule of recognition which differs from, and conflicts with, the ultimate rule of recognition of the legal system of each of the EU's member states. According to EU law, in particular, EU law is supreme and the law of each member state holds sway only subject to it and by its leave. According to English law, by contrast, English law is supreme and the law of the EU holds sway only subject to it and by its leave (principally under the European Communities Act 1971). Yet this divergence between the EU and the English rules of recognition, and between their respective constitutional arrangements, leads to very little day-to-day conflict between the two legal systems in respect of the rest of their law (just as there is very little conflict between Alcazar-era law and Tapioca-era law in San Theodoros). Each system is pretty good, indeed, at giving effect to the laws of the other by dexterous use of its own constitutional arrangements. And the English courts, giving effect to most of EU law pretty much on EU law's own terms (apart, of course, from the ultimate rules) therefore make EU law largely effective, in the Hartian sense, in England.

---

[40] The scenario is Hergé's, from *Tintin and the Picaros* (London 1976).

Much the same is true, although with differences of degree and detail, in all the other EU member states.

It follows that EU law does not need its own state apparatus, its own petty officials, its own police or bailiffs or trading standards officers, to meet Hart's conditions for qualifying as a legal system. The EU has its own elite of law-applying officials at the European Court of Justice in Luxembourg, and they have their own customary rules *in foro* by which they are recognized as officials of the EU legal system. Their work in that capacity is effective across the whole gamut of non-official European populations mainly thanks to the machinery of the domestic legal systems of the several member states, which all put their own effectiveness at the day-to-day disposal of the EU. In each EU member state, at least two legal systems are concurrently in force, the first largely effective through its own mechanisms, the second largely effective through the mechanisms of the first.

What could be a simpler, or more amply corroborative, application of Hart's explanation of the nature of law? Why would anyone imagine that EU law is a problem case for him? Perhaps it is just that, as Neil MacCormick says, Hart 'rather gives the basis for [this application of his work] than exploits it to the full himself'.[41] Of course, it would be anachronistic to expect Hart to have dwelled on the application of his ideas to EU law in particular, since the emergence of a distinct EU legal system can most plausibly be dated to the years immediately following the publication of *The Concept of Law*.[42] Nevertheless perhaps MacCormick is right that the wider 'polycentric potentialities' of his thinking, of which the polycentricity of legal life in the EU is a mere illustration, are not 'highlighted' by Hart himself?[43]

Actually, even this strikes me as doing Hart an injustice. It is not quite true, as MacCormick goes on to claim, that Hart's 'representation of law as a union of primary and secondary rules ... was principally based on domestic law', where 'domestic

---

[41] MacCormick, 'Beyond the Sovereign State', *Modern Law Review* 56 (193), 1 at 9.

[42] The claim to supremacy which is characteristic of a legal system is first made by the ECJ in *Flaminio Costa* v *ENEL* [1964] ECR 585.

[43] MacCormick, 'Beyond the Sovereign State', above note 41, at 9.

law' might naturally be contrasted, as MacCormick himself contrasts it, with EU law.[44] Hart focused rather on *municipal* law, by which he meant, as I read him, legal systems that mark out their own jurisdictions in at least partly territorial terms (by contrast with public international law, canon law, and on some interpretations, shari'a law, which do not).[45] Not all municipal legal systems are domestic legal systems. Nor, *a fortiori*, are they all state legal systems, let alone those of 'sovereign states'.[46] When Hart first introduces the idea that different countries have different legal systems he already puts the word 'country' in inverted commas as a way, I think, of signaling his forthcoming rejection of the Westphalian model in which all municipal law is necessarily the domestic law of a sovereign state.[47] And when later he comes to interrogate the 'state sovereignty' as a supposed precondition of municipal law, he notes (a) that all states have legal systems but not all legal systems have states;[48] and (b) that many territories, whether state territories or not, are legally polycentric; ie fall under the territorial jurisdiction of several municipal legal systems at once, each maintaining its territorial effectiveness thanks to some kind of comity with the others (even though, we should add, each cannot but claim its own supremacy, and so must present itself as merely licensing the others).[49]

EU law is an example of municipal law in Hart's sense, and indeed a very good example of it for his purposes. In one fell swoop it bears out, if any legal system does, the following theses that Hart endorsed: that a municipal legal system need not be the legal system of a state;[50] that it need not have its own apparatus of

---

[44] Ibid.
[45] CL, 17, 79, 122.
[46] For corroborating comments see Roger Cotterrell, 'Law and Community: A New Relationship', *Current Legal Problems* 51 (1998), 367 at 381.
[47] CL, 3.
[48] CL, 216: a state is differentiated by 'two facts', only one of which is possession of a legal system.
[49] CL, 217–18: one possibility is a 'federal legislature on the model of [the US] Congress'. On this model federal law and state law co-habit and give effect to each other (more or less) peacefully by each conceding certain subject-matters to the other in their respective constitutions.
[50] CL, 216.

enforcement or 'centralized sanctions';[51] that there need not be any territory in which or population over which it is the only municipal legal system in force;[52] and perhaps most importantly, that there need be no customary rules *in pays*, but only customary rules *in foro*, for it to qualify as a legal system.[53] Sociologists of law may marvel at the possibility of such socially disengaged law. Romantics may wring their hands at the sight of it. It may defy what Tamanaha 'learned law was...in the course of [his] legal training'.[54] But it is grist to Hart's mill. It confirms his point that

---

[51] CL, 95: 'most [legal] systems have, after some delay, seen the advantages of...centralized official "sanctions"'. Most, but not all. Cf CL, 3–4, where Hart's first thought, later revised, is that a lack of 'centrally organised...sanctions' puts a question mark over the status of some arrangements as legal systems.

[52] CL, 217–18.

[53] CL, 113.

[54] Tamanaha, *A General Jurisprudence*, above note 24, xi–xii. Tamanaha here is reflecting not on the law of the EU, but on that of the state of Yap in the Federated States of Micronesia, about which he testifies from personal experience as Yap's one-time Assistant Attorney General. He writes: 'many people were ignorant of the [state and federal] law, and feared or avoided it...[t]he law in Micronesia was like an alien presence in their midst, mostly irrelevant, taking care of tasks related primarily to the operation of the government, occasionally intruding on their lives in various unwelcome ways'. This example is also grist to Hart's mill. That people 'fear or avoid the law' is one way in which law, for Hart, can be effective. The 'irrelevance' of most law to most people is also neither here nor there; where a law doesn't apply to Joe Public (instead 'tak[ing] care of tasks related primarily to the operation of the government') it can't be made ineffective by Joe Public's ignoring it. Compare Tamahana's remarks in his *Realistic Socio-Legal Theory*, above note 2, at 136. Here he suggests that a lot of state law in Yap *does* apply to Joe Public but simply 'ha[s] never been [so] applied' by state officials. That marks an interesting difference, but I doubt whether it significantly changes the complexion of the problem under discussion here. To my ears it suggests that the officials of the state legal system in Yap are regarded (under their own custom *in foro*) as having legal powers to leave certain matters to be sorted out other than under their legal system's own rules and/or other than via their legal system's own institutions. That much is true in every legal system known to me: not every law is enforced, not every crime is prosecuted, many disputes are settled by negotiation or mediation or arbitration, etc, and all of this is officially approved. The widespread use of such powers to disapply state law does not show that state law is ineffective; on the contrary, it shows state law's considerable efficacy in determining whether alternative resolutions are to be sought and can be relied upon. (An extra feature in Yap *may* be that a distinct customary legal system is also in force to which the situations to which state law turns a blind eye are effectively remitted. If that is

many features that have often been taken to be part of the nature of law are no such thing, even though they are widespread features of law. If Hart's account of the nature of law was in some respects over-inclusive, afflicted by false positives, we can now see one possible reason why. He was trying to correct the false negatives returned by the often hidden classificatory assumptions of others, mapping legal systems too closely to states, or for that matter to (independently identifiable) societies.

4. Purely customary law

Yet Hart himself is often accused of returning false negatives, and not only by those who mistakenly think he has problems with EU law and similar non-state law. He is also accused of having sidelined (as 'pre-legal'[55] or 'primitively legal'[56]) a whole world of more purely customary social arrangements. The charge is a bit overstated. Hart's explanation of the nature of law is readily capable of accommodating, as legal systems, purely customary social arrangements so long as they include customary officials. More specifically they need to have officials who shape the rules of the system (including rules about who count as officials and hence who contributes to shaping the rules) through their attempts to apply them. But this condition—roughly, that there needs to be custom *in foro* as well as custom *in pays*—is more easily satisfied than some of Hart's critics appear to think. The officials need not be state officials, since if Hart is right there need be no state. Moreover, although there do need to be official law-appliers, there do not need to be official law-enforcers. Securing compliance might well be left to custom *in pays*.[57] And although there does need to be a mechanism for law-making, there is no reason to assume that it has to be legislative law-making. The same officials who apply the rules may be capable of changing them (and where officialdom is small enough, changing them

true, then what we are witnessing is precisely the kind of comity among legal systems that is also characteristic of the EU.)

[55] *CL*, 41, 92.
[56] Ibid 4, 84.
[57] Hart gives the example of Roman law (until the Late Empire): *CL*, 244.

intentionally) by shifts in their own rule-applying customs, including their own customary interpretations of custom *in pays*.[58] To take a fairly well-documented example, the customary system known as *xeer* that prevails in much of Somalia (where there is little or no state) would seem to qualify quite straightforwardly as a legal system on the Hartian analysis. Clan elders (*oday*) perform the law-applying function and take themselves to be following rules created by previous *oday* decisions, including agreements with other *oday*, when they do so. Thereby they have gradually built up a body of law that is in force, with some local variations, over a huge territory, including law about who serves as an *oday* for whom and when *oday* decisions qualify as precedents that regulate later *oday* decisions and so forth. In Hart's terms, there are rules of recognition, change, and adjudication, and there are official (*oday*) customs that make those rules. Effectiveness across the wider population is secured mainly by respect for *xeer* itself, and hence for *oday*, without state involvement.[59] So for Hart, although almost purely customary, *xeer* is not difficult to classify as law.

The 'questionable cases', for Hart, are mainly ones in which there are only customary rules *in pays*, and nobody in the role of *oday*. Perhaps there are no elders, gurus, sages, or others from whom guidance is popularly sought. Or perhaps there are elders or the like, but they do not apply or purport to apply any of the customary rules *in pays*: they exercise only the arbitration function that Hart discusses under the heading of 'scorer's discretion'.[60] Or perhaps there are elders and they do apply some of the customary rules *in pays* but they do not have any customary rules *in foro* by which they distinguish the customary rules *in pays* that they will apply as elders from those that they will not; or by

---

[58] Hart says, at *CL* 93, that the 'simplest form' of what he calls 'a rule of change' is one empowering a legislator or legislature. The simplest, not the only. Cf *CL*, 3–4, where Hart's first thought, later revised, is that a lack of a legislature makes it questionable whether some arrangement is a legal one. I include the parenthetical remark about intentionality to meet a condition that Hart sometimes says a 'rule of change' of a legal system needs to meet.

[59] I rely on Joakim Gundel, *The Predicament of the 'Oday': The Role of Traditional Structures in Security, Rights, Law and Development in Somalia* (Nairobi 2006).

[60] *CL*, 139.

which they add more specificity (by way of interpretation) to the customary rules *in pays* that they do apply; or by which they mark themselves (elders) out as those entitled to make authoritative applications of customary rules *in pays*.[61] You can see here a significant number of possible extra features, which, as they build up, bring the case progressively closer to that of a legal system as Hart explains it. No doubt that is why Hart does not lump all such cases together under the plain residual heading 'non-law'. He thinks that many possible customary arrangements are classificatorily indeterminate ('questionable'), so that it might be reasonable to call them either primitively legal or pre-legal, this terminological vacillation implying that in a sense they are law but in a sense they are not.

Second-order indeterminacy probably makes it silly to debate the question of exactly which range of examples lie in this indeterminate zone. But there is clearly an important question of whether there is any classificatory frontier (be it rife with indeterminacy or not) in this vicinity. Obviously, Hart thinks that there is. He thinks that all law by its nature belongs to legal systems—that it is law only relative to some rule of recognition—and that some measure of institutionalization (minimally, the existence of *fora* that are capable of having customary rules *in foro*) is required to constitute the relevant kind of system. Thus one dimension in which law differs from some things that are akin to it, for Hart, is the dimension of institutionalization. Is he right about this? As Lacey poses the question:

> [D]oes it make sense to seek a theory of the 'legal order' – that is, prevailing legal norms – independent of a theory of the 'legal regime', i.e. the institutions that generate and enforce those norms?[62]

Lacey is evidently in the 'no' camp. To this extent she sides with Hart, as I do, against those who say that there is no connection

---

[61] To appreciate some of the possible configurations more concretely, consider the lives of the G/wi, !Kung, and other San peoples in the Kalahari, as documented by several contributors to Eleanor Leacock and Richard Lee (eds), *Politics and History in Band Societies* (Cambridge 1982). Remarks by Lee at 53 are particularly salient: !Kung bands or camps do have leaders, claims Lee, but no officials. Indeed there is some animosity towards the very idea.

[62] Lacey, 'Analytical Jurisprudence', above note 11, at 946.

between law and institutionalization, that custom *in pays* without custom *in foro* can still be law in the fullest sense.[63]

Hart's work speaks for itself on this point. I will not attempt to add any defence beyond the various corroborative applications of Hartian thinking that I have sketched in this chapter, and at some other points in this book. Allow me, however, to end by mentioning some reasons that sociologically inclined writers have given for rejecting as under-inclusive the Hartian view that a legal system is, *inter alia*, an institutional arrangement (itself governed by norms of the system) for managing the norms of the system. These reasons are strange and suggest some serious breakdowns of communication across academic disciplines, even when the disciplines are asking the same questions.

(a) Functionalism. 'For most social scientists,' says Fernanda Pirie,

the study of law outside the familiar realms of the western world has meant examining the institutions, practices and understandings that serve to maintain order and resolve disputes.'[64]

This reminds us that there is still a major current of social-scientific (including sociological) thinking according to which everything in social life should be classified according to, and only according to, its social function. Armed with this initial restriction on what qualifies as a valid classification, some have concluded that something should be classified as law if and only if it serves the same social functions as law.[65] But that is an odd

---

[63] Although Hart would probably say 'apply' where Lacey says 'enforce' since he doesn't regard enforcement, on reflection, as a necessary feature of a legal system. For some reason (not I think this one) Lacey regards the quoted remark as raising a challenge to Hart. Perhaps she is thinking, with Neil MacCormick and Joseph Raz, that Hart's version of 'institutionalization' was a bit too minimal, that what is required is not just officials but organizations too. See MacCormick, 'Law as Institutional Fact', *Law Quarterly Review* 102 (1974), 90; Raz, 'The Institutional Nature of Law' in *The Authority of Law* (Oxford 1979).

[64] Fernanda Pirie, 'Law before Government: Ideology and Aspiration', *Oxford Journal of Legal Studies* 30 (2010), 207 at 207.

[65] In her 'Legal Pluralism', *Law and Society Review* 22 (1988), 869 at 870, Sally Merry writes: '[L]egal pluralism... [is] a situation in which two or more legal systems co-exist in the same social field.... Recent work defines "legal system" broadly to include the system of courts and judges... *as well as nonlegal forms of*

conclusion to draw. A better conclusion to draw is that the social sciences have no use for the classification of anything as law. For law is not a functional kind. It is a modal kind. There is no social function, nor any combination of social functions, that distinguishes law from any of its near neighbours. Rather, law is distinguished from many of its near neighbours (those that have social functions at all) by how it serves the many social functions that it, in common with those near neighbours, serves or is capable of serving. Law is not 'whatever resolves disputes' but a special *way* of resolving disputes, and for doing a huge range of other things besides, by the use of rules largely effective across a general population, and officials who apply them and who claim authority and supremacy in doing so. These (and the several other) distinguishing marks of law are all in the 'how' and not in the 'why' list. So if it is a necessary condition for Hart's work to be 'of use to social scientists and socio-legal scholars'[66] that it should portray law as a functional kind then Hart's work, which rightly denies that law is a functional kind,[67] can never be of use to social scientists. But that is not, as some think, because Hart's horizons are narrow. Rather it is because of the narrow horizons of those particular social scientists who have no use for (or interest in) any classifications other than functional ones.

(b) Law's supposed superiority. By denying that some customary arrangements are law, or law in the fullest sense, one is sometimes thought to be denigrating them, condescending to them, or otherwise looking down one's nose at them. In Chapter 5 of *CL*, Hart sadly played into the hands of those who press this objection. As Lacey says:

---

normative ordering' (emphasis added). So a 'legal pluralist' situation can arise where there are no legal 'forms of normative ordering' but only non-legal ones. Why would anyone be even slightly surprised to find that there can be many of *those* in the same 'social field'? Therein lies one possible case for having a legal system, viz. to help deal with a *melée* of nonlegal ones. As Raz explains (*Practical Reason and Norms*, above note 18, 152–4) it is part of the nature of a legal system that it is an 'open system' capable of giving effect to norms other than its own, while asserting its supremacy over all of them (ie its right to decide which prevail).

[66] Lacey, 'Analytical Jurisprudence', above note 11, at 945.
[67] *CL2e*, 248–9.

His [chapter five] fable of secondary rules of recognition, adjudication and change as emerging to 'cure the defects' of a system composed exclusively of primary rules carries, it has been argued, an implicit evaluation of other sorts of legal order—customary systems, for example—as less advanced or civilized.[68]

Hart was probably thinking about things that may sometimes be *experienced* or *perceived* as defects by those living under some customary arrangements. He was in the business of making the emergence of law rationally intelligible, making it such that we could understand why populations might have drifted (for better or worse) in the direction of having legal systems.[69] But since he was not in the business of either defending or criticizing law, he should not have given the impression, as he did to some readers, that he himself regarded the emergence of law as a blessing. Nor should he have suggested, as he did with the expressions 'pre-legal' and 'primitively legal' that the move to law is always a kind of progress, a step forward in human civilization.

Of course Hart did think, and he was right to think, that law in capable of bringing some blessings under some circumstances. Acquiring a legal system is a necessary condition of coming to live under the rule of law, and depending on what else is going on, there can be advantages to living under the rule of law. The 'defects' he mentioned in Chapter 5 were rule-of-law defects. But having a legal system, as Hart pointed out later in *The Concept of Law*, is only a necessary, not a sufficient, condition of living under the rule of law.[70] So getting a legal system is only the first step towards curing the advertised defects of 'pre-legal' life.

---

[68] Nicola Lacey, 'H.L.A. Hart's Rule of Law: the Limits of Philosophy in Historical Perspective', *Quaderno Fiorentini* 36 (2007), 1203 at 1209–10. Lacey is careful not to endorse the objection. Those endorsing it include Peter Sack, 'Homosexuality, Earthquakes and Hart's Concept of Primitive Law', *Bulletin of the Australian Society of Legal Philosophy* 8 (1984), 2; Peter Fitzpatrick, *The Mythology of Modern Law* (2nd ed, London 2002), 192–210; and Morton Horwitz, 'Why is Anglo-American Jurisprudence Unhistorical?', *Oxford Journal of Legal Studies* 17 (1997), 551 at 582–3.

[69] That comes across particularly in *CL*, 89.

[70] *CL*, 202: for the rule of law to prevail, legal systems and legal rules must 'satisfy certain [obviously, additional] conditions'.

Besides, the rule of law is not the only ideal worth pursuing. It is, as Hart also emphasized later in the book, 'compatible with very great iniquity'.[71] Sometimes it may do more harm than good. The rise of the rule of law may sometimes go hand-in-hand, for example, with a loss of mutual trust across the wider population, or some other kinds of alienation. If we are going to have a legal system we have, perhaps, the beginnings of a case for having the rule of law too; but it does not follow that we should want to have a legal system. Indeed, as Hart should have stressed, there is no special kudos that attaches to the mere fact of having a legal system, and it is not always a step forward for a customary society to acquire one. Societies with legal systems have no legitimate claim to moral superiority over those without.

So it cannot be said of a broadly Hartian explanation of the nature of law that it privileges some ways of living, and thereby marginalizes the others, where that is taken to suggest some kind of relative devaluation. That would be true only on the assumption that law in general, law wherever it may be found, is a good thing. Why should we assume that? An anarchist who regards law as having no redeeming features at all could embrace Hart's explanation of law's nature.[72] Indeed, the part of Hart's explanation that concerns us right now (the part according to which there cannot be law without officials) is exactly the part that an anarchist *must* embrace in order to explain why she stands so completely opposed to law. Since this part of Hart's explanation is compatible with and helps to explain an absolute disparagement for law's presence, how can it also entail a relative disparagement for law's absence? Much as Hart may have brought it upon himself, the objection that he privileges some social arrangements over others, merely by classifying some of them as law and others not, is seriously confused.[73]

(c) The province of legal theory. In objecting to the marginalization of official-free customary arrangements, some critics are objecting not

---

[71] *CL*, 202.

[72] Except possibly for his curious and anomalous 'germ of justice' idea (*CL*, 202), discussed in Ch 9 above.

[73] For other routes to the same conclusion, see Leslie Green, 'The Concept of Law Revisited', *Michigan Law Review* 94 (1996), 1687 at 1698.

to their supposed devaluation but merely to the absence of attention to them in the literature, or in some parts of it. Non-institutionalized customary arrangements are said by William Twining, for example, to 'deserve sustained attention' by 'our discipline', meaning 'the discipline of law' and in particular its 'theoretical part'.[74] Twining is doubtless right about that. Yet it does not follow from the fact that these arrangements deserve the attention of legal theorists that they are legal systems. They may deserve the attention of legal theorists because they reveal that law's social functions can also be served by things other than law, or because they show that societies with legal systems have no legitimate claim to moral superiority over those without, or for any of a vast number of similar reasons in which the fact that these things are not legal systems is precisely the source of their interest for legal theorists. Many other things (morality, etiquette, games, cuisines, mafias, religions, voluntary associations, personal relationships, trade practices, etc) also deserve the attention of legal theorists for similar reasons. To set about understanding the nature of law, to put the matter more generally, one needs constantly to juxtapose it with nearby things that are not law, and to isolate the various axes or dimensions in which it differs from its many neighbours.

Differentiation is possible only against a background of commonality. If there is no general jurisprudence, as I said before, there is no special jurisprudence. The same is true at the next classificatory level up: if there are no wider classifications, such as 'structure of governance' or 'set of social arrangements' or 'institutional normative system', to which law belongs in common with at least some things that are not law, then law is not a proper subject of study at all. And in that case there is no room for legal theory of any kind, anthropological, sociological, historical, philosophical or otherwise. So legal theory cannot but extend its reflective horizons to at least some types of non-law (and, if Hart is right, especially to indeterminate examples that are law in a sense but not law in the fullest sense).[75]

---

[74] William Twining, 'A Post-Westphalian Conception of Law', *Law and Society Review* 37 (2003), 199 at 199–200. See also Roger Cotterrell, *The Sociology of Law: An Introduction* (London, 1984), 29–31.

[75] It is quite another matter to suggest, as Twining sometimes seems to suggest, that all legal theorists should have the same special interests that he has. Twining

LAW IN GENERAL 297

(d) A variety of concepts of law? Brian Tamanaha has the most philosophically ambitious proposal for drawing the circle of law more widely than Hart does (although more narrowly, he would add, than some functionalists do). What counts as a legal system is, for Tamanaha, parasitic on local understandings. The first step is to ask: 'How do people classify their own social arrangements?' Do *they* regard this thing they have as law? The theorist's task is then to accommodate each of the (as it were) indigenous classifications within 'a core concept of law' that restricts itself to the ground on which all of the indigenous classifications overlap. 'Law,' he says, 'is whatever people identify and treat through their social practices as "law" (or recht, or droit, etc.).'[76]

This proposal is extremely hard to make sense of. At first sight, the inverted commas around the word 'law' might make one suppose that Tamanaha is interested in grouping together whatever stuff people around the world call by the name of 'law'. And some other things he says reinforce that impression.[77] But a moment's reflection shows that this can't be what he has in mind, or indeed what anyone should have in mind when they investigate the nature of law. The word 'law' refers to many things other than law. Are we supposed to accommodate, for

---

veers dangerously close to a Dworkinian diktat about what is 'interesting' when he chides contemporary philosophers of law for working on 'issues most of which seem generally remote from the concerns of world leaders and "Southern" peoples' (Twining, *General Jurisprudence*, above note 25, at 12). Why should I follow Twining in regarding those concerns as paramount or even relevant? Why tackle today's problems, the possibly transient concerns of the early twenty-first century, at the expense of the timeless problems that were also of interest to Plato, Confucius, and Maimonides? We all have our different fish to fry. Personally I am particularly intrigued, for example, by the differences and similarities between legal systems on the one hand and games on the other, mainly because of the importance of showing that law is not a game. I suppose I could imaginably chide Twining for working on 'issues most of which seem remote from the concerns of FIFA referees'. But I wouldn't dream of doing so (except in jest!) because his interests strike me as no less legitimate than mine. Alas Twining, like Dworkin, may not be inclined to return the compliment.

[76] Tamanaha, *A General Jurisprudence*, above note 24, 194, emphasis omitted.
[77] He says, eg, that the 'core concept' should reflect 'shared fundamental features abstracted from phenomena to which the label "law" has been conventionally attached'. Tamanaha, *A General Jurisprudence*, above note 24, 196, emphasis omitted.

example, the laws of thermodynamics, Kant's 'moral law', or the laws of cricket in our account of the nature of law? Surely not. Conversely, not everyone refers to law by the word 'law'. Tamanaha's parenthetical extension of his data set to include what is identified as '*droit*' or '*recht*' shows that the use of the word 'law' is not his focus. To have translated 'law' as '*droit*' or '*recht*' or anything else, one must already have mapped word to idea; one must already know that there is a common something to which these diverse words and their cognates refer.

So what Tamanaha wants us to search for, before we attempt our own explanation of the nature of law, are presumably various indigenous ideas (aka concepts) of law. The mystery then only deepens. What counts as a concept or idea *of law*? How can someone have a different concept or idea of law, as opposed to simply having a different concept or idea full stop (which is not a concept or idea of law)? And even if there can really be different concepts that are all somehow concepts of law, which I doubt, how can we possibly identify them as concepts of law before we know what counts as law; ie before identifying the very 'common something' that, according to Tamanaha, we are supposed to be using the various concepts to find?[78]

And why, anyway, should we imagine that everyone who lives under law also has the (or a, if there can be more than one) concept of law? Or even that every legal official has that concept? Quite possibly, for example, many Somalians, including many *oday*, have the concept of *xeer* but not the concept of law. To have and use the concept of something, one need not know every further classification to which it belongs; one can clearly have and use the concept of a duck without having or using the concept of a bird, and the concept of a cup without having or using the concept of a receptacle. Equally clearly it doesn't follow from

---

[78] For a variation on the same theme, but with the circularity more apparent, consider Günther Teubner, 'The Two Faces of Janus: Rethinking Legal Pluralism' *Cardozo Law Review* 13 (1992), 1443. Whereas Tamanaha searches for law in the way in which people carve up their own social worlds, Teubner searches for it in 'the line which the discursive practice of law draws between itself and its environment' (at 1452). So to work out which things are law we need to (1) work out which things are law; and then (2) work out how those things *think or claim* that they differ from other things. Given (1), why (2)?

one's lack of the concepts of bird and receptacle that one hears no birdsong and uses no receptacles.

Are things different with law? Some people associate Hart with the view that they are. They associate him with the view that in understanding social forms and social practices, of which law is taken to be an example, what is needed is a 'hermeneutic approach', an approach that respects and incorporates into our understanding the way that participants in those forms and practices understand what they are doing.[79] Hart's famous claim that legal rules have an 'internal aspect' is often taken to exemplify this approach. It is doubtful whether that is what it exemplifies.[80] But be that as it may: in explaining this 'internal aspect', doesn't Hart argue that there are legal rules only if at least some people (namely the law-applying officials who make the rule of recognition) think of the law as law? In which case surely the officials, at least, need to have the concept of law?

No. This seriously misrepresents where the internal aspect fits into Hart's thinking. He says that *rules* have an internal aspect, by which he means that rule-users are people who accept the rules, for whatever further reason, as reasons for action. I don't share this view about rules myself.[81] But perhaps it does follow from this view, and indeed perhaps it is also true, that one cannot be a rule-user unless one has the concept of a rule.[82] What certainly doesn't follow, however, is that one cannot be a law-user until one has the concept of law. Legal systems are systems of rules with officials who manage the rules in certain ways by using them in certain ways. To be those officials, they may need to know that they are using rules but they do not need to know that they are doing so as the officials of a legal system. They do not even need to know, it seems to me, what a legal system is. It is possible to have law without having the concept of law and to have the

---

[79] See Peter Hacker, 'Hart's Philosophy of Law', in P.M.S. Hacker and J Raz (eds), *Law, Morality and Society: Essays in Honour of H.L.A. Hart* (Oxford 1977), at 9; Neil MacCormick, *H.L.A. Hart* (2nd ed, Stanford 2008), 203.

[80] Although Hart embraced the idea in the introduction to his *Essays in Jurisprudence and Philosophy* (Oxford 1983), 13–14.

[81] It is inconsistent with the view presented in Chs 1 and 6 above.

[82] See Krygier, '*The Concept of Law*' above note 2, at 174–5.

concept of law without having law. So there is little to be said for Tamahana's move of trying to work out who has law and who does not by asking who takes themselves to have it. 'If we take Tamanaha seriously,' as Simon Roberts says, 'we effectively turn our backs on [his] ... project [of trying to work out what law is] altogether.'[83] We stop trying to understand law in all of its colourful variety and start trying to understand concepts in all of their colourful variety instead.

There is much interesting work to be done in the sociology of concepts, on how different populations organize their thought, and in particular on how some do without classifications that others find essential. But that is quite different from working in the sociology of law, on how different populations organize their norms of behaviour and associated institutions, and in particular on how some do without institutions (institutions of law) that others find essential. Those who do without the institutions do not necessarily do without the classifications, nor (more problematically for Tamanaha) *vice versa*. I can imagine that some readers may be disappointed to find that both the institutions and the classifications—both law and the idea of it—are only contingent features of human civilization, that they may rise and fall at different times and in different places and for different reasons, and not always in tandem. Some readers may even think that this lack of an eternal hold over human affairs makes these objects—law and the idea of it—somehow less worthy of serious study. If so, that only goes to show that not everyone is suited to life as a social scientist or a philosopher. Social scientists, such as sociologists and anthropologists and social psychologists, study the contingent and variable (but often intriguingly patterned) features of human civilization, including, *inter alia*, the amazing variety of institutional and non-institutional normative systems and the no less amazing variety of schemes under which they are classified. Philosophers study, *inter alia*, the timeless necessity of all this contingency—the universal and invariant truth, for instance, that law and the idea of law are both equally contingent and

---

[83] Simon Roberts, 'After Government? On Representing Law Without the State', *Modern Law Review* 68 (2005), 1 at 21.

variable features of human civilization, features that might one day, perhaps, be lost and even forgotten.

Maybe *that* is the universal truth about law that Lacey wants us to remember when she suggests that there is nothing universal about law. Does she mean to associate Hart's 'theoretical claim to universality' with what she elsewhere calls 'the conception of law's universality'?[84] If so, she could hardly be more wrong about Hart's theoretical claim. Hart did not claim, and did not provide any reason for anyone to suppose, that law is universal, or indeed that the concept of law is universal. He only claimed, and gave us reason to think, that there are things both interesting and true to say about law in general, law as such, law wherever it may be found. They are universal truths about a decidedly non-universal thing. They will still be interesting and true, I think, even if some day law is nowhere to be found except in the history books. And if Hart is right about this, as I think he is, it is a quite separate question whether we should anticipate that day with dread, with joy, or (most likely, it seems to me), with mixed feelings.

[84] Lacey, 'Philosophy, Political Morality, and History: Explaining the Enduring Resonance of the Hart-Fuller Debate', *New York University Law Review* 83 (2008), 1059 at 1073.

INDEX OF SUBJECTS

absurdity 3–4, 8–9
adjudication (*see also* **courts, judges**)
  institutions of, *see* institutions, adjudicative
  justice in 256–61
  legal positivist view 34–7, 256–67
  rule of 70, 103–6, 116–21, 290, 294
administrative law 98, 101, 110, 115, 209n
agency
  concerted, natural v artificial 62–5, 130–2
  institutional 62–65, 239–42
  moral 239, 241–2
  of orchestra or team 62–5, 72–4, 130
  types of, in law-making 82
anarchism 14, 28–9, 32, 138, 295
artefacts
  laws as 54, 180
  law as a genre of 178–85, 190–3
attitude
  as an aspect of law's nature 277
  'internal' 15, 299
  of acceptance 138
  of law-applying officials 126n, 127–8, 136, 138, 145n
authority
  in law-applying 209
  in law-making 43, 86, 87
  intentionality of 86
  law, part of the nature of 87
  legal 15, 16, 169
  legislative 86–7
  moral 125–7, 131, 142–4, 147

  of Basic Norm (or *Grundnorm*) 10, 15
  of case law 81–2, 86–7
  of customary law 86–7
  of God 1n, 14, 15
  of judges 81–2
  of law 142–4, 169
  of officials 86

Basic Norm (or *Grundnorm*) 717, 107n, 109n, 281n
belief
  and attitude 127–8
  (*see also* attitude)
  false 17
  of law-applying officials 127–8, 138
  legal systems as systems of 179
  norms of 149
  of norm-users 25
  v claims 127–8
bindingness
  legal (of case law) 74, 84, 148, (of customary law) 66, 87
  moral (of law) 52–3, 163, 168–72, 174, 178, (of promises, oaths, etc.) 143n, 190–1
  of morality 149–53
  positivity and 7–9

case law
  as positive law 85–8
  authority of, *see* authority
  bindingness of, *see* bindingness
  conformity with rule of law 200–1
  development of 84–5, 118–21

case law (*cont.*)
  distinguishing 40–1, 80–2, 258
  formulation v use 75–9
  implicit law 86
  in common law 84–5
  in constitutional law 118–19, 122, 124
  interpretation of,
    see interpretation
  overruling 40, 75, 80–1, 84
  stare decisis 40, 84, 123
  v customary law 67, 74, 75, 79–82, 88, 118
  v legislated (or statutory) law 74–9, 118
claims of law
  made by officials 125–32, 145–8
  moral 56n, 132–9
  to correctness v to authority 139–44, 147–8
  to justice 141–2
  to supremacy 278, 286n, 287, 293
  v aims of law 168–9
  v claims about law 132–3
clarity
  as desideratum of rule of law 29–32, 193, 231
  as 'formal' merit 30, 198–204
  as public good 231
  bearing on content of law 199–200
  legal positivism 29
  of immoral laws 219
  of language v of rule 199–200
command
  of God 1–7, 10n, 11–17
  theory of law 43, 55–6, 68, 178, 250
common law 54, 59n, 82–5, 141
concepts
  individuation of 194
  interpretive, concept of law as 166

  multiplication of 52n, 193–4, 228, 297–300
  negative and positive criteria 169
  sociology of 300
  v what is conceptualized 276n, 297–300
conflict
  among legal norms 35, 46, 79–80, 82, 123, 188, 285
  among norms of justice 243, 245, 247–8
  among rules of recognition 101n, 110n, 285
  between justice and other virtues 245–6, 252
  between legal systems 285
  between statutes 93–4
  moral 33–4, 171, 192, 243–4, 252, 260
  of intentions 60–1
  of interpretations 67, 123n
  social 260, 265
constitution
  amendments 92–4
  as element of every legal system 89
  canonical form 70, 83, 90–2, 98, 102, 122, 124n
  claim to justice 140–4
  conventions of 96, 114, 117, 118
  crisis of 96n
  first 9–10, 109n, 281n
  founding of union 91
  interpretation of 120–4
  living reality of 108–9, 119–21
  nature of 97–8
  place of courts in 92–9
  rules of adjudication in 118–22
  rules of recognition, *see* rules of recognition

INDEX OF SUBJECTS

United Kingdom 89–101, 109, 117, 94n, 123n
United States 93, 96n, 102, 110–24, 145–8
unwritten 70, 83, 89–124
written 56, 70, 85, 94n, 97–110, 116–124
constitutionalism (ideology) 94
constitutional law
  customary 92, 96–8, 106–8, 118–22
  interpretation of 45–6, 121–2
  legislated 90–5, 110–15
  v administrative law 98–9, 101, 110, 115
  v constitutional text 121–4
  v conventions of the constitution 96–7, 117–18
cooking (norms of) 154–62
courts (*see also* **judges, law-applying officials**)
  as adjudicative institutions 259
  as artificial persons 81
  as central to the nature of law 257
  as constitution-makers 94, 95, 97, 124
  as guardians of constitutional law 94, 94
  as law-applying institutions 92, 96, 98, 185–6
  as law-making institutions 41, 46–7, 75, 121, 185–6, 261, 289
  as makers of rules of recognition, *see* rules of recognition
  as political institutions 92, 94
  higher courts 58, 117, 284
  of inherent (or original) jurisdiction 100n, 117, 180, 185

custom
  of officials (*in foro*) 66, 69, 72, 82, 83, 102, 118, 286–92
  of wider population (*in pays*) 66, 83, 288–92
customary law
  authority, *see* authority
  bindingness, *see* bindingness
  conformity with rule of law 200–1
  in constitutional law, *see* constitutional law
  in foro v *in pays*, *see* custom
  in international law 66
  made by attempts to follow or apply 67–8, 75, 186, 283
  normativity 67, 68
  norms 66, 71, 72
  not expressly made 67–72
  positive law 85–8
  product of multiple agency 72–4
  purely 289–92
  rules of recognition, *see* rules of recognition
  stare decisis as doctrine of 84–5
  v case law, *see* case law
  v legislated (or statutory) law 65–7, 70, 71, 73, 102, 104n, 108

descriptive sociology, *see* **philosophy**
detachment 15–17, 154–61, 169
discretion 39, 290
duty (or obligation)
  in recipes and games 157–8
  justice and 140
  moral v legal 133–4, 137, 142, 146–7, 162, 170–4
  not-merely-claimed-or-supposed ('NMCS') 134–7
  of friends, *see* friendship

INDEX OF SUBJECTS

duty (or obligation) (*cont.*)
  of judges, moral or
    professional 34, 39, 74, 79,
    146, 213–14, 258
  presumptive 170
  to obey the law, moral 161,
    171, 173–4, 176
  v non-categorical
    requirement 55–6
  v permission 54, 55, 105n, 123n
  v power 105–106, 209

equity 254–6, 258

faith
  God's commands 4, 5, 6
  justification 7
  leap of 5, 6
  reason 3–7, 12, 13n
  value of 5, 6, 13
form
  merits of 30
  of justice 249–52
  of law 198–201, 249–51
  v content 29–34, 198–201
  v mode 205–7, 210
  v source 30–1
  v substance 201–4
formality *see* **form; justice; rule of law (ideal)**
friendship
  duties or obligations of
    154–7
  justice in 253–4
  reasons for 5–6
  rule of law in 192
functions
  in social-scientific
    explanation 292–3, 297
  of law 49, 73, 193, 206–20,
    226–30, 272–3, 278, 290,
    292–3, 296
  v modes 205–11, 217, 293

games
  compared with law 52–3, 136,
    157, 161–2, 170, 207, 212,
    228, 278, 296, 297n
  concerted agency in 130
gaps (in the law) 34–5, 47n
God
  commands of 1–6, 10n, 12,
    14–17
  knowledge of 1n, 17
  love of 6–7, 14, 16
  personification of goodness 3–5,
    9, 11, 13–17
  reasons for faith in 6–7, 12
  Socratic challenge to belief
    in 1–3, 5, 9, 17
  study of, relevance to study of
    law 7–18, 280n
Grundnorm, *see* **Basic Norm**

institutions
  agency of, *see* agency
  adjudicative 257–67, 269
    (*see also* courts)
  and the rule of law, *see* rule of
    law (ideal)
  as essential feature of law 9,
    278, 291–2, 296, 300
  delegate 98–101, 110
  intentions of 60–2
  justice 252, 258–61
  law-applying, 117, *see also*
    courts; officials
  law-making 61, 62, 64, 65,
    73, 110
  of inherent or original
    power 68, 73, 98–105,
    109–16
  of unlimited power 100n
  social 260
  sovereign 68
interpretation
  concept of 122

constitutional 119–24
intention in 42–5
legal positivist view of 42–7, 50
of case law 59, 75–9, 85
of customary law 67
of law generally 42–47,
  57–60, 75–79, 119–124,
  139–142, 291
of legislation and legislated
  law 57–60, 85, 123n
of the legal world (or legal
  consciousness), 10–11, 28,
  184–185, 253–254
retrieving v innovative 121–124
source-based rules of 44,
  46, 47
styles of (originalist, textualist,
  etc.) 42–4, 120–1, 123n

**judges (*see also* courts,
law-applying officials)**
and justice 191–2, 258n, *see also*
  adjudication
as legislators 37–8, 54, 81,
  84, 86
ideal, stylized 191
law-making by 37–42,
  70–5, 121
legal powers of 40
moral and professional
  obligations, *see* duty (or
  obligation)
officials v practitioners 191
possible reasons for being
  one 5–6, 138
pretences v errors 71, 79–80,
  127–8, 138
role in case law 74–82, 85–6
role in common law 83
role in constitutional law 119–24
role in customary law 70–1
v arbitrator 254, 257, 258n,
  259, 262

violation of rule of law by
  208–10
judicial review 94n, 123, 210
jurisdiction
boundaries of 270–1, 280
errors of jurisdiction 133n,
  209n
inherent (or original), *see* courts
legal positivist account 31
territorial 287
justice
administration of 192, 238, 268
as allocative 230, 243–9, 254–6,
  259, 261–7
distributive v corrective 243–9,
  269
formal 246–50, 255
forms of, *see* form
in adjudication, *see* adjudication
moral virtue 239–46, 252
natural (*audi alterem partem*,
  etc.) 231
part of morality 216, 223,
  233–4, 239–46, 268
priority of 252, 259–69
procedural 248–9, 250n, 263
proportionality 242, 243, 265
special relationship to law 27,
  48–51, 141, 229–32, 238–240,
  249–59, 261, 267–9
v humanity 244–6
v rule of law (or legality) 192,
  216, 231–2

law
administration of 203, 208,
  232, 257–9, 267–8
artefacts, genre of 178–85,
  190–3
as classification 276–9, 289,
  293, 300
authority, *see* authority
case law, *see* case law

law (*cont.*)
  claims of, *see* claims of law
  central v deviant cases
    162–75
  central v limit cases 53, 162–75,
    228–9, 291
  classification of (types of
    law) 54, 82
  command theory of, *see* command
  common, *see* common law
  concept(s) of 166, 169, 179,
    193, 194, 227, 228, 270,
    297–301
  constitutional, *see* constitutional
    law
  co-ordination by 13–14, 73,
    88, 172, 206
  customary, *see* customary law
  escapability of 160–74
  fidelity to 209, 253, 258n
  form(s) of, *see* form
  ius v *lex* 52–3, 193–4, 228
  legislated (or statutory), *see*
    legislated or statutory law
  making v applying 41, 46–7,
    70, 185–6, *see also*
    law-applying officials
  modal kind v functional
    kind 206–7, 211, 217,
    220n, 293
  moral claim of, *see* claims of law
  most distinctive activity 185
  natural, *see* natural law
    (traditions of thought)
  personification of 126–32
  positive (or posited) 9–11, 20,
    27–9, 32, 34–9, 42–3, 53,
    85–8, 254
  pure theory of 8, 9, 14
  social control by 222, 226–7,
    270–3, 276
  social functions of 49, 73, 193,
    272–96 (*see also* functions)
  social nature of 279–89
  'specific social technique' 207,
    208
  universal v parochial
    criteria 183–4
  universality of 301
  validity of, *see* validity
  v *the* law 184–5
law-applying officials
  (*see also* **courts, judges**)
  as essential to law 74, 209, 286,
    289, 295
  as law's representatives 69,
    127–32, 138–9, 168
  as makers of rule of recognition,
    see rules of recognition
  as makers of constitution 92,
    97–8
  error by 15–16, 121, 133
  insincerity of 136–8, 168–9
  law-making by 118, 180,
    185–6, 283, 289–90
laws (or legal rules)
  as sub-units of law 181
  common content (directions to
    apply coercion) 178
  common form 29, 251
  membership of legal
    systems 181
  power-conferring v
    duty-imposing 105–6
  'ruliness' 254–6
  v laws of chess, logic, nature,
    etc. 177
  v legal rulings 27–8, 74–8, 104,
    178, 186, 188–90, 192, 193,
    208–211, 255
  v principles 38n
legalism (ideology) 32–4, 192,
  196–7, 205, 211–12,
  217, 220
legality (ideal), *see* **rule of law
  (ideal)**

legal norms
  distinguishable only as norms
    of legal systems 178–9
  morally significant
    implications 162, 189,
    190, 193
  positivity of all 27–8
  problem of their
    normativity 159–60

legal positivism
  adjudication, view of, *see*
    adjudication
  and rule of law, *see* rule of
    law ideal
  distinctive thesis of 9, 19–53
  hard v soft (or exclusive v
    inclusive) 21–2, 50,
    179n, 189
  interpretation, view of,
    see interpretation
  'no necessary connection'
    thesis 48–51, 144–5,
    221–4, 237
  'normative' variant
    (positivity-welcomers) 26–9
  theory v thesis 33, 49,
  tradition v position 7, 19–25,
    51, 174
  v global positivism about
    norms 24–5
  v natural law 7–11, 51–3, 174–6

legal power; *see also* **authority**
  constitutional (or inherent or
    original) 105, 111–15
  delegated 99;
    irrevocably delegated 110,
    117, 143
  judicial 40–1, 58, 69, 80, 81,
    139, 188, 209n
  law-making 43, 44, 69,
    198, 261
  rule of change 103
  rule of recognition 103

legal reasoning (or legal argument)
  may create new legal norms 40,
    74, 79, 188
  may have moral premises 39,
    187–9
  moral obligation of judge to
    proceed by 39, 74, 79, 190
  place of interpretation in 46–7, 76
  ratio decidendi 78, 80
  reasoning with the law v
    reasoning about the law 39–40
  v ordinary moral reasoning 39

legal system
  artefact of the genre law 181
  at least one customary norm for
    each 68
  basic unit of law 181
  constitution of each, *see*
    constitution
  law-applying officials essential
    to 257
  municipal 89, 287–8
  no law without 179, 226, 291
  not a concerted agent 131
  of state 89n, 287
  purely customary 257
  rule of recognition of each,
    see rules of recognition
  system of rules and rulings 209,
    211

legislated (or statutory) law
  constitutional, *see* constitutional law
  expressly made 56–9
  intentionally made 59–62
  interpretation of,
    see interpretation
  judicial, *see* judges
  judicial review of 123
  retroactive 38, 41, 54n
  rule of recognition not, *see* rules
    of recognition
  speech-act 57n
  v case law, *see* case law

INDEX OF SUBJECTS

legislated (or statutory) law (*cont.*)
 v customary law,
  see customary law
legislatures 36–41, 60, 68–9, 130, 257, 290n

morality
 as mere point of view 8, 25n, 155n
 bindingness, *see* bindingness
 conflict within, *see* conflict
 inescapability of 149–53, 156, 159, 175
 invariant parts of 153
 justice as part of, *see* justice
 necessary connections with law, *see* legal positivism
 of law, internal v external 195–7, 206, 211, 217–19
 rule of law as, *see* rule of law (ideal)
 v prudence 137
 v religion 2–3, 5, 8

natural law (tradition of thought) 7–11, 23, 51–3, 174–6, 205, 224n, 228

obligation, *see* **duty (or obligation)**
officials (*see also* **law-applying officials**)
 attribution of actions to institution 65, 168
 authority of, *see* authority
 custom of, *see* custom
 in common law variant of ideal 83
 in ideal of the rule of law 209, 213–14;
 possession of concept of law 299–300
 state 289

 v practitioners 191
 v subjects, non-officials 66, 85, 96n, 166n, 227, 276, 284

philosophy
 back-room conception 24
 descriptiveness 275–8
 of law 22–4, 177, 184, 271
 v history of ideas 19
 v lexicography 177, 194
 v sociology 270–5, 279–80, 300–1

pluralism
 legal 292n
 social 263
 value- 32–4, 216, 239–42, 268–9

presupposition 9–11, 14–17, 105, 270–2, 281n
point of view (or viewpoint) 2–5, 8, 69, 158, 162–3, 170–1
positivism, *see* **legal positivism**
procedure 201–5, 210, 248–9, 263

reasoning, *see* **legal reasoning**
Rechtstaat 29 (*see also* **rule of law (ideal)**)
recognition, rule of, *see* **rules of recognition**
rule of law (ideal)
 and legal postivism 29–34, 38, 41–2,
 as complete morality for law 32–4, 235–6
 compatible with iniquity 218–20
 common-law conception 83
 connection with the nature of law 52, 196n, 222–9, 294–5
 exaggeration of importance 192–4 (*see also* **legalism (ideology)**)

formal conceptions 30–2,
    197–205
institutional aspects 210
liberal case for 214–16
modal ideal 205–11, 217
moral ideal 216–18, 233–7
narrow ('asymmetrical')
    interpretation 213–16
neutrality 217–19, 225
procedural aspects 201–4
relationship with justice,
    229–32 (*see also* justice)
v 'rule of rules' 209–10
value of 214–16, 218,
    233–4
wide interpretation
    195, 211
rules (*see also* **laws (or legal rules)**)
allocative 261
conflict of 123n
games 157, 161
immoral 144, 147, 163–73,
    222, 234, 258
internal aspect of 158,
    159, 299
legal, *see* laws
moral value of having or
    using 27–8, 48–9, 189–90,
    193, 232, 251–2
rules of recognition
conflicts among 101n, 110n
constitutions and constitutional
    law 83, 103, 107–9,
    117–18
curing defects of pre-legal
    life 294
customary character of 68–74,
    102, 107–9, 282–5
creation by case law 118
duty-imposing 69, 103
European Union 285
identifying v regulating 103–6
law or non-law 69, 107–17

made by courts/law-applying
    officials 69, 101–102, 104,
    118, 179–80, 186, 283, 289
number of such rules per legal
    system 101n, 110n, 283n
parochiality of 183–5
ultimate v lower-level
    101n, 102
United Kingdom 104
United States (federal) 116
v Basic Norm 109n, 281n
v criteria for correct use of the
    concept of law 181–5
v rules of adjudication and
    change 70, 103–6, 116, 118
rulings, *see* **rules, laws, legal norms**

social institutions 259–66
social rule (*see* also **custom,**
    customary law)
rule of recognition as, *see* rule of
    recognition
v concerted action 73, 283
v convention 72–3
v social habit 67–9, 72
society 162–3, 278–89
sovereignty
in command theory of law 68,
    178, 180, 251
Parliamentary 93n, 95,
    100n, 113n
self-embracing v
    continuing 95n
state 282, 287

validity
Basic Norm (or *Grundnorm*)
    9, 10
fiction 107
inflexions of 52–3
legal 9–11, 21, 22, 30n, 32–3,
    38, 47n, 49, 50–3, 101n,
    113n, 167n

validity (*cont.*)
  norms 20–5, 30, 31, 38, 40, 41,
    47n, 51–3
  one problem about law among
    others 33
value
  faith, *see* faith
  positivity 26–9
  law 49–50
  moral, as a validity condition of
    law 276
  of rules, *see* rules
  rule of law, *see* rule of
    law ideal
virtue, moral
  justice as 239–40, 242–6
  legality as 216
  variety of 240–2

INDEX OF NAMES

Alexy, R, 125–6, 138–45, 147
Aristotle, 242–3, 246–9, 254–6
Austin, J, 20, 43, 48–9, 55, 68–9, 178–81, 184, 273, 281, 284

Bellamy, R, 94–7
Bentham, J, 20, 26–7, 36, 43, 48–9, 66, 200–1

Coleman, J, 20, 48
Cornell, D, 125
Craig, P, 198–205

del Conte, Anna (chef), 154–6
Derrida, J, 125
Dicey, AV, 96, 114, 117–18
Diplock, Lord (judge), 141–3
Durkheim, E, 278
Dworkin, R, 17–18, 37–42, 46, 54–5, 73, 85–6, 120–1, 125–32, 144–8, 165–7, 181–5, 190, 192, 224–5, 235, 270–5, 280

Finnis, J, 125, 162–74, 228
Fuller, L, 30–1, 33, 194, 195–220, 222–6, 233–7

Goff LJ (judge), 141–4, 147

Hart, HLA, 10, 20, 27–8, 30–1, 33, 35, 37–9, 43, 48–50, 55, 68–70, 73–4, 90, 101–9, 117–18, 138, 157–60, 163, 169–72, 174, 177–90, 193–4, 206, 215–19, 221–37, 250–1, 257, 272–3, 274–301
Hazan, M (chef), 154–8

Hayek, F, 196, 200
Hobbes, T, 20, 26, 48, 49
Holmes, OW, 127–9, 142, 145;
  as Justice Holmes (judge), 145–8
Honoré, T, 274

Johst, Hanns (playwright), 237

Kant, I, 8, 159, 241, 298
Kelsen, H, 8–18, 20, 27, 35, 48, 105, 107, 178–81, 184, 206–7, 281, 284
Kierkegaard, S, 2–8
Korsgaard, C, 159–60
Kramer, M, 137
Krygier, M, 272

Lacey, N, 275, 278–80, 282, 291, 293, 301

MacCormick, N, 14–15, 286–7
Mauss, M, 278

Pirie, F, 292
Plato, 1

Rawls, J, 259–67
Raz, J, 8, 14–15, 20, 27–8, 35, 48, 87–8, 108, 125–32, 138–45, 156, 165, 169–70, 174, 177, 197, 199, 204, 210–11, 213, 215–17, 228
Roberts, S, 300

Selznick, P, 125
Shklar, J, 196
Simmonds, N, 223, 232, 237

Socrates (in Plato), 1–4
Solomon (biblical figure), 254, 261

Tamanaha, B, 281–282, 288, 297–300

Tönnies, F, 278
Twining, W, 296

Waldron, J, 105, 109, 198
Weber, M, 278–9

Printed in Poland
by Amazon Fulfillment
Poland Sp. z o.o., Wrocław